W9-AVA-303

LONGSTREET HIGHROAD GUIDE
—— TO THE ——

NEW HAMPSHIRE MOUNTAINS

BY CAROL CUSHING

LONGSTREET
ATLANTA, GEORGIA

Published by
LONGSTREET PRESS, INC.
a subsidiary of Cox Newspapers,
a subsidiary of Cox Enterprises, Inc.
2140 Newmarket Parkway
Suite 122
Marietta, Georgia 30067

Great efforts have been made to make the information in this book as accurate as possible. However, over time trails are rerouted and signs and landmarks may change. If you find a change has occurred to a trail in the book, please let us know so we can correct future editions. *A word of caution:* Outdoor recreation by its nature is potentially hazardous. All participants in such activities must assume all responsibility for their own actions and safety. The scope of this book does not cover all potential hazards and risks involved in outdoor recreation activities.

Printed by RR Donnelley & Sons, Harrisonburg, VA

1st printing 1999

Library of Congress Catalog Number 98-89177

ISBN: 1-56352-503-8

Book editing, design, and cartography
by Lenz Design & Communications, Inc., Decatur, Georgia

Cover illustration by Harry Fenn, *Picturesque America,* 1872

Cover design by Richard J. Lenz, Decatur, Georgia

Illustrations by Danny Woodard, Loganville, Georgia

Photographs by Carol Cushing

The publisher would like to thank Houghton Mifflin for permission to reprint an excerpt from *Stone Walls* from *Old and New Poems* by Donald Hall. Copyright © 1990 by Donald Hall. Reprinted by permission of Ticknor & Fields/Houghton Mifflin Company. All rights reserved.

In October the leaves turn
on low hills in middle distance, like heather, like tweed,
like tweed woven from heather and gorse,
purples, greens, reds, grays, oranges, weaving together
this joyful fabric,
and I walk in the afternoon sun, kicking the leaves.

In November the brightness washes from the hills
and I love the land most, leaves down, color drained out
in November rain,
everything gray and brown, against the dark evergreen,
everything rock and silver, lichen and moss on stone, strong bones of
stone walls showing at last
in November cold,
making wavy rectangles on the unperishing hills.

—Donald Hall, excerpted from *Stone Walls*

Contents

New Hampshire

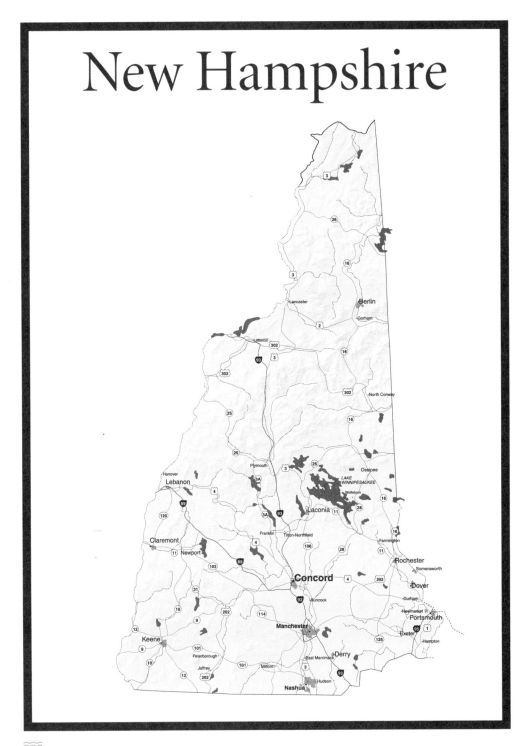

How Your Highroad Guide is Organized

North Country
Pages 15–39

White Mountain
National Forest
Pages 41–193

Lakes Region Lowlands
Pages 249–289

Western Highlands
Pages 195–247

How to Use Your Longstreet Highroad Guide

T he *Longstreet Highroad Guide to the New Hampshire Mountains* includes a wealth of detailed information about the best of what the New Hampshire Mountains have to offer, including hiking, camping, fishing, canoeing, cross-country skiing, mountain biking, and horseback riding. The *Longstreet Highroad Guide* also presents information on the natural history of the mountains, plus interesting facts about New Hampshire flora and fauna, giving the reader a starting point to learn more about what makes the mountains so special.

This book divides New Hampshire's mountains into four major areas: the North Country, the White Mountain National Forest, the Western Highlands, and the Lakes Region. The White Mountain National Forest is so dense with mountains and attractions that it has been further subdivided into six sections of its own. There are two additional chapters. One presents an overview of the natural history of New Hampshire's mountains, and the closing chapter lists New Hampshire's long trails and scenic drives.

Hunting is permitted in much of the state, and there are legal seasons for black bear, moose, deer, turkey, pheasant, and waterfowl. Both hunting and fishing require a current New Hampshire license. Fishing licenses may be obtained from local stores and sporting goods dealers, and hunting licenses are available from district licensing agents, Fish and Game Department headquarters in Concord, and some town clerks. An excellent resource for hunters is the free booklet *Hunting Digest,* published annually by the New Hampshire Fish and Game Department and available at the department's headquarters at 2 Hazen Drive, Concord, NH, 03301. Phone (603) 271-3421. The maps in the book are keyed by figure numbers and referenced in the text. These maps are intended to help orient both the casual and expert mountains enthusiast. Below is a legend to explain symbols used on the maps. Remember, hiking trails frequently change as they fall into disuse or new trails are created. Serious hikers may want to purchase additional maps from the U.S. Geological Service before they set out on a long hike. Sources are listed on the maps, in the text, and in the appendix.

A word of caution: The mountains can be dangerous. Weather can change suddenly, rocks can be slippery, and wild animals can act in unexpected ways. Use common sense when in the mountains so all your memories will be happy ones.

Legend

Symbol	Description	Symbol	Description	Symbol	Description
	Amphitheater		Wheelchair Accessible		Misc. Special Areas
	Parking		First Aid Station		Town or City
	Telephone		Picnic Shelter		Physiographic Region/ Misc. Boundary
	Information		Horse Trail		Appalachian Trail
	Picnicking		Horse Stable		Regular Trail
	Dumping Station		Shower		State Boundary
	Swimming		Biking		Interstate
	Fishing		Comfort/Rest Station		U.S. Route
	Interpretive Trail		Cross-Country Ski Trail		State Highway
	Camping		Snowmobile Trail		State Route
	Bathroom		Park Boundary		Township Road

Preface

Welcome to the mountains of New Hampshire. No matter what season you've chosen to visit, the rolling hills and bald peaks of the northern Appalachians will be wearing an elegant costume. Each season has its own winsome face and each is uniquely inviting.

In summer, the mountains cloak themselves in a forest wrapper of absolute green, while in the winter, snowy fields paint white patches here and there and ice-covered lakes sparkle among the evergreen conifers and the silvery hardwoods. It's a Currier and Ives landscape complete with red barns and gurgling streams, all draped in what looks like dollops of marshmallow fluff.

Later, spring brings a long-awaited light and airy feel to the back roads and mountainsides, where roaring brooks and maple sap run with equal exuberance. Then autumn, the fairest of them all, spreads out a party-colored tapestry of red and orange and yellow, with deep green accent points, like an impressionist painting, come to life.

For a small state, New Hampshire is disproportionately rich in ambience. And, lucky for the outdoor person, she is also loaded with mountains. In fact, with the exception of a stretch of coastal lowlands in its southeastern corner, the state is virtually all Appalachian highlands, the northern end of the 1,300-mile mountain range that runs up the eastern coast of North America, from Alabama to Newfoundland.

The big picture of New Hampshire's topography lies stretched out on a long table at the State Library in Concord. There, in a dimly lit room on the second floor, the curious can get a feel for the lay of the land. Over 100 years ago, C.H. Hitchcock, a state geologist, fashioned this 20-foot long, raised relief map of New Hampshire's topographical features. The visitor's strongest and most lingering impression of this three-dimensional model is the state's essential and nearly universal lumpiness. New Hampshire is nearly all mountains—not Alps, mind you, but respectable mountains nonetheless.

Fully three-quarters of the state is sculpted into ridges and knobs and monadnocks—a term that describes a lone mountain surrounded by a lower, eroded surface. The crown jewels of this rumpled landscape are the White Mountains, those rugged, muscled shoulders of the northern Appalachians. The highest peaks among them, the mighty Presidential Range, rear up near the place where New Hampshire narrows into a slim wedge and penetrates north into Quebec. In all, New Hampshire boasts 48 peaks towering over 4,000 feet—a relief, or vertical distance between the highest and lowest points, that is greater than many parts of the Rockies.

Several major river systems have used their erosive power to help sculpt these highlands. The largest are the Connecticut and the Merrimack river systems that flow generally south through the state before turning east to the Atlantic. Their pictur-esque valleys have collected the richest and most rock-free soil in the state and naturally, most of the state's population. These valleys first became farming country and then, the population and industrial centers of the state.

The Connecticut River, which forms the border between New Hampshire and Vermont, has its source near the Canadian border in a string of lakes named, collec-tively and appropriately, the Connecticut Lakes. All of New Hampshire's west-flowing streams and rivers flow into this system. The more easterly Merrimack River arises from the joining of the Pemmigewasset and Winnipesaukee rivers at Franklin and forms the state's broad and populous central valley. Two other large rivers, the Androscoggin and the Saco, flow east into Maine and on to the Atlantic, while several smaller rivers drain directly into the sea along New Hampshire's abbreviated, but picturesque seacoast.

The mountains through which these rivers run have long provided recreational opportunities and spiritual enrichment to residents and visitors alike. But, this human history is but a blink in time compared with the history of the mountains themselves. Under this placid covering of forest and human civilization lies a com-plex and tumultuous geological past.

—Carol Cushing

Acknowledgments

This guide represents much more than the work of one author. It is a distillation of experience, expertise, and a love for the outdoors shared by hundreds of other people—from scientists to volunteer naturalists, from staffers at conservation organizations and state departments to servers at tiny cafes tucked away in the White Mountains. It carries the imprint of foresters, biologists, ecologists, geologists, conservationists, hikers, and site managers who enthusiastically shared materials, maps, and anecdotes. Some spent hours in the field with me, and none ever seemed to tire of my questions, phone calls, or visits.

First, a warm thanks to Marge McDonald, project director for the Highroad Guides series, who entrusted me with putting together the New Hampshire guide and came all the way from Georgia to New Hampshire to buy me lunch. Editors Pam Holliday and Richard Lenz, of Lenz Design, have earned my gratitude for their unfailing patience and encouragement and their deft ability to gather up spelling errors and excess commas and throw them out, like bath water, preserving the proverbial baby in the process. Thanks also to Lenz Design for its excellent maps, illustrations, and layout. The glossary was compiled by Nancy Bazilchuk and Rick Strimbeck, authors of the *Longstreet Highroad Guide to the Vermont Mountains*. I am deeply indebted to Eugene Boudette, New Hampshire state geologist, who first recommended me for this project and has provided hours of ongoing support throughout its completion. Maps, information, field trips, and an intensive and ongoing course in geology are only a few of his generous contributions. Thanks also to J. Dykstra Eusden Jr., of Bates College, and Brian K. Fowler, president of North American Reserve, for unraveling other geological mysteries. This guide also reflects the accumulated knowledge of all those geologists, present and past, who published work on New Hampshire's geological quadrangles in words that the lay person can understand. In the area of forest ecology, I have depended on the expertise of Tom Wessels, director of the Environmental Biology Program at Antioch New England Graduate School, and on foresters Lynne Levine and Geoffrey Jones.

The author is indebted to several libraries and the natural history publications of other writers. The New Hampshire State Library, the Baker Free Library, the Concord Public Library, and the library at Antioch New England Graduate School have all helped me.

Several of New Hampshire's environmental organizations have lent invaluable support throughout this project. The Society for the Protection of New Hampshire Forests, aside from sharing its library and offering field trips, has provided information and encouragement through David Anderson, Richard Ober, Rosemary Conroy, Paul Leveille, Kristin Loomis, Trish Churchill, and Annie McCullough.

The Audubon Society of New Hampshire has also been an invaluable resource for this project. Thanks especially to Stephen Walker, Rebecca Suomala, Chris Martin, David Govatski, Bob Quinn, and Jenny Ashley for tours, information, and advice, and for including the author in pertinent projects throughout this year. The Nature Conservancy and its staff have helped with conservation issues and with information about specific properties. Thanks to Peter Benson, Janet Johnson, and the Concord office staff. Thanks to Meade Cadot, director of the Harris Center, for generously sharing his wealth of natural history and land conservation knowledge, and also to David Van Luven of the New Hampshire Natural Heritage Inventory. I am grateful for help from Jason Tremblay of the U.S. Army Corps of Engineers in regard to Edward MacDowell Lake, and to the staff at the University of New Hampshire's Cooperative Extension.

Several private enterprises have helped move this project along. Thanks to the Mount Washington Cog Railway, the Mount Washington Auto Road, the All Outdoors shop in Manchester, and to the proprietor of the Colonial Motel in North Conway, who took extra pains to provide a safe, clean, and quiet place to land, after long days on the trail.

No single entity has been of more service in compiling this guide than the State of New Hampshire itself. Thanks to Betty Lund of the Bureau of Travel and Tourism, who offered access to the bureau's files and armloads of booklets and brochures. Mary Goodyear and Bob Spoerl, of the Parks and Recreation Department, did the same and were always willing to field my questions. Thanks to Michael Walsh, manager of Monadnock State Park, for sharing his knowledge about several state parks, and to the New Hampshire Fish and Game Department for providing hunting and fishing information.

Sincere thanks goes to the rangers and staff of the White Mountain National Forest. They never failed to answer my questions or return my calls. If the Forest Service had a dollar for every time I called or visited one of its Ranger Station Visitor Centers, their budget pressures would be considerably lessened. The Appalachian Mountain Club and its staff at the Pinkham Notch and Crawford Notch visitor centers were invariably ready with whatever information I needed. The club's *White Mountain Guide*, now in its 26th edition, became an indispensable resource for this work, both at home and in the field. Thanks, as well, to David Hook and Ase Thomas of the Dartmouth Outing Club, Tim Symonds of the Monadnock-Sunapee Greenway Trail Club, and John Flanders of Friends of the Wapack, for their time and knowledge. I am also indebted to a few good friends. Thanks to Peter Miller, who hiked a few of his favorite trails with me and shared many of his experiences and observations about others. Gratitude goes also to Marie Brockway for the personal tour of the New Hampshire Indian Museum. Thanks, as well, to my friend, Carol Foord, who intrepidly hit the icy trails with me in early March.

Finally, the author and every other hiker in New Hampshire owes an overwhelming debt of gratitude to all the professionals and volunteers who maintain the hundreds of miles of trails in the state. The winter of 1998 brought a devastating ice storm, which totally obscured many trails. When I began hiking in March, I doubted some would be passable for years. To my amazement, in one hiking season, most have been miraculously restored to good condition. More remarkable still, most of the trail work was done by volunteers, performing a labor of love.

—Carol Cushing

New Hampshire Physiographic Regions

Northern Highlands

Upper Androscoggin Lowlands

Whitefield Lowlands

White Mountains Kilkenny Region

Central White Mountains

Connecticut Valley

Southern White Mountains

Conway Lowlands

Eastern Uplands

Ossipee Lowlands

Ossipee Mountains

Winnipesaukee Lowlands

Western Highlands

Belknap Mountains

Eastern Uplands

Connecticut Valley

Coastal Lowlands

Keene Lowlands

Merrimack Valley

The Natural History of
New Hampshire's Mountains

W hen you look at the green, rolling landscape of today's New Hampshire, it is difficult to imagine the land's dynamic geological past. A soft veneer of fine forests and grassy valleys hides a lot of the clues, but beneath this surface—and not very far beneath it—the distorted rocks speak volumes.

Take a look at any of the hundreds of road cuts along the state's major highways, where road builders have blasted their way through the bedrock. There you'll see, written in stone, a record of the tremendous forces that have molded the bedrock on which you stand. Sheer walls of fractured and folded metamorphic rock rise there beside the highway—in places, shot through with once-molten material, such as dark basalts or silvery granitics. These veins of igneous rock, called dikes, were forced up into the cracks of older metamorphics and speak of unimaginable strain and upheaval.

[*Above:* Mt. Chocorua in the Sandwich Range is one of the most beloved peaks in the White Mountains]

Geologic Time Scale

Era	System & Period	Series & Epoch	Some Distinctive Features	Years Before Present
CENOZOIC	Quaternary	Recent	Modern man.	11,000
		Pleistocene	Early man; northern glaciation.	1/2 to 2 million
	Tertiary	Pliocene	Large carnivores.	13 ± 1 million
		Miocene	First abundant grazing mammals.	25 ± 1 million
		Oligocene	Large running mammals.	36 ± 2 million
		Eocene	Many modern types of mammals.	58 ± 2 million
		Paleocene	First placental mammals.	63 ± 2 million
MESOZOIC	Cretaceous		First flowering plants; climax of dinosaurs and ammonites, followed by Cretaceous-Tertiary extinction.	135 ± 5 million
	Jurassic		First birds, first mammals; dinosaurs and ammonites abundant.	181 ± 5 million
	Triassic		First dinosaurs. Abundant cycads and conifers.	230 ± 10 million
PALEOZOIC	Permian		Extinction of most kinds of marine animals, including trilobites. Southern glaciation.	280 ± 10 million
	Carboniferous	Pennsylvanian	Great coal forests, conifers. First reptiles.	310 ± 10 million
		Mississippian	Sharks and amphibians abundant. Large and numerous scale trees and seed ferns.	345 ± 10 million
	Devonian		First amphibians; ammonites; Fishes abundant.	405 ± 10 million
	Silurian		First terrestrial plants and animals.	425 ± 10 million
	Ordovician		First fishes; invertebrates dominant.	500 ± 10 million
	Cambrian		First abundant record of marine life; trilobites dominant.	600 ± 50 million
	Precambrian		Fossils extremely rare, consisting of primitive aquatic plants. Evidence of glaciation. Oldest dated algae, over 2,600 million years; oldest dated meteorites 4,500 million years.	

The energy required to bend, fold, or melt solid rock is difficult to comprehend. Nonetheless, in this rock record, geologists see the undeniable evidence and have pieced together an incredible scenario—the story of how this tiny state on the edge of the North American continent came together.

Five hundred million years ago, none of New Hampshire's bedrock was yet part of the modern North American continent. It is not even clear where, at that time, the continent lay on the surface of the globe. In any case, it was ocean that filled the space now occupied by New Hampshire. Over the eons, sedimentary and volcanic rocks accumulated on the floor of this ocean until upper Ordivician time, 500 million years ago, when a titanic force called an *orogeny,* or mountain building event, pushed them up onto the edge of the continent. The tremendous heat and pressure of that event cooked and compressed these rocks, transforming them into the metamorphic and igneous rocks of northwestern New Hampshire. But, this was only the first of several herculean crunches that mashed together this part of the world.

For many millions of years after this first orogeny, relative quiet reigned. Gradual but unremitting erosion poured thousands of feet of material into the sea. It accumulated, layer upon layer, slowly becoming sedimentary rock under the pressure of its own weight and that of the ocean. Later, after a lot more cooking, this would constitute some of New Hampshire's most resistant rocks, the Littleton Formation.

Then, about 385 million years ago, came the most profound event of all. It continued intermittently over the next 100 million years. During that immensity of time, a protracted series of orogenic pulses welded these offshore, sedimentary rocks onto the continent and thrust them up out of the sea to become the ancient Appalachian Mountains, a Himalayan-sized range of glistening peaks that some say stood 25,000 feet high.

The fierce power of these processes transformed the sedimentary rocks of the Littleton Formation into new and much harder forms—the metamorphic gneisses and schists that we see in outcrops and road cuts today. Some rock was completely melted and intruded into the metamorphics, becoming the Concord, two-mica granite for which New Hampshire is now famous.

These tremendous mountain-building events were worldwide and, before they were over, they had compressed all the earth's continents together into the one great supercontinent geologists call Pangaea. What unimaginable earthly forces could possibly push all this real estate around? To understand what happened—what still happens—we need to look at a relatively young, but now widely accepted, theory in the science of geology. It is called plate tectonics.

The earth's crust was once thought to be solid and relatively stationary, but now geologists have proven that it actually consists of a dozen or so major plates that fit together like the pieces of a jigsaw puzzle. These plates carry both continents and ocean floor and are jostled around on the surface of the globe by forces deep within the earth's mantle, forces that are not yet clearly understood. These tectonic plates push and crunch against one another or slide by one another, or, in many places, one dives beneath another, back into the earth to be remelted.

In any case, wherever two or more plates come together, sparks fly. If they butt into one another, as the Indo-Australian plate and the Eurasian plate are now doing, the crust wrinkles and lofty mountains arise. If they slide by one another, as the Pacific plate and the North American plate are now doing, the earth shivers and shakes and buildings fall. And if one dives beneath the other, as is happening all around the edge of the Pacific plate, the immense heat and pressure builds great chains of volcanoes as a way to vent some of the energy.

Where does all this force come from? It is the work of the earth's internal furnace, fired by the decay of isotopes like uranium and potassium, which is constantly melting crustal rock and extruding it out of cracks in the earth's surface called rifts. The most impressive of these rifts forms a nearly continuous seam around the globe, in the middle of the ocean basins. As the molten rock is pushed out of the rift into the sea, it hardens and becomes new sea floor. Then, it is pushed to either side of the rift and very slowly by man's sense of time—only a few centimeters a year—is added to the ocean floor.

The creation of more sea floor on a finite globe means that constant readjustment is required at the edges of the plates. The basalt rock of the ocean floor is generally heavier than the lighter continental materials so, when the sea floor meets a continental plate, the heavier oceanic rock often dives under the lighter continental rock, in a process called subduction. At the same time, a reciprocal process called obduction often scrapes some oceanic crust off the top of the subducting plate which then ramps up or flips over onto the land.

Geologically speaking, the supercontinent Pangaea remained intact for a relatively brief time, only about 50 million years. About 180 million years ago, the same forces that put it together began to tear it asunder. This pulling apart of Pangaea opened the present day Atlantic Ocean, which is still widening at the rate of a few centimeters a year. The stretching also opened up cracks in New Hampshire, continental rifts where molten rock welled up and rolled out over the land. Most of these volcanics have long since eroded away, but granitic plutons now fill the empty magma chambers of the ancient volcanoes and serve as frozen testimony to their existence. These granitic plutons are Conway Granite, the second and newest kind of granite in New Hampshire. Once buried miles beneath the surface, it now forms the base of the White Mountains.

The millions of years since these cataclysmic events have witnessed the more quiet processes of upwarping and erosional sculpture that, nonetheless, have left massive marks upon the land. Geologists believe that erosion has removed many vertical miles of New Hampshire's bedrock, so that we now stand on a surface that was once 7 to 12 miles deep within the crust.

New Hampshire, we can see, is a complex product of many geological processes—

crustal accretion, metamorphosis, volcanics, and erosion. Nowhere can it be said that geology is simple. The bedrock of New Hampshire resembles nothing so much as a giant slice of fruit cake where granitic rocks form round or oblong intrusions into a fine background matrix of metamorphics.

New Hampshire calls itself the Granite State, but this is only partially correct since granitics—those gray and pink, sugary-textured rocks that make such beautiful buildings or gravestones—make up only about half the state's bedrock. The other half is made up of metamorphics, like schist and gneiss. Granite is a kind of igneous rock, meaning it was once melted. Metamorphics, on the other hand, have only been partially melted or heated to a point where they recrystallized. The third category of rocks, sedimentary, is virtually missing from New Hampshire.

The millions, even billions of years it takes to form bedrock are vast chunks of time for humans to try to understand. Perhaps it is easier for us to wrap our thinking processes around a more recent and equally formative geomorphological event, the Pleistocene Epoch. This geologic period, also known as the Ice Age, which, incidentally, is not necessarily over yet, has been a time of alternating advances and retreats of great ice sheets over the northern latitudes. The most recent of North America's ice sheets, the Laurentide, named for the area in Canada where it originated, was at its peak a mere 18,000 years ago. This icy colossus stood more than 1 mile thick over the entire state of New Hampshire. In fact, it blanketed all of the northeastern United States, reaching as far south as Long Island, New York.

Glaciation occurs whenever the climate cools sufficiently for snowfall to exceed snowmelt, allowing vast quantities of snow to accumulate. When the depth of snow reaches 100 to 200 feet, the sheer weight of its mass changes the bottom layers to ice, a special kind of ice with a pliable, plastic texture. This malleable ice squeezes out from under the mass and slowly flows across the landscape. It takes the path of least resistance around mountains and down valleys until it thickens enough to roll right over mountain summits. First, it pushes soil and rocks out of the way, then eventually it picks them up and carries them along, incorporating them into its towering mass. All this debris turns into a gigantic scouring tool with which the glacier reworks the landscape.

After several tens of thousands of years, the plucking and polishing and grinding of this frozen behemoth considerably alters the land. Left behind are the many glacier-made landforms that we find in New Hampshire today. U-shaped valleys with oversteepened sides mark the troughs where the ice completely filled the valleys and milled away at the walls. In New Hampshire, many of these valleys are called notches, and clear examples can be seen in Crawford and Franconia state parks.

Other fascinating glacial mementos are the erratic boulders, huge stones plucked from one place and carried along by the ice, in some cases for great distances, and then dropped in a new location. In Madison, New Hampshire, a ponderous boulder, the size of a small freighter, rests incongruously in the quiet, shady woods. Eighty-three feet long and several stories high, the Madison Boulder is the largest known glacial erratic in New England. But, if you look around the state, you'll see thousands of smaller erratics—large, rounded boulders sitting by themselves in places where no human or team of animals could ever have moved them.

Wherever bedrock is exposed, as it is on many of the bald peaks in New Hampshire, you may find long grooves, trending northwest-southeast, carved into the rock. These glacial striations were etched by the tough rocks embedded in the bottom of the glacier as it ground its way across the mountaintop. Many striations have eroded away but some very nice ones remain visible atop Mount Kearsarge in Warner, New Hampshire.

In any case, before the Laurentide ice sheet melted away some 14,000 years ago, glaciers had left an indelible mark on the landscape and the life forms of New Hampshire. Biologically speaking, what remained after its recession was virtually a clean slate—an ecological frontier on which plants and animals could slowly reassert their presence over time.

Return of Life to the Landscape

By 14,000 years ago, after sweeping the landscape clean of all its soil and vegetation, the Laurentide ice sheet had completely melted away. Left behind at its southernmost extent was an immense ridge of rocky debris geologists call a terminal moraine. That ridge is now called by various names; Long Island and Nantucket Island are two of them. Left along the glacier's former edges are other piles called lateral moraines and spread over the entire area the glacier once covered are various other landforms, including eskers, kames, drumlins, and deltas—places whose origins tend to be forgotten and which, today, are seen as just other hills.

Even where there are no discrete and obvious piles, the melting ice left its traces spread uniformly over the land, a blanket of rocky rubble and pulverized stone called ground moraine, or glacial till. It was simply dropped in place as the ice melted. This poor, rocky stuff could never really be called soil, but after several thousand years of chemical breakdown and enrichment with organic remains, it has become a thin veneer of meager earth, the best approximation to soil that New Hampshire can come up with. Soil does lie a little thicker in the valleys, but a glance at any of the state's many road cuts will reveal how sparsely it coats most of the bedrock.

Immediately following the glacier's retreat, New Hampshire was a bleak and frigid landscape much like today's Arctic regions, with winds howling down the treeless slopes and canyons, blowing the dusty, pulverized rock into dunes. Immense lakes of meltwater filled the valleys of the Merrimack and the Connecticut rivers, which were held in by dams of glacial debris at their southern ends.

For a couple of thousand years after the glacier retreated, the only life-forms that were able to eke out a living were Arctic plants and animals that had previously held on near the southern edges of the glacier. This tundra community of lichens, mosses, sedges, and tiny willows crept slowly north behind the glacier and formed a tenuous, green fuzz over the land, slowly enriching the thin soil as it went.

Following the first plants came grazing animals from the south—mastodon, giant beaver, elk, and woolly mammoth—and close on their heels crept the Pleistocene predators—bear, dire wolf, and saber-toothed cat. But, these and other Ice Age animals succumbed rather quickly. Scientists agree that both extinction and evolution are significantly affected by climate, which is determined by continental size and position, which are determined by plate tectonics. But, it is not yet clear that the demise of these Pleistocene megafauna, as these big animals are known, was caused by the warming climate. Some believe it was hastened by excessive hunting by the early humans present in the region 12,000 years ago.

BLACK SPRUCE
(Picea mariana)
Growing up to 40 feet tall, the black spruce is identified by its four-sided, blue-green needles and purple-brown cones.

At last, the climate warmed enough so that the permafrost melted. A few other large, cold-country animals like musk oxen and caribou did manage to hang on but were forced to move farther north. In response to the warming climate and increased moisture, trees came edging north, first in the lower valleys, then later moving up the mountain slopes. First came the conifers, spruce and fir, that today still dominate the higher and more northern parts of New Hampshire. Then some pioneer deciduous trees—aspen, birch, and alder—began to creep up the valleys from the south. For a few thousand years, the climate became even warmer than it is today, welcoming more southern species like pines and oaks to colonize New Hampshire.

The mixed hardwood-conifer forest you see around you today claimed dominance a mere 3,000 years ago. Today, northern New Hampshire forests are dominated by one of two groups of trees: the northern hardwood group of American beech, sugar maple, and yellow birch or the boreal conifers, spruce and fir. Either group can appear alone or mixed with the other, depending on the climate in each particular habitat. The hardwoods generally prefer warmer, drier sites while the conifers dominate in spots that are cooler and wetter.

Southern New Hampshire is a different story. Characterized as a transition forest, it has elements of both northern and southern tree types. Oaks, white pine, and hemlock dominate here, but, at higher elevations, many other species such as ash, black birch, and even the southern sassafras are found scattered among trees northern hardwood and boreal groups.

Climate plays a huge role in what grows where, and climate in the mountains is determined as much by elevation as by latitude. How far up is every bit as important as how far north. For every 1,000 feet of elevation, the average temperature decreases 3 degrees Fahrenheit and the average precipitation goes up about 8 inches annually. Add to this the effects of aspect—that is, which direction the slope faces—and you can clearly see that mountains, by raising and turning the land toward or away from the sun, add significantly to climate variation, and thus to the variety of plant and animal life.

In any discussion of mountains and climate in the Northeast, one mountain in particular always comes up. At 6,288 feet, Mount Washington, diminutive by Rocky Mountain or Alp standards, is often said to have the worst weather in the world. In 1934, the weather station atop this mountain clocked the highest wind speed ever measured—231 miles per hour. In fact, in any year, January's wind speed averages nearly 50 miles an hour, and in any month of the year, the visitor can routinely expect snow, high winds, and subfreezing temperatures.

How could this be? There are certainly higher mountains and colder climates, and in terms of latitude, northern New England is about the same as the balmy south of France. But here there is a peculiar convergence of the low pressure systems that travel toward the Northeast from the Pacific, the Atlantic, and the Gulf of Mexico. A map of storm tracks shows them all drawing together over New England, like iron filings to a magnet. Polar air that often circulates over Hudson Bay to the north tends to get sucked in behind each of these storms and pulled south to New England.

TRAILING ARBUTUS
(Epigaea repens)
Massachusetts, the state flower of
has fragrant spring flowers.
the trailing arbutus

Whenever cool, moisture-laden air meets a mountain, it climbs, cools even more, and drops its moisture as rain or snow. Since Mount Washington rears its rocky summit higher than anything else in the region, it snags and wrings the moisture from every cloud that passes over.

On Mount Washington, hiking safety and preparedness cannot be overstressed. In the last 100 years, dozens of hikers have lost their lives when the weather took an unexpected turn. Carry extra clothing and foul weather gear, even on what looks to be a grand day. Better yet, be prepared to change plans at the first hint of a change in the weather.

Biodiversity

Biodiversity is the glue that holds together the life systems on planet earth. The term has been variously defined but, simply stated, means the variety of plant and animal species and their interdependent ecological communities. Diversity depends on many factors, the most elemental of which is latitude. The farther from the equator and the closer to the poles you travel, the fewer species you find. Since New Hampshire sits about halfway between the equator and the North Pole, it naturally has more species than northernmost Canada and fewer than, say, Colombia.

Wide diversity of flora and fauna also depends upon many other factors, two of which are the time that species have had to evolve and the favorability and diversity of the environment. As we have seen, in New Hampshire both time and favorable conditions have been severely limited by the relatively recent onslaught of the Laurentide ice sheet. Yet, amazingly, New Hampshire, because of its variety of habitats—from acidic bogs to pine barrens, from seacoast to alpine meadows—manages to host over 60 species of mammals, more than 200 birds, 65 fish, 40 reptiles and amphibians, nearly 3,000 species of plants, and a whopping 11,000 known kinds of insects.

Today's Forest and Plant Communities

Plants are the basis for all living communities, and because New Hampshire has such a variety of habitats—lakes, rivers, swamps, mountains, and seacoast—over 30 different plant communities can be found. The largest and most obvious plants in the state are trees.

Although the forests may look like they have been here forever, today's forest is a relatively new development. One hundred and fifty years ago, the seemingly endless carpet of green that now covers roughly 80 percent of the state was, instead, nearly 80 percent cleared and open land. By that time, European settlers had already been chopping and hacking and sawing at the land for more than 150 years, in their heroic attempt to wrench a living from its stony soil. Native Americans before them, in a much smaller and more widely distributed way, had also regularly cut and burned sections of the forest to improve their hunting and agricultural endeavors. Consequently, old growth, a concept more readily connected to the tropical rain forest or the temperate rain forest in the Pacific Northwest, is limited to rare and precious pockets in New Hampshire

A few small areas of old growth did, however, manage to escape the logger's saw blade, largely because they were difficult to access. Norton Pool in Pittsburg, New Hampshire; the Great Gulf Wilderness; a glacial cirque northeast of Mount areas of ton; and The Bowl Natural Area in the Sandwich Range Wilderness are t'

9

old growth that somehow avoided both fire and logging. They stand in mute but eloquent testimony to the great forests of the past.

For the most part, though, New Hampshire's forests consist of various stages of successional growth, often referred to as second growth, though in truth it may be the second, or third, or fourth forest to spring up since an area was originally cleared. Many factors are at work in determining what grows where—and when. Climate, soil composition, disturbance, and topography that creates rain shadows or south-facing slopes, all play roles in whether a mountainside is covered by a sunny slope of oak and beech or a damp, shady pocket of conifers.

Thanks to this variation of tree types, fall foliage in New Hampshire is breathtaking. October brings throngs of people from great distances to gaze over vistas cloaked in a hundred hues of orange and yellow and red, accentuated by the contrast of deep green conifers. It is an experience one cannot adequately describe or remember from one year to the next so that, invariably, each autumn seems to outshine the last.

Forest Disturbances

Just as New Hampshire's geology is a product of continental collisions, her forests are a product of various disturbances too. From the impressive climatic effects of a glacier to the seemingly small work of the gypsy moth, nature is constantly reshaping and readjusting the mix of the forests.

Fire has long been a natural shaper of forest composition. Fire suppression, which seemed like a good idea in the early part of the twentieth century, is now seen by foresters as a practice that needs rethinking. Some species, like the pitch pine, actually need fire to keep down the competition. Because they are relatively fire-resistant, they thrive in fire-prone areas where other species cannot. Suppressing natural fires also encourages the accumulation of dead wood on a forest floor, which adds to the fuel available to feed conflagrations like the one in Yellowstone National Park in 1988.

Another natural agent of forest disturbance comes dressed in a rich, brown fur coat. The coat's luxuriance nearly spelled an end to its wearer—the beaver. Nearly extirpated from the state by the early 1800s, the beaver has returned in healthy numbers to New Hampshire's streams and ponds. This most ancient worker of the land dams up brooks, creates ponds, and cuts down trees. Eventually he moves on, leaving behind meadows where the ponds have filled in and small openings punched into the otherwise closed forest canopy. This becomes habitat for many other kinds of wildlife and opportunities for various kinds of plant succession.

The reordering of the forested landscape is also the work of a multitude of much smaller creatures. An army of insects and fungal diseases makes its living by attacking trees. Gypsy moths, Dutch elm disease, and chestnut blight are but a few of the natural enemies that wreak varying amounts of havoc upon New Hampshire's forests.

Weather, too, has taken its toll on the forest. In 1938, an unusual but devastating hurricane turned inland and roared up the Connecticut Valley, flattening millions of trees in its path. On a smaller scale, winter ice storms and high winds can leave behind shocking amounts of uprooted and broken trees. In January of 1998, a punishing ice storm battered parts of New Hampshire, leaving toppled trees and broken limbs to temporarily scar the landscape.

BEAVER
(Castor canadensis)

Nature's wounds heal over time, but no natural force since the coming of the glacier has disturbed forest cycles as much as have human beings. Three hundred years ago, the first European settlers looked out over a fearsome, primeval forest and saw not a benevolent and peaceful vista, but instead, a formidable enemy to be subdued and conquered so that civilization could march on, unimpeded. At first, the damage came slowly as the land was laboriously cleared by hand for farming and the grazing of pasture animals, but later came industrial exploitation of the forest for its timber. The belief seemed to be that a limitless supply of trees stretched on over the western horizon and that they existed for no other purpose than to enrich whoever could grab the wood and run with it.

By the beginning of the twentieth century, unrestricted and irresponsible logging had taken a sad toll. Clear-cutting and miles of logging roads caused devastating erosion of the thin mountain soils, and slash piles were easily ignited by sparks from passing locomotives, causing ruinous fires in the early 1900s. Some people began to look at the forest in a new, more concerned, light.

Evolution of Modern Land Use

About this time, in what now seems a happy coincidence, the White Mountains and their clean air were becoming ever more widely appreciated for their recreational appeal. In the summers, the railroads brought more and more smoke-weary and heat-oppressed city dwellers to vacation in the cool, clear air of the north country. For decades, the well-to-do had been coming for entire summers to stay in the many grand hotels in Bethlehem and other northern New Hampshire towns. The mountain environment was becoming a valuable resource in a whole different way.

The visible destruction left in the wake of irresponsible logging and devastating fires drew people's attention and created the desire to salvage what was left of this magnificent landscape. In 1901, the Society for Protection of New Hampshire Forests, one of the oldest conservation organizations in the nation, was f the next 10 years, the society and others lobbied the federal government to pass the Weeks Act, a 1911 piece of legislation that made national forests a reality in the East. The White Mountain National Forest (WMNF), which was formed then, is still the largest east of the Rocky mountains and south of Canada, covering nearly 800,000 acres, an area larger than the state of Rhode Island.

Setting aside national forests does not protect the land from exploitation of its resources. National forests are managed for multiple uses, including timber harvesting, outdoor recreation, watershed protection, and healthy fish and wildlife populations. In 1964, in order to protect areas of national forests that are important for ecological or recreational reasons, Congress passed the Wilderness Act. In the WMNF, this act led to the establishment of wilderness areas, 15 percent of the forest that is protected from logging, road-building, and motorized vehicles. In addition to four designated wilderness areas, another nine scenic areas and many restricted-use areas in the WMNF protect places of outstanding or unique natural beauty or places particularly vulnerable to damage.

Today, New Hampshire owes its conservation movement to an interesting amalgam of private and public interests. Over the past 100 years, through donations, easements, and outright purchase, two private groups—Audubon Society of New Hampshire and the Society for the Protection of New Hampshire Forests—have, between them, protected thousands of acres of land from development. The state also boasts active chapters of national and regional environmental organizations such as the Appalachian Mountain Club, the Sierra Club, and The Nature Conservancy.

Various local groups, too, practice particularly effective conservation. Hiking clubs, watershed protection groups, and groups formed to care for various special places or individual species have put together a patchwork of protected areas that spreads over the state. In addition to these national and local groups, New Hampshire state agencies cooperatively oversee over 200 state forests, state parks, and other natural areas. Together these agencies manage the land for the multiple purposes of responsible forestry, wildlife habitat, recreation, protection of threatened and endangered species, and protection of water quality. For a small state, New Hampshire boasts a hefty conservation ethic.

Undoubtedly, the biggest factor ensuring that New Hampshire still has this wealth of places and species to protect is the astounding resurgence of her forests. Just how has New Hampshire become the second most forested state in the nation next to Maine? How did the state go from being 80 percent cleared to 80 percent forest? The facts—not to make total virtue out of happenstance—are that various social and 'storical events contributed significantly to the beautifully restored forests and sel tain vistas seen in New Hampshire today.

new tr responsible for the forest comeback was the opening of the West to the middle of the nineteenth century, adventurous settlers were using sportation corridors through the mountains to move on to what were quite literally greener pastures. New Hampshire farmers got wind of more fertile, less rocky, and less heartbreaking lands in the South and Midwest, lands where the biggest crop could be something other than stones. After the Civil War, many former soldiers who had seen some of these lands abandoned New Hampshire's stony fields and harsh winters and moved away.

New Hampshire began to develop enterprises and industries more suited to the natural resources it possessed. The power of falling water and a large immigrant work force brought the textile mills and other kinds of manufacturing. Since most of the tall timber was gone, much of the timber industry had also moved on to the forests of the Midwest.

In the absence of logging and tilling, New Hampshire's rocky soils did what they naturally do best—they returned to forest. Today they are part of the 26 million acres that has come to be called The Northern Forest, an amazing tract of trees that spreads over upper New England and New York. Much of it is still a working forest where some timber and lots of paper pulp are harvested within responsible limits. Stretching from the Atlantic coast of Maine to Lake Ontario, this is one of the largest contiguously forested expanses in the country, and it continues on into Canada. Eleven million acres of it has been declared an International Biosphere Reserve.

Because the forests are back, New Hampshire has again become home to thousands of moose and white-tailed deer. Black bear now gorge on wild blueberries in the fall and sleep in their snowy dens in the winter woods. The beaver, an animal once nearly trapped out of the state, is once again hard at work, rearranging New Hampshire's rural landscape. Bird watchers delight in spotting the 182 species of birds that breed in New Hampshire and many more that winter here or pass through on their semiannual migrations.

Since 1524, when Italian explorer Giovanni da Verrazano first beheld Mount Washington from his sailing ship off the coast of New England, New Hampshire's mountains have intrigued and inspired human beings. Lying within a day's drive of over one-quarter of the country's population, they are visited by over 4 million people a year. But, with more than 1,200 miles of hiking trails in the White Mountain National Forest alone, it is still possible to find solitude.

Mountains are for people to wander over—and to wonder at. They provide a necessary irregularity, a unique landscape in an otherwise mechanized and standarized world. The rocky, gray peaks and forested valleys of New Hampshire draw people into them, and out of themselves, to reestablish a vital connection to nature.

North Country

FIGURE NUMBERS

6 Connecticut Lakes

7 Lake Umbagog
National Wildlife Refuge

8 Nash Stream Forest Area

9 Lancaster Area

North Country

The region of New Hampshire known as the North Country is an irregularly shaped protrusion reaching north into Canada. Here, New Hampshire shows its true north woods character in a land of rolling contours, clear lakes, tumbling streams, and pointed conifers. This remote section straddles the 45th parallel—the midpoint between the equator and the North Pole—and for 200 years, its landscape and the lifestyle of its residents have reflected that here, timber is king. Over 80 percent of the land is still used to grow trees that provide wood pulp to giant paper-product companies, whose stewardship has helped to keep this a land of trees and wildlife and very little development.

A strict definition of the North Country might include only the area north of NH 110 and 110 A, but for ease of organization, this guide includes everything north of the White Mountain National Forest (WMNF) under this heading. On a map, the

[*Above:* Beaver Brook Falls is a spectacular waterfall, especially in the spring]

state appears to protrude noticeably above the 45th parallel, which, west of here, divides Canada from Vermont and New York in a perfectly straight line. But this is only one of many distinctions, both physical and cultural, that give this heavily wooded region its own special character.

Unlike most of New Hampshire, which is divided into incorporated towns or cities, this region has large swaths of land labeled "location," "purchase," or "grant." These tracts were long ago granted to certain colonists by British colonial governors, or purchased by others from the state early in its history. Since then, they have had neither a sufficient population nor an inclination to become formal towns. In a region that remains as thinly populated now as it ever was, the only significant concentrations of people cluster around the towns where lumber and paper mills have determined the industrial economy for nearly 200 years.

The cultural ambience of the region reflects its history and its people, many of whom are loggers, hunters, or fishermen—and often all three. These are self-suffi-cient folks—people who are at home on the rivers, in the forests, and on the back roads that cover most of the region. From this rural background springs an attitude of political independence that first drew the nation's attention in 1832, when this loosely governed area declared itself an independent republic.

Local residents resented the long-simmering border dispute between the United States and Canada, which had ignored their needs for an established government. In response, The Indian Stream Republic—the area that is now the town of Pittsburg—took over its own destiny for three years. This brief experiment had limited success, and ended when opposing factions within the tiny republic—prodded by the two giants to the north and south—launched the Indian Stream War, a minor dust-up with no fatalities. In 1842, the border question was finally settled with a treaty negotiated by Daniel Webster and Britain's Lord Ashburton, and New Hampshire sat up and took proper notice of its northernmost community. The geographic shape of the short-lived Indian Stream Republic accounts for much of that bulge north of the 45th parallel.

A certain independence of spirit continues to assert itself in the North Country, even yet. In the tiny voting district of Dixville Notch, for example, all two dozen or so voters show up at the polls late on the night before election day, so Dixville Notch can be the first precinct in the nation to tally and report its ballots, shortly after midnight.

Geologically, the North Country is very different from the granitic White Mountains that lie to the south. The bedrock here is almost all dark gray, metamorphic schists, slates, and phyllites that were scraped off the top of a subducting crustal plate. Long ago, this was the edge of the continent, and southeast lay nothing but ocean. The rock shows distinct layers, formed of silt and clay that settled to the sea bottom hundreds of millions of years ago. There, it slowly hardened to rock, and was later pushed ashore by the process of plate tectonics.

The regional vegetation, too, differs from that to the south. Dark spires of spruce and fir trees rise above the mixed deciduous forests, becoming more numerous as you travel north into the latitude and the elevation in which they thrive. Although the mountains are fewer and more widely spaced here than in the White Mountains to the south, the land between them is higher, providing a consistent minimum elevation of 1,500 to 2,000 feet.

Historically, the North Country has been the most remote and least visited section of the state. Colebrook and the mill towns of Berlin and Groveton remain the only substantial centers of commerce in a sea of lakes, forests, and rivers. In recent decades, however, a modest tourist economy has sprung up beside the thriving wood products industry, catering to those who come for the fine hunting, fishing, and recreational activities. Summer welcomes hikers and canoeists, and winter in the North Country offers a cross-country skiing and snowmobiling paradise.

Because most of the land is owned by paper companies, and managed in long cycles for its wood products, the North Country is virtually all forest in various stages of growth. The region is a piece of a much larger entity, the Northern Forest. This vast, 26-million-acre blanket of green stretches across New York, Canada, New Hampshire, Vermont, and Maine, constituting the largest continuous wild forest east of the Mississippi River.

All these trees make the North Country a must-visit, if wildlife viewing is one of your goals. The region's backcountry is home to moose, black bear, deer, beaver, mink, fisher, snowshoe hare, and pine marten. Occasionally, a rare lynx drops in from Canada. Northern bird species such as boreal chickadees, gray jays, black-backed woodpeckers, and spruce grouse are commonly seen in this region, especially at higher elevations.

Most visitors, however, come looking for moose. This big brown member of the deer family, is so ubiquitous, it is difficult to travel down US 3, from the Canadian border to Pittsburg, without encountering at least one of the lumbering creatures as it feeds on vegetation at the edge of the woods or licks road salt from the mud at the side of the road. This area is so "moose-y" that the road is often called "Moose Alley."

Hobblebush

Hobblebush (*Viburnum alnifolium*) gets its odd name from the tendency of its branches to droop over and take root, thus "hobbling," or tripping up, the unwary passerby. This common member of the honeysuckle family is widely dispersed in the understory of New Hampshire's cool, moist woodlands, and at no time of the year is it uninteresting. In May, this shrub produces wide white clusters of fragrant flowers in the brightly lit spring woods. In July and August, these clusters turn to bunches of brilliant red berries. As summer wanes to autumn, the berries turn dark, and the lovely heart-shaped leaves develop a deep purple mixed with their summer green. Then, all winter long, the large showy buds of the hobblebush stick up pertly like fuzzy, beige rabbit ears from the ends of bare twigs. Hobblebush serves as food and cover for wildlife ranging from small rodents to the mighty moose.

Connecticut Lakes

Lake Francis, the southernmost of the Connecticut lakes, is more than 2,000 acres in size and offers Lake Francis State Park as a quiet north woods camping experience.

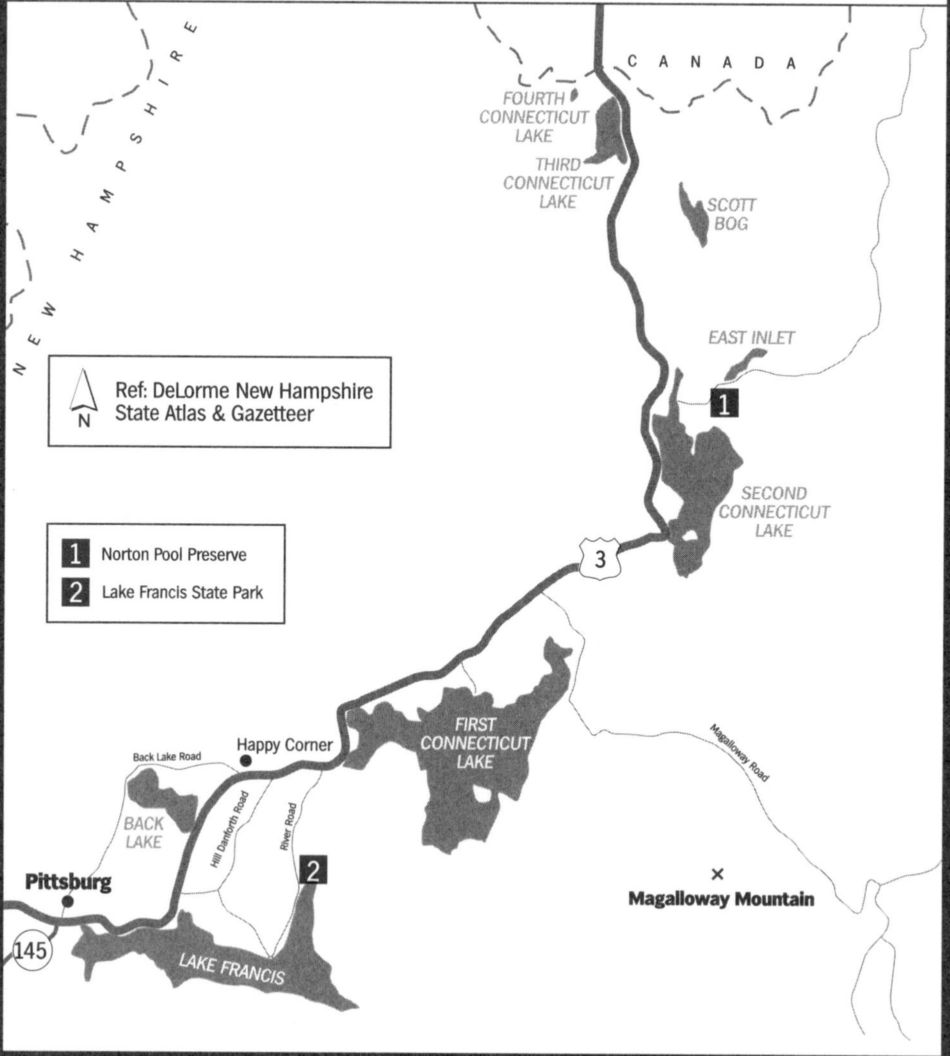

NEW HAMPSHIRE

CANADA

FOURTH CONNECTICUT LAKE

THIRD CONNECTICUT LAKE

SCOTT BOG

EAST INLET

1

SECOND CONNECTICUT LAKE

Ref: DeLorme New Hampshire State Atlas & Gazetteer

N

3

1 Norton Pool Preserve

2 Lake Francis State Park

FIRST CONNECTICUT LAKE

Magalloway Road

Back Lake Road   Happy Corner

Hill Danforth Road

River Road

BACK LAKE

2

Pittsburg

× Magalloway Mountain

145

LAKE FRANCIS

Needless to say, alert and cautious driving is a must. Colliding with a thousand pounds of moose may not only kill the animal, it may kill people as well.

Roads in the North Country are few in number but are well maintained. The only one that goes all the way to the border with Canada is US 3, which follows the Connecticut River all the way to its source at Fourth Lake. NH 16 runs partway up the eastern side of the state, and NH 26 provides a scenic, east-to-west crossover between the two. Most other roads are unnamed, unpaved, and primarily maintained by the paper companies as logging roads. If these aren't gated, they are open to the public, with the provision that logging trucks have the right of way.

While much of the North Country is managed for wood products, several state parks and private conservation areas here have reserved land for wildlife and recreational purposes. Hunting and fishing are prime attractions in the Pittsburg area, which boasts many lodges and camps, and offers ample fishing and boating access to all the lakes and streams in the area. Although hiking trails are fewer here than in the higher mountains to the south, some short hikes to interesting viewpoints are described in the following sites.

The Connecticut Lakes

The upper end of the Connecticut River, which forms the border between New Hampshire and Vermont, takes a sharp turn to the east near the 45th parallel. Here, it is collected into five lovely lakes, some behind dams belonging to the New England Power Company. Collectively called the Connecticut Lakes, these dark jewels reflect the deep green boreal forests that line their shorelines. As you travel north, each in turn becomes smaller and more remote. The last of the string, Fourth Lake, sits right on the U.S.-Canadian border, and is little more than a marshy pond that collects the tiny rivulet that is the ultimate source of one of New England's most important rivers.

North of Pittsburg, US 3 skirts the shoreline of Lake Francis, then runs along the edges of First, Second, and Third Connecticut lakes. The threatened common loon can often be seen bobbing on the surface of these waters, and trout and salmon swim in their cold depths. Once north of First Lake, US 3 runs up the middle of a narrow band of green, the Connecticut Lakes State Forest. The moist boreal habitat comes right down to the road, and hoof-trampled patches of mud along its edge are a graphic indication of heavy moose traffic. This stretch of road constitutes "Moose Alley." Drive with caution, and if you see a moose, pull over and enjoy. Do not try to approach the animal, however. Despite their phlegmatic appearance, these are wild animals whose behavior can be unpredictable.

▓ LAKE FRANCIS

[Fig. 6] Lake Francis, the southernmost of the Connecticut lakes, is captured behind Murphy Dam. Its more than 2,000 acres of uncluttered surface gives visitors a chance to get off on their own, to feel the cool northern breezes, play hide and seek with the local trout, or perhaps listen to the eerie call of a loon.

Several private campgrounds and lodges are located on the shores of both Lake Francis and Back Lake, another small body of water on the west side of US 3. A free, public boat ramp for Lake Francis is located 0.6 mile north of Murphy Dam, or campers can stay overnight in Lake Francis State Park, situated around the north end of the lake.

LAKE FRANCIS STATE PARK

[Fig. 6(2)] Pickerel, salmon, and three kinds of trout lurk beneath the waters off Lake Francis State Park. Bring your own boat or rent a canoe at this quiet north woods camping area, where flush toilets take a little of the edge off the rusticity. Forty tent sites, five of which are walk-in for ultimate privacy, offer a quiet central location from which to explore the Connecticut Lakes region.

Directions: From the junction of NH 145 and US 3 in Pittsburg, go 5.5 miles north on US 3 to River Road and the sign for Lake Francis State Park. Turn right and go 2.3 miles to the entrance.

Activities: Camping, swimming, picnicking, fishing, boating.

Facilities: Lake, canoe rental, tent sites. No hook-ups, but small, self-contained RVs can be accommodated. Boat launch, flush toilets, planned showers, picnic tables.

Dates: Mid-May to mid-Dec.

Fees: There is a fee to camp.

Closest town: Pittsburg, 7.8 miles.

For more information: New Hampshire Department of Parks and Recreation, 172 Pembroke Road, Concord, NH 03302. Phone for camping reservations (603) 227-3628.

EAST INLET AND NORTON POOL PRESERVE

[Fig. 6(1)] Not far from the source of the Connecticut River, other small mountain streams begin to kick their share of runoff into the flow. One of these, the East Inlet, comes down from the farthest northern reaches of New Hampshire, and is pooled behind an old dam into a long, narrow strip called Norton Pool. This quiet water lies in the center of a 427-acre nature preserve, surrounded by a spruce-fir forest. A portion of the forest at the far eastern end of the preserve contains a virgin stand of stately old balsam fir (*Abies balsama*) that has never felt the logger's saw. Natural disasters and diseases have reduced some of the oldest red spruce (*Picea rubens*) in the area, but their progeny stand all around. It is difficult to imagine all the layers and layers of fallen trees that lie beneath the thick carpet of undisturbed moss on this forest floor, let alone the thousands of smaller ecological interrelationships that thrive in this remote forest. Thanks to conservation efforts, this virgin stand will be allowed to continue in its natural cycle of evolution. In 1987, this precious piece of land and water was donated by Champion International into the capable hands of The Nature Conservancy and the New Hampshire Fish and Game Department. Its quiet serenity is now available to anyone who drives in and launches a canoe.

WOOD DUCK
(Aix sponsa)

Wildlife abounds here. Moose, beaver, otter, and mink are often spotted from the water, especially at dawn or at dusk. A small boat is the only way to get truly into this refuge—to see around the corners and into the coves of this long mirror-still stretch of water. Norton Pool is a birder's paradise too, just the spot to find nesting warblers and the rare black-backed woodpecker (*Picoides arcticus*). This area is both high enough and north enough for this and other boreal species—spruce grouse, Canada jay, and the boreal chickadee—to be seen lurking in the shoreline vegetation or higher up the slopes.

Directions: From Deer Mountain Campground just north of Second Lake, go 0.6 mile south on US 3. Turn left onto an unnamed gravel road. After 0.4 mile, bear right for 1 mile, then bear left for 0.7 mile to launch area on the left, near the Nature Conservancy and the New Hampshire Fish and Game signs.

Activities: Canoeing, fishing, wildlife viewing.

Facilities: Boat launch.

Dates: The gravel road is closed in the winter and during mud-season, Mar.15 to May 30.

Fees: None. A New Hampshire fishing license is required to fish.

Closest town: Pittsburg, 16 miles.

For more information: The Nature Conservancy, 2&1/2 Beacon Street, Concord, NH 03301. Phone (603) 224-5853.

FOURTH CONNECTICUT LAKE

[Fig. 6] From Lake Francis, US 3 continues north, passing near First, Second, and Third Connecticut Lakes. These are all lovely lakes, adjacent to the road, and all with fine picnic areas and free boat launching facilities. Fourth Lake, however, the last in the string, and the source of the Connecticut River, is tucked half a mile back in the woods, on the west side of the road. Fourth Lake is actually more of a quiet pond, full of cattails and rushes, sporting an old beaver lodge. Trickling down one side of this shallow bowl in the rocky terrain is the ultimate inflow stream, a tiny trickle that will eventually flow 407 miles through these small lakes, down the border between New Hampshire and Vermont, across Massachusetts and Connecticut, and finally empty into Long Island Sound and the Atlantic Ocean.

The short hike into this secluded spot is an intriguing international experience. After parking at U.S. Customs near the border, stick your head inside the door and tell the official, as a courtesy, that you are hiking to Fourth Lake. There will be no

Blackflies

More than 40 species of the often-cursed blackfly are known to occur in New Hampshire. The good news is that only two, *Prosimulium mistum* and *Simulium venustum*, leave behind that vicious calling-card for which they are infamous—a large, itchy, and painful welt near the hairline or around exposed wrists and ankles.

Blackflies breed only in clean, running water, and only the female bites and only in the daytime. Another species, *Simulium jenningsi*, arrives later, in August and September, but seems to prefer swarming around the head and getting in the eyes to actual biting.

There really is no practical, regional control measure for this springtime nuisance, although a local nontoxic measure has been used with some success at the Balsams Resort (*see* page 24). The best defense is to cover your head with a bug net and wear long sleeves and pants until this "wrath of the north woods" dissipates in early June. Chemical repellents are useful, especially if applied to clothing and net around neck, wrists, and ankles. Blackflies are most active in May during the daytime, so early morning and late evening are the best times to be outside.

papers, no questions, and no hassles. Then head for the large Nature Conservancy sign out back. The trail is a bit steep at first, but this is the worst portion. The rest involves skipping around bushes and over rocky ledges where, every 100 yards or so, an engraved brass plate in the rock has "Canada" printed on one side, a line down the middle, and "United States" printed on the other. On the way to the lake, the trail skips back and forth a dozen times over the longest unguarded border in the world. At the lake, another small loop skirts around the boggy edges of the pond, where you can locate the trickling inflow that eventually becomes the Connecticut River.

Trail: 1.4-miles (round-trip) from U.S. Customs parking lot to Fourth Connecticut Lake. After 0.6 mile, a sign points left to the lake, and near the edge, a loop trail runs around the periphery.

Elevation: 2,360 feet to 2,670 feet.

Degree of difficulty: Moderate. Steep in spots.

Surface and blaze: Surface is rocky and muddy in places. There are no blazes but trail is clearly delineated.

Coleman State Park

[Fig. 8(1)] For trout fishermen who like to roll right out of their tents or trailers and into their boats, Coleman State Park is the place to set up camp. In the northeastern corner of this 1,500-acre piece of the north woods sits Little Diamond Pond, 51 acres of smooth-as-glass trout water. The nights here are filled with starry skies, the smell of balsam fir, and the predawn calls of common loons. The camping facilities are rustic—pit toilets, no showers—but the sites are grassy and you would be hard pressed to get your camp any closer to the fish. The free boat launch provides access to Little Diamond Pond for small boats and canoes. At dusk and dawn, when the fish are rising for insects, a few tiny boats scattered about the surface of the pond move in and out of a shroud of mist settling over the water, and contemplation becomes an outdoor sport as well.

BLACK FLY
(Simulium spp.)
Found near running water, these biting flies are the curse of human visitors to the mountains and forests.

Directions: From the junction of US 3 and NH 26 in Colebrook, go 6.8 miles east on NH 26 to the Coleman State Park sign. Turn north on Diamond Pond Road (no road sign) and go 5.7 miles, following state park signs, to Coleman State Park.

Activities: Camping, fishing.

Facilities: Campground, pond, boat launch, firewood, pit toilets.

Dates: Memorial Day to Labor Day. (Weekends only before mid-June)

Fees: There is a charge to camp overnight and a lesser charge for day use only. There is no additional charge to use boat launch, but anglers must have a New Hampshire fishing license.

Closest town: Colebrook, 12.5 miles.

For more information: New Hampshire Division of Parks and Recreation, 172 Pembroke Road, Box 856, Concord, NH 03302. Phone (603) 271-3254

Beaver Brook Falls

[Fig. 8(2)] There are two ways to get from Pittsburg down to Colebrook. NH 145 is the most direct, and this smaller road also serves up a wonderfully big surprise. Eleven miles south of Pittsburg, a startlingly high waterfall splashes down Lovering Mountain. It's a cascade that can hardly be missed, even from a moving automobile. The State of New Hampshire and the Colebrook Kiwanis Club maintain an attractive picnic area here, where sheltered tables and grills provide a lovely spot to stop for lunch or dinner. In this little amphitheater, surrounded by woods echoing with birdsong, Beaver Brook Falls either trickles or roars, depending on the season, down the wall behind you. On your way across the footbridge to the base of the falls for that obligatory photograph, notice the impressively large balsam fir and spruce trees along the path.

Directions: From US 3 in Pittsburg, go 11.1 miles south on NH 145 to Beaver Brook Falls Scenic Area on the left.

Activities: Picnicking, viewing the falls, angling in the stream.

Facilities: Covered picnic tables and charcoal grills, falls, path.

Dates: Picnic area seasonal. Falls available year-round, most spectacular in spring.

Fees: None.

Closest town: Colebrook, 2.5 miles.

For more information: New Hampshire Department of Parks and Recreation, 172 Pembroke Road, Concord, NH 03302. Phone (603) 271-3254.

Dixville Notch and The Balsams Resort

Dixville Notch [Fig. 8(4)] is a dramatic, narrow cleft that cuts east and west for about 2 miles through the dark rock of the North Country—the metamorphic schists of Sanguinary Mountain and Mount Gloriette making up its north and south walls. When the Laurentide Glacier flowed over this high ground, it carved a swath through the ancient rock, but not the typical U-shaped valley of glaciers. This is a tighter place, allowing only the passage of a road and the beginnings of two rivers. From the high point of the notch the Mohawk River runs west to the Connecticut River, and the Clear Stream rolls east, down to the Androscoggin.

Dixville Notch, both the township and the rock formation, are named for Colonel Timothy Dix, who was granted this land in 1807. The township now has the distinction of being the first precinct in the nation to report its voting results on election day. This little community shows its independence in other ways as well, producing much of its own electricity and all of its own steam heat from wood waste products. It also supports its own post office, fire department, and its own telephone company. The population numbers fewer than 40, but the area employs over 800 people.

Just west of the notch, an anomaly jumps out of the rustic scenery—the sweeping acres of manicured grounds surrounding the venerable Balsams Grand Resort Hotel. The Balsams takes its name from the graceful and aromatic balsam firs whose dark green spires etch a jagged line into the skies surrounding the resort's 15,000 acres.

The Balsams [Fig. 8(3)] is where outdoor sport meets four-star elegance. Perhaps nowhere else in New Hampshire do vigorous recreation, natural history, and elegant resort facilities blend together in such a beautiful setting. The lodging and the dining are superb here, but The Balsams also aims to fill every other need a vacationer could possibly have. Outdoor winter sports include nordic and downhill skiing, snowshoeing, snowmobiling, skating, and snowboarding. Summer brings swimming, hiking, tennis, golf, canoeing, fishing, and croquet. There is a full-time naturalist on staff to answer questions, plan or lead hikes, and set up programs. Advice and equipment for golf, tennis, biking, and fishing are also available.

The Balsams has even figured out a way to contend with northern New England's spring scourge—the infamous black fly. In a cooperative effort with the University of New Hampshire, The Balsams uses a nontoxic protein substance with outstanding effectiveness on its grounds, which seems to have rendered those nasty black fly bites a thing of the past.

When guests reluctantly leave the magnificent gardens, tennis courts, golf courses, heated pool, and the mountain profiles reflected in exquisite Lake Gloriette to head inside red-roofed buildings, they find other pleasures waiting. There are programs and live entertainment, children's activities, and day camps offered daily, and a dining room like none other. Here, guests have the same table and wait staff for their entire stay, and meals are chosen only after a tour around a huge tiered table upon which is displayed a fresh sample of every entree, every salad, and every dessert—a visual preview that whets the appetite and makes the selection easier for some and more difficult for others.

Skiing—both alpine and nordic—is free of charge for guests at The Balsams, and nonguests may buy day tickets. Sample any of the 75 kilometers of cross-country trails, or board the shuttle for a short ride to The Balsams Wilderness alpine ski area, complete with lodge, lifts, and ski patrol. Rental equipment is available for either kind of skiing. In the summer, hiking and biking trails are maintained and maps or guided tours are available at the resort's Mountain Bike and Nature Center.

Lots of wildlife inhabit The Balsams' 15,000 wooded acres, and guidebooks to the area's flora and fauna are available from the hotel's naturalist. One of the more exciting stories is the return of the endangered peregrine falcon. Only in the last

White Birch

Betula papyrifera is the familiar chalky white–trunked tree with peeling bark that Native Americans once fashioned into lightweight, water-tight canoes. Called white birch, paper birch, or canoe birch, this lovely white-barked tree stands in striking contrast to the dark green evergreens among which it is often found. Though not a particularly long-lived tree, the white birch is hardy enough to persist into high elevations where most other hardwoods cannot.

White birch is found at nearly every elevation below tree line and has been designated the state tree of New Hampshire. At least three things distinguish it from the similar gray birch (*Betula populifolia*). The white birch has an ovate leaf, whereas the gray birch's leaf is more heart shaped; the white has groups of two or three catkins on winter twigs while the gray has only singles; and peeling bark is a hallmark of white birch, while the bark of the gray birch does not peel at all.

Although this natural sloughing of bark is a wholesome thing, human peeling of birch bark can cut so deep that it kills the tree. Resist this urge and allow these trees to continue to brighten the forest.

decade or so, since the banning of DDT, has this lightning-fast hunter of the air returned to nest on the Abenaki Cliffs, which rise abruptly to 2,700 feet behind The Balsams' stucco buildings. Pull out a lawn chair and pair of binoculars on an early summer day and watch the parents hunt food for their growing chicks, who stand waiting on the ledges high above.

Directions: From the junction of US 3 and NH 26 in Colebrook, go 10.2 miles east on NH 26.

Activities: Skiing, alpine and nordic, snowmobiling, snowshoeing, skating, golf, tennis, volleyball, swimming, fishing, boating on Lake Gloriette, hunting with guide, hiking, hayrides, and more.

Facilities: Four-star resort with facilities for all of the above.

Dates: Open year-round with the exception of Mar. to early May, and Columbus Day to just before Christmas.

Fees: Guest fees include use of all facilities. There is a charge for rentals and guides. There is a charge for nonguests to use trails.

Closest town: Colebrook, 10.2 miles.

For more information: The Balsams Grand Resort Hotel, Dixville Notch, NH 03576. Phone (800) 255-0600.

🌸 TRAILS NEAR THE BALSAMS

Trails for hiking, mountain biking, snowmobiling, and cross-country skiing surround The Balsams Resort. A few of the state's 600 miles of snowmobiling trails also run through The Balsams' property. Seventy-five kilometers of cross-country ski trails are detailed on a map available at the cross-country center, and a comprehensive map of the 32 hiking and biking trails can be found in the hotel's lobby. This is an excellent guide in which trails are color-coded for their ease, length, and primary use, and many have comments from the hotel's natural historian about their features. For example, one trail rambles by an old quarry where lime-rich soil—a rarity in New Hampshire's mostly granitic soils—is home to plants that require calcium, such as the beautiful maidenhair fern (*Adiantum pedatum*). Another leads to Two Town Pond, where moose may be spotted early in the morning, munching on aquatic vegetation. Others lead to Sanguinary Ridge and Table Rock, each above 2,700 feet, on opposite sides of this narrow notch, where the views of the region are spectacular.

Dixville Notch State Park

[Fig. 8(5)] Almost immediately after NH 26 passes through the narrow opening of Dixville Notch, it enters tiny Dixville Notch State Park. Relatively undeveloped, this 137-acre state park straddles the road and runs up the ridges on either side. Two of its features are Huntington Cascades and a newly developed wildlife viewing area.

CASCADE BROOK PICNIC AREA AND HUNTINGTON CASCADES TRAIL

[Fig. 8(6)] Shortly after entering Dixville Notch State Park from the north, a wayside picnic area appears on the right, or west, side of the road. Here the Huntington Cascades Trail leads 0.3 mile into the woods, tracing the fall of Cascade Brook down the eastern slopes of Dixville Peak. The lowest of the cascades is reached in about five minutes; walk another five minutes uphill to view the second. Depending on the time of year, the water either pounds wildly or gurgles softly down the steplike rock formations in the stream bed. The upended, almost vertical layers of rock are schists and phyllites that tend to break evenly, creating stair steps down which the water tumbles.

Directions: From The Balsams, go 1.2 miles east on NH 26 to the Cascade Brook Picnic Area on the right.

Activities: Picnicking, hiking, viewing Huntington Cascades.

Facilities: Picnic tables, pit toilets, trail.

Dates: Open all year.

Fees: None.

Closest town: Errol, 10 miles.

For more information: New Hampshire Division of Parks and Recreation, 172 Pembroke Road, Concord, NH 03302. Phone (603) 271-3254.

Trail: 0.6-mile (round-trip) trail up Cascade Brook past two cascades.

Elevation: 1,400 feet to 1,550 feet.

Degree of difficulty: Easy.

Surface and blaze: Forest floor, some rocks. No blazes.

DIXVILLE NOTCH WILDLIFE VIEWING AREA

[Fig. 8(5)] Just east of the Cascade Brook Picnic Area on NH 26 is a relatively new wildlife viewing area, situated in a 5-acre piece of regenerating forest. Although clear-cuts may at first be unsightly, the regrowth that immediately follows them supports a wider variety of wildlife than did the forest that was cut. This area, cut in 1990, is growing back in birch, cherry, mountain ash, spruce and fir. Moose and deer love this stage of regrowth, when they find abundant buds and tender bark for winter food. Wood warblers, sparrows, and purple finches find food and nooks to nest in here, and the trees are still short enough for them to be seen darting in and out.

Several private and public organizations have cooperated to put together a self-guided walk along the edge of the site, with informative plaques and a large, gazebo-like viewing platform at the end. The flat, hard-packed path is wheelchair-accessible and only about a hundred yards long. The wildlife mix, of course, will continue to vary as this forest grows up and changes its composition. Now, however, it is a good place to come at dawn or dusk to sit quietly and wait for moose, or to watch a wide variety of birds that breed here in the summer or stop over on their spring and fall migrations.

Directions: From The Balsams, go 1.4 miles east on NH 26 to the sign for Wildlife Viewing Area on the right.

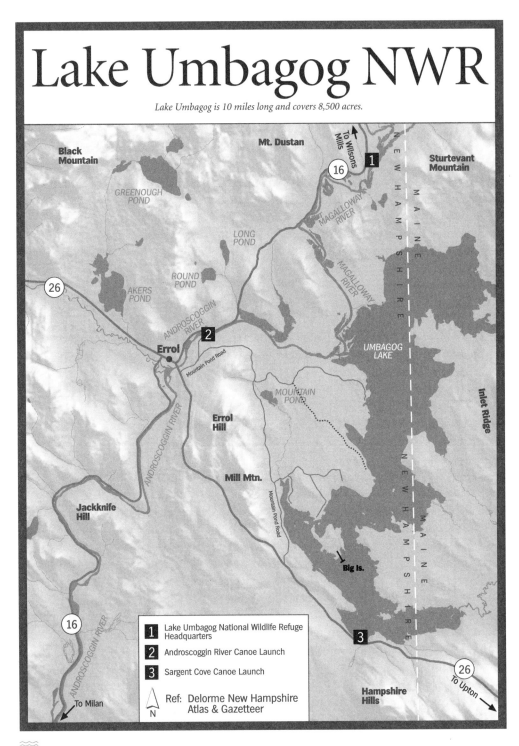

Lake Umbagog NWR

Lake Umbagog is 10 miles long and covers 8,500 acres.

Black Mountain

Mt. Dustan

To Wilsons Mills

16

1

Sturtevant Mountain

NEW HAMPSHIRE

MAINE

GREENOUGH POND

MAGALLOWAY RIVER

LONG POND

ROUND POND

AKERS POND

MAGALLOWAY RIVER

26

ANDROSCOGGIN RIVER

2

UMBAGOG LAKE

Errol

Mountain Pond Road

MOUNTAIN POND

Inlet Ridge

ANDROSCOGGIN RIVER

Errol Hill

Mill Mtn.

Mountain Pond Road

NEW HAMPSHIRE

MAINE

Jackknife Hill

Big Is.

16

1 Lake Umbagog National Wildlife Refuge Headquarters

2 Androscoggin River Canoe Launch

3 Sargent Cove Canoe Launch

3

26

To Upton

Ref: Delorme New Hampshire Atlas & Gazetteer

N

ANDROSCOGGIN RIVER

To Milan

Hampshire Hills

Activities: Short walk, wildlife viewing.
Facilities: Path, informative plaques, viewing platform
Dates: Open year-round.
Fees: None.
Closest town: Errol, 9.8 miles.
For more information: New Hampshire Fish and Game Department, 2 Hazen Drive, Concord, NH 03301. Phone (603) 271-3211.

Lake Umbagog National Wildlife Refuge

[Fig. 7] To Native Americans, Umbagog meant "clear water." To the moose and eagles, falcons and loons, Lake Umbagog has meant survival, across the bridge of time from the days of plentiful, undisturbed habitat, to the present, when humans are realizing that preserving habitat like this is imperative.

Lake Umbagog, 10 miles long and covering some 8,500 acres, sits astride the New Hampshire-Maine border just east of Errol. Its pristine waters are shallow enough so that moose and waterfowl may feed at the edges, and large birds of prey, like bald eagles and osprey, may swoop down to catch fish near the surface. Just as important, in terms of its designation as a National Wildlife Refuge, are the marshy wetlands and boggy islands that form an apron all around the lake. It is here among the tall cattails that loons and other waterfowl build nests and find food and cover for their young. The forested perimeter of this relatively undeveloped lake provides habitat near water, which is necessary for wood ducks. Nesting and migrating wood warblers also find safety and food in the marshy wetlands. Because it is relatively undisturbed, Lake Umbagog has been the most productive breeding area for common loons in the state, and holds the highest concentration of nesting osprey in all of New England.

But the real wildlife glamour story on this lake is the return of *Haliaeetus leucocephalus*, the bald eagle. This majestic and fierce-eyed raptor—the symbol of America—was hit hard by the mid-20th century use of the pesticide DDT. It weakened the eagles' eggshells, which broke long before their young could hatch. A large old white pine on an island at the edge of Lake Umbagog had long been home to New Hampshire's last nesting eagles in 1949, but stood vacant for the next forty years.

In 1989, after decades of eagle restoration work on the part of federal, state, and private organizations, it still seemed little short of a miracle when a pair of bald eagles returned, and to the very same white pine on that little island at the edge of Lake Umbagog. The first male had been captured in Alaska and then released in New York state, and the female was believed to have hatched in Maine. Year after year, these two mated and produced young. Now, others have replaced them, and as of 1998, the total number of chicks fledged from this—New Hampshire's only eagle nest—was 13.

Lake Umbagog National Wildlife Refuge, established in 1992, is a relatively young endeavor, and it has plans to keep growing. So far, it either owns or has easements on more than 7,500 acres, including nearly all the shoreline on the New Hampshire side of the lake, and much along the Magalloway and Androscoggin rivers.

A new headquarters is located on NH 16, about 5 miles north of Errol. During business hours, staff is available with information, maps, and advice, but the best way to experience the refuge is to get right into it. You can launch a canoe or small boat into the Magalloway River, next to the refuge headquarters, and paddle out to the lake, or you can drive around to Sargent Cove, at the south end of Lake Umbagog, and launch at the public access site. Another good launch site is on the Androscoggin River, just east of the dam, in Errol.

The eagles' nest pine—roped off during breeding season—is located on one of a group of small islands where the Magalloway River enters and the Androscoggin River exits Lake Umbagog. Look for a tall dead pine with a gargantuan nest of sticks. Whatever your water route through this remarkable refuge, plan to make a day of it, binoculars in hand, exploring the coves and islands and reedy edges of this wildlife paradise.

Directions: To reach the Lake Umbagog National Wildlife Refuge Headquarters and canoe launch, go 5.8 miles north on NH 16 from its junction with NH 26 in Errol. Parking is limited and none is allowed overnight. To reach the launch site at Sargent Cove, on the south end of the lake, go 7.6 miles east on NH 26 from its junction with NH 16 in Errol. To reach the launch into the Androscoggin River, go 0.2 mile east on NH 26 from NH 16 in Errol. Turn left onto Errol Dam Road which ends at the launch.

Activities: Wildlife viewing, canoeing and boating, fishing. Ice fishing.

Facilities: Lake, launch sites, refuge headquarters, private campgrounds in the area.

Dates: Open year-round. Headquarters hours vary.

Fees: None.

Closest town: Errol, 5.8 miles.

For more information: Lake Umbagog National Wildlife Refuge, Box 280, Errol, NH 03579. Phone (603) 482-3415.

Thirteen-Mile Woods

[Fig. 8(7)] South of Errol, along the Androscoggin River, NH 16 runs through a long strip of very special land called Thirteen-Mile Woods. Although most of it is privately owned, the state holds conservation easements here because this unique stretch of road and river is recognized as one of the premier wildlife viewing areas in the North Country. Like "Moose Alley" farther north (*see* page 19), it is difficult *not* to see a moose here in the spring or early summer. But this remarkable corridor of water and woods is perfect habitat for a wealth of other creatures as well.

The combination of shallow, open water; shrubby edge, and spruce-fir forest provides homes for deer, black bear, otter, and plenty of bird species—big and small. The northern, or boreal, species of birds—spruce grouse, black-backed and three-toed woodpeckers, and boreal chickadees—are often spotted here. Sometimes, without even trying, you will see the much larger osprey or bald eagle, both of which fish along the river where shallow water riffles over

These male peregrine falcon chicks wait for food from their parents.

the rocks. Look also for the common loon, bobbing on the surface, then disappearing below in pursuit of a fish.

This strip of scenic roadway and river is meant to be enjoyed. Several wayside areas beckon the traveler to pull over for a spell and have a picnic, cast a line or a canoe into the dark water, or just let quiet contemplation win the hour. If you can linger a bit longer, Mollidgewock State Park offers camping along the river, 3.5 miles south of Errol.

Directions: From Errol, drive slowly down NH 16 through Thirteen-Mile Woods which officially ends about a mile beyond the Dummer-Cambridge town line.

Activities: Scenic driving, wildlife watching, fishing, canoeing, picnicking, camping.

Facilities: Road, wayside pullouts, picnic tables, boat access points, camping.

Dates: Scenic drive open year-round. Camping, Memorial Day to Labor Day.

Fees: There is a fee to camp and a New Hampshire fishing license is required to fish, but waysides and boat access are free.

Closest town: Errol, up to 13 miles.

For more information: New Hampshire Division of Parks and Recreation, 172 Pembroke Road, Concord, NH 03302. Phone (603) 271-3421. Mollidgewock State Park, phone (603) 482-3372.

Nash Stream Forest Area

Both the township and rock formation of Dixville Notch are named for Colonel Timothy Dix, who was granted the land in 1807.

1 Coleman State Park		**6** Cascade Brook Picnic Area & Huntington Cascades Trail	
2 Beaver Brook Falls		**7** Thirteen-Mile Woods	
3 The Balsams Resort		**8** Sugarloaf Trail	
4 Dixville Notch		**9** Percy Peaks Trail	
5 Dixville Notch State Park and Wildlife Viewing Area		Nash Stream Forest	
		Trail	

VERMONT

NEW HAMPSHIRE

145

3

102

26

3

Colebrook

Diamond Pond Road

Kidderville

Dixville Peak

26

GREENOUGH POND

AKERS POND

Errol

NASH BOG POND

PHILLIPS POND

Sugarloaf × **Mountain**

LOWER TRIO POND

16

ANDROSCOGGIN RIVER

North Percy Peak ×

× **South Percy Peak**

Percy

CHRISTINE LAKE

110

● Crystal

Ref: DeLorme New Hampshire State Atlas & Gazetteer

N

The Nash Stream Forest, The Percy Peaks, and Sugarloaf Mountain

[Fig. 8] The Nash Stream Forest covers nearly 40,000 acres of land, which varies from lakes and bogs, to glacial outwash, to glistening mountaintops. In 1988, it constituted a fairly typical, privately owned piece of a much larger entity—that 26 million-acre swath of green, stretching over four states, known as the Northern Forest. When this particular piece of wild woods became threatened with development around 1988, a remarkable cooperative effort between state, federal, and private conservation organizations kept it intact and available for multiple public uses.

The Percy Peaks stand sentinel at the southwestern corner of the Nash Stream Forest, their twin humps of granite flashing silver slabs of rock at the sun. As you drive north on US 3, just beyond Lancaster, their profiles appear on the northern horizon like a giant "M". Other mountains are scattered around the periphery of the Nash Stream Forest, and running down the center is the Nash Stream.

Nash Stream and its tributaries were once held back by dams owned by the lumber companies. In the spring, the backed-up water was released in a churning torrent that carried a juggernaut of tumbling, winter-cut logs down to the mills at Groveton. The loose glacially deposited gravels and sands of the Nash Stream Valley became a brown soup that ran wild and treacherous for a few weeks each spring, with any aquatic life completely scoured away. Now the streams run clear in the bottoms of their rocky beds, brook trout lie in the shadows, and logging is conducted carefully along the lines of ecosystem management. Nash Stream Forest is now a state-owned area dedicated to the protection of watersheds, wildlife habitat, education and research, recreation, and timber management.

The best way to get the big picture at Nash Stream is to climb to the summit of one of its mountains. Two relatively short, but reasonably stiff, hikes—one to North Percy Peak, the other to the summit of Sugarloaf Mountain—are accessible from the seasonal Nash Stream Road, which runs the length of the property. This graded gravel road is open from May to December.

Directions: From Lancaster, go north to Groveton on US 3. Turn east on NH 110 and go 2.7 miles to Emerson Road. Turn left on Emerson Road, following Nash Stream signs, for 2.2 miles to Nash Stream Road. Turn left on Nash Stream Road and go 0.6 mile to a gate, and another 2.2 miles to parking on the right. The Percy Peaks Trail begins here.

Activities: Hiking, mountain biking on road, fishing, hunting.

Facilities: Trails, gravel access road, parking.

Dates: Road is open late May to Dec.

Fees: None.

Closest town: Percy.

For more information: New Hampshire Division of Forests and Lands, 172 Pembroke Road, Concord, NH 03302. Phone (603) 271-2214.

PERCY PEAKS TRAIL

[Fig. 8(9)] South Percy Peak is cloaked in dark forest to its summit, but its twin cone, North Percy Peak, displays large slabs of exfoliating granite that make for a tough, but eminently rewarding, 2.2-mile climb. The summit opens up a 360-degree view of the whole Nash Stream drainage to the north. Christine Lake lies shimmering below, as well as numerous other ponds. If you scan the forested acres carefully, you may pick out the geometric shapes of old clear cuts, now returning in the lighter greens of birch and aspen. In late summer, *Sorbus americana,* or mountain ash— more shrub than tree at the summit—throws sprays of brilliant orange-red berries across the pale rock.

Directions: Follow directions to the Nash Stream Forest. The Percy Peaks Trailhead leaves the Nash Stream Road about 25 yards north of the parking area.

Trail: 4.4 miles (round-trip) to the summit of North Percy Peak.

Elevation: 1,242 feet to 3,410 feet.

Degree of difficulty: Strenuous.

Surface and blaze: Forest floor and rocky ledge. Granite slabs near the summit can be slippery when wet or icy. Blazes absent on the forested, lower end, but orange paint blazes a trail over the rocks near the top.

SUGARLOAF TRAIL

[Fig. 8(8)] Sugarloaf Mountain, situated five miles north of the Percy Peaks and still within the Nash Stream property, is another spectacular way to get an overview of the area and a startling eyeful of North Percy Peak to the south. From Sugarloaf's granite peak, on a clear day, you can see the Presidential Range to the south as well as the Green Mountains of Vermont. On your way to the trailhead, 8 miles up the Nash Stream Road, you will see some private camps which have been grandfathered into the Nash Stream Forest Reserve. The Sugarloaf Trailhead sign is just left of one of these camps.

Directions: Follow the directions for the Nash Stream Forest, page 33. At the turn onto Nash Stream Road, go 8.3 miles north, 60 yards beyond the spot where it crosses the Nash Stream. Park off the road and look for the Sugarloaf Trail sign to the left of a camp.

Trail: 4.2 miles (round-trip) to the summit of Sugarloaf Mountain.

Elevation: 1,530 feet to 3,710 feet.

Degree of difficulty: Strenuous.

Surface and blaze: Forest floor, rocky ledge near top. Blazes rare.

TIMBER RATTLESNAKE
(Crotalus horridus)

Weeks State Park

[Fig. 9(1)] Mount Prospect in Lancaster, at 2,058 feet elevation, is certainly not one of New Hampshire's giants, but this modest summit arguably offers one of the best overviews for the least effort in the northern White Mountains. A paved road climbs less than 2 miles to the top, which is capped by Weeks State Park, an enchanting, 420-acre slice of tranquility and scenic vistas that was once the home of the pioneer conservationist, John Wingate Weeks.

In 1913, Weeks built this mountaintop retreat in Lancaster, where he grew up in love with the White Mountains. He served as congressman, senator, and secretary of war under Presidents Harding and Coolidge, but is best known for his work on the Weeks Act, passed in 1911. This legislation led to the first purchases of conservation land in the East, and awarded Weeks with the honorary title of "Father of the Eastern National Forests."

The Lodge, as his home is known, is on the National Register of Historic Places and is open for tours. Its living room, which measures 30 by 70 feet, has walls of picture windows that wrap the visitor in breathtaking mountain panoramas on all sides. The Presidentials, all the Kilkenny Ranges, the Jefferson Valley, the Franconia Range, and the Green Mountains of Vermont are all in view, a perspective seldom seen from any one peak. The Lodge, made of fieldstone and stucco, is stuffed with examples of the best craftsmanship of its time, along with mementos of Weeks's Washington days and his collection of over 100 preserved birds. The beautiful stone fire tower nearby is still used, and visitors are welcome to climb up and gasp at an even wider view. It is outside the buildings, however, where the magic of this place really begins to sink in. One treat is driving the 1.5-mile auto road to the top of Mount Prospect. This New Hampshire Scenic Byway features two magnificent overlooks that have panorama boards identifying all the mountains on the horizon. When the road is gated, during the off-season, visitors are welcome to walk this easy grade to the summit.

Mount Prospect also has a small network of trails, two of which coincide with the New Hampshire Heritage Trail, a 230-mile walking path that, when completed, will run the length of the state. A map of Mount Prospect's trails may be purchased at the Weeks Lodge.

Directions: From the junction of US 3 and US 2 in Lancaster, go 2.4 miles south on US 3 to the state park entrance on the left, or east, side of the road.

Activities: Scenic drive with informative overviews, hiking, visiting Weeks's home, viewing bird specimen collection, cross-country skiing, snowmobiling. Evening programs in summer.

Facilities: Paved scenic road, historic home and visitor center, photo and bird collections, trails, fire tower, parking, restrooms, summit picnic area.

Dates: Open Wed. through Sun. mid-June to Labor Day, and fall weekends to Oct. 12th.

Fees: Road, trails, fire tower, picnicking, and programs are free. There is a charge to tour the Weeks Lodge.

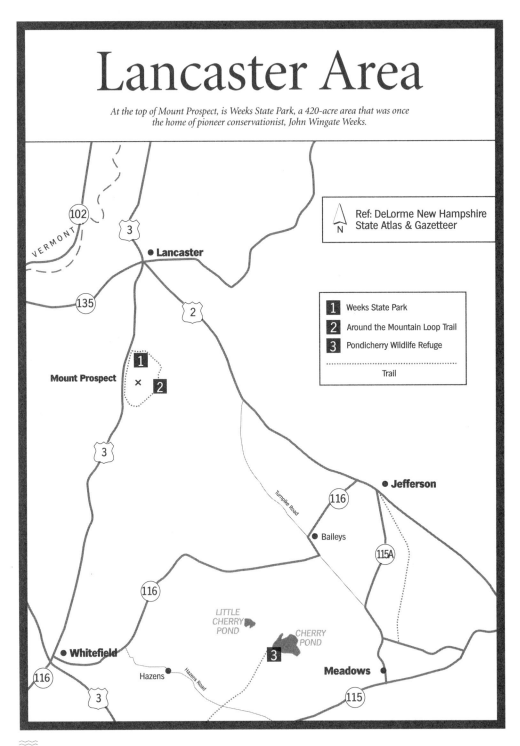

Lancaster Area

At the top of Mount Prospect, is Weeks State Park, a 420-acre area that was once the home of pioneer conservationist, John Wingate Weeks.

Ref: DeLorme New Hampshire State Atlas & Gazetteer

102

3

● Lancaster

VERMONT

135

2

1 Weeks State Park

2 Around the Mountain Loop Trail

3 Pondicherry Wildlife Refuge

Trail

1

Mount Prospect × **2**

3

● **Jefferson**

Turnpike Road

116

● Baileys

115A

116

LITTLE CHERRY POND

CHERRY POND

3

Meadows

● **Whitefield**

Hazens   Hazens Road

116

3

115

Closest town: Lancaster, 2.4 miles.

For more information: New Hampshire Division of Parks and Recreation - North Region, RFD 2, Box 241, Lancaster, NH 03584. Phone (603) 788-3155.

AROUND THE MOUNTAIN LOOP TRAIL

[Fig. 9(2)] The longest of the Mount Prospect trails, at 3 miles, follows easy grades on wide roads designed for shared use by hikers, cross-country skiers, and snowmobilers. The Around the Mountain Loop offers a variety of woods walking through stands of white cedar, red oak, and sugar maple, plus scenic overlooks, historic stone walls and cellar holes, and a trip through a maple-sugaring area. The trail is marked with white wooden signs and begins at the entrance to the Mount Prospect Ski Area, 0.2 mile north of the entrance to Weeks State Park.

Trail: 3-mile loop around the base of Mount Prospect.

Elevation: 1,300 feet to 1,620 feet.

Degree of difficulty: Easy.

Surface and blaze: Forest floor. Wooden signs.

Pondicherry Wildlife Refuge

[Fig. 9(3)] "Pondicherry" is the time-honored name for this 310-acre National Natural Landmark, where Cherry Pond and Cherry Mountain sit close enough together that the mountain spreads its reflection halfway across the pond's still water. Beyond Cherry Mountain lies a more breathtaking vista that includes the entire Presidential Range to the east, the Pliny Range to the north, and the Franconia Ridge to the southwest. From a canoe in the center of this remote pond, surrounded by spectacular mountains, the feeling is one of absorption, enfolding into a natural scene as it must have looked 500 or even 1,000 years ago.

The birding isn't bad here either. In fact, it is the main attraction. The diverse habitat of the Pondicherry Refuge brings together an amazing variety of bird species, reflected in a 1997 New Hampshire Audubon Society survey that recorded 140 different species breeding here, with many others winging through on spring and fall migrations. This is a place where you can stand in one spot and hear a loon warble, see a hawk soar, spot two species of boreal woodpeckers, or get caught up in virtual storm of migrating warblers—all this alongside a marsh emitting the weird squawks and "chunks" of rails and bitterns skulking in the reedy vegetation.

This confluence of habitats happened naturally, thanks to the work of that tireless master landscaper, the beaver. Long ago, beavers dammed up the headwaters of the Johns River into Cherry and Little Cherry ponds. Surrounding the ponds are various kinds of wetlands, from swamps to marshes to fens to bogs. Wherever the land gets a little drier, the classic boreal forest takes over—spruce, balsam fir, tamarack, white cedar, and balsam poplar, a tree usually found far north of New Hampshire. *Populus balsamifera* is the northernmost of New World hardwoods, and its leaf, more oval than those of other aspens or poplars, has a strong balsam odor. The tamarack is also an odd species—a conifer that sheds its needles every autumn—but not before turning to a lovely golden cone against the green of surrounding fir and spruce. The Pondicherry Wildlife Refuge overlaps the Jefferson and Whitefield town line, and is accessed near the Whitefield Airport. New Hampshire Audubon and the New Hampshire Fish and Game Department manage the refuge, and have kept trails and improvements to a minimum.

Directions: From the junction of US 3 and NH 116 in Whitefield, go 1.7 miles east on NH 116 to a small airport sign on the right. Turn right here onto Hazen Road (no sign) and go 1.4 miles to a larger airport sign on the left. Turn left here onto Airport Road. Go 0.6 mile to Whitefield Airport, then another 0.8 mile, bearing right, then left along Airport Road to pull-off parking on the right, a few hundred yards beyond the biomass power plant. Pondicherry Trail is directly across the road.

Activities: Hiking, canoeing, birdwatching.

Facilities: Trails.

Dates: Open year-round.

Fees: None.

Closest town: Whitefield, 4.5 miles.

For more information: Audubon Society of New Hampshire, 3 Silk Farm Road, Concord, NH 03301. Phone (603) 224-9909. New Hampshire Fish and Game Department, 2 Hazen Drive, Concord, NH 03301. Phone (603) 271-3211.

TRAILS IN THE PONDICHERRY WILDLIFE REFUGE

Trails in the Pondicherry Refuge are cleared, but relatively unmarked. The main trail, Pondicherry Trail, follows an abandoned railroad bed into the refuge from Airport Road. A multiuse trail for skiers, hikers, or snowmobilers, it is wide and smooth enough so that a canoe can be pulled in on portage wheels. In 1.5 miles, the trail crosses an active set of railroad tracks, along which a train rolls about three times a week. Turn right along these tracks to walk beside Moorhen Marsh, or go straight across these tracks, and the outlet for the Johns River, to a right turn onto the unmarked Shore Path, which borders Cherry Pond for 0.3 mile. This little trail runs atop an "ice push rampart," a natural berm, produced by hundreds of years of winter ice pushing at the edges of this pond.

To visit the even more remote Little Cherry Pond, go another 200 yards straight on Pondicherry Trail (the unused railroad bed) to a trail that leads left for 0.6 mile through a wet area to Little Cherry Pond. The rewards here are the carnivorous pitcher plant (*see* page 66) or perhaps a moose feeding in the shallows.

Pondicherry Trail: 1.5 mile (one-way) trail on an old rail bed into Pondicherry Wildlife Refuge.

Elevation: No elevation gain.

Degree of difficulty: Easy.

Surface and blaze: Grass and gravel. No blazes.

Shore Path: 0.3-mile walk along the edges of Cherry Pond with excellent views of mountains and waterfowl.

Elevation: No elevation gain.

Degree of difficulty: Easy.

Surface and blaze: Forest floor. No blazes.

Little Cherry Pond Trail: 0.6-mile hike through wetland vegetation to remote Little Cherry Pond.

Elevation: No elevation gain.

Degree of difficulty: Easy. Can be wet.

Surface and blaze: Forest floor, moss, mud in spots. No blazes.

Moose Brook State Park

[Fig. 12(12)] West of Gorham and just outside the White Mountain National Forest (WMNF) sits Moose Brook State Park, 740 acres of quiet picnic, swimming, and camping area. The campsites, available on a first-come, first-serve basis, are large, wooded, and private. Moose Brook has been dammed in two places, resulting in one pond for swimming and another for contemplative fishing.

A few miles upstream, at its headwaters, Moose Brook tumbles down a boulder-strewn ravine called Ice Gulch, which, like King Ravine, is called a rock glacier. During the last glacial retreat, a lingering tongue of ice remained in this little valley. Frost-broken rocks tumbled off the walls onto its surface and were strewn along the valley bottom as the ice continued to move downslope.

Situated between two segments of the WMNF, Moose Brook State Park makes an excellent home base for hikers and anglers who plan to stay a few days. Both the Crescent Range and the Presidentials look close enough to touch, and the Androscoggin River, Moose Brook, and several other nearby streams are reputedly home to bass, trout, pickerel, and salmon. The park also offers hot showers and a short nature trail.

Directions: From the junction of US 2 and NH 16 N west of Gorham, go 1.2 miles west on US 2 to Jimtown Road. Turn north and follow brown state park signs to park entrance.

Activities: Camping, picnicking, swimming, fishing.

Facilities: Campsites, picnic tables and fireplaces, ponds, restrooms, hot showers.

Dates: Mid-June to Labor Day.

Fees: There is a charge for use.

Closest town: Gorham, 2 miles.

For more information: Moose Brook State Park, RFD 1, 30 Jimtown Road, Gorham, NH 03570. Phone (603) 466-3860.

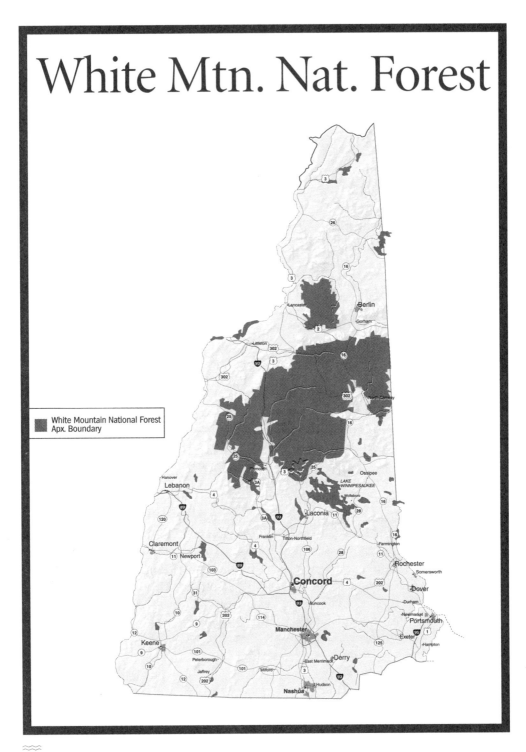

White Mtn. Nat. Forest

White Mountain National Forest
Apx. Boundary

White Mountains

The beautiful White Mountains—New Hampshire's crowning jewels—shoulder their way into the skies over most of the northern part of the state. The tallest ranges are concentrated in a wide elliptical area between the Lakes Region and Coos County, and lie mostly within the borders of the White Mountain National Forest (WMNF). At the center of the national forest, the mighty Presidentials—the grandest of the White Mountains—are topped by 6,288-foot Mount Washington, the highest mountain in the Northeast.

The origin of the name, White Mountains, lies buried in obscurity, but one story is that these frosty peaks, visible from sea-going ships 80 miles away, were given that designation by early sailors who used the shining summits of the Presidentials, which are covered in snow from October until June, as a navigational landmark.

[*Above:* Mountain ash is found in the White Mountains]

Geologic Origins

Thanks to over 200 years of geological study, the origin of the mountains themselves is a little less obscure than their naming—though far more impressive. Briefly, while many of the White Mountains are underlain with massive intrusions of granite, the lofty Presidential range is made up almost entirely of the more resistant metamorphic schists and quartzites of the Littleton Formation.

The whole region under the White Mountains has been slowly uplifted, while eons of erosion have carved deep valleys into the softer surrounding granites. More recently—during the last 1.6 million years—pulses of Pleistocene glaciation have added their own interesting, though relatively superficial, touches. Cirques, U-shaped valleys, and *roche moutonées* are all the work of these glaciers.

Drainages

Many of New Hampshire's major rivers begin as cascading white rivulets in the White Mountains. The Upper Ammonoosuc River rises in the Kilkenny region, while the headwaters of both the Saco and the Pemigewasset-Merrimack rivers come pouring off the southern slopes of the White Mountains. North of the Presidentials, the Ammonoosuc, the Israel, the Peabody, and the Moose rivers all tumble in a headlong rush to meet larger rivers. Alongside the Kancamagus Highway that cuts east and west through the White Mountains, the Swift River runs wild and foamy, thoroughly living up to its name.

Notches

Here in the White Mountains, what might elsewhere be called a pass or a canyon, more often than not, is quaintly referred to as a notch. The most notable of these spectacular clefts in the mountains are Kinsman, Franconia, Crawford, Pinkham, and Dixville notches. These relatively easy routes snaking through the White Mountains were discovered by early settlers, often with Native American help. Soon they became the most commonly used routes. Rivers ran through them, and soon also, rolled the roads. Today's modern highways naturally follow the same pattern.

Notches tend toward the scenic, and two of New Hampshire's more beautiful—Franconia and Crawford—are now set aside as state parks within the White Mountain National Forest. Tourist attractions have, for the most part, been kept to a minimum and sit back subtly out of sight. Trailheads, parking places, visitor centers, and campgrounds—all geared to the outdoor and hiking enthusiast—are particularly well situated in Franconia Notch around a pleasant parkway section of I-93.

Blue flag (Iris versicolor) in the lower wetlands of the White Mountain National Forest.

White Mountain Vegetation

On Mount Washington, where the tree line is about 4,500 feet—far lower than expected for this 44-degree latitude—there is said to occur some of the worst weather in the world. A peculiar combination of geography, elevation, and climate bestows upon this highest of the White Mountains some remarkable patterns of arctic vegetation.

Notwithstanding the particular climatic idiosyncrasies of Mount Washington and its surrounding high peaks, increased elevation alone has a profound effect on the local flora and fauna. On average, for every 1,000-foot gain in elevation, the temperature drops 3 degrees Fahrenheit, and precipitation increases by 8 inches. At the highest elevation, wind also adds its desiccating and deforming effects, so that, as you climb up many of the White Mountains, every 1,000 vertical feet you travel is akin to moving north 200 miles. By the time you reach the top of 6,288-foot Mount Washington, you have been transported, vegetationally, to the alpine tundra of Northern Labrador.

Generally speaking, by 2,500 feet, the northern hardwood association of beech,

Throughout New Hampshire there are erratic boulders, huge stones plucked and carried by glaciers and dropped in random locations.

sugar maple, and yellow birch begins to give way to a boreal mix dominated by red spruce, balsam fir, and a few white birch. By 3,000 feet, the birch are getting scarce and the spruce and fir trees have become noticeably shorter, beginning to display that "reaching-downwind" shape produced by the constant buffeting of the wind. At 4,000 feet, the conditions have become even less hospitable and true alpine vegetation takes over. Now, black spruce and balsam fir tuck in low to the ground to get out of the unremitting winds. These prostrate, ground-hugging plants are known as *krummholz,* and are barely recognizable as trees. *Krummholz* is a German term for "crooked wood," and it very aptly applies to these dwarfish, gnarled, and often quite old, trees.

In and around these low conifers are found the other tiny alpine plants that also survive above tree line. They adopt a low, matlike profile in order to stay warm and maintain a tenuous foothold in the crevices of broken rock atop the highest peaks. Every year, in June and July, they put forth a crazy quilt of delicately colored blossoms, flowers that can be seen in the Alpine Garden (*see* page 102).

Animal life also changes dramatically as elevation increases. The typical woodland species—white-tailed deer, moose, black bear, raccoon, fox, and fisher—stick to their wooded habitat, seldom venturing above treeline. Skittering among the rocks and the alpine plants are a few species of small rodents, some spiders, and two species of rare butterflies (*see* page 90). Nesting birds are limited to dark-eyed juncos and the American pipit, the rest staying below in the shelter of the forest.

The White Mountain National Forest

[Fig. 10] In the early 1900s, after the timber interests had had their way with the trees and the land in the White Mountains, they left behind a bleak landscape of stubble and slash. Frequent fires among this slash threw a pall over this once-pristine place where people had fled for respite from city smoke and grime. A public outcry demanded passage of the Weeks Act, named for its sponsor, Congressman John W. Weeks, later a senator, then President Harding's secretary of war. The Weeks Act enabled the government to set aside national forests for the first time and one of its first and most gratifying achievements was the beginning of the White Mountain National Forest.

Today, the White Mountain National Forest (WMNF) covers nearly 800,000 acres—an area larger than Rhode Island. Twelve hundred miles of hiking trails wend their way through regenerated forests, over lofty peaks, and along roaring brooks, providing plenty of backcountry and opportunity for the nearly 7 million annual visitors to get closer to nature.

Like the nation's other national forests, this one too is managed for multiple purposes: recreation, protection of watersheds and wildlife habitat, hunting and fishing, and of course, timber. Less than 0.5 percent is cut in any season, however, and some of the cutting actually enhances forest growth and wildlife habitat. Despite these other uses, the WMNF has recognized mountain recreation as its most important resource.

In 1964, the passage of the Wilderness Act resulted in the WMNF setting aside 115,000 acres in five designated wilderness areas. These special areas, four of which are in New Hampshire—the fifth is in Maine's section of the WMNF—will never be logged or developed. In

BALD EAGLE

(Haliaeetus leucocephalus)
It is believed that bald eagles mate for life. The 40-inch-long bird, which can have a 7½-foot wingspan, builds a large nest in trees, cliffs, or on the ground that can weigh up to 1,000 pounds. Eagles eat carrion, fish, and waterfowl.

45

addition, nine scenic areas and two experimental forests are off limits to cutting. The Hubbard Brook and Bartlett experimental forests are reserved for long-term forest and ecological research. Nonetheless, this is a forest for people to enjoy. Trails, scenic roads, and campgrounds are the places where most activity is focused. Despite all the attention to human visitors, the WMNF still manages to serve the needs of its wildlife. Trout and bass swim the streams, dozens of species of birds send their songs echoing through the woods, countless amphibians, reptiles, and invertebrates reside in lakes and ponds, and a very visible contingent of charismatic megafauna—deer, moose, and black bear—roam the woods and are frequently seen crossing roads.

The WMNF may be reached from a number of directions on good highways built to withstand the punishment of winter weather and summer traffic. Interstate 93 and NH 16 approach from the south, US 302 and NH 25 come in from the west, and NH 112, the most spectacular of them all, cuts right through the heart of the WMNF as the famous Kancamagus Highway.

Twenty-one organized campgrounds are located in the WMNF, some of which take reservations and others that operate on a first-come, first-serve basis. Some campgrounds are suitable for recreational vehicles, but none has hookups. All offer basic tent sites and running water and many have handicap accessibility. Reservations must be made at least five days in advance. There are also over 50 backcountry shelters and cabins, and the Appalachian Mountain Club (AMC) operates eight cabins at which reservations are required.

A relatively new trial program of fees has been instituted as a way of asking those of us who use the forest to help defray the expense of its upkeep. This WMNF permit is essentially a parking fee for those who stay all day or overnight. It does not apply to those driving through the forest or stopping at an overlook. It only applies where there are signs reading "Vehicles parked here must display a parking pass." If you don't have one, don't worry. An envelop will be left for you to mail in your fee later. These passes are parking stickers and can be purchased at any visitor center and many sporting or general stores around the area.

Although some reorganization is underway, there are currently six WMNF Visitor Centers in the New Hampshire portion of the national forest. Here you will find friendly, helpful people and lots of information: maps, hiking and camping information, details on trail conditions, and weather updates. The centers are located in attractive buildings with various educational displays, bookshops, and restroom facilities.

Directions: Enter New Hampshire from any direction and head to the national forest on I-93, NH 16, US 3, US 302, or US 2.

Activities: Scenic driving, hiking, vista and rock formation viewing, camping, fishing, swimming, canoeing, cross-country skiing, snowshoeing.

Facilities: Scenic highways, trails, overlooks, campgrounds, streams, and rivers.

Dates: Campgrounds, state parks, and some roads closed in winter. Trails open year-round.

Fees: There is a charge for campgrounds and state parks. For parking in the national forest, you must display the WMNF parking pass. A New Hampshire fishing license, obtainable at many sporting goods or general stores, is required to fish.

Closest towns: Conway, Gorham, Lincoln, Littleton, and Plymouth are scattered around the periphery of the park at various distances, none over 30 miles away.

For more information:

ANDROSCOGGIN RANGER STATION
300 Glen Road
Gorham, NH 03581
Phone (603) 466-2713 or TDD (603) 466-2856
Directions: From US 2 in Gorham, go 2.5 miles south on NH 16 (Glen Road).

SACO RANGER STATION
RFD # 1 Box 94
Conway, NH 03818
Phone (603) 447-5448 or TDD (603) 447-1989
Directions: From NH 16 in Conway, go 100 yards west on NH 112 (Kancamagus Highway).

LINCOLN WOODS VISITOR CENTER
Route 112
Lincoln, NH 03251
(no phone)
Directions: From I-93 in Lincoln, go 5.4 miles east on NH 112 (Kancamagus Hwy.)

WMNF / LAKES REGION ASSOCIATION VISITOR CENTER
Unit 2 Exit 23 Plaza
New Hampton, NH 03256
Phone (603) 744-9165
Directions: From I-93 in New Hampton, go 0.2 mile to Exit 23. Plaza on right.

AMMONOOSUC VISITOR CENTER
Box 329
Bethlehem, NH 03574
Phone (603) 869-2626 or TDD (603) 869-3104
Directions: From I-93, go 3.5 miles east on US 3 to Trudeau Road. Turn north for 1 mile.

PEMIGEWASSET VISITOR CENTER
RFD # 3 Box 15
Plymouth, NH 03264
Phone (603) 536-1315
Directions: From I-93, take Exit 25. Bear left to NH 175. Turn north for 1 mile.

For more information regarding camping reservations in national forest campgrounds, phone (800) 280-2267. For handicap camping facilities, phone (603) 528-8721 or TTD (603) 528-8722. Regarding AMC hut reservations, phone (603) 466-2727.

WMNF Kilkenny Region

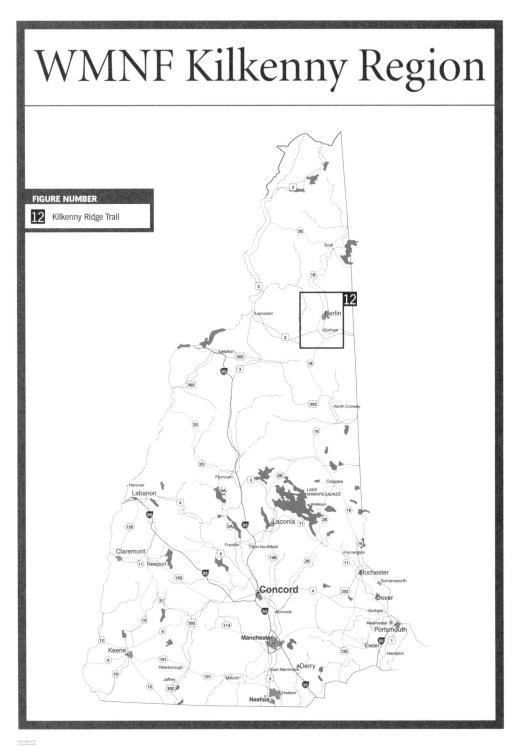

FIGURE NUMBER

12 Kilkenny Ridge Trail

WMNF Kilkenny Region

The Kilkenny Region is the northernmost outpost of the White Mountain National Forest (WMNF), and its most remote and least visited section. At the heart of this region sits The Kilkenny, an area bounded more by the almost mythical image it conjures than by any distinct borders. The region covers parts of Berlin, Randolph, Milan, and Stark as well as the uninhabited township of Kilkenny, and this wild region remains as sparsely settled as it was 200 years ago.

The name, Kilkenny, fairly rolls off the tongue. Mention it to local people and their eyes look long into the distance as they remember that their grandfathers always used to hunt there or that it's a place where they used to go fishing. There are no roads that traverse the whole region. A few short, dirt roads poke in at the edges, but if you want to sample its remote interior, you must do it on foot.

This is not to say that the area has never been logged; of course it has. Its center—

[*Above:* Wild lupine (*Lupinus perennis*) grows on Mount Cabot]

The pollen of goldenrods (Solidago) is too heavy to blow in wind. It is carried by insects.

a basin bounded on all sides by groups of mountains—is so invitingly flat, relatively speaking, that it was totally cut over early in the last century. In 1903, the piles of slash left scattered in the wake of this careless logging ignited in a devastating fire that burned 25,000 acres. This and similar conflagrations provided the public with the final impetus to demand protection for the White Mountains. Congressional adoption of the Weeks Act in 1911 allowed the federal government to begin buying up the land that would become the White Mountain National Forest.

One is left to surmise the origin of the name Kilkenny. Perhaps some homesick Irishman likened the unremitting green of the place to his Kilkenny County home on the Emerald Isle. There is also an Irish legend about the Kilkenny Cats—two belligerent felines who allegedly fought so ferociously there was nothing left but their tails.

This Kilkenny, however, has a peaceable nature, and today the area is once again covered in lush, second-growth forest. Northern hardwoods, including beech, yellow birch, and sugar maple, mingle with boreal spruce and balsam fir, and crystalline brooks tumble down ravines filled with jumbled granite blocks. The Upper Ammo-

Four Thousand Footers

In the northern Appalachians, New Hampshire runs away with the prize for having the largest number of mountains topping 4,000 feet in elevation. In and around the White Mountains, a whopping 48 of them punch their way into the skies, and because humans cannot seem to resist a challenge, the sturdier hikers among us try to climb them all. If they do, they can become a member of the Four Thousand Footer Club, an offshoot of the Appalachian Mountain Club (AMC). This club, which bases membership on the honor system and has no regular meetings, provides the necessary documentation forms and an honorary patch for completion. Members are, of course, driven by greater goals than simply personal achievement. Primary among them are the promotion of safe and responsible enjoyment of the mountains and the overall conservation of wild lands.

For the compulsive "peak bagger" who finishes this White Mountain list with energy to spare, there are two other little tasks—the New England Four Thousand Footers and the New England Hundred Highest. These are higher rungs on the same ladder, so to speak, and the Four Thousand Footer Committee gives out patches to those who climb these mountains.

noosuc River rises in the heart of the region and is joined by the Nash Stream from the north, to flow westward to the Connecticut River.

Geologically, the region is dominated by the younger granites of New Hampshire's most recent magma intrusions, a mere 180 million years ago. These intrusions are often outlined by ring dikes of quartz syenite (*see* Lakes Region, page 249) that mark the location of ancient volcanoes. Mount Starr King is largely made of this rock. The lava from these volcanoes has been almost totally erased from the landscape by erosion, exposing at the surface the beautiful, pinkish granites that formed deep within the crust below them. These granites are both harder and younger than the surrounding granites. They have undergone less erosion, so they now stand high as the region's present-day mountain ranges.

The Pilot Range, on the west side of the Kilkenny, includes Terrace Mountain, Hutchins Mountain, The Horn, and The Bulge. The highest, Mount Cabot, is the only 4,000-footer in the region. To the southwest lies the Pliny Range: Mount Starr King, Mount Waumbek, and Mount Weeks. On the east, beyond the valley of the Androscoggin River, the Mahoosuc Range rolls along the horizon, and to the south, the view is dominated by the mighty Presidentials.

The longest road into the Kilkenny is an 18-mile gravel loop consisting of York Pond Road and Bog Dam Road, a route that reaches the U.S. Fish Hatchery, then continues from there in a loop through the forest and over many streams and wetlands. There is, of course, the occasional cutover section because the White Mountain National Forest, like all the nation's others, is used as a timber resource. The few open vistas

Kilkenny Ridge Trail

The Kilkenny Ridge Trail system runs roughly north and south for more than 20 miles.

1. South Pond Recreation Area
2. Devil's Hopyard Trail
3. Kilkenny Ridge Trail
4. Rogers Ledge
5. Unknown Pond Trail
6. Mt. Cabot Trail
7. Starr King Trail
8. Lookout Ledge
9. Ledge Trail
10. Mahoosuc Trail
11. Austin Brook Trail
12. Moose Brook St. Pk.

········· Trail
– – – – – Appalachian Trail

CHRISTINE LAKE

Stark

110

S. Pond Road

SOUTH PONDS

West Milan

CEDAR POND

MUD POND

110B

Milan

ANDROSCOGGIN RIVER

16

WHITE MOUNTAIN NATIONAL FOREST

UNKNOWN POND

York Pond Road

Mt. Cabot

HEAD POND

JERICHO LAKE

110

16

Mt. Starr King

Jefferson

2

Jefferson Highland

Stag Hollow Road

Bog Dam Road

Randolph Hill

Randolph

Appalachia

Valley Road

Bowman

Berlin

Success Pond Road

ANDROSCOGGIN RIVER

Mt. Hayes

10

North Road

Mt. Crag

11

MASCOT POND

Gorham

2

MOOSE RIVER

2

16

Ref: Delorme New Hampshire Atlas & Gazetteer

N

you come upon show the seemingly endless miles of forest climbing the slopes of the surrounding mountains. Sighting wildlife in this remote area is highly probable.

Kilkenny Ridge Trail

[Fig. 12] The best way to see the heart of the Kilkenny Region is to go on foot. The Kilkenny Ridge Trail system runs for more than 20 miles, roughly north and south, through the region, accessed from either end via NH 110 or US 2. The visitor can hike small sections by entering at either end or by approaching the Kilkenny Ridge Trail from the east or west on side trails. To hike the whole trail requires three to four days. Though this trail is fairly well maintained by the U.S. Fish and Wildlife Service and its volunteers, it receives relatively little foot traffic. There are several primitive campsites for backpackers along the way—at 4.6 miles, 6.8 miles, 9.6 miles, and 16.5 miles.

This is primarily a woods walk over relatively even terrain but along the way are several short, strenuous climbs to breathtaking overviews of the surrounding mountain ranges and backcountry. Several highlights of this trail are discussed in the following pages.

Directions: The northern end of the Kilkenny Ridge Trail begins at the South Pond Recreational Area in Stark. From NH 110, 4 miles east of the covered bridge in Stark, turn south on South Pond Road. Go 2.4 miles to South Pond Recreational Area entrance and parking. At 1.3 miles, a gate is locked from mid-Oct. until mid-June, and also every night. Foot travel is welcome anytime, but when the gate is closed, you must park at this gate and walk the remaining 1.1 miles in. The access path to the Kilkenny Ridge Trail takes off from the western end of the beach at South Pond. The trailhead is located 0.7 mile down this path. Hikers may leave their cars at the recreation area parking lot overnight if they have the required WMNF parking pass.

Activities: Hiking, snowshoeing.

Facilities: Trail, primitive campsites.

Dates: Hiking trail is open year-round but not cleared in winter. Gate locked mid-Oct. to mid-June and every night.

Fees: There is a charge to enter the South Pond Recreation Area from mid-June to mid-Oct.

BLACK RACER
(Coluber constrictor)
The racer holds its head up while gliding swiftly along the ground, and vibrates the tip of its tail against vegetation when threatened.

Roche Moutonnée

Seldom has one type of landform had so many names as the *roche moutonnée* or "sheepback" or "stoss and lee topography." All three terms are used to describe the kind of hill or mountain that shows a gradual slope on its northwestern side and a sharp cliff face on the southeast. In New Hampshire, this landform is the result of the Pleistocene glaciers which moved northwest to southeast, thousands of years ago, sliding up over the former slope, then plucking large chunks of rock off the latter one. This plucking happened because the thin layer of water that rode under the glacier seeped into crevices, froze, expanded, and split off blocks on the down-ice side. The normal flow of the ice over this region then pulled these chunks away to the southeast, in the direction of its flow. After a time, the southeastern side became steepened into the kind of sheer faces you see on Cannon Mountain or Cathedral Ledge. Smaller hills (*roche* is French for "rock") whose profiles are softened with forests tend to resemble grazing sheep (*mouton* in French) with their lowered heads to the northwest and their sharply-angled derrieres facing southeast.

Closest town: Stark, 6.4 miles.

For more information: WMNF Androscoggin Ranger District, 300 Glen Road, Gorham, NH 03581. Phone (603) 466-2856. Or see the AMC *White Mountain Guide*.

Trail: 20.6-mile backpacking trail from South Pond in Stark to Mount Waumbek in Jefferson.

Elevation: 1,100 feet to 4,170 feet.

Degree of difficulty: Moderate to strenuous.

Surface and blaze: Variable from forest floor, to rocky ledge, to stream crossings. Blazes are yellow.

░ SOUTH POND RECREATION AREA

[Fig. 12(1)] At the northern terminus of the Kilkenny Ridge Trail, a string of ponds lie along the drainage of Pond Brook. The last and largest of these, South Pond, is the centerpiece of this Forest Service park. A long, sandy beach with a bathhouse and a wooded picnic area offer quiet views across the pond and a restful place to spend an afternoon. The area's woodlands are home to pileated woodpecker and various wood warblers. A flat access trail to the Kilkenny Ridge trailhead runs 0.7 mile along the west side of the pond, and is an easy stroll on a path lined with mountain maple (*Acer spicatum*), wood sorrel (*Oxalis montana*), and forget-me-nots (*Myosotis scorpioides*).

Directions: Follow directions to Kilkenny Ridge trailhead, page 53.

Activities: Swimming, fishing, picnicking, hiking.

Facilities: Beach, bathhouse, picnic tables, grills, trail. A park caretaker is in residence from June to Labor Day.

Dates: Mid-June to mid-Oct.

Fees: There is a charge to enter the park from Mid-June to mid-Oct.

Closest town: Stark, 6.4 miles.

For more information: WMNF Androscoggin Ranger District, 300 Glen Road, Gorham, NH. Phone (603) 466-2856.

SNOWSHOE HARE
(Lepus americanus)
A shy boreal species that is more active at night. Dark brown in summer, white in winter.

DEVIL'S HOPYARD TRAIL

[Fig. 12(2)] This relatively short detour off the Kilkenny Ridge Trail near South Pond takes the hiker up a narrowing gorge between two cliffs that hang with ferns and mosses. False hellebore, red trillium, and Indian cucumber root line the stream that runs alongside the trail. Soon this stream bed actually becomes the trail, as the gurgling brook dives beneath a jumble of granite chunks that fill its bed. Good hiking boots and some careful scrambling are in order here as the rocks can be slippery and covered with moss. Keep this spot in mind for a hot day when it is so cool in here that ice often remains beneath the rocks of the upper end year-round.

Directions: Follow directions to Kilkenny Ridge Trail, page 53. From South Pond, take the access trail at the west end of the beach for 0.7 mile to a sign indicating a right turn to Devil's Hopyard.

Trail: 2.6-mile hike (round-trip) up a stream bed in a sheer-walled gorge.

Elevation: 1,200 to 1,600 feet.

Degree of difficulty: Moderate. Modest elevation gain but footing can be tricky.

Surface and blaze: Forest floor to mossy blocks of granite. No blazes but trail is evident.

ROGERS LEDGE

[Fig. 12(4)] Besides the blessed solitude, one of the rewards of hiking the Kilkenny Ridge Trail is the view from the top of Rogers Ledge. The whole southwest side of this 2,945-foot mountain is a sheer cliff looking out over the vast, unpopulated Kilkenny and three other ranges of mountains: the Mahoosucs, the Pilots, and the Presidentials.

Named for Robert Rogers, who led Rogers' Rangers for the British during the French and Indian War, this outlook is 4.1 miles down the trail from South Pond, but only the last 0.6 mile is steeply uphill. For the backpacker, there is a turn-off to a primitive campsite 0.5 mile farther down the trail. This is truly backcountry and hikers must be prepared with warm clothing, camping equipment, food, water purification equipment, and stamina.

Directions: Follow directions to Kilkenny Ridge trailhead, page 53.

Trail: 4.1-mile hike (one-way) on Kilkenny Ridge Trail from South Pond to the summit of Rogers Ledge.

Elevation: 1,100 feet to 2,945 feet.

Degree of difficulty: Strenuous.

Surface and blaze: Forest floor and rocky ledge. Yellow blazes.

UNKNOWN POND

[Fig. 12] This remote, 10-acre pond lies undisturbed at the heart of the Kilkenny backcountry. To the backpacker who has hiked 6.8 miles down the Kilkenny Ridge Trail, its isolated beauty and primitive campsite will be more than enough reason to call it home for the night. White birch and a carpet of ferns are the setting where this gem of a pond reflects sky, clouds, and the surrounding peaks. A stunning view of The Horn, a bald and rocky 3,905-foot summit to the west, is ample reward for the long trek.

Two approaches to this lovely pond are possible. The backpacker can hike down from the north enjoying the solitude of the Kilkenny Ridge Trail, or if a day hike is more in order, the visitor might take the 3-mile (one-way) hike in from Mill Brook Road on the Unknown Pond Trail.

KILKENNY RIDGE TRAIL TO UNKNOWN POND

Directions: For Kilkenny Ridge Trail approach, follow directions to Kilkenny Ridge Trailhead at South Pond Recreation Area, page 53. Hike 6.8 miles to Unknown Pond.

Trail: 6.8-mile backpack (one-way) down Kilkenny Ridge Trail, over Rogers Ledge, to Unknown Pond.

Elevation: 1,100 feet to 3,300 feet.

Degree of difficulty: Strenuous.

Surface and blaze: Forest floor, rocky ledges. Yellow blazes.

UNKNOWN POND TRAIL TO UNKNOWN POND

[Fig. 12(5)] This 3-mile hike (one-way) is more suitable to day-hiking plans and affords the visitor the same stirring views of Unknown Pond and The Horn.

Directions: From NH 110 in Stark, 0.4 mile east of the covered bridge, turn south on Mill Brook Road (Forest Road 11). Go 3.8 miles south to a gate. Park and walk 0.6 mile farther on this road to a sign on the left where Unknown Pond Trail begins.

Trail: 6-mile (round-trip) hike to Unknown Pond.

Elevation: 1,050 feet to 3,300 feet.

Degree of difficulty: Moderate.

Surface and blaze: Forest floor, some rocks.

MOUNT CABOT

[Fig. 12] Mount Cabot, the principal peak in the Pilot Range, bears two distinctions. It is the only 4,000-footer in the Pilot Region and is the highest peak in the north country. Those who tally all the 4,000-foot peaks they've conquered are called "peak-baggers," and they often travel long distances to add 4,170-foot Mount Cabot to their list.

Formed of Conway Granite, Mount Cabot is part of the huge "lens" of granite that intruded the earth's crust underneath the volcanoes of the Jurrassic Period, 180 million years ago. Look for granite outcrops and boulders with a pinkish hue along the trek to the top of this hill. This color, plus the coarse, oatmeal-like texture of the rock, help to identify the Conway type.

The true summit of Mount Cabot is wooded and affords little in the way of view, but a fair overlook exists 0.4 mile southeast of the summit where a fire tower used to stand. Here, the old fire warden's cabin offers primitive shelter to hikers on a cold, blustery day. The best view, however, is from Bunnel Rock, an overlook 1 mile below the summit on the Mount Cabot Trail.

A backpacker hiking the Kilkenny Ridge Trail will find Mount Cabot and its primitive shelter 9.6 miles along the trail, or about halfway between the trail's northern and southern ends. It is possible, and much more popular, to access this mountain via the Mount Cabot Trail out of Jefferson. This is a day hike, albeit a long one, of 3.9 miles (one-way), mostly over old logging roads. The approach to this trailhead is a bit complicated, but fields of wild lupine (*Lupinus perennis*) and buttercups (*Ranunculus* spp.) await those who give it a try.

The Mount Cabot Trail follows old roads in a fairly straight line up the mountain, but does cross other trails along the way. A detailed trail map from either the AMC or the Randolph Mountain Club (RMC) is strongly recommended, as blazing and signs are minimal.

PIPSISSEWA
(*Chimaphila umbellata*) The Cree Indians named this plant "pipsisikweu," meaning "it breaks into small pieces" because of their belief in its ability to break down kidney stones and gallstones.

For more information: Randolph Mountain Club, Randolph, NH 03570. Phone (603) 466-2438. Appalachian Mountain Club, Pinkham Notch Visitor Center, Box 298, Gorham, NH. Phone (800)-262-4455.

KILKENNY RIDGE TRAIL TO MOUNT CABOT

[Fig. 12(3)] **Directions:** For the Kilkenny Ridge Trail approach to Mount Cabot, follow the directions to Kilkenny Ridge trailhead at South Pond Recreation Area, page 53. Hike 9.6 miles south to Mount Cabot.

Trail: 9.6-mile backpack (one-way) down Kilkenny Ridge Trail to Mount Cabot.

Elevation: 1,100 feet to 4,170 feet.

Degree of difficulty: Strenuous.

Surface and blaze: Forest floor, rocky ledges. Yellow blazes.

MOUNT CABOT TRAIL TO MOUNT CABOT'S SUMMIT

[Fig. 12(6)] This alternate, day-hiking route to Mount Cabot approaches the mountain from the southwest, mostly over old logging roads. It begins in Jefferson, off US 2, and is the most popular way to ascend the 2,600 feet to the top. The trail proceeds through a young forest with a floor covered in ferns and wildflowers. If a 3-mile hike (one-way) better fits your plans, Bunnell Rock has a better view than at the top of Mount Cabot and is 0.9 mile below the summit. An old fire warden's cabin 0.4 mile below the summit is maintained by local volunteers and is available year-round as a primitive shelter, on a first-come, first-serve basis.

Directions: From the junction of US 2 and NH 116 in Jefferson, go 0.3 mile west on US 2 to North Road. Turn right on North Road for 2.3 miles to Gore Road. Turn right on Gore Road for 1.4 miles to Garland Road. Bear left on Garland Road for 0.5 mile to Pleasant Valley Road (gravel). Turn right on Pleasant Valley Road for 0.8 mile to Arthur Hill Road. Turn right on Arthur Hill Road for 0.4 mile to a metal gate and the trailhead sign. Park off the road in the designated place 50 yards prior to this gate without blocking any driveways. This trailhead is on private land and hiking here is at the discretion of the owner.

Trail: 7.8-mile (round-trip) hike to the summit of Mount Cabot or 6.0 miles (round-trip) to Bunnell Rock.

Elevation: 1,500 feet to 4,170 feet.

Degree of difficulty: Strenuous.

Surface and blaze: Logging roads, forest floor, some rocks. No blazes.

MOUNT STARR KING

[Fig. 12] After leaving Mount Cabot, the Kilkenny Ridge Trail winds south and west, stringing together the mountains of the Pliny Range. The trail officially ends on 4,006-foot Mount Waumbek, the tallest of this group. Unfortunately, the summit of this mountain is forested and the view is just a frustrating peek off to the east, but only 1 mile west, its neighbor, Mount Starr King, provides a splendid vista of the entire Presidential range. The Kilkenny Ridge Trail ends here on Mount Waumbek, but the Mount Starr King Trail connects Waumbek to Starr King, then descends to US 2.

Mount Starr King is named for the nineteenth-century Boston clergyman, Thomas Starr King, who explored and wrote glowing descriptions of the majesty of the White Mountains. His book, *The White Hills: Their Legends, Landscape and Poetry,* drew many visitors to New Hampshire, and later both this mountain and King Ravine on Mount Adams were named for him.

It is a pleasure to hike up Mount Starr King. Though the hiker gains more than 2,500 feet, the 2.6-mile trail never really gets steep or rocky. It climbs at a nice, even pace, first through an airy forest of sugar maple and yellow birch. Then it winds a narrow path through fragrant spruce, fir, and white birch to the summit—the conifer needles underfoot cushioning the tough quartz syenite that forms this mountain.

In June, this hike is a garden walk along a forest floor carpeted with foamflower (*Tiarella cordifolia*) and wood sorrel (*Oxalis montana*). Be aware, however, that this is a 3,907-foot mountain that can get chilly and windy at the top. Come fortified with lots of water, a snack, and extra clothing.

KILKENNY RIDGE TRAIL TO STARR KING TRAIL TO MOUNT STARR KING

[Fig. 12(3)] The Kilkenny Ridge Trail ends atop Mount Waumbek where it meets the eastern terminus of the Starr King Trail. One more mile on this trail brings the hiker to a magnificent view and a route down out of the Pliny Mountains to US 2 in Jefferson.

Directions: For the Kilkenny Ridge Trail approach to Mount Starr King, follow the directions to the Kilkenny Ridge Trailhead at South Pond Recreation Area, page 53. Hike 20.6 miles down the Kilkenny Ridge Trail to the summit of Mount Waumbek and the last mile over to Mount Starr King on the Starr King Trail.

Trail: 21.6-mile, 3- to 4-day, backpacking trip through the Kilkenny, offering mountain outlooks in the Pilot and the Pliny ranges.

Elevation: 1,500 feet to 4,170 feet.

Degree of difficulty: Strenuous.

Surface and blaze: Forest floor, rocks, stream crossings. Yellow blazes.

STARR KING TRAIL TO MOUNT STARR KING

[Fig. 12(7)] This is the southwestern day-hike route to the summit of Mount Starr King, a pleasant climb through mixed forest to a breathtaking view south over the Presidentials. The trail continues another mile beyond this summit to the top of Mount Waumbek where it meets the southern terminus of the Kilkenny Ridge Trail.

Trail: 5.2-mile (round-trip) hike to the Summit of Mount Starr King or a 7.2-mile (round-trip) hike to the summit of Mount Waumbek.

Elevation: 1,450 feet to 3,907 feet to Mount Starr King or 1,450 feet to 4,006 feet to Mount Waumbek.

Degree of difficulty: Moderate.

Surface and blaze: Forest floor, some rocks.

Randolph and Gorham Area

A broad swath of relatively open country separates the Kilkenny section of the White Mountain National Forest (WMNF) from the Presidential section to the south. It runs east and west at an elevation around 1,500 feet, which would make it high country in most parts of New Hampshire. Here, it seems more like lowlands, compared with the neighboring mountains. Crouched between the Crescent Range looming on the north, and the mighty Presidentials that fill the southern horizon, this stretch of sloping valley is lower because it is geologically older. The granitic rocks underlying this valley intruded the area about 385 million years ago, and thus have had a few hundred million years longer to erode than have the newer granites

Randolph Mountain Club

Since 1910, the Randolph Mountain Club (RMC) has been luring hikers and mountain scenery buffs to the tiny town of Randolph. The club maintains over 100 miles of trails, marked by their neatly lettered white signs, that point the way into the mountain ranges that surround Randolph. The trails offer access primarily up the northern slopes of Mounts Madison, Adams, and Jefferson in the Presidential Range, or into the Crescent Range north of US 2. The club also manages two overnight cabins and two Adironcack-style shelters in the mountains, all of which welcome hikers on a first-come, first-serve basis. One of the cabins, Gray Knob, with a year-round caretaker and a wood stove, sits at 4,400 feet elevation in the Presidentials.

Every summer, the RMC holds an annual rendezvous and picnic and every week they offer guided hikes. Their hiking guide, *Randolph Paths,* and their detailed trail map are authoritative sources on hiking the area and are available by writing Treasurer, Randolph Mountain Club, RR 1, Box 1570, Randolph, New Hampshire 03570, or calling (603) 466-5425 or (603) 466-2438.

that form the bulk of the White Mountains.

Through this swath of relatively low terrain run two rivers—the Androscoggin and the Moose. As always, where the rivers are, so come the railroads, and the highways, and the towns. In this case, though, no large population center ever sprang up; perhaps the winters are too cold. Instead, only a few tiny villages and one middle-sized town interrupt the miles of sloping farmland and the million-dollar view.

The village of Randolph sits just north of US 2 on Durand Road, formerly a piece of the old Route 2. Despite its diminutive profile, this town enjoys a certain quiet distinction among hikers as the home of the Randolph Mountain Club (RMC). This 90-year-old organization of dedicated volunteers maintains over 100 miles of hiking trails, both within and outside of the WMNF. Many of these trails head south into the Presidentials from two trailheads located on the south side of US 2, between Randolph and Bowman. Others lead north into the Crescent Range. This range takes its name from the arcurate ridge formed by Mounts Randolph, Crescent, and Black Crescent. These heights are made up primarily of a granitic porphyry that contains large crystals of quartz and biotite.

Immediately south of the Crescents, on the southern shoulder of Mount Randolph, Lookout Ledge provides a stunning view south into the Presidential Range, and visible from here is King Ravine, a dramatic cleft between the northern slopes of Mounts Madison and Adams. This boulder-strewn gulch is a much larger version of the Devil's Hopyard (*see* page 55), a ravine in the Kilkenny that is also strewn with huge chunks of angular rock. This phenomenon, referred to by geologists as a "fossil rock glacier" occurs when gigantic pieces of rock from the mountains above drop onto a glacial remnant left behind by the receding ice sheet and are gradually carried down valley. As the dying tongue of ice creeps down the ravine, it carries the rocks with it and deposits them, helter-skelter along the ravine. So deep and protected are the crevices and caves beneath the rocks that ice often remains there year-round.

Of the many hiking destinations north of US 2 in the Randolph-Gorham area, (see the Randolph Mountain Club's *Randolph Paths* or its map of *The Randolph Valley and Northern Peaks)*, three short treks offer much more in the way of vista than they demand in the way of exertion. Lookout Ledge, Mascot Pond, and Mount Crag all begin near US 2, the east-west highway that runs through the region.

LOOKOUT LEDGE AND THE LEDGE TRAIL

[Fig. 12(8), Fig. 12(9)] Lookout Ledge in Randolph offers a wonderful view south into the Presidential Range of the White Mountains. To get to it involves a 1.3-mile climb up from the site where the old Durand House used to stand. From 1877 to 1961, this hotel with its cleared front slopes offered guests a grand vista and a quiet mountain escape. Though relatively short, this climb is rather steep in places and hiking boots are in order.

Directions: From the junction of NH 16N and US 2 in Gorham, go 4.6 miles west on US 2 to Durand Road East. Turn right and go 0.1 mile. Turn left (it remains Durand Road) and go 1 mile to a blue sign on the right marking the site of the old Durand House. Park on the right just beyond this sign and look for white RMC sign and orange-blazed trail to Lookout Ledge.

Trail: 2.6-mile (round-trip) climb to Lookout Ledge.

Elevation: 1,420 feet to 2,350 feet.

Degree of difficulty: Moderate. Steep in spots.

Surface and blaze: Narrow trail, forest floor and some rocky surfaces. Orange blazes.

MASCOT POND AND THE MAHOOSUC TRAIL

[Fig. 12, Fig. 12(10)] Whatever the beginning of this hike may lack in pristine ambience, it certainly makes up for in local color and interesting biology. In the first 0.5 mile, you walk over the Androscoggin River on a footbridge that is slung underneath a railroad trestle, then cross over a canal on top of a hydroelectric dam. At Mascot Pond, another surprise lies in store. The pond sits just below the bare cliffs of Leadmine Ledge, on the south side of Mount Hayes. For a few years in the 1880s, the old Mascot Mine operation blasted lead-bearing ore from the cliff above this pond, then abandoned the place when the mineral ran out. Those were the days before reclamation was expected, and today, the cliffside remains littered with broken rock and abandoned mine shafts.

This mess might offend some human eyes, but other species have come to call it home. Several kinds of bats, seeking caves for winter hibernation, have for the last few years, set up winter quarters inside one of the mine shafts. In addition to the

AMERICAN CRANBERRY
(Vaccinium macrocarpon)

fairly common little brown bat, The Nature Conservancy has also found numbers of long-eared bats, big brown bats, and even a few pipistrelles and endangered small-footed bats, hibernating in this old mine shaft. Because New Hampshire has little limestone—where caves normally develop—this is the closest thing to a cave that this area can come up with. It now has the distinction of being the largest bat hibernaculum in the state.

The Nature Conservancy has covered the shaft with a gratelike gate that keeps people out, and allows the bats to come and go at will. This protects humans from falls and the bats from disturbance. Hibernating bats are living off the fat they stored away in the fall. If they are awakened, they fly around, using up precious energy, and since there are no insects to eat in the winter, they can starve to death before spring.

Below this backdrop of Leadmine Ledge, Mascot Pond provides a placid mirror for the sky and serves as home for several beaver families whose conical lodges are anchored around its edges. There is a sandy beach on the north side of the pond, a birch and balsam woods on the opposite shore, and sundry boulders scattered around on which to sit for a spell and enjoy a picnic lunch. Over the treetops, the peak of Mount Madison is just barely visible to the south.

Directions: From the junction of US 2 and NH 16 in Gorham, go north on NH 16 for 0.4 mile to a railroad bridge over the road. Park there on the right near a white sign that reads "To Mahoosuc Trail 0.5 mile."

Activities: Hiking, picnicking, swimming.

Facilities: Trail, beach.

Dates: Open year-round.

Fees: None.

Closest town: Gorham, 2 miles.

For more information: New Hampshire Department of Resources and Economic Developement, 172 Pembroke Road, Concord, NH 03302. Phone (603) 271-3456. The Nature Conservancy, 2 1/2 Beacon Street, Concord, NH. Phone (603) 224-5853.

MAHOOSUC TRAIL TO MASCOT POND

[Fig. 12(10)] The Mahoosuc Trail is an Appalachian Trail (AT) connector that runs from Gorham to the summit of Mount Hayes. The initial 1.3 miles lead to Mascot Pond for a view of Leadmine Ledge to the north and Mount Madison to the south. A white sign in the parking lot directs you up the metal stairs to a footbridge under the railroad bridge. On the other side of the river, bear right on a dirt road for 0.4 mile, then cross over the hydroelectric dam between the two buildings and turn left down a another dirt road for 100 yards to the sign and blue blazes of the Mahoosuc Trail. Approximately 0.7 mile along this trail, a white sign on the right directs you to the pond.

Activities: Hiking, swimming, picnicking.

Trail: 2.6-mile (round-trip) hike to Mascot Pond.

Elevation: 700 feet to 1,060 feet.

Degree of difficulty: Easy.

Surface and blaze: Wooden foot-bridge, concrete dam, woods road, forest floor. Mahoosuc Trail has blue blazes.

MOUNT CRAG

[Fig. 12] With a summit of only 1,412 feet, Mount Crag is a short mountain for these parts, but it makes a good climb for families and offers a splendid view of the Androscoggin River valley as it runs east into Maine. From the viewpoint at 1.3 miles, you can also see the much higher Carter Range to the south. Like many trails in this middle ground between sections of the WMNF, this one begins on private land, at a curious little turnstile. It travels a grassy old road, some open lawns, and a tall and pleasant forest. After crossing Austin Brook, you reach the lookout.

AUSTIN BROOK TRAIL TO MOUNT CRAG

[Fig. 12(11)] This 1.2-mile hike begins with passage through a white wooden turnstile that seems to serve no other purpose than to be charming. It ends 680 feet higher at the cliff atop Mount Crag. Taking over 1 mile to gain this modest elevation, this is primarily a flat walk, through a fern-carpeted forest. Remember that this is private land and the owner's forbearance rests upon the continued courteous behavior of visitors.

Directions: From the junction of US 2 and NH 16S in Gorham, go 5.8 miles east on US 2 to Meadow Road. Turn left and cross the Androscoggin River. After 0.9 mile, turn left again onto North Road and go 0.5 mile to a white fence and turnstile on the right. Pull-out parking is on the other side of North Road. Pass through the turnstile and follow the blue-blazed Austin Brook Trail to Mount Crag's summit.

Trail: 2.4-mile (round-trip) hike to the summit of Mount Crag.

Elevation: 732 feet to 1,412 feet.

Degree of difficulty: Easy.

Surface and blaze: Forest floor and logging roads. Stay with blue-blazed Austin Brook Trail when the Yellow Trail with yellow blazes turns off at 0.4 mile.

FISHER
(Martes pennanti)
A boreal species, the shy fisher is an adept climber and swimmer that eats porcupines and snowshoe hares.

WMNF Carter Region

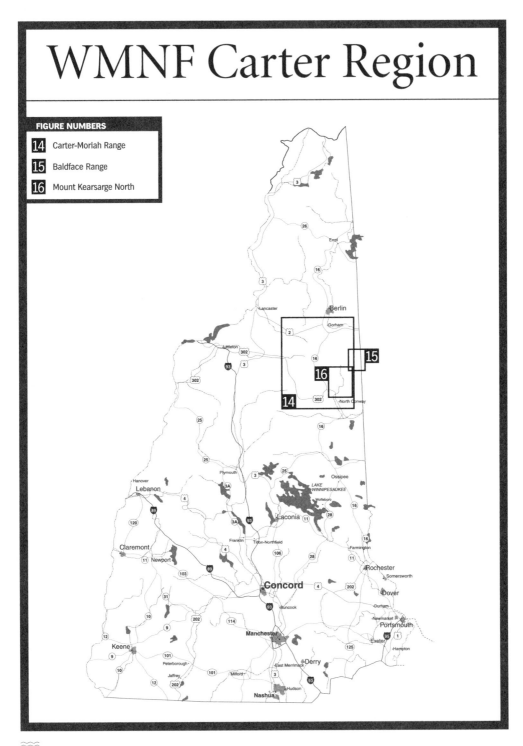

FIGURE NUMBERS

14 Carter-Moriah Range

15 Baldface Range

16 Mount Kearsarge North

WMNF Carter Region

T he Carter Region is the easternmost portion of the White Mountain National Forest, and a little more than half of it lies in New Hampshire. The remainder continues on across the border into Maine. New Hampshire's piece is organized around two long mountain ranges—the Carter-Moriah and the Baldface ranges—that run roughly parallel down the full length of the region and trend northeast to southwest. These two ranges, alone, could provide hiking and other outdoor recreation enough to last for a lifetime, and some of their more outstanding trails and features are the subject of this section.

Between these two belts of mountains lies the unpopulated Wild River valley. This tumbling stream more than lives up to its name during spring runoff—or, for that matter, anytime it rains. The water pours off the flanks of the surrounding mountains, then tears north, to the Androscoggin River. Other streams and rivers have

[*Above:* A beautiful winter sunset in the White Mountains]

Carnivorous Plants

Among other impoverishments, bogs are very short on nitrogen, a critical plant nutrient. The round-leaf sundew (*Drosera rotundifolia*), and the northern pitcher plant (*Sarracenia purpurea*), have evolved some elegant ways to make up for this deficiency. They actually eat insects.

The sundew has leaves covered with red, glandular hairs. They secrete a sticky substance that traps any hapless insect that comes to investigate. The sundew then digests the insect's nitrogen-rich body. The pitcher plant is a little more subtle but just as deadly. Its liver-colored leaves form a receptacle that catches rainwater in a little pool. The leaves exude nectar to lure insects down inside where they cannot crawl back out because the leaves are covered with downward-pointing hairs. The insects drown in the water and are digested by enzymes there. Additionally, the pitcher plant's "pitcher" is now known to house nitrogen-fixing bacteria, which can take nitrogen right from the air and convert it to a form the plant can use. Thus covering all the bases, this plant thrives in the nitrogen-poor world of the bog.

their headwaters in these mountains too, and the crystal clear waters of the Peabody and the Ellis rivers, running north and south out of Pinkham Notch, exemplify the effectiveness of the WMNF as a protector of water quality.

New Hampshire's portion of the Carter region is bordered on the west by NH 16, on the north by US 2, and on the east by the New Hampshire/Maine border. Ignoring this merely political border, the forest rolls onward into Maine's Evans Notch region. Just as the forest remains unperturbed by this ecologically invisible line dividing two states, so too, should the visitor, because the only road running down this eastern flank—NH or ME 113—weaves across the border several times—when it isn't closed for the winter. For that reason, this guide will give some directions to New Hampshire sites that take the visitor briefly into Maine.

One of the more breathtaking vistas in the Carter Region is the approach to the area from the south, driving into Pinkham Notch on NH 16. Just north of Jackson Village, the whole world seems to open up as the broad Ellis River valley spreads its arms in welcome. To the west tower the mighty Presidentials with Tuckerman and Huntington ravines, on the side of Mount Washington, facing east and shining white with snow, long into late spring. On a high southern shoulder of Mount Washington, silhouetted against the sky, sits another long-loved landmark. Glen Boulder rests solidly on its deceptively precarious perch, as it has for thousands of years, while seeming to threaten an imminent tumble down into the valley. The rock, however, hasn't budged in millennia, and remains precisely where the glacier left it. A better perspective of its immensity is possible by hiking up the short, but very steep, Glen Boulder Trail from NH 16 (*see* page 102).

Along the eastern side of this magnificent view runs Wildcat Mountain, a long and humpy ridge that includes five separate summits labeled, a tad unimaginatively, A, B, C, D, and E peaks. The highest of them, A Peak, rises 4,422 feet. On one portion of its eastern slope lies the Wildcat Ski Area, a year-round recreational area run privately on land leased from the Forest Service.

ROUND-LEAF SUNDEW (Drosera rotundifolia) Insects attracted to a sweet sticky fluid on the tips of the sundew's hairy leaves become stuck among the hairs that bend like tentacles to smother the victim.

The Jackson Area

The town of Jackson has had a few names. It was New Madbury in 1790, then Adams in 1800. After the election of 1828, it was changed to Jackson, reputedly because all but one of its citizens voted for Andrew Jackson. This last name seems to have stuck, but who knows what changes the future might bring.

Today, driving through the bright red covered bridge into Jackson Village is like entering another world. For nearly 200 years, this area of white-steepled churches and long, green lawns has provided a quiet and comfortable base from which to explore the White Mountains. Two-thirds of the town of Jackson is within the borders of the WMNF, and this gracious village offers superlative amenities without spoiling the view.

Most of the accommodations here are in old inns with sprawling lawns and mature perennial gardens, making the overall feeling of this place one of unhurried restfulness. There is, however, enough to do to work up a healthy appetite, and fine dining is available. An 18-hole golf course rolls over hills and hollows and sports its own little covered bridge over a stream. There are rivers and ponds to fish, bike trails to ride, cross-country trails to ski, and fall foliage to view, or if outlet shopping is your wish, Conway is just a few miles south on NH 16.

Last and most attractive of all, the WMNF, which virtually surrounds the village, offers nearly 1,200 miles of trails to hike and no less than 48 exciting 4,000-footers to climb. If equipment or lessons are required, there are rentals and instructors located close by for everything from golf, to fishing, to skiing, to kayaking, to mountain biking (*see* Great Glen Trails, page 74).

Directions: From the junction of US 302 and NH 16 in Glen, go 2.4 miles north on NH 16 to red covered bridge on right. Turn right, driving through the covered bridge, into Jackson Village.

Activities: Downhill and cross-country skiing, golfing, biking, hiking, fishing, dining, and lodging.

Facilities: Inns, restaurants, golf course, ski trails, biking trails. Rivers, ponds, hiking trails, and WMNF, all nearby.

Dates: Most facilities open year-round.

Fees: There is a charge for lodging, meals, golfing, and skiing. Activities within the national forest are generally free but a parking permit is required.

Closest town: Jackson Village or Conway, 8 miles south.

For more information: Jackson Chamber of Commerce, Box 304, Jackson, NH 03846. Phone (800) 866-3334 or (603) 383-9356. Internet address is www.jacksonnh.com.

Appalachian Mountain Club Visitor Center

[Fig. 14(8)] For anyone visiting the White Mountains of New Hampshire, a stop at the Appalachian Mountain Club's Pinkham Notch Visitor Center is an absolute must. The Appalachian Mountain Club (AMC) was founded in 1876 and is the oldest organization of its kind in this country. This nonprofit environmental group focuses on the protection, enjoyment, and wise use of the mountains, rivers, and trails of the Northeast. It maintains trails and shelters, publishes books and maps, and conducts workshops, youth programs, and outdoor research. The club also pursues a vigorous conservation agenda.

The AMC is the best source of maps and hiking guides for the WMNF. Its *AMC White Mountain Guide* is an indispensable resource for hiking in the White Mountains. It is packed with information about hundreds of trails, comes with a fistful of topographical maps, and is still small enough to fit in a pocket of your backpack. Of use too, if you're planning a longer trek, is the *AMC White Mountain Guidebook/ Guide to the Presidentials.*

The AMC manages eight backcountry shelters, situated a day's hike apart in some of the most beautiful country in the White Mountains. With advance reservations, the hiker can expect a warm bunk and nutritious meals at these huts. For a base closer to the center of things, there is also a lodge adjacent to the Pinkham Notch Visitor Center, and a hostel in Crawford Notch, on the other side of the Presidentials. Reservations are necessary at any of these accommodations in the busiest months of July and August.

Many of the trails in the WMNF and many of those discussed in this guide were built and are maintained by the AMC. With both professional and volunteer trail crews, the club maintains a total of 1,200 miles of hiking trails in the Northeast, 350 miles of which are part of the Appalachian Trail (*see* page 295). Numerous other trails in the WMNF are maintained by the U.S. Forest Service, and others are maintained by various volunteer hiking clubs. No matter who takes care of the upkeep on a particular trail, there is a general color coding of blazes to inform the hiker of the trail's overall type. White blazes signify that the trail is part of the Appalachian Trail, the 2,160-mile-long trail that runs from Georgia to Maine. Blue blazes denote those trails that connect to the AT, and yellow blazes mark all the other trails on national forest land.

The AMC's Pinkham Notch Visitor Center is a bustling hub of hiker activity where a friendly and helpful staff stands ready with whatever information and advice the visitor needs. The main building holds a cafeteria, a book and map store, and postings about weather and upcoming programs. Filling a large table there is a wonderful graphic relief map of the Presidential Range, its geology clearly explained in lay terms on posters around the edges.

WHITE-THROATED SPARROW
(*Zonotrichia albicollis*)

Several AMC hiking trails take off from various places around the visitor center—at the rear of the main building, at the south end of the parking lot, or across the street. All are clearly signed and blazed. Many of the other trails discussed below take off from parking areas along NH 16 and US 2, which are posted with brown hiker signs. These trails are of varying lengths and degrees of difficulty. Pick up a copy of the *AMC White Mountain Guide* and choose a hike to match your fitness and your footwear. Many of these mountain trails are muddy, rocky, and rough. Be sure to take along lots of water, extra food and clothing, and the appropriate topographic map for the area. Whatever hike you choose, careful planning will enhance your enjoyment.

The AMC runs a hiker's shuttle service daily from June to October. Vans make regular stops at 13 trailheads throughout the Presidential Range, Franconia Notch, and along NH 16. This means the visitor can plan a hike that ends in a different place than it begins, and have a way to get back to his or her car. Schedules are posted at trailheads and reservations are recommended.

Directions: From the junction of US 302 and NH 16 in Glen, go 12.3 miles north on NH 16 to AMC Visitor Center sign on left.

Activities: Hiking, lodging, gathering trail and map information, shopping, showers, eating.

Facilities: Trails, parking, restaurant, showers, information desk, displays, programs, bookstore.

Dates: Open year-round.

Fees: There is a charge for lodging, meals, showers, and store items. Information, trails, and programs are free.

Closest town: Jackson, 10 miles.

For more information: AMC Pinkham Notch Visitor Center, Box 298, Gorham, NH 03581. Phone (800) 262-4455. For lodging or shuttle reservations, phone (603) 466-2727.

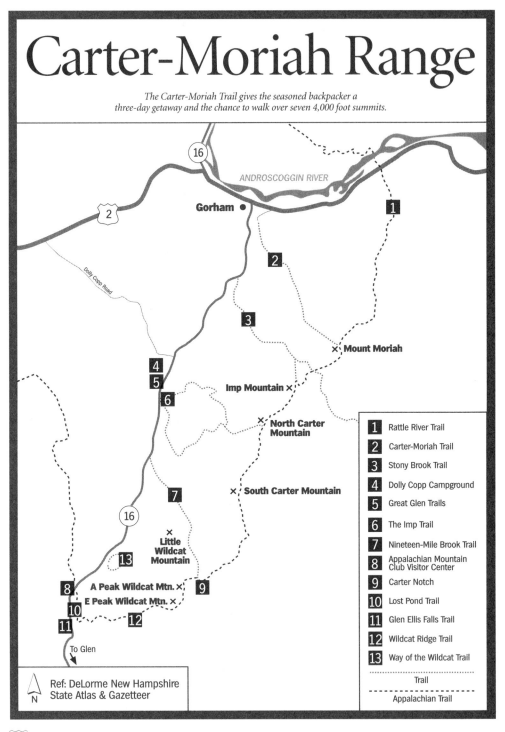

Carter-Moriah Range

The Carter-Moriah Trail gives the seasoned backpacker a three-day getaway and the chance to walk over seven 4,000 foot summits.

ANDROSCOGGIN RIVER

16

2

Gorham ●

1

2

Dolly Copp Road

3

×͏ Mount Moriah

4
5
6

Imp Mountain ×

× North Carter Mountain

1	Rattle River Trail
2	Carter-Moriah Trail
3	Stony Brook Trail
4	Dolly Copp Campground
5	Great Glen Trails
6	The Imp Trail
7	Nineteen-Mile Brook Trail
8	Appalachian Mountain Club Visitor Center
9	Carter Notch
10	Lost Pond Trail
11	Glen Ellis Falls Trail
12	Wildcat Ridge Trail
13	Way of the Wildcat Trail

× South Carter Mountain

7

16

×
Little
Wildcat
Mountain

13

8
A Peak Wildcat Mtn. ×
E Peak Wildcat Mtn. ×
9

10
11
12

To Glen

N
Ref: DeLorme New Hampshire
State Atlas & Gazetteer

············· Trail

- - - - - Appalachian Trail

The Carter-Moriah Range

[Fig. 14] The Carter-Moriah Range of mountains runs northeast to southwest for about 15 miles down the eastern edge of the valley that holds the Peabody and Ellis rivers, roughly parallel to NH 16. Their southern peaks form the eastern wall of Pinkham Notch. Although eight of the mountains in this range are higher than 4,000 feet, they tend to be dwarfed by comparison with those lofty Presidentials "across the street."

Geologically, these are tough, metamorphic rocks of the Littleton Formation. Here and there, they are cut with a few dikes and sills of younger igneous rocks, but for the most part, these are metamorphic schists and quartzites. Many of their peaks are wooded, but Carter Dome, Mount Hight, Mount Moriah, and Shelburne Moriah Mountain all offer excellent views of the Wild River valley to the east and the Presidentials to the west.

The Carter-Moriah Trail, which is part of the AT, runs almost 14 miles down the range, from the town of Gorham to Carter Notch. In several places, this long trail is accessible via side trails from NH 16 on the west, while other side trails from the east connect it to the Highwater Trail and the Wild River Trail that run down the Wild River valley. Primitive shelters and campsites, plus the roomier AMC Carter Notch Hut, are available along the way for the hiker who chooses to make this extended backpacking trip. Day hikes of various lengths and degrees of difficulty are accessible from the many trailheads scattered along NH 16 and US 2, and descriptions of some of them follow.

GLEN ELLIS FALLS TRAILHEAD

[Fig. 14(11)] This trailhead, located less than 1 mile south of the AMC Pinkham Notch Visitor Center, is a wonderful introduction to the Pinkham Notch area. The parking lot on the west side of the road is a good spot to stop and get your bearings and to make plans for how to explore this spectacular area. Near the parking lot are picnic tables and restroom facilities, and a footpath leads under the road to three trail choices on the east side of NH 16. While one of them, the Wildcat Ridge Trail, is a strenuous climb to the Carter Notch Hut, the other two, Lost Pond Trail and the trail to Glen Ellis Falls, are easy family hikes.

Directions: From the junction of NH 16 and US 302 in Glen, go 11.5 miles north on NH 16 to the Glen Ellis Trailhead parking lot on the west side of the road.

Activities: Hiking, picnicking, falls viewing.

Facilities: Trails, picnic tables, restrooms, parking, map, water.

Dates: Open year-round.

Fees: None.

Closest town: Glen, 11.5 miles

For more information: AMC Pinkham Notch Visitor Center, Box 298, Gorham, NH 03581. Phone (800) 262-4455. WMNF Androscoggin Ranger District, 300 Glen Road, Gorham, NH 03581. Phone (603) 466-2713.

WILDCAT RIDGE TRAIL

[Fig. 14(12)] After crossing under NH 16 on the footpath, the Wildcat Ridge Trail, a leg of the AT, leads straight ahead, across the Ellis River, to a strenuous climb of about 5 miles. This route winds up and down over the five undulating peaks of Wildcat Mountain until it meets the Nineteen Mile Trail, at 4.9 miles, and turns right for a short distance to the Carter Notch Hut. Advance reservations assure the visitor of a hot meal here and a bunk for the night.

Trail: 5-mile hike (one-way) over the multiple peaks of Wildcat Mountain to Carter Notch Hut.

Elevation: 1,600 feet to 4,422 feet.

Degree of difficulty: Strenuous.

Surface and blaze: Forest floor, rocky ledges. Blazes are blue briefly, then white.

LOST POND TRAIL

[Fig. 14(10)] This relatively flat trail crosses the Ellis River, after the footpath under the highway, then turns left and runs north beside NH 16. It passes a quiet pond and crosses over a beaver wetland on a boardwalk before ending at the AMC Pinkham Notch Visitor Center, a distance of 0.9 mile, one-way. Just before the bridge leading to the center, a side trail turns upslope and leads to two lookouts: Lady's Lookout at 0.1 mile and Square Ledge at 0.5 mile. These give good views of the Presidential Range to the west.

Trail: 1.8-mile (round-trip) hike from Glen Ellis Falls to Pinkham Notch Visitor Center. This is a short segment of the AT.

Elevation: No elevation gain.

Degree of difficulty: Easy.

Surface and blaze: Forest floor, the river crossing may be difficult in high water. Blazes are white.

TRAIL TO GLEN ELLIS FALLS

[Fig. 14(11)] A trail of rock stairs turns right off the Wildcat Ridge Trail, after the underpass but before it crosses the river. This 0.3-mile walk down to Glen Ellis Falls offers a look at this lovely falls from the top—where it foams around orange-colored boulders and through tight crevices—to the bottom—where it plunges into a deep green pool. Informative plaques along the route tell the glacial history of the origin, while the cool spray makes rainbows in the dappled sunlight.

Trail: 0.6-mile (round-trip) walk down several flights of stone steps to the base of Glen Ellis Falls.

Elevation: 1,800 feet to 1,700 feet.

Degree of difficulty: Easy.

Surface and blaze: Stone steps. No blazes.

WILDCAT MOUNTAIN

[Fig. 14] This long, slinky mountain was named for the bobcat, an animal still known to sun itself on Wildcat Mountain's south-facing ledges. The humpy profile of Wildcat is made up of at least five summits, the highest of which is A Peak at 4,422 feet. The Wildcat Ridge Trail runs over all five of them on its way to the Carter Notch Hut (*see* page 72).

On the northern side of Wildcat Mountain, ski trails trace broad, white paths up the mountain in the winter. Come summer, they are bright green swaths winding through the forest, welcoming visitors to ride the multicolored gondola cars up to the top, between D and E Peaks. The view there stretches all the way to Canada or to the Atlantic Ocean, and a glance to the west reveals Mount Washington, with its rocky summit often in the clouds. Often as late as June, snow may still glint from Tuckerman Ravine on its northeastern flank.

At the base, Wildcat offers a shop, a restaurant, and a nice family stroll along the Way of the Wildcat Trail, an easy 0.5-mile walk along the beginnings of the Peabody River, with a short side trip to Thompson Falls. A trail guide packed full of history of the Pinkham Notch area is available inside the base lodge.

Directions: From Pinkham Notch Visitor Center, go 0.9 mile north on NH 16 to Wildcat Mountain sign and parking lot on right.

Activities: Downhill skiing in winter. Hiking, picnicking, and gondola rides in other seasons.

Facilities: Ski slopes, gondolas, gift shop, restaurant, hiking and history trail, picnic tables, restrooms.

Dates: Skiing, Dec. to Mar. Summer activities, mid-June to Oct.

Fees: There is a charge to ski or ride the gondola. Way of the Wildcat Trail is free.

Closest town: Glen, 13.2 miles.

For more information: Wildcat Mountain, Box R, Jackson, NH 03846. Phone (603) 466-3326.

WAY OF THE WILDCAT TRAIL

[Fig. 14(13)] This easy family stroll is actually more of a history walk than a nature walk. The trail guide available inside the base lodge contains a wealth of historical and ecological information, everything from forest ecology, to logging history, to a tall story about the miraculous birth of the Peabody River, a feeder of which gurgles along beside the trail. A short side trail leads to the lovely Thompson, Falls, making the whole loop a little over 1 mile. Though the flow coming down these pebbled streams usually looks pretty benign, these innocent looking streams can become wild in a hurry. Col. Joseph Thompson for whom Thompson Falls is named, drowned in the Peabody River during a storm.

Trail: 0.5-mile loop trail through the woods and beside a pond. 1.2 miles total with side trip to Thompson Falls.

Elevation: No change in elevation.

Degree of difficulty: Easy.

Surface and blaze: Forest floor. Yellow blazes.

GREAT GLEN TRAILS

[Fig. 14(5)] Often, visitors arrive in this wild and beautiful country unprepared to charge off on a 10-mile mountain hike by themselves. They may never have been on a mountain bike or a pair of cross-country skis, but decide they want to try it. Perhaps the fly-fishing bug bites them after their first glimpse of a lone fisherman on the side of the road, casting graceful loops of line over a still pond or a riffling stream. Some may think that snowshoes are items from the distant past until they arrive in a place where they become a necessity for crossing open country. Now there's a place where the visitor can sample and learn how to participate in all these sports and more, without investing in or lugging along lots of equipment, and without taking unnecessary risks.

Great Glen Trails is a private enterprise within the national forest, managed by the same folks who run the Mount Washington Auto Road from Glen House, across the street (*see* page 97). Great Glen Trails offers access to biking, canoeing, kayaking, fishing, skiing, and snowshoeing trails and rental equipment. Moreover, there are instructors who will teach you how to do all of these things. Everything except backpacks and hiking boots is provided for guided tours that will take the visitor hiking up Mount Washington, fishing in many nearby streams and ponds, or off to the backcountry on a 10-day canoe trip.

Great Glen maintains miles of biking, hiking, and skiing trails at the foot of Mount Washington, on hundreds of gorgeous, rolling acres in the Peabody River valley. A huge fish pond lies low in the valley, reflecting the tallest mountain in the Northeast, a grand spot to learn the fine art of fly-casting. If you only want to walk the trails and admire the scenery, that is free.

Great Glen Trails is housed in a new post-and-beam building, the interior of which is lit by the warm colors of native New Hampshire pine. There's a gift shop and helpful staff on hand to answer questions.

Directions: From the AMC Pinkham Notch Visitor Center, go 2.9 miles north on NH 16 to the Great Glen Trails sign on the left.

Activities: Hiking, fishing, canoeing, kayaking, cross-country skiing, snowshoeing, biking, lessons for all of the above, and guided hikes and tours.

Facilities: Trails, equipment to rent, buildings, staff and instructors, maps, parking, restrooms.

Dates: Open year-round.

Fees: There is a charge for equipment rental, lessons, and skiing. Hiking trails are free.

Closest town: Gorham, 4 miles.

For more information: Great Glen Trails, Pinkham Notch Box 300, Gorham, NH 03581. Phone (603) 466-2333. Online: www.mt-washington.com.

NINETEEN-MILE BROOK TRAIL

[Fig. 14(7)] "Brook" really seems like an understatement for this rushing torrent that goes on for miles, tumbling around and over boulders the size of a small garage.

Sugar Maple

The sugar maple (*Acer saccharum*), is one of New Hampshire's most valuable trees, and at midelevation, also one of the more numerous. Sugar maples, along with American beech and yellow birch, make up the dominant forest group known as the northern hardwood association, which covers many hillsides in northern New England. Sugar maples can grow 80 feet tall and 2 to 3 feet in diameter, and have historically been an economic staple, in both the timber industry and the agricultural market. The best maple syrup comes from boiling down the sweet sap that, every spring, runs up under the bark of these stately trees. Because of the attractiveness and sturdiness of its wood, maple has long been used for fine furniture. *Acer saccharum* is often called "hard rock maple" both for its hardness and—according to one forester who loves these trees—because of the appearance of its bark, which tends to look gray and sugary, like the fine-grained texture of New Hampshire granite.

The Nineteen-Mile Brook is actually one long, continuous waterfall, sending a cool rush of fresh air up to the trail, even on the hottest day. At times you walk right on the edge of the flow, and at others, suspended high on the slope above its swirling waters.

This trail runs 3.8 miles (one-way) to the Carter Notch Hut, making a long but pleasant day hike up and down, or a brisk ending to a overnight hike begun elsewhere. It intersects the Carter Dome Trail and the Wildcat Ridge Trail for other possible destinations. Lovely Carter Notch, elevation 3,288 feet, cradles two small scenic ponds and is surrounded by high peaks, making it a great base for further exploration of the Carter Moriah Range. Reservations are necessary at the AMC's stone hut at Carter Notch, which dates from 1914, and except for one weekend in October, this hut is open year-round to accommodate the ever increasing enthusiasm for winter hiking. Great care and the use of crampons are recommended in the winter, however, as places along this streamside trail can become quite icy.

Directions: From AMC Pinkham Notch Visitor Center, go 3.8 miles north on NH 16 to a brown hiker sign and parking on right. Kiosk gives trail and hut information.

Trail: 7.6-mile (round-trip) hike from NH 16 to Carter Notch, along the wildly beautiful Nineteen-Mile Brook.

Elevation: 1,500 feet to 3,288 feet.

Degree of difficulty: Strenuous.

Surface and blaze: Forest floor and rocks. Blazes are blue.

THE IMP TRAIL

[Fig. 14(6)] The name "Imp" sounds as if it might be applied to a sprightly, little rock formation, but instead, it is the name of a rather somber, stiff profile on the west side of North Carter Mountain. It can be seen both from NH 16 and from the

Dolly Copp Campground, but the hiking trail that climbs up over it gives a different view, this one to the west over the Presidentials. This loop trail takes off from NH 16, climbs 2.2 miles to the viewpoint, then another 4.1 miles back to NH 16 (a point 0.3 mile south of the trail's beginning), for a total loop of 6.6 miles. To climb to the viewpoint, then return the same way, is a 4.4-mile option.

Directions: From the AMC Pinkham Notch Visitor Center, go 5.9 miles north on NH 16 to a brown hiker sign and parking on the right.

Trail: 6.6-mile loop over the cliff bearing the Imp Profile or a 4.4-mile up-and-back hike to the viewpoint.

Elevation: 1,250 feet to 3,165 feet.

Degree of difficulty: Strenuous.

Surface and blaze: Forest floor, rocky ledges, several stream crossings. Blazes are yellow.

🏕 DOLLY COPP CAMPGROUND

[Fig. 14(4)] In the early 1800s, the Copp family farmed this land in the Peabody River valley, where today a large national forest campground serves as a base for visitors. Once, Dolly Copp sold homemade apple-butter, cheeses, and candles to the tourists who passed by on their way to the Glen House Hotel or to Mount Washington. She even put up guests in her home for $0.25 a night. Dolly was a farmer's wife for 50 years—that is until she packed up her things and moved to Maine to be with her family, reputedly saying on departure, "Fifty years is long enough to live with one man."

The Dolly Copp Campground is one of the largest in the national forest system, accommodating hundreds of people each night. The campsites, however, are spacious and wooded, and the minimal amenities provided enhance the outdoor experience. In an attempt to remain rustic, this camp has no hookups or showers. For a shower, the visitor must go back to the AMC visitor center to use the coin-operated ones there. Most of the sites are available on a first-come, first-serve basis, with a few that can be reserved during the peak season.

This campground puts the visitor right in the heart of the White Mountains, with easy access to dozens of hiking, biking, and skiing trails, good fishing spots, and scenery as grand as it gets. A free picnic area, also named for the spunky Dolly Copp, is right on NH 16, 0.7 mile north of the campground entrance.

Directions: From Gorham, go 4 miles south on NH 16 to the Dolly Copp Campground sign on the right.

Activities: Camping, fishing, hiking, and picnicking.

Facilities: 177 campsites, flush toilets, water, phones, picnic tables, fire rings, programs, short nature trail, handicap accessibility.

Dates: Mid-May to mid-Oct.

Fees: There is a charge to camp.

Closest town: Gorham, 4 miles.

For more information: Androscoggin Ranger Station, 300 Glen Road, Gorham, NH 03581. Phone (603) 466-2713. To reserve a campsite by credit card, phone (800) 280-2267 or TTY (800) 879-4496.

STONY BROOK TRAIL

[Fig. 14(3)] With a 3,150-foot elevation gain and a distance of 5 miles each way, this is a hike for the physically fit. The 360-degree view from atop 4,049-foot Mount Moriah offers a look back down the entire Carter-Moriah Range. To the north, you look out over the Mahoosuc Range and the Androscoggin River valley; to the east, down into the Wild River valley; and to the southwest, of course, the lofty Presidentials fill the horizon. The trail begins on a bridge over the beautiful Stony Brook and follows this sparkling stream a good deal of the way. It intersects the Carter-Moriah Trail at 3.5 miles where you turn left toward the summit of Mount Moriah.

Directions: From US 2 in Gorham, go 1.4 miles south on NH 16 to Stony Brook Road on the left. Parking is on the left upon entrance to this road, and the trailhead is 25 yards farther up the road, on the left.

Trail: 10-mile (round-trip) hike up Stony Brook and Carter-Moriah trails to the summit of Mount Moriah.

Elevation: 900 feet to 4,049 feet.

Degree of difficulty: Strenuous.

Surface and blaze: Forest floor, rocky ledges. Blue blazes, then white.

CARTER-MORIAH TRAIL

[Fig. 14(2)] The 13.8-mile Carter-Moriah Trail affords the seasoned backpacker a three-day getaway, and a chance to walk over the summits of no fewer than seven 4,000-footers. They are strung out along the Carter-Moriah Range, and several have open peaks from which to appreciate the grandeur of the whole region. The trail begins near Gorham and ends at Carter Notch Hut, where the hiker can pick up the Nineteen-Mile Trail back to NH 16. Another option is to hike the trail in reverse, from south to north. This makes for a shorter uphill hike on the first day, and a longer downhill hike on the third day.

For a good deal of its length, the Carter-Moriah Trail is part of the AT, with its familiar white blazes. There are two organized camping areas along the route, spread at roughly 6.5-mile intervals: the AMC's Imp Campsite, between Mount Moriah and North Carter, and the Carter Notch Hut, at Carter Notch. In planning ahead, do remember to make reservations at the camping areas. Water is a bit scarce on this long hike so come prepared with lots of water-carrying capacity and the ability to purify spring or stream water when available.

Directions: From NH 16 in Gorham, go 0.6 mile east on US 2 to Bangor Road. Turn right onto Bangor Road for 0.6 mile to parking at its end. Trailhead is on the left.

Trail: 17.6-mile backpacking route along the ridges of the Carter-Moriah Range.

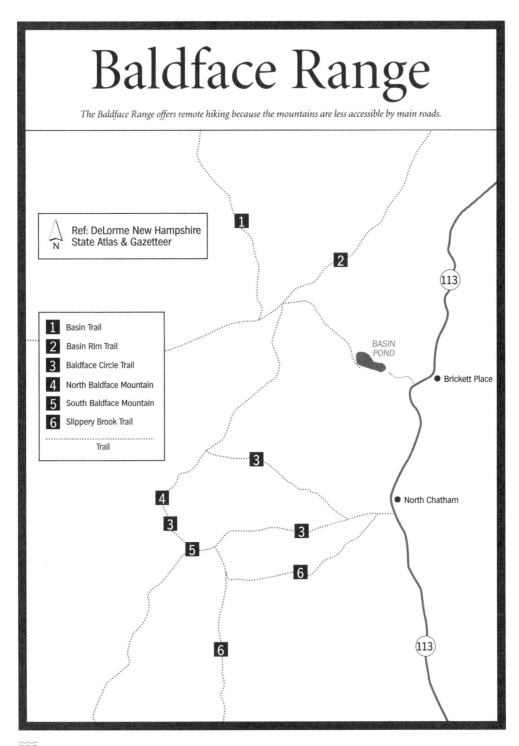

Baldface Range

The Baldface Range offers remote hiking because the mountains are less accessible by main roads.

Ref: DeLorme New Hampshire
State Atlas & Gazetteer
N

1 Basin Trail
2 Basin Rim Trail
3 Baldface Circle Trail
4 North Baldface Mountain
5 South Baldface Mountain
6 Slippery Brook Trail

Trail

BASIN POND

● Brickett Place

● North Chatham

113

(This includes the trip down to NH 16 from Carter Notch.) Climbs seven 4,000-footers. Allow 3 days.

Elevation: 850 feet to 4,675 feet, gaining and losing elevation several times.
Degree of difficulty: Strenuous.
Surface and blaze: Forest floor, rocky trails and ledges, stream crossings, some scrambling.

RATTLE RIVER TRAIL

[Fig. 14(1)] The Rattle River Trail, another challenging section of the AT, takes the hiker on a 5.5-mile trek (one-way) to the summit of 3,735-foot Shelburne Moriah Mountain. This is the northernmost peak in the Carter-Moriah Range, and it offers one of the best views in the region. After 4.3 miles, turn left on the Kenduskeag Trail, another portion of the AT, and hike 1.3 miles farther to the top. This summit has flat, open ledges affording magnificent views of the Androscoggin Valley and the northern Presidentials, as well as the rest of the Carter-Moriah Range stretching south. For about 4 miles, the trail follows the Rattle River, passing the Rattle River Shelter at 1.6 miles. At the headwaters of one of the river's feeder streams, the trail continues steeply uphill to the Kenduskeag Trail.

Directions: From NH 16 in Gorham, go 3.5 miles east on US 2 to the trailhead and parking on the south side of the highway.
Trail: 11-mile (round-trip) hike via the Rattle River and the Kenduskeag trails to the summit of Shelburne Moriah Mountain.
Elevation: 800 feet to 3,735 feet.
Degree of difficulty: Strenuous.
Surface and blaze: Forest floor, rocks, and rocky ledges. Several stream crossings. Blazes are blue, then white.

The Baldface Range

[Fig. 15] On the east side of the Wild River valley, the mountains of the Baldface Range are a little lower in elevation than the Carter-Moriahs, averaging 3,000 to 3,500 feet. They are also a little less accessible by main roads and, consequently, a lot less frequently visited. This adds up to an opportunity for more remote hiking, but also some greater elevation gains because the trails begin at a lower elevation.

There are different kinds of rock to look at here. While the Carter-Moriah Mountains are made of predominantly older, metamorphic rock types, in the Baldface Range, various kinds of granitic rock have intruded, and so have some leftover volcanics.

The best way to approach this eastern side of the Carter Region is to drive east from Gorham on US 2, right over the state border into Maine. About 2 miles into the

Pine Tree State, turn south on NH-ME 113, so named because it winds back and forth across the border, following the valleys of the Wild River and of Evans Brook.

Entering Maine's section of the WMNF on this less-traveled road is a very different experience than coming into the forest's more populated sections in New Hampshire. There are no towns of any size, and the road winds along through a green tunnel of trees. The vistas remain so until the surprising encounter of Evans Notch. Unlike the grand, open vista of Pinkham Notch, on the other side of the Carter Region, Evans Notch appears suddenly, through openings in the trees, as immense walls of rock that seem to lean inward, towering over a deep, narrow chasm on the right side of the road. This notch divides the watersheds of the Androscoggin River to the north and the Saco River to the south and makes a beautiful drive down to where the road re-enters New Hampshire.

After about 11 miles of uninterrupted WMNF, Maine-style, NH-ME 113 passes back across the border, and right into another dramatic vista—Basin Pond. This jewel of a lake sits a mile off the road, in an amphitheaterlike setting of high, forested mountain walls.

▒ BASIN POND

[Fig. 15] Situated at the lower end of Evans Notch is a bowl-shaped cirque carved by the last glacier into the side of Mount Meader. Basin Brook drains this steep headwall, but where it would flow out to the east, an earthen dam backs the water up into a quiet pond. Surrounded by the dark, forested walls of the basin rim, the pond's glassy surface is broken only by the dipping of an occasional canoe paddle and the spreading circles of surfacing fish.

The mix of habitats here—forest, lake, grassy fields—attracts a nice variety of bird life. Thrushes and scarlet tanagers call from the forests around the pond, while swallows and least sandpipers take advantage of the water and the shoreline. The peaceful setting invites the visitor to just sit down and watch those widening circles that fish make when they are feeding, but for those wanting more action, there are some other things to do here. A hiking trail climbs to the top of that imposing rim that surrounds the pond on three sides and winds along its length. There's a boat launch for small boats or canoes and picnic tables to spread supper out on.

If this feels like home for a day or so, adjacent to the pond are two national forest campgrounds with spacious, wooded sites. The Basin Campground has flush toilets and reservations are accepted, while the more rustic Cold River Campground has vault toilets, a few spots for RVs, and operates strictly on a first-come, first-serve basis.

Directions: From the junction of US 2 and NH 16 in Gorham, go 11.6 miles east on US 2 to NH-ME 113. Turn right on 113 and go 11.1 miles to the sign on the right for the Basin Area. Signs for the two WMNF campgrounds are here as well.

Activities: Hiking, boating, camping, fishing, picnicking.

Facilities: Trails, boat ramp, campgrounds, picnic tables and grills. Campgrounds are handicap accessible.

Atlantic Salmon

Historically, Atlantic salmon (*Salmo salar*), once spawned by the millions in many of the streams of New England, before their numbers began declining at the hand of man. The remarkable life cycle of *Salmo salar*, "the leaping fish," has perhaps been studied more than that of any other fish, yet still there are many things we do not understand. Hatching in the cold waters of small streams, salmon may stay from one to several years in freshwater before migrating down to the sea. For two or three years in the ocean, they eat, grow, and lay down fat stores to sustain them on their arduous migration back to the streams of their birth. How each fish is able to find the particular stream in which it was hatched has long been a mystery, but it is believed that the fish can detect, or smell, the specific chemical mix of their own native stream.

Once the salmon has re-entered freshwater, it no longer takes in food, but struggles upstream against all obstacles, on the all-important mission of reproduction. It becomes thin and tattered and the males undergo a grotesque reshaping of their bodies. After spawning, the overwhelming majority of the fish then die, but occasionally, an Atlantic salmon female lives to swim back downstream to repeat the years-long cycle all over again.

Salmon are innately able to negotiate stream barriers up to 18 feet high, but man-made dams, locks, and other obstructions, together with river and ocean pollution, and siltation of spawning streams, have wreaked havoc on salmon populations. As early as 1800, some New England rivers no longer held any Atlantic salmon, once so important to the diet of early Americans.

In recent decades, conservation efforts have resulted in the construction of fish ladders to help salmon get upstream around dams, screens to help keep them out of the turbines, and an amazing restoration of New England rivers to cleaner conditions. However, salmon, like many other North Atlantic fish, have continued to decline from the silting in of streams, the warming or acidification of waters, and especially, from overfishing. As we learn more about salmon biology, efforts continue to save this historically important, endangered species. Our world will be a richer place when their silvery sides and forked tails once again move freely up and down our rivers.

Dates: Facilities and campgrounds open mid-May to mid-Oct. Basin area is open for hiking or fishing year-round.

Fees: None for use of pond, trails, or picnic area. There is a fee for camping.

Closest town: North Chatham, 2 miles.

For more information: WMNF Androscoggin Ranger District, 300 Glen Road, Gorham, NH 03581. Phone (603) 466-2713. For camping reservations, phone (800) 280-2267 or (800) 879-4496 (TTY).

BASIN TRAIL TO BASIN RIM TRAIL LOOKOUT

[Fig. 15(1)] The 2.3-mile Basin Trail leads around the pond and up the headwall to the longer Basin Rim Trail that runs along the ridgetop between Mount Meader and West Royce Mountain. A right turn onto this trail leads 0.1 mile to a spectacular view of Basin Pond, 1,000 feet below. The Basin Trail leaves the Basin Pond parking area, and after 1 mile, a short, optional loop leaves the trail and leads to Hermit Falls. At 2.3 miles, turn right onto the Basin Rim Trail for a 0.1-mile hike to the overlook.

Trail: 4.8-mile (round-trip) hike to a lookout at the top of the rim surrounding Basin Pond, with an optional short side trip to Hermit Falls.

Elevation: 650 feet to 2,000 feet.

Degree of difficulty: Strenuous. Last 0.4 mile is steep.

Surface and blaze: Forest floor, some rocky scrambling.

NORTH AND SOUTH BALDFACE MOUNTAINS

[Fig. 15(4), Fig. 15(5)] These two rocky summits are named Baldface because they expose acres of bare rock at their summits, which can be clearly seen from NH-ME 113. At 3,591 and 3,569 feet, respectively, well below the local tree line of about 4,500 feet, they would normally be cloaked in forest. However, in 1903, there was a devastating fire here that destroyed the trees and exposed the soil atop these mountains to such tremendous erosion that most of it was washed downslope. The fact that nearly 100 years later, these peaks remain "bald" shows how long it takes to build new soil. Even now, the weathering of rock and the growth of lichens are working away at soil-building, but it could be another thousand years before trees once again cover these mountains.

Geologically, North and South Baldface and some of the other mountains in the vicinity are made of different material from the ranges west of here. Whereas Rangeley and Littleton metamorphics dominate the Presidentials and the Carter-Moriahs, these hills show outcrops of younger granites—Kinsman Quartz Monzonite and Mount Osceola Granite. To the hiker, this changes the texture underfoot and lightens the color of the rocks and the soil.

Because of their miles of open rock, the Baldfaces are a magnet to hikers who like to look out over grand vistas. There are two ways to handle the difficult approach to the summits. One offers a challenge to the experienced hiker in terms of difficulty and steepness, the reward being the miles of exposed rock surfaces with 360-degree panoramic views. The other approach cheats a little by letting your automobile gain some of the elevation, and also circumvents the worst of the steep areas.

BALDFACE CIRCLE TRAIL

[Fig. 15(3)] This 9.8-mile loop is for the physically fit hiker seeking a challenge. A day-long trek, involving some very steep rock faces and lots of exposure, it is as beautiful as it is difficult.

In all, this route includes about 4 miles of open and semiopen ledges, from which the hiker is treated to spectacular views of the Wild River valley and the Carter-Moriah Range to the west. Chandler Gorge, a narrow flume full of pools and cascades, is found a little more than 1 mile into the trail, and located at 2 miles is the WMNF's Baldface Shelter.

The Baldface Circle Trail leaves NH 113 and ascends the steep eastern slope of South Baldface. It then traverses 1 mile over open rock to North Baldface, and circles over more open ledge to return via the Eagle Link Trail to the Baldface Circle Trail and back down to the road. Allow at least seven hours for the whole trip.

Because of its unforested, wide-open nature, this trek over the two highest peaks in the Baldface Range has been called one of New England's finest mountain hikes. For the same reason, this route can expose the hiker to extremes of wind and weather. Be prepared, as always, with food, lots of water, extra clothing, and rain gear.

Directions: From US 2 in Gilead, ME, go 13.3 miles south on NH-ME 113 to the AMC's Cold River Camp parking area on the left, or east, side of 113. Park here and walk 0.2 mile back north on 113 to the trailhead on west side of the road.

Trail: 9.8-mile loop over the summits of South Baldface and North Baldface.

Elevation: 500 feet to 3,591 feet.

Degree of difficulty: Strenuous.

Surface and blaze: Forest floor, some very steep rock faces, miles of open ledge. Yellow blazes.

SLIPPERY BROOK TRAIL

[Fig. 15(6)] This 9-mile (round-trip) alternate route to South Baldface Mountain's summit does not cut off much in the way of mileage, but it does have two advantages. The trail starts at an elevation of 1,700 feet, leaving the hiker to climb 1,200 fewer feet than on the Baldface Circle Trail. It also avoids the roughest part of that sheer climb up the mountain's eastern face by approaching it from the south. An up-and-back hike, as opposed to a loop, this trek begins at the end of slippery Brook Road (called Town Hall Road as it leaves NH 16 A in Lower Bartlett), then turns left onto the Baldface Knob Trail, to the Baldface Circle Trail, to the summit of South Baldface. It returns the same way. Like the Baldface Circle Trail, this approach affords spectacular views in all directions from the bald summit of South Baldface.

Directions: From the junction of US 302 and NH 16 A in Intervale, go north on NH 16 A for 1.8 miles to Town Hall Road. Turn right and go 7 miles on this road which becomes Slippery Brook Road. Go straight, avoiding any left-hand turns, to the end of Slippery Brook Road, and park at the gate. The Slippery Brook Trail begins on the left, 200 yards north of the gate. Follow this to the Baldface Knob Trail and turn left. Go to the Baldface Circle Trail and turn left again to the summit of South Baldface Mountain.

Trail: 9-mile (round-trip) hike to the summit.

Elevation: 1,700 feet to 3,569 feet.

Degree of difficulty: Strenuous.

Surface and blaze: Forest floor, exposed ledges, several stream crossings.

RED-SPOTTED NEWT
(Notophthalmus viridescens viridescens)

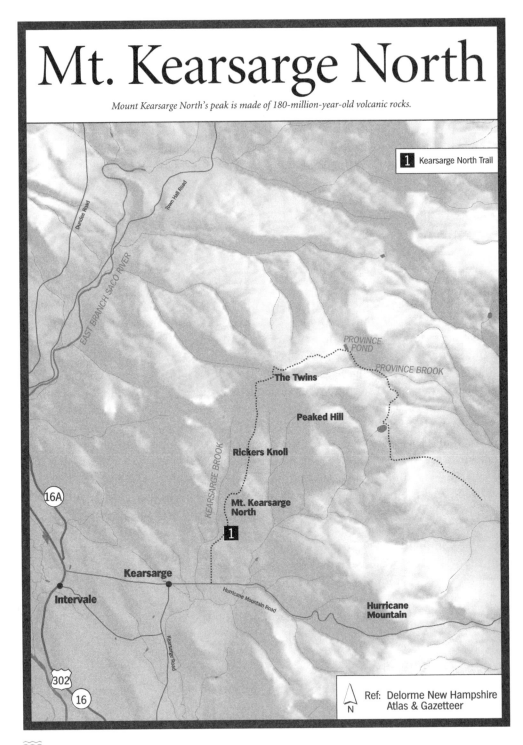

Mt. Kearsarge North

Mount Kearsarge North's peak is made of 180-million-year-old volcanic rocks.

1 Kearsarge North Trail

Dundee Road

Town Hall Road

EAST BRANCH SACO RIVER

PROVINCE POND

PROVINCE BROOK

The Twins

Peaked Hill

KEARSARGE BROOK

Rickers Knoll

16A

Mt. Kearsarge North

1

Kearsarge

Intervale

Hurricane Mountain Road

Hurricane Mountain

Kearsarge Road

302

16

N Ref: Delorme New Hampshire Atlas & Gazetteer

Hermit Thrush

The lilting song of the hermit thrush (*Catharus guttatus*), echoes through the mixed hardwood and conifer forests of New Hampshire's mountains. *Catharus guttatus* has been called the American nightingale, for its haunting, flutelike music. A series of phrases, each one beginning with a single note, and each slightly higher up the scale than the last, signals that a male hermit thrush is either courting or he is guarding his territory while his mate incubates their eggs. Amid this concert, he finds time to feed her on the nest and to help feed the chicks once they've hatched.

The hermit thrush seems a bit hardier than the other North American thrushes. It migrates north earlier in the spring, stays later in the fall, and occasionally one will stay all winter. Its conservation status looks brighter than its equally melodious cousin, the wood thrush, and it also experiences less nest parasitism from cowbirds. In this era of worry about declining songbird numbers, *Catharus guttatus* seems to be holding its own.

MOUNT KEARSARGE NORTH AND KEARSARGE NORTH TRAIL

[Fig. 16] In a small state like New Hampshire, it seems that there should be enough mountain names to go around, but here is one with the same name as that double-humped monadnock that rises above Warner and Wilmot, 70 miles to the southwest. The reasons why the name of this conelike peak was changed from the Native American *Pequawket* are lost to obscurity—gone, like the hotel that once topped the mountain but blew away in 1883.

Kearsarge North's beautiful peak is made of 180-million-year-old volcanic rocks, something of a rarity around here. It has easily survived the vicissitudes of human nomenclature and hotel building, and its summit offers up one of the finer views in the White Mountains. Though the trail to the top gains almost 2,700 feet, most of it is not very steep, and it has become a favorite for families. A fire tower at the top begs climbing for a panoramic view of the Carter and Presidential ranges to the north and west, and the smaller Green Hills of Conway to the south. About 2 miles up, the trail takes to open ledges for a long stretch, where Mount Chocorua, the Moat Mountains, and Cathedral Ledge are all visible. The vegetation runs to blueberries and mountain laurel (*Kalmia latifolia*), a member of the heath family that sprays delicate pink blooms around the understory in June. Near the summit stand some beautiful red pines.

Directions: From NH 16 and US 302 in Intervale, turn east on Hurricane Mountain Road. Go 1.5 miles to pull-off parking on the left at the Mount Kearsarge North trailhead.

Trail: 6-mile (round-trip) hike to the summit of Mount Kearsarge North.

Elevation: 600 feet to 3,268 feet.

Degree of difficulty: Strenuous.

Surface and blaze: Forest floor, some open ledges, can be a little wet in spots. Blazes are yellow and scant, but trail is clearly delineated.

WMNF Presidential Region

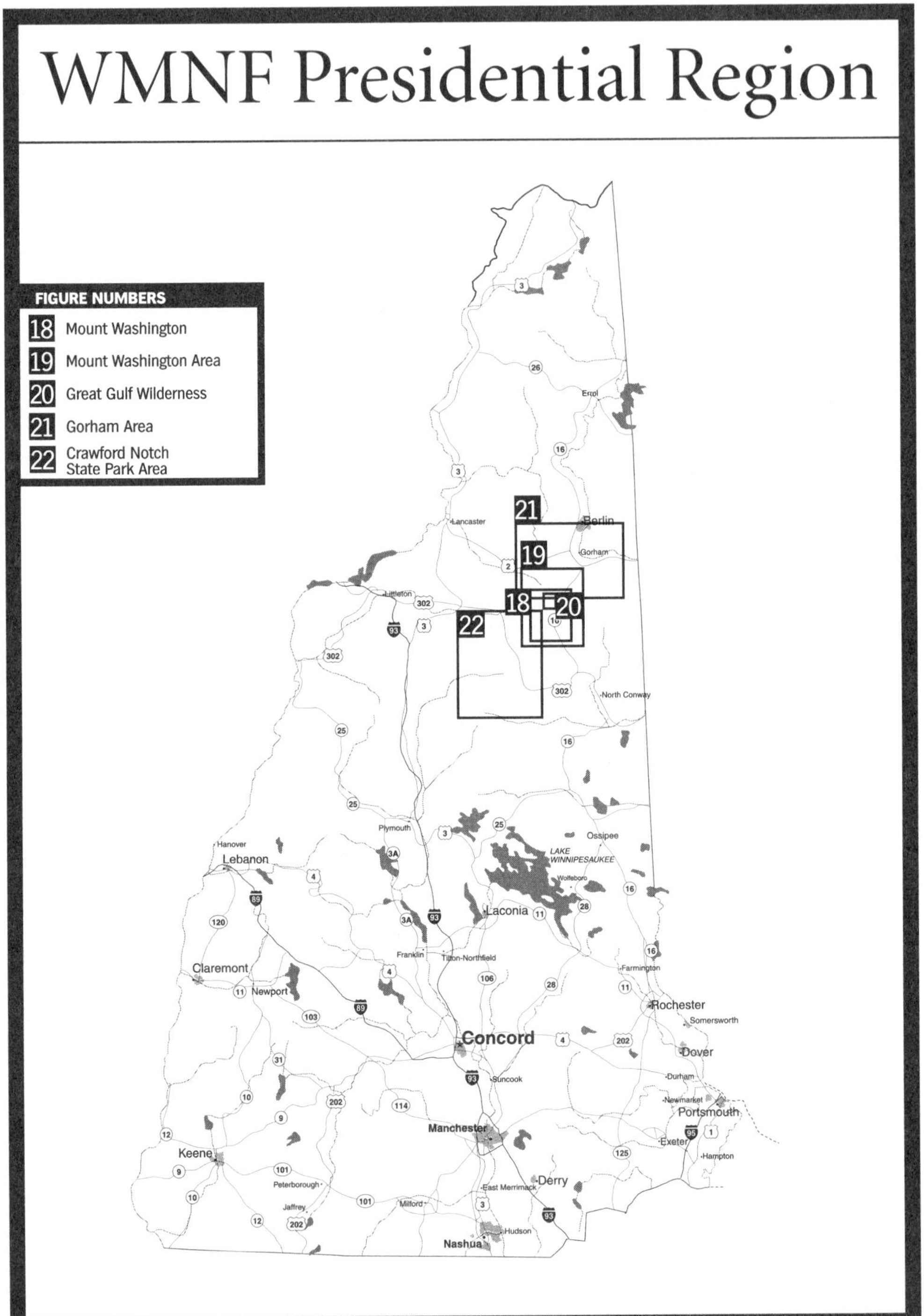

FIGURE NUMBERS

18 Mount Washington
19 Mount Washington Area
20 Great Gulf Wilderness
21 Gorham Area
22 Crawford Notch State Park Area

WMNF Presidential Region

The centerpiece of the White Mountain National Forest is the area surrounding the mighty Presidential Range. These mountains, the highest in the Northeast, wind a 12-mile course down through the region, with imposing, treeless summits that are often speckled with snow well into May. These peaks, visible offshore from the Atlantic, are believed to have inspired the name White Mountains, and still stand as a fitting symbol for the whole group.

The massive ridge of the Presidentials runs northeast to southwest, between Gorham and the valley of the Saco River. There the last in the line, Mount Webster, drops off abruptly into a deep defile called Crawford Notch. The individual mountains of this range began to acquire their Presidential names around 1784, when Dr. Jeremy Belknap, an early New Hampshire historian, named the tallest one for George Washington. Previously, the Native Americans had called this stunning peak

[*Above:* A view of the Presidentials from the town of Jefferson]

Agiocochook, meaning "dwelling place of the great spirit." The loss of this spiritually evocative name was much lamented, by Indians and Europeans alike. But a trend had begun, and over the following two centuries, seven of these fine peaks came to bear the names of American presidents. The latest name change was in 1962, when the former Mount Pleasant was renamed for Dwight D. Eisenhower.

Confusion invariably arises in the naming business, and the case of the Presidentials illustrates the point. Some mountains in this chain are named for statesmen other than presidents—Mounts Clay, Webster, and Franklin, for example. Mountains outside the range are also named for presidents, such as Mounts Lincoln and Garfield.

To further muddy the issue, New Hampshire contains a number of presidential sound-alikes—such as Mounts Carter, Hayes, Jackson, and Clinton—all named for people other than the presidents who bear those names.

Fortunately, experiencing these beautiful peaks does not require the memorization of their names, but just for the record, the seven Presidentials within the Presidential Range, north to south, are: Madison, Adams, Jefferson, Washington, Monroe, Eisenhower, and Pierce.

These mountains present an equally impressive vista whether seen from the north, off US 2; the east, along NH 16; or from the west, off US 302. Unlike the pointed pinnacles of younger mountains, these grandfathers sit ponderously upon the land. Their muscular shoulders fill the horizon and seem to shrug off both vegetation and human perturbation. Yet, from a distance, these rounded slopes look soft and welcoming. They have always fascinated people, and for hundreds of years, Mount Washington's summit has beckoned the more adventurous to make the arduous trek to the top. Before the Europeans came, the awe Native Americans felt toward this mountain made most of them reluctant to climb to the top of such a holy place. Some obviously did, however, because they showed Darby Field of Durham, New Hampshire, the way up in 1642, when he became the first white man known to gain Mount Washington's summit.

Surprisingly, these highest mountains in the Granite State are not made of granite at all. With the exception of a granitic intrusion here and there, these lofty behemoths are composed of metamorphic schists, quartzites, and gneisses, which were laid down as layers of mud and sand by an offshore ocean 400 million years ago. These alternating layers of sediment slowly became mudstones and sandstones, and then were compressed, heated, and pushed onto the North American continent by the process of Plate Tectonics. Later, they were folded and lifted as high as 25,000 feet above sea level, heights approximating today's Himalayas.

Since then, several vertical miles of their original height have been eroded away. What we see now, when we look at these ancient hills, are only the roots of mountains—their exposed innards—that once lay miles below the surface. Even though this massive erosion has deprived us of the grandeur of this once-shining sierra, it has given geologists an opportunity to see processes that normally go on deep within the crust. Only at great depth does solid rock, under incredible heat and pressure, become as malleable as modeling clay, able to bend and fold into great loops like ribbon candy. In many places, the folds of layered rock got so high that they fell over on themselves, pulling the older, bottom layers of rock on top of younger layers.

The erosion that wore away miles of rock, and exposed these inner cores, took hundreds of millions of years. More recently, geologically speaking, the Pleistocene Ice Age added a finishing patina to the Presidentials. Only 18 thousand years ago, the mile-thick Laurentide Ice Sheet covered the tops of even the highest of these mountains under a moving blanket of ice. Compared with the erosion of former eons, the ice scraped off very little additional height, but it did round the tops and scoop great gouges out of the sides of these mountains. The glacier dumped till all over their slopes and erratically dropped boulders, plucked from elsewhere, on their summits. Today, however, one of the most striking features atop these summits is more a result of the climate that ensued soon after the glaciers retreated.

For several thousand years after the great ice sheet had retreated, the climate was one of great and frequent temperature fluctuations. Alternating freezing and thawing shattered the surface rock into a jumble of angular chunks. Water that seeped into cracks during the thaws would subsequently freeze and expand to break the rock apart. The jagged and jumbled surface that resulted, now greenish with lichens and alpine plants, is known as *felsenmeer,* a German term meaning "sea of rocks."

The whole of Mount Washington's summit, and that of its fellow Presidentials, is covered with this irregular jumble of angular blocks. The surfaces of the individual rocks are rough, too, studded with various kinds of tough, erosion-resistant crystals. Hundreds of millions of years ago, andelusite, sillimanite, garnet, and other crystals formed when the tectonic pressure cooker deep within the crust melted and recrystallized some of the rocks' material. Now, even on the flatter surfaces of these angular chunks, crystals form bumps and ridges that snag the boots of unwary hikers.

This is rugged territory. The summits of many of the Presidentials are 1,500 feet above tree line, creating the largest alpine tundra region east of the Rockies and south of the Canadian Arctic. Because of the peculiarities of climate here, the Presidentials constitute a large slice of subarctic habitat thrust southward into the United States, and with it come several kinds of plants and insects found nowhere else in the region.

Sixty-three different species of alpine plants, sedges, mosses, and shrubs grow on the subarctic slopes of the Presidentials. One plant, the dwarf cinquefoil (*Potentilla robbinsiana*), grows nowhere else in the world. Most of these alpine plants have evolved an arctic survival strategy of growing low to the ground and close together to conserve heat and moisture from the freezing and desiccating wind. Almost without exception, they are evergreen perennials that avoid the energy-consumptive task of growing new leaves each year. Their tiny, perennial leaves are often waxy to conserve water, and they stand ready to photosynthesize whenever they are granted a brief

BLACK BEAR
(Ursus americanus)

period of warmth and sun.

Although these tough, leathery leaves protect alpine plants from the worst weather in the world, they are surprisingly vulnerable to the hiking boot. They cling tenuously to the thinnest of soils and are easily disrupted. Once dislodged, they require decades to reestablish themselves, so an oft-repeated warning in this part of the world is "Stick to the trails and walk in single file." (*see* Alpine Gardens, page 102).

Animal life in this alpine habitat tends to be small and scarce. Below tree line you find the usual complement of northern woodland animals: deer, moose, bobcat, bear, fox, raccoon, and dozens of nesting birds. But the slopes above that line, where the trees end and the terrain is exposed to the cruel elements, become the domain of just a few small, scurrying creatures. Shrews and white-footed mice find refuge in rock crevices and under the low mat of alpine vegetation. By far, the most prevalent mammal in this realm of rock is the red-backed vole (*Clethrionomys gapperi*), a chubby little rodent distinguished from a mouse by its shorter tail and smaller ears.

Few birds nest in this inhospitable habitat. Only the dark-eyed junco (*Junco hyemalis*), and the American pipit (*Anthus spinoletta*), find this a suitable place to raise a family. Insects, spiders, and butterflies are more common, especially on a warm, sunny day when rising thermals blow some nonresidents up the mountain. Two rare butterflies, however, actually do inhabit these bare mountaintops. The White Mountain fritillary (*Brenthis montinus*) is found solely on Mount Washington, and nowhere else in the world. The White Mountain butterfly (*Oeneis melissa semidea*) is found elsewhere in this range of mountains and has the peculiar habit of lighting on a rock, folding up its brown mottled wings, and lying on its side—thus avoiding the wind and becoming practically undetectable on the mottled rock.

This mountain range, impressive though it is, is not the only notable feature of the Presidential Region. Both Crawford Notch State Park and Mount Washington State Park lie within its borders, as well as the Presidential-Dry River Wilderness and the Great Gulf Wilderness. The region teems with waterfalls, scenic vistas, rock formations, cross-country skiing trails, and dozens of hiking opportunities.

Still, without question, Mount Washington is definitely the jewel in this rocky crown. Perched atop this summit since 1932, the Mount Washington Weather Observatory provides round-the-clock weather and atmospheric information for the U.S. Weather Service. Almost invariably, conditions atop the mountain differ radically from those at the base. Also occupying the summit is the tiny 52-acre Mount Washington

Black Bear

More than 5,000 black bears (*Ursus americanus*), live in the mountains and woodlands of New Hampshire. During the warmer months, the lucky visitor may catch sight of a mother bear with one or two cubs, feeding on the lush spring vegetation or, later, gorging on the berries and other fruits of summer. Weighing 200 to 400 pounds, black bears are hard to miss if they are out and about in the daytime, but this animal—who would truly rather avoid human contact—generally prefers to feed at night. All summer and fall, black bears are busy feeding on insects, larvae, and berries—storing up a thick layer of fat for the colder months when food is in short supply.

As winter approaches, the bear seeks out a dry and cozy den beneath a rock or an uprooted tree, where it will spend two to four months in a state of semihibernation. Its body temperature and heart rate fall, but unlike the woodchuck—a true hibernator—the black bear can arouse from this deep sleep, come out for awhile, then return to its den. In these tight winter quarters, females give birth to their young in January or February, and then they spend the next two years raising the cubs before mating again. Black bears, when left undisturbed, are generally not dangerous to people, but they should never be approached or fed. If a garbage dump or a bird feeder becomes an attraction to a wild bear, it should be removed until the bear has moved on to more appropriate food sources.

State Park, which offers visitors shelter from the wind, a cafeteria, gift shop, and a museum full of Mount Washington history. So, even beyond its exciting geology, record height, and violent weather, the top of Mount Washington is well worth a visit.

Hiking on this mountain has a history all its own. Since Darby Field's first ascent in 1642, the seemingly irresistible challenge to carry oneself on foot to the top of this peak has lost none of its allure. Caution, however, is in order on any of Mount Washington's trails, as not all of these journeys have ended happily. This fact is sadly illustrated by the plaque inside the summit building listing the names of those who have lost their lives on these slopes. Nevertheless, with proper clothing and supplies, and the willingness to turn back when the weather takes a bad turn, the overwhelming majority of hikers have a safe and awe-inspiring trip. For the hardiest among them, new cold-weather equipment has made winter ascents relatively common.

Not only hikers visit the top of this awesome mountain. During the short but glorious summer, the summit of Mount Washington is accessible to virtually everyone, via either a breathtaking trip on the famous Cog Railway or by driving or riding the van—called a stage—up the Mount Washington Auto Road. Whatever your route of travel, on a clear day, the view from the top takes in five states, two countries, and the Atlantic Ocean.

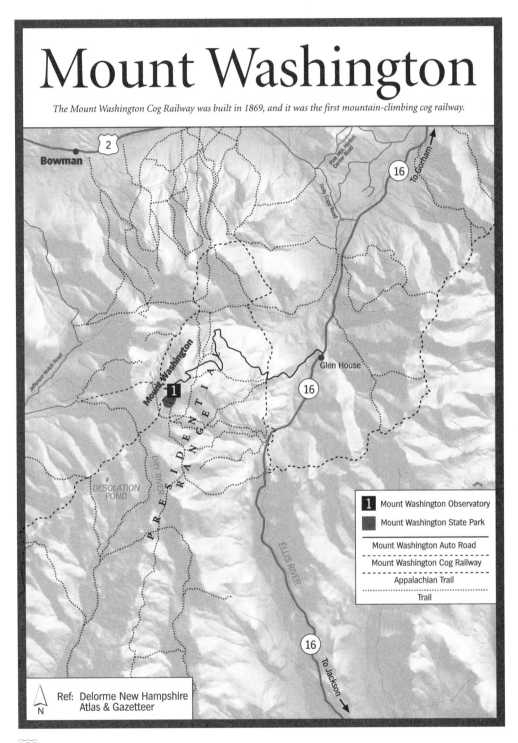

Mount Washington

The Mount Washington Cog Railway was built in 1869, and it was the first mountain-climbing cog railway.

Legend:

1 Mount Washington Observatory

■ Mount Washington State Park

— — — Mount Washington Auto Road
- - - - Mount Washington Cog Railway
- - - - Appalachian Trail
·········· Trail

Ref: Delorme New Hampshire Atlas & Gazetteer

N

Mount Washington

Whichever way you choose to ascend Mount Washington, you will pass rather quickly through four major vegetational zones on a trip botanically equivalent to traveling 600 miles north to Labrador. The summit is socked into clouds or fog on more than half the days of every year, so visibility is never guaranteed. But, on that rare day of clarity, the view of the rest of the Presidential Range—sometimes the whole of northern New England—is drop-dead gorgeous.

All of Mount Washington—at 6,288 feet, the Northeast's highest mountain—lies within the borders of the White Mountain National Forest. Fifty-two acres at its summit are leased to the State of New Hampshire for Mount Washington State Park. The Park headquarters and the Mount Washington Observatory are housed in the beautiful, low-slung Sherman Adams building. Adams was a former New Hampshire congressman and governor and an avid outdoorsman who campaigned hard for the building of this modern facility atop the mountain. Completed in 1980, its low profile and broad verandas hug the stony ground unobtrusively, and its earth-colored materials blend in artfully with the austere alpine surroundings.

Sharing the summit are a cluster of radio and television towers, the Cog Railway and stage stops, buildings to house observatory personnel, and a rugged, old stone building called the Tip Top House. This was the last of the hotels to occupy the top of the mountain in the 1800s, when tourists, who endured a grueling horse and buggy ride up the rutted Carriage Road, would have sorely needed a place to spend the night.

There are no longer any overnight accommodations atop Mount Washington, but the state park's Adams building, open in the summer, does offer food service, a place to store hikers' backpacks, a gift shop, a museum, and a home for the Mount Washington Observatory. The first thing the visitor has to decide is how to get to the summit.

From May to the middle of October, there are four ways to ascend Mount Washington: ride the 130-year-old Mount Washington Cog Railway, take the Mount Washington Stage van, drive up the Auto Road, or hike up one of the many trails. From October until May, the only way up is on foot. Although hiking this mountain requires caution in any month, winter hiking demands the highest level of fitness and preparation. The hiking routes and descriptions discussed in this guide will pertain only to hiking in the warmer season. For information on winter hiking, see *Winterwise* by John Dunn, or *Winter Adventure: A Complete Guide to Winter Sports* by Peter Stark and Steven Krauzer.

▨ MOUNT WASHINGTON STATE PARK

[Fig. 18] Perched atop the tallest mountain in the Northeast sits Mount Washington State Park. At only 52 acres, this park is diminutive in size, but long on location. It is surrounded by nearly 800,000 acres of White Mountain National Forest and offers a view that, on a clear day, stretches all the way to New York, the Atlantic Ocean, and Canada.

The weather outside may be ferocious at times, but inside the cozy Sherman Adams building there is warmth, food, and a place to contemplate the awesome power of nature. Send a post card from the top of Mount Washington at the tiny post office, or visit the Mount Washington Museum on the lower level. Here you find lots of information about the human history this mountain has silently witnessed—an odd story that spans over 250 years and involves wild weather, luxurious hotels, and lots of derring-do.

The historic Tip Top House, a stone-built hotel dating from 1853, has been restored and is open for visitors to tour. If the weather is accommodating, look for the metal U.S. Geological Survey benchmark, reading 6,288 feet, embedded in the rock at the highest point on the summit. At the Adams building, spacious outdoor viewing platforms look out in all directions from what seems like the top of the world. On many days, a visitor may look down on the clouds that fill the ravines and valleys around the mountain.

Beyond the small circle of buildings and parking lots, the mountain's surface consists of intriguing rocks, lichens, and alpine flora that invite exploration. But on any trip to the summit of Mount Washington, cold or inclement weather is always an imminent possibility. Take along warm clothing and rain gear, even in the middle of summer, and keep an eye on the weather at all times.

Directions: To reach the state park situated on the summit of Mount Washington, follow the directions that follow, either to the Cog Railway station, the entrance to the Auto Road, or any of the hiking trailheads.

Activities: Viewing New England, exploring the unique terrain of Mount Washington's summit, touring the museum and Tip Top House, shopping, food service.

Facilities: Cafeteria, gift shop, post office, restrooms, museum, Tip Top House.

Dates: Facilities open from mid-May to mid-October.

Fees: Admission to the Sherman Adams building is free. There is a small fee to tour the museum and the Tip Top House.

Closest town: Glen, 23 miles.

For more information: Mount Washington State Park, Box D, Gorham, NH 03581. Phone (603) 466-3347.

MOUNT WASHINGTON OBSERVATORY

[Fig. 18(1)] The legendary weather atop 6,288-foot Mount Washington offers a unique vantage point for the Mount Washington Observatory. Since 1932, when it began operation in a building that had to be held down by chains, this private, nonprofit weather observatory has been monitoring the weather, informing regional radio and television stations and the U.S. Weather Service, and conducting cold weather research. More recently, it has branched into public education in intriguing ways. It broadcasts daily weather reports, publishes the quarterly newsletter *Windswept,* and broadcasts a regular radio program called *The Weather Notebook* to inform and educate the public. If you are a member, you may tour the Observatory, or if you are a teacher or camp operator, you may arrange a tour for your class or camp group. The observatory offers summer seminars, as well as winter "Edutrips," where fit and hardy participants ride to the top of the mountain aboard a large snow tractor and stay for a weekend to learn about subjects such as natural history, meteorology, and winter photography.

Mount Washington claims to have the worst weather in the world—at least the worst that is consistently monitored. The staff at the observatory readily admit that the winds of Antarctica or of the high Himalayas might reach the world record of 231 miles per hour, set here in 1934, but no one is stationed in those places to measure them. A 1997 storm in Guam claimed wind speeds of 236 miles per hour, and although it looked as if Mount Washington's record might be broken at last, those measurements were later proven wrong. Mount Washington's 1934 record remains the highest ever measured.

Situated at the juncture of three converging weather tracks, Mount Washington seems to pull bad weather from the skies. In January, the wind speed *averages* over 50 mph, and snow depths *average* 250 inches a year. It has snowed here in every month of the year and temperatures at the summit are routinely 20 degrees colder than the surrounding valleys.

It isn't just snow and wind that make the weather unusual on top of this mountain. There is also fog. Combined with the low temperatures and high winds, this fog results in the creation of tons of rime ice, which coats everything on the summit in ghostly, wind-driven shapes. Four- or five-foot-thick ice stretches in long fingers away from the howling wind, like solid white flags that refuse to flutter. The ever-present fog in the winter is one of the biggest hazards to humans atop this summit, often creating a totally disorienting whiteout in which people have perished, only yards from the summit buildings. The combination of wind and low temperature routinely produces wind chill equivalents of 50 degrees below zero.

The observatory occupies one end of the Sherman Adams building atop the mountain and monitors conditions around the clock from its weather room. Staff and volunteers, who come to work in a Caterpillar tractor during the winter, stay for a week at a time. Dials mounted on the observatory's weather wall record readings from instruments outside. From the observation deck, in summer, you can watch the anemometer, or wind gauge, spinning atop a small tower, and just imagine the staff coming out hourly in the winter to beat rime ice off the equipment. Beneath the tower and the weather room are snug living quarters where the staff stay during their weeklong tours of duty on the mountain.

Directions: To reach the Mount Washington Observatory, follow the directions either to the Cog Railway station, page 96; the entrance to the Auto Road, page 97; or to any of the hiking trailheads listed.

Activities: Watching the weather equipment from the deck of the Sherman

CEDAR
WAXWING
(Bombycilla
cedrorum)

Adams building, viewing informative displays inside. Members of the observatory or school and camp groups may arrange tours of the weather room. Weekend seminars are offered.

Facilities: Sherman Adams building has food, restrooms, a gift shop, a museum, and informational displays about the observatory.

Dates: Adams building facilities open mid-May to mid-Oct.

Fees: There is a fee for observatory membership and charges for transportation to the summit on the Cog Railway, the Auto Road, or the Mount Washington Stage.

Closest town: Glen, 23 miles.

For more information: Mount Washington Observatory, Box 2310, North Conway, NH 03860. For general information or to arrange a summer seminar, call (800) 706-0432. To arrange a group tour call (603) 466-3388. For information about winter Edutrips, call (603) 356-8345.

MOUNT WASHINGTON COG RAILWAY

[Fig. 18] Climb aboard the Mount Washington Cog Railway for a trip back in time. Completed in 1869, this was the world's first mountain climbing cog railway, and today, it remains the only one still powered entirely by steam. It takes about an hour for the chugging and belching little steam engine to propel each car to the top of the mountain, and during that interval, the world of automobiles and buses and planes drifts away. The 3-mile route travels over trestles, crawls up impossible inclines, and winds around curves that look like the end of the earth. "Jacob's Ladder," the steepest section, climbs a 30-foot trestle with a mind-boggling 37 percent grade. This translates to traveling 37 feet up for every 100 feet forward. Passengers are invited to stand in the aisles and be astonished by their slanted angle.

Each trip this little train makes up the mountain requires a thousand gallons of water, a ton of coal, and significant amount of sweat on the part of the fireman and brakeman. Going up, the fireman frantically shovels two thousand pounds of coal into the little steam engine that turns the gear wheel on the bottom of the train. On the way down, gravity poses the opposite problem and braking becomes the key issue. This solution, too, is relatively low-tech. A brakeman at the front of the train manually turns the wheels that loosen or tighten the brakes to provide a safe and reasonable rate of descent.

When you first board the Cog, the sound of steel teeth dropping rhythmically into the cog rack between the rails under the train can be a little disconcerting. Soon, however, the scenery grabs your attention and the ratchetty sound becomes mere background chatter, even a little comforting. Wider and wider circles of mountain real estate open up to view. On a cloudy day, the dramatic play of the weather is entertaining in itself.

There is hardly a better vantage point for observing the dynamic relationship between elevation and vegetation than through the windows of a Cog Railway car. Though this is the warm western side of the mountain, placing the levels a little higher, the sequence of forest zones remains the same. First, the northern hardwoods grade into spruce and fir with a lingering sprinkle of birch and mountain ash. Then comes the short forest where even these hardy species begin to grow lower to avoid the fierce wind and cold. Next, there is a brief band of *krummholz*, a stunted forest made up of woody plants that hug the ground to escape the weather. Above this point, suddenly, the forest is gone. In every direction lies only a sea of greenish, angular, lichen-covered rocks.

The colorful Cog Railway experience provides a different perspective on this mountain, a leap into the past that remains forever in the visitor's mind. Plan a day around it. The basic trip requires about three hours, for the trip up and back, and the stop at the top which lasts about 20 minutes. Trains run hourly in the peak months and deliver the visitor to all the attractions of Mount Washington's summit. Come prepared for cold or inclement weather at the top and perhaps, a little sprinkling of coal dust en route.

Directions: From Twin Mountain, go 4.7 miles east on US 302 to Fabyan. Turn left at Cog Railway sign onto Base Road and go 5.5 miles to parking at the railway station.

Activities: Three-hour train ride to Mount Washington's summit. Museum and weather observatory viewing , shopping, food.

Facilities: Train, museum, gift shop, weather observatory, restaurants at base and summit, restrooms, parking.

Dates: May through Columbus Day. Call for reservations and information; times change throughout the season.

Fees: There is a charge to ride.

Closest town: Twin Mountain, 10.2 miles.

For more information: Mt. Washington Cog Railway, Route 302, Bretton Woods, NH 03589. Phone (800) 922-8825 or (603) 278-5404.

MOUNT WASHINGTON AUTO ROAD

[Fig. 18] Perhaps the easiest way to Mount Washington's summit is to travel up the Mount Washington Auto Road. Although it runs through national forest and state park lands, this 8-mile road to the top of New England was built by private companies and remains privately owned and operated. The road climbs 4,600 feet in just 8 miles and, for much of its route, runs right along ridge lines, with views in all directions. On many days the view is straight down into the clouds.

Completed in 1861, it was initially traveled by horseback, in carriages, or on foot.

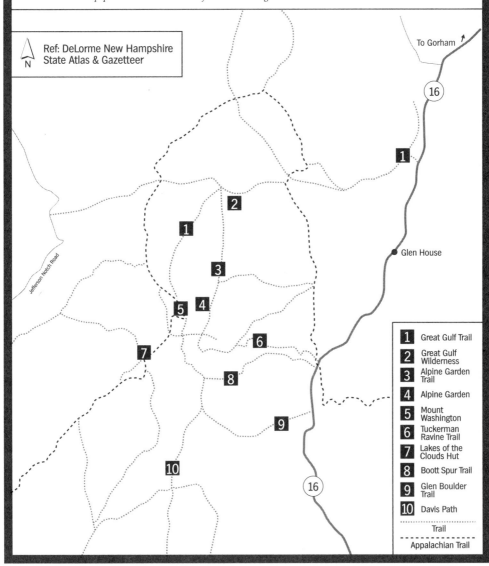

Mount Washington Area

The most popular trail to the summit of Mount Washington is the 4.2 mile Tuckerman Ravine Trail.

N

Ref: DeLorme New Hampshire
State Atlas & Gazetteer

To Gorham

16

Glen House

Jefferson Notch Road

1   Great Gulf Trail

2   Great Gulf Wilderness

3   Alpine Garden Trail

4   Alpine Garden

5   Mount Washington

6   Tuckerman Ravine Trail

7   Lakes of the Clouds Hut

8   Boott Spur Trail

9   Glen Boulder Trail

10   Davis Path

······· Trail

– – – Appalachian Trail

In 1899, the first Stanley Steamer steamed up the road, driven by Mr. Stanley himself.

Since then, the auto road has been climbed by almost every kind of conveyance imaginable—dog teams, solar vehicles, llamas, unicycles, and roller skates, to name a few. Each year America's oldest motorsports event, "The Climb to the Clouds," sends race cars around these edgy turns at 90 miles per hour. When it's not serving as a race track, which is most of the time, this incredible piece of engineering is the most popular way to get to the summit.

You can drive your own car up the road, accompanied by an audiocassette tour that comes with the price of admission. This offers the opportunity to make leisurely stops along the way at pull-outs, where the scenery cries out for photographs. In June, the tiny blossoms of alpine plants are in full glory, and in every season, the summits of the northern Presidentials—Jefferson, Adams, and Madison—trail off to the northeast.

If full-time viewing and a hands-free ride better suit your needs, book a trip on the Mount Washington Summit Stage, a comfortable van that allows the visitor to fully enjoy the spectacular scenery while the driver/tour guide negotiates the tight turns and the 12 percent grades. Either way, each breathtaking turn opens up a new vista across the tops of the Northeast's highest mountains.

The audiocassette tour relates some of the road's and the mountain's colorful history, along with news of how history is still being made. Each year, the auto road hosts several kinds of races in which runners, auto racers, and bicyclists compete to see who can make it to the summit first, perhaps topping a record set the year before.

Directions: From the junction of US 302 and NH 16 in Glen, go 15.1 miles north on NH 16. To drive up the auto road, turn left at the entrance. To ride the stage, turn right into the Glen House, headquarters for the stage service.

Activities: An 8-mile trip (one-way) up the auto road.

Facilities: Road, tour vans. Restaurant and gift shop at Glen House.

Dates: Mid-May to late Oct., weather permitting. Road is open to private cars during the day and vans are available daily.

Fees: There is a charge, either to drive the road or to ride the stage.

Closest town: Gorham, 4 miles.

For more information: Mount Washington Auto Road, Box 278, Gorham, NH 03581. Phone (603) 466-3988.

Hiking in the Presidential Region

The fourth way to reach the summit of Mount Washington—and, for the hiker, the most challenging and gratifying one—is to simply put one foot in front of the other, and walk a little less than one vertical mile into the sky. People have been doing it since the early 1800s, when the first trail to the top was blazed by Abel and Ethan Allen Crawford (*see page 116*).

At least 15 trails ascend to the top of this mountain and, for the last 200 years, its summit has proven nearly irresistible to hikers. However, Mount Washington is not the only destination in the Presidentials; in this region of stark beauty lie all the other peaks of the range, and the equally attractive gulfs and valleys and ravines between them. The area is laced with miles of hiking trails to wander, streams to fish, backcountry camping to enjoy, and immeasurable amounts of nature with which to commune.

A few hikes of varying difficulty will be discussed here, but for an in-depth look at the whole region, the visitor will want to own a copy of the Appalachian Mountain Club's *White Mountain Guide, 26th Edition.* It comes complete with minute descriptions of hundreds of hikes and also with excellent topographic maps. This book is available at AMC's Pinkham Notch or Crawford Notch Visitor Centers.

THE EASTERN SLOPES OF THE PRESIDENTIALS

There could hardly be a better spot from which to begin hiking in the Presidentials than the Appalachian Mountain Club (AMC) Visitor Center, located in Pinkham Notch (*see* page 68). Several trails lead up the mountains or into the wilderness from this centrally-located point, and the Visitor Center also offers the latest weather and trail information, as well as food, lodging, supplies, and, best of all, expert advice.

TUCKERMAN RAVINE TRAIL TO THE SUMMIT OF MOUNT WASHINGTON

[Fig. 19(6)] Directly behind the Visitor Center begins the most popular and direct trail to the summit of Mount Washington, the Tuckerman Ravine Trail. The first part of this trail is so wide and worn that its blue blazes are really unnecessary. Be aware, though, that many trails diverge from this one, and pay close attention to signs. No portion of the Tuckerman Ravine Trail gets unbearably steep, but it is 4.2 miles to the summit. It has also been carefully routed around the potential snow and ice hazards which persist into early summer, so it is important on the upper stretches to stick to this route.

The trail leads straight up the Cutler River drainage into the head wall of Tuckerman Ravine, the great, northeast-facing cirque that, most years, provides the bravest of skiers with a bowl of icy snow well into May. Because there is no ski lift, skiers must lug their skis and boots all the way up this trail and all the way up the ravine. Still, for many, this trek has become a sacred rite of spring.

The Hermit Lake primitive campsite is located at the base of the cirque and requires reservations with the AMC. Beyond the campsite, the Tuckerman Ravine Trail continues another 1.8 miles to the summit of Mount Washington. It scrambles up the right side of the ravine and emerges onto the treeless slopes above. The last part of the hike climbs over the rough and tumbled rock of Mount Washington's cone.

An early treat along this well-worn path is the encounter with Crystal Cascade, just 0.4 mile from the Visitor Center. Here, a wooden staircase leads a few yards to the right of the trail, affording a bird's eye view of the Cutler River as it comes tumbling down a sheer wall of rock. On the upper trail, hikers get an awesome look down into the massive bowl of Tuckerman Ravine. While this is a bit humbling, nothing compares with the stunning view of open sky and bare rock when you reach the summit.

Directions: From the junction of US 302 and NH 16 in Glen, go 12.3 miles north on NH 16 to the AMC Pinkham Notch Visitor Center on the left. Trail begins behind the visitor center.

Trail: 8.4-miles (round-trip) from Pinkham Notch to the summit of Mount Washington.

Elevation: 2,038 feet to 6,288 feet.

Degree of difficulty: Strenuous.

Surface and blaze: Wide, eroded road, then rough rock. Blazes are blue. Rock cairns near the summit.

BOOT SPUR TRAIL TO THE SUMMIT OF MOUNT WASHINGTON

[Fig. 19(8)] The cirque of Tuckerman Ravine is cradled between two promontories on the eastern slope of Mount Washington. The north wall, Lion Head, resembles that animal's noble profile when seen from NH 16 north of the notch, and the south wall is part of Boott Spur, the great southeast arm of Mount Washington, named for Francis Boott, one of the first botanists to explore the area.

OSPREY

(Pandion haliaetus) Also known as the fish hawk, the osprey hovers over water before plunging in feetfirst to grasp the fish with its talons.

Boott Spur Trail diverges left from the Tuckerman Ravine Trail at 0.4 mile, just 150 yards beyond Crystal Cascade, and runs to the Davis Path, then on to Mount Washington's summit via the Crawford Path. The distance one-way is 5.4 miles. This attractive route follows the Boott Spur ridge line and offers a slightly longer, but less traveled, alternative to Tuckerman Ravine Trail. Unlike the Tuckerman, it breaks out of the trees in several places, offering views to make a hiker gasp. The disadvantage in foul weather is that this trail is much more open and exposed to the elements. Stay alert to changing weather conditions and be prepared to head for the woods.

Directions: Follow the directions to the Tuckerman Ravine Trail. The Boott Spur Trail diverges left from the Tuckerman Ravine Trail at 0.4 miles, just 150 yards beyond Crystal Cascade, and runs to the Davis Path, then on to Mount Washington's summit via the Crawford Path.

Trail: 10.8-mile (round-trip) trek to Mount Washington's summit via Boott Spur, Davis Path, and Crawford Path Trails.

Elevation: 2,038 feet to 6,288 feet.

Degree of difficulty: Strenuous.

Surface and blaze: Wide, eroded road to rough, rocky terrain. Blue paint blazes give way to rocky cairns above tree line.

GLEN BOULDER TRAIL AND DIRETTISSIMA TRAIL TO GLEN BOULDER

[Fig. 19(9)] Looking up from the road through Pinkham Notch, Glen Boulder seems precariously poised atop the southeastern end of Boott Spur, but it is actually much more stable than it looks. Perched high above the west side of the road, it is one of the first landmarks seen as you drive north on NH 16. It has stood sentinel to the notch for thousands of years, since the Laurentide Glacier dropped it here.

The most direct way to a place where you can lay your hand upon this rock is the Glen Boulder Trail, which leaves from the Glen Ellis Falls parking area on NH 16. This short but steep trail travels almost due west and arrives at the boulder in 1.6 miles, one-way. An attractive alternative is to take the Direttissima, a link trail as charming as its name, which leaves a parking lot just south of the AMC Visitor Center in Pinkham Notch and joins the Glen Boulder Trail partway up the mountain. This little-used trail ambles through a mossy woods, gently accomplishing some of the climbing in an oblique way before joining the Glen Boulder Trail. Via either route, this is an interesting hike for families with older children. It takes about 3 hours (round-trip) and climbs about 1700 feet.

Directions: To Glen Boulder Trail from Pinkham Notch Visitor Center, go 1.8 miles south on NH 16 to the Glen Ellis Falls parking area. For the Direttissima approach, go 0.2 mile south of this center to parking on the west, just south of the bridge over the Cutler River.

Trails: The Glen Boulder Trail is a 3.2-mile (round-trip) climb to Glen Boulder. The Direttissima-Glen Boulder route is a 4.4-mile (round-trip) alternative to the same destination.

Elevation: Glen Boulder Trail, 1,975 feet to 3,729 feet. Direttissima Trail approach, 2,025 feet to 3,729 feet.

Degree of difficulty: Strenuous.

Surface and blaze: Forest floor to rocky ledge. Blazes are yellow.

TRAILS TO THE ALPINE GARDEN

[Fig. 19(4)] Imagine a flower garden where 2-inch plants grow half-inch blossoms, where soil is all but nonexistent, and where the wind howls all the time. Clinging to the rocks on the high, eastern flank of Mount Washington, between Lion Head and Nelson Crag, is just such a patch of vegetation, called the Alpine Garden. For a brief period every June and July, during the region's ephemeral summer, this dense mat of tiny flowers paints the shoulder of the mountain pink, white and yellow. This ultimate in rock gardens, made up of alpine plants and tundra shrubs normally found far north of New Hampshire, has fascinated botanists for nearly 200 years.

More than 60 species of subarctic plants, sedges, mosses, and shrubs make up this unusual community. Most are subarctic plants at the extreme southern end of their range, but one, the mountain avens (*Geum peckii*), grows only in the White Mountains and in Nova Scotia. Another—the real celebrity of the area—dwarf cinquefoil

(*Potentilla robbinsiana*), is found only here on Mount Washington and, possibly, in the Franconia Range.

The plants of the alpine garden share the peculiar characteristics of snow-patch vegetation. They are, almost without exception, evergreen perennials that grow very close to the ground and often have tough, waxy leaves. Lying under the snowpack for much of the year helps them avoid freezing and desiccation, while evergreen foliage provides the ability to photosynthesize as soon as the sun hits their leaves in the spring. When these plants are not covered with snow, the tough, waxy coating on their leaves protects against moisture loss to the omnipresent winds.

Nature seems to have prepared these plants for everything except the hiker's boot. Once knocked loose from their tenuous hold on the thin soil, it takes decades for these delicate plants to regenerate. The Alpine Garden Trail is marked with cairns and signs, and the practice of sticking to the trail is nowhere more important.

At times, the flowers in this peculiar garden are almost outshone by the rocks surrounding them, as the sun glints off the mica in the schist that forms much of Mount Washington. Between these sparkling flecks are great patches of brilliant chartreuse and orange-colored lichens that paint leopard spots of color over this otherwise gray world. As you step gingerly from rock to rock among the flowers and grasses, there is an overwhelming sense of quiet here, far above the busy world below. Only the steam whistle of the Mount Washington Cog Railway, on the other side of the summit, periodically shatters the stillness.

The Alpine Garden Trail intersects several other trails ascending the mountain from the east, and may be approached in those ways. If a shorter hike is in order, the trail may also be reached from the Mount Washington Auto Road. It actually intersects the road at about mile 6, but there is no parking there. It is best to park in a relatively flat area—fondly called the "cow pasture"—at 6.7 miles. From here you can hike a brief way downslope on the Huntington Ravine Trail to intersect the Alpine Garden Trail.

Directions: Follow directions to the Mount Washington Auto Road, page 97, and drive 6.7 miles up to a parking area on the left side of the road. Follow the Huntington Ravine Trail, marked by large rock cairns, 0.3 mile downslope, crossing over the Nelson Crag Trail, to the intersection with the Alpine Garden Trail. Amble right or left on this trail across the mountain, carefully exploring the vegetation.

Trail: 0.3-mile descent from "cow pasture" parking area on the Huntington Ravine Trail, to the Alpine Garden Trail, then a flat, 1-mile browse across the Alpine Garden.

Elevation: 5,700 feet to 5,300 feet.

Degree of difficulty: Strenuous getting downslope, then easy. The Alpine Garden Trail is moderately flat, but the 400-foot descent over 0.3 mile on the Huntington Ravine Trail has some tricky footing and requires sturdy footwear.

Surface and blaze: Rugged rocks. Signs and large cairns mark the trails.

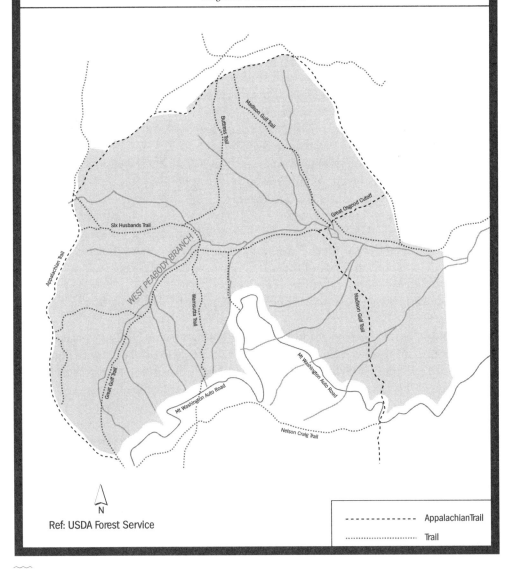

Great Gulf Wilderness

Since the Wilderness Act of 1964, the Great Gulf has been a federally designated wilderness area.

Ref: USDA Forest Service

N

- - - - - - - Appalachian Trail
.... Trail

THE GREAT GULF TRAIL TO THE GREAT GULF WILDERNESS

[Fig. 19(1), Fig. 20] The largest glacial cirque in the White Mountains is the Great Gulf, an imposing gouge out of the Presidentials between Mount Washington and its neighbors to the north. The Mount Washington Auto Road runs precipitously close to its edge most of the way up the mountain, with a view across this great void straight into the faces of Mounts Clay, Jefferson, Adams and Madison. Hiking and camping in the more than 5,000 acres of the Great Gulf is an experience that offers more solitude than the busier trails.

Since the Wilderness Act of 1964, the Great Gulf has been a federally designated wilderness area. "Wilderness" is defined by that law as "an area retaining its primeval character and influence, without permanent improvements or human habitation, which is protected and managed to preserve its natural conditions." All but one of the camping shelters in this area have been removed, and while the trails are maintained, no new structures will be built there. Primitive camping is encouraged, according to WMNF backcountry camping rules.

What does wilderness designation mean? It means that no timbering, no mining, no buildings, and no motorized or mechanized vehicles will ever be permitted here. For the hiker, it means certain restrictions on his activities: no wood or charcoal fires, no trash left behind, no camping groups of more than 10 people, and no camping within 200 feet (in some places, 0.25 mile) of trails or bodies of water. These prohibitions are intended to prevent people from loving their wilderness to death, and in places where this has become a clear possibility, there may be fencing put up long enough for vegetation to reestablish itself.

But the Great Gulf Wilderness is a big place, and it is possible to find solitude here among patches of old-growth forest, crystalline waterfalls, and along the West Branch of the Peabody River, which drains the Great Gulf. Trails branch off to all the northern Presidentials and several primitive tent sites are along the Great Gulf Trail, which cuts through the middle. Camp at these, or find a suitable place off by yourself, but remember to leave the land as you found it.

The Great Gulf Trail runs right up the middle of this great expanse, to Spaulding Lake. It connects with several other trails so that the hiker can plan a wilderness trip of several days without covering the same ground twice. The trail is accessed off NH 16, and in 1.4 miles, reaches the wilderness boundary. The blazes on the initial segments of this and other trails in the Pinkham Notch area are often the same as those on local ski trails. They are plastic squares nailed to trees, whereas hiking blazes are painted rectangles—white for the Appalachian Trail, blue for trails connecting to the AT, and yellow for all other U.S. Forest Service trails. The Great Gulf Trail has infrequent blue paint blazes, but the trail is wide and evident.

Any backpacking trip or day hike into the Great Gulf Wilderness must be carefully planned with proper equipment, food, water, and a good topographical map.

Directions: From the junction of US 2 and NH 16 in Gorham, go 2.6 miles south

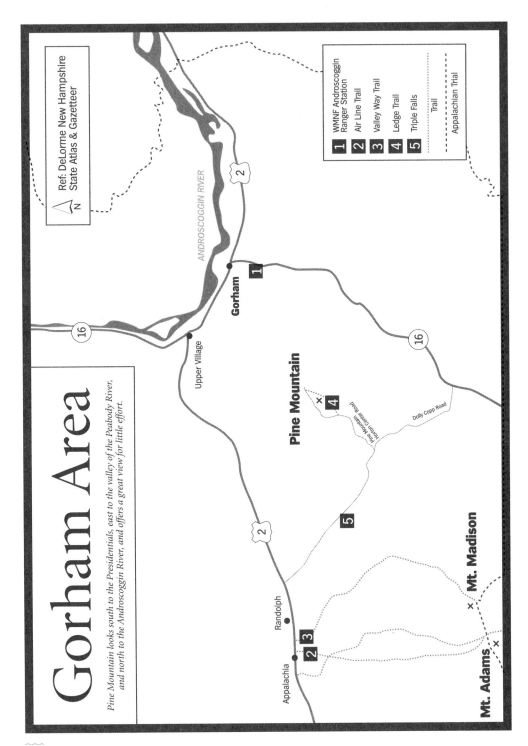

Gorham Area

Pine Mountain looks south to the Presidentials, east to the valley of the Peabody River, and north to the Androscoggin River, and offers a great view for little effort.

Ref: DeLorme New Hampshire State Atlas & Gazetteer

N

ANDROSCOGGIN RIVER

2

16

1 WMNF Androscoggin Ranger Station

2 Air Line Trail

3 Valley Way Trail

4 Ledge Trail

5 Triple Falls

.... Trail

– – – Appalachian Trial

Gorham

1

16

Upper Village

Pine Mountain

4 ×

Pine Mountain Horton Center Road

Dolly Copp Road

2

5

Randolph

2 3

2 ×

Appalachia

Mt. Madison

×

× **Mt. Adams**

×

on NH 16 to Great Gulf Wilderness parking on the right.

Trail: 6.5-mile trail from NH 16 to Spaulding Lake, through the Great Gulf Wilderness. Connects to several other wilderness trails, offering access to all of the northern Presidentials.

Elevation: 1,350 feet to 4,228 feet at Spaulding Lake.

Degree of difficulty: Varies from easy along the river, to strenuous, climbing any of the headwalls or mountains.

Surface and blaze: Forest floor, suspension bridges, stream crossings, rocky ledge. Blazes are blue.

PINE MOUNTAIN ROAD AND LEDGE TRAIL TO PINE MOUNTAIN

[Fig. 21, Fig. 21(4)] Pine Mountain near Gorham is the last little blip in elevation as the northern end of the Presidential Range drops off into the Androscoggin River Valley. At 2,410 feet, it is dwarfed by the rest of the string, but for this very reason, it is a good little mountain to hike up with the family. Seldom does the hiker get so much in the way of view for so little in the way of climbing.

The summit of Pine Mountain looks south to the northern Presidentials, east to the valley of the Peabody River, and north to the Androscoggin. One hundred acres at the top of this mountain is owned by the Congregational Church, which operates the Horton Center there, a retreat and educational camp. It also owns the road from the base on Pinkham B Road to the Ledge Trail, which constitutes the first part of the hike.

The usual midelevation bird songs accompany the first leg of this trip. Black-throated green warblers, hermit thrushes, and scarlet tanagers sing your way up the easy 0.9 mile of gravel road you must take to the Ledge Trail. Here, the trail turns right into the woods and begins a rather steep ascent to accomplish the last 600 vertical feet, over 0.7 mile, to the summit. Dark-eyed juncos, fluttering their white-sided tails, signal the increase in elevation.

Pine Mountain is an abrupt knob with rocky cliff sides visible from the gravel road. Though privately owned, both the road and the summit are open to foot travelers who do not disturb any camp or church activities that may be in progress.

Directions: From the junction of US 2 and NH 16 in Gorham, go 4 miles south on NH 16 and turn right at the Dolly Copp Campground entrance. This is Pinkham B Road (though it may not be marked). Go 2 miles northwest, avoiding the turns into the campground and into Barnes Field, to a parking area on the left. Opposite this is Mountain Center road that climbs 0.9 mile to the Ledge Trail cutoff.

Trail: 3.2-mile (round-trip) hike to the summit of Pine Mountain. Follows a gravel road for a little over half the way.

Elevation: 1,650 feet to 2,410 feet.

Degree of difficulty: Moderate.

Surface and blaze: Gravel road, forest floor, some ledge. No blazes but trail is evident.

TOWN LINE BROOK TRAIL TO TRIPLE FALLS

[Fig. 21(5)] Whether on the way home from Pine Mountain, or just driving along

Pinkham B Road near Gorham, take a few minutes to stop at Triple Falls for a surprising triple treat. This must be one of the tiniest trails in the state, running a mere 0.2 mile off the road and steeply uphill along the Town Line Brook. First, you climb past Proteus Falls, a subtle sheet of water flowing over and around smooth gray granite. Erebus, the next in line, resembles a veil of water that breaks into several streamers, like silvery tresses flowing down the rock. Last in line and highest up the hill is Evans Falls, and this one you can get close to—and perhaps cool your face or your feet on a hot afternoon. A side trip up this lovely little stream is worthwhile any time, but Proteus, Erebus, and Evans are particularly spectacular after a rain.

Directions: From the Pine Mountain Road trailhead, go 0.8 mile northwest on Pinkham B Road and watch for trail sign on left.

Trail: 0.2-mile hike up a somewhat steep slope beside Town Line Brook.

Elevation: 1,475 feet to 1,725 feet.

Degree of difficulty: Moderate.

Surface and blaze: Forest floor. No blazes.

THE WMNF ANDROSCOGGIN RANGER STATION VISITOR CENTER

[Fig. 21(1)] The Androscoggin Ranger Station Visitor Center, an invaluable source of information, is located on NH 16, 2.5 miles south of its junction with US 2, in Gorham. The friendly staff are hiking, fishing, and camping experts, and they stand ready to field all your questions, or direct you to someone who can. This Ranger Station, responsible for search and rescue operations over a wide area of the WMNF, knows when and where it is safe to hike, what the trails are like, and how to plan everything from a short family afternoon to a multiple-day backpacking excursion.

Weather and trail information, camping availability, and books, maps, and educational displays are laid out here in an attractive new building with a red roof. Out front are gardens full of native New Hampshire plants and benches where the visitor can relax or plan the next adventure.

Inside, the store offers books, maps, and small camping items for sale. The required WMNF parking permit may also be obtained here. Among the educational displays are a table relief map of the Presidentials and an interactive area with puppets for children.

Directions: From the junction of US 2 and NH 16, in Gorham, go 2.5 mile south on NH 16 to a sign for the visitor center on the right.

Activities: Planning hikes or camping, checking the weather, viewing educational displays, shopping for books and maps.

Facilities: Free camping and hiking information, helpful staff, educational displays, restrooms.

Dates: Open year-round.

Fees: None for advice and information. Items in store are for sale, and there is a charge for the required WMNF parking permit.

Closest town: Gorham, 2.5 miles.

For more information: Androscoggin Ranger Station, 300 Glen Road, Gorham, NH 03581. Phone (603) 466-2713.

THE NORTHERN SLOPES OF THE PRESIDENTIALS

US 2 traverses the wide, sloping valley north of the Presidential Range, and offers some of the more awesome views of this range along the southern horizon. But the green forests and gray hills refuse to remain passive scenery. They seem to draw visitors in for a closer look—urge them to step out of their cars and wrap themselves up in the mountain experience. A network of hiking trails heads south from several trailheads along this road, and leads those on foot into the heart of the White Mountains.

The town of Randolph and the Randolph Mountain Club (RMC) have a long hiking tradition, and the RMC (*see* page 60) built many of the trails into these mountains. Its Randolph Path, which required six years to complete, was finished in 1899 and is still in use today. Several trailheads, where this and many other paths start out together, are strung out along US 2, marked with brown hiker signs. The trailhead names, Appalachia, Bowman, and Randolph East, are left over from the days when these were also stops along the railroad, whose tracks have been removed. Now, these old station stops are parking areas for hikers, maintained by the cooperative efforts of the WMNF and private clubs. The Randolph Mountain Club maintains many miles of these trails and also operates two lodges in the northern Presidentials, Gray Knob and Crag Camp, both on the slopes of Mount Adams.

For more information: Randolph Mountain Club, Randolph, NH 03570. Phone (603) 466-2438. Maps are available. Or see the Randolph Mountain Club's *Randolph Paths* or its map, *The Randolph Valley and Northern Peaks.*

Several trails leading into the northern Presidentials take off from the trailhead called Appalachia. The two that follow, Valley Way and Air Line, were both constructed in 1895. They are still popular routes today, though not as heavily used as some of the trails out of Pinkham Notch, on the eastern side of Mount Washington. They, and myriad others, are clearly shown on the excellent topographical maps that accompany the newest *AMC White Mountain Guide, 26th Edition.*

VALLEY WAY TRAIL TO MADISON HUT AND THE SUMMITS OF MOUNTS ADAMS AND MADISON

[Fig. 21(3)] It took J. R. Edmunds two years to put this trail together out of pieces of other earlier trails. Between 1895 and 1897, he worked with the mountain's contours, rather than against them, as he fashioned a path that conforms fairly closely with the Snyder Brook. This trail is still the easiest and most direct route from NH 2 to the Madison Hut, one of the AMC's overnight lodgings, and the summits of Adams and Madison are both accessible from here. This is the route that AMC staffers use to pack in food and supplies for the hut's guests. It is more protected by a wooded canopy than some of the other trails fanning out from the Appalachia Trailhead. The distance to Madison Hut is 3.8 miles with a gain of 3,550 feet. From there, another 0.4 mile via the Osgood Trail brings you to the summit of Mount Madison, and another 0.6 mile via the Air Line puts you at the summit of Mount Adams.

The Valley Way begins at the Appalachia parking area, and together with the Air Line, crosses an old railroad bed to a fork where it turns left, passes under some power lines and heads into the woods.

Directions: From Gorham, go 5.5 miles west on US 2 to the "Trails Parking" sign on the left, which is the Appalachia Trailhead. All trails depart from one entrance and split off at clearly signed intersections along the way. Follow signs for Valley Way.

For more information: AMC Reservations, Box 298, Gorham, NH 03581. Phone (603) 466-2727.

Trail: 3.8-mile (one-way) mostly wooded trail to Madison Hut, with connections to the summits of both Mount Madison and Mount Adams.

Elevation: 1,306 feet to 4,825 feet for Madison Hut. Mount Madison is 5,366 feet, and Mount Adams is 5,799 feet.

Degree of difficulty: Strenuous.

Surface and blaze: Forest floor, some rocks. Blue blazes.

AIR LINE TRAIL TO THE SUMMIT OF MOUNT ADAMS

[Fig. 21(2)] Mount Adams, at 5,799 feet, is second only to Mount Washington in elevation. In fact, if hiked from the north, there are 231 more feet to gain than hiking Mount Washington from Pinkham Notch. The most direct way to the Adams' summit is an old and venerable trail called the Air Line, built in 1895 by Laban Watson and Eugene Cook. It was one of the first trails to follow an exposed ridge line, and this remains one of its most spectacular features. As this trail ascends the Durand Ridge and follows the Knife Edge, it puts the hiker out in the open for much of the rest of the trip. The view down into King Ravine at the rock glacier there is breathtaking. There are boulders below the size of small houses, and in the deepest trenches beneath them, the snow never melts.

The Air Line's exposure, which makes for these inspiring views, also makes the hiker vulnerable to the area's famous capricious weather. A good map and a careful eye on the weather are in order. If a storm comes up, seek shelter below tree line. One escape to shelter is the Air Line Cutoff at 3.5 miles, which runs into the trees and crosses over to the Valley Way, just below Madison Hut.

The Air Line leaves the Appalachia parking area, together with several other trails, crosses an old railroad bed, splits off to the right under the power lines, and heads into the woods. Like the Valley Way, there are many other trails diverging from it initially, so care must be taken to read and follow signs. The hike to Mount Adams' summit is 4.3 miles (one-way).

Directions: From Gorham, go 5.5 miles west on US 2 to "Trails Parking" sign on the left at the Appalachia Trailhead. All trails depart from one entrance and split off at clearly-marked intersections along the way. Air Line turns right at the intersection

Beaver

North America's largest rodent (*Castor canadensis*) has had an enormous impact on the shape of New Hampshire's landscape. For thousands of years, this animal, which requires ponds of water for its lifestyle, has been damming streams and cutting down certain kinds of trees. After a beaver family uses all it can of the resources of one location, it moves on, creating a patchwork of habitats that evolve from forest stream, to pond, to meadow, and eventually back to forest again.

The beaver has two kinds of tooth enamel—a tough orange enamel coating the front of its teeth and a softer, lighter-colored enamel on the back. Differential wearing of these two materials produces a sharp beveled edge, which the animal uses to chew down a small tree in a matter of minutes.

Why do beavers cut down trees? Its not because they eat the wood. Beavers eat the softer, more nutritious leaves, buds, and cambium, or inner bark, of the smaller branches near the top. After these smaller sticks are whittled clean of bark, they then become building materials, stuffed meticulously into the beaver's dam or lodge.

Beavers prefer hardwoods—aspen, alder, maple—to evergreen trees. When beavers move on from an area, the character of the forest has changed, and wildlife move in that favor the coniferous woods left behind.

Beavers are large animals, some weighing up to 60 pounds, and they wear a luxuriant brown coat of fur. It was this attribute that nearly did them in. So many beavers were trapped in the 1700s to make the felt hats then fashionable in Europe that the animal was virtually extirpated from the state. The carnage slowed when the high silk hat came into fashion, but unhappily, it was nearly 100 years before beavers again repopulated New Hampshire's streams and ponds.

Beavers are back now in healthy numbers, and once again, they are busily rearranging the landscape. Look closely as you pass by ponds or lakes for their conical lodges and downstream dams made of mud and sticks, and ponder the fact that each branch or twig has been carefully placed by an industrious beaver. Because repairs are constantly necessary, the work never ends, and each evening, beavers will return, doing whatever they can to hold their watery world together.

under the power lines.

Trail: 8.6-mile (round-trip) hike up the Air Line Trail to the summit of Mount Adams, following exposed ridge tops.

Elevation: 1,306 feet to 5,799 feet.

Degree of difficulty: Strenuous.

Surface and blaze: Some forest floor, but the upper third of this trail is on exposed and rocky ridges. Both footing and weather can be troublesome. Go armed with good boots, rain gear, maps, and a planned escape route to shelter. Blazes are blue.

Crawford Notch State Park Area

Crawford Notch State Park encompasses nearly 6,000 acres within the White Mountain National Forest that can be used for camping, hiking, swimming, fishing, and sightseeing.

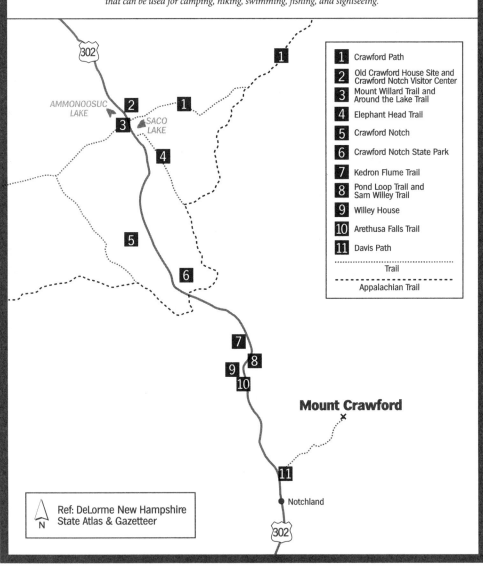

1 Crawford Path
2 Old Crawford House Site and Crawford Notch Visitor Center
3 Mount Willard Trail and Around the Lake Trail
4 Elephant Head Trail
5 Crawford Notch
6 Crawford Notch State Park
7 Kedron Flume Trail
8 Pond Loop Trail and Sam Willey Trail
9 Willey House
10 Arethusa Falls Trail
11 Davis Path
·········· Trail
--------- Appalachian Trail

AMMONOOSUC LAKE

SACO LAKE

Mount Crawford

Notchland

Ref: DeLorme New Hampshire State Atlas & Gazetteer
N

CRAWFORD NOTCH AND THE WESTERN SLOPES OF THE PRESIDENTIALS

[Fig. 22(5)] The western approach to the Presidential Range first takes the visitor on a beautiful ride down US 302, toward Crawford Notch. Soon after turning south onto US 302, the tourist accommodations of Twin Mountain and the golf greens of Bretton Woods begin to give way to a less cluttered world. To the east, the last large building you pass is the elegant and historic Mount Washington Hotel, the last of the grand White Mountain establishments that dominated tourism in the 1800s (*see* page 125). This current incarnation, very much alive and operating, sits regally against its backdrop of mountains. With flags flying from its red roof, it seems to float there like a luxury liner, cruising across the meadows.

As US 302 re-enters the WMNF, the landscape becomes broad vistas and green forests once again. This area of the forest has a particularly appealing variation of color, shape, and texture, one that only the subtle mixture of hardwoods and conifers can create. Dark green spruce and balsam fir stand among the rounder and paler birch and maple trees. Seen from the road, these woods are a tapestry of myriad shapes and textures and a palette of variegated greens.

Crawford Notch is one of New Hampshire's classic glacier-sculpted notches. Running 3 miles south from the narrow opening known as the "Gate of the Notch," this U-shaped trough through the mountains was formed when massive amounts of glacial ice squeezed through a preexisting valley. The smooth rock surfaces, on the steep walls of Mounts Webster, Willard, and Willey, show where the ice smoothed and polished the rock as it passed through.

Within this valley, the tough metamorphic rock that makes up the Presidentials ends abruptly, where Mount Webster's cliffs dive into the valley of the Saco River. This mountain, which forms the notch's east wall, is the last concentration of metamorphic gneisses and schists for about 15 miles. Beginning with the bedrock under the Saco River Valley, the much younger granites of the White Mountain Plutonics stretch southwest and include the igneous rocks of Mount Willard, on the west side of the notch. These granites, though younger by more than 200 million years, have worn low. They are softer and more vulnerable to erosion than the cliffs of Mount Webster which, made of 400 million-year-old metamorphics, stand high and triumphant. This shows that younger doesn't necessarily mean tougher.

Much of the bedrock of the Saco River Valley is buried in a wide apron of glacial outwash. The clean gravels, boulders, and sands that result when water erodes Conway Granite are unquestionably beautiful. These pinkish materials are strewn about in the clear-running, braided streams that make up the Saco River, and the pools and grottoes hidden among its large rounded stones beckon the visitor to stop, look, listen, and feel.

OLD CRAWFORD HOUSE SITE AND CRAWFORD NOTCH VISITOR CENTER

[Fig. 22(2)] Just before the Gate of the Notch are some significant small buildings, clustering around the site where the old Crawford House, in its many incarnations, looked boldly down the valley for nearly 150 years. The Crawfords, possibly the most famous family in White Mountain history, owned a virtual string of inns and lodgings at various places along this valley, and provided overnight accommodations to the tourists who inundated these mountains in the 1800s. The last Crawford House burned down in 1977.

Now this significant curve in the road is once again a hub of activity. The Appalachian Mountain Club (AMC) purchased the site and the remaining buildings in the early 1980s and established the Crawford Notch Hostel, where hikers may set up a base from which to explore the surrounding mountains. The AMC also refurbished the old railway station here, which serves as a visitor center and a stop for the Conway Scenic Railroad train from North Conway. The train toots through here on four days of the week during the summer.

Right down to its yellow paint, this quaint little railroad depot was authentically restored and opened in 1985 as the AMC's Crawford Notch Visitor Center. Inside, light streams through beautiful stained-glass window transoms onto historical displays about the railroad, the hotel, and the Crawfords. From June through October, the staff will help you find books, maps, and small hiking supplies. They can answer questions about the colorful history of the place or where to plan a hike.

At precisely 1 p.m., four days a week, a familiar whistle announces the arrival of the Conway Scenic Railroad train, which brings tourists up from North Conway aboard the same mode of travel that brought them here in the nineteenth century. They disembark to explore while engineers maneuver the two locomotives around and hook them up to the south end of the train for the trip back. The nostalgic sounds of the whistle seem to strip a hundred years away in an instant, as the train disappears through a slot cut into the hills, on its way back down the valley.

The old station remains as a charming token of the days when the railroad was king. In its new embodiment, it has kept its rich mahogany ceiling, but has relinquished its old plumbing and added a ramp which offers access to handicapped people.

Directions: From the junction of US 3 and US 302 in Twin Mountain, go 8.8 miles south on US 302 to the little yellow train station on the west side of the road, labeled Crawford's.

Activities: Information gathering, viewing historical and natural history displays, purchasing books and maps, hiking.

Facilities: Helpful staff, store with maps, books, small hiking supplies, and snacks, weather board, educational displays, trails, restrooms.

Dates: Memorial Day to Columbus Day.

Fees: None for information. Store items are for sale.

Closest town: Twin Mountain, 8.8 miles.

For more information: About the visitor center, AMC, Box 298, Gorham, NH 03581. Phone (603) 466-2727. About the train, Conway Scenic Railroad, Box 1947,

North Conway, NH 03860. Phone (800) 232-5251. About AMC Crawford Notch Hostel reservations, phone (603) 466-2727.

TRAILS FROM THE CRAWFORD NOTCH VISITOR CENTER

For families with younger children or those with limited time, several short and relatively easy hikes take off from the Crawford Notch Visitor Center. One circles a small lake, one climbs Willard Mountain for a wonderful look down the notch, and another climbs to the top of the intriguing rock formation known as Elephant Head.

ELEPHANT HEAD TRAIL

[Fig. 22(4)] At the Gate of the Notch, south of the visitor center, the walls of Webster and Willard mountains pinch the highway in a narrow pass. Bulging out of the eastern wall is a rock formation that looks like an immense gray elephant, charging right out of the wooded hillside. Time and geological forces have conspired to place white quartz features in a rocky gray matrix, creating this illusion. Look long enough and you can even see the wrinkles in his leathery nose and the shadows where his big ears hang.

A short, 0.3-mile hike places the visitor at the top of the elephant's forehead, where the view stretches north to the Mount Washington Hotel, and south through Crawford Notch. More significantly, from up here, one looks down on the highest point in the valley, a divide where two small and insignificant-looking lakes, Saco and Ammonoosuc, are headwaters for the two rivers of the same names. When the Crawford House was still standing, its guests were told that the peak of its roof was actually the divide—that a raindrop falling on one side of the roof drained west to the Connecticut River via the Ammonoosuc, while a drop on the other side traveled down the Saco River to the Atlantic Ocean.

Below, Saco Lake flanks the east side of the road while Ammonoosuc Lake glimmers in the woods behind the AMC Hostel. The summer hiker who happens to be enjoying a picnic lunch atop the Elephant Head around 1 p.m., Tuesday through Friday, will also have a bird's eye view of the arrival of the Conway Railroad train into Crawford's Station below.

Directions: Take the Webster-Jackson Trail east off US 302, between the visitor center and the Elephant Head, for 0.1 mile, to the turn off for Elephant Head.

Trail: 0.6-mile (round-trip) hike to the top of Elephant Head.

Elevation: 1,900 feet to 2,020 feet.

Degree of difficulty: Easy.

Surface and blaze: Grassy forest floor, raised boards lead over wet areas, rocky ledges at the top. Blazes are blue.

WILD SARSAPARILLA (Aralia nudicaulis) Roots of the sarsaparilla were brewed by early settlers for root beer and medicinal tea.

AROUND THE LAKE TRAIL

[Fig. 22(3)] Tiny Ammonoosuc Lake nestles in the woods just northwest of where the Crawford House once stood. A flat, woodsy trail runs around the perimeter of this cool, clear pond—the lower headwaters of the Ammonoosuc River—and a side loop, the Red Bench Trail, offers a view of the Gateway of the Notch. This was once a favorite destination for hotel guests, and one wonders if, a hundred years ago, on the way to this path, they too stopped in the meadow behind the hotel. In July, it is lush with wildflowers and ripe, red raspberries.

Directions: From the visitor center, walk north to the AMC Hostel and find the trail leading off the circular drive behind the building.

Trail: 1.2-mile loop (1.8 miles including the Red Bench loop) around Ammonoosuc Lake.

Elevation: 1,900 feet to 2,000 feet.

Degree of difficulty: Easy.

Surface and blaze: Forest floor, yellow blazes.

TRAIL TO MOUNT WILLARD

[Fig. 22(3)] Mount Willard stands opposite Mount Webster on the west side of Crawford Notch. Near its summit, there are southeast-facing ledges that, for the effort of a relatively short 1.6-mile hike, offer a stupendous view of the notch and the surrounding mountains. The classic U-shape of Crawford's glacier-carved valley is nowhere more evident.

Directions: In back of the visitor center, cross the railroad tracks to the sign for the Mount Avalon Trail. After 100 yards on the Mount Avalon Trail, turn left, following the Mount Willard Trail to the summit.

Trail: 3.2-mile (round-trip) hike to the summit of Mount Willard.

Elevation: 1,900 feet to 2,800 feet.

Degree of difficulty: Moderate.

Surface and blaze: Forest floor and rocks. Trail is eroded in places. Blazes are rare, but trail is evident.

DEER MOUSE
(Peromyscus maniculatus)

CRAWFORD PATH

[Fig. 22(1)] The Crawfords, Abel and his son Ethan Allen, are famous not only for their inn-keeping, but also for their trailblazing. In 1819, they cut the first trail up Mount Washington. The Crawford Path has been nationally recognized as the oldest continuously used hiking trail in America. In 1994, it was designated a National Recreational Trail. For a few decades after 1840, the trail was used as a bridle path, but then was restricted to foot travel only in 1870.

The Crawford Path climbs up Mount Pierce to the AMC's Mizpah Hut, then follows ridgelines over

Mounts Eisenhower, Franklin, and Monroe, passes the Lakes of the Clouds Hut, and ends on the summit of Mount Washington. In 1821, Ethan Allen Crawford also built the first structure on this summit, a shelter for those he led up the mountain on guided walks. Ethan Allen was a legend even then. He was a big man—6 feet 3 inches in the days when a man of that height was rare—and his strength and determination eventually earned him the nickname "Giant of the Mountains."

The Crawford Path has many destinations. Beyond Mount Pierce, it bears the white blazes of the Appalachian Trail, the 2,160-mile network of trails that runs from Springer Mountain, Georgia to Mount Katahdin, Maine. With prior reservations, the hiker may plan an overnight backpack, stopping at Mizpah or Lakes of the Clouds Huts. On this same trail, visitors can opt for something as short as a 15-minute sprint up to Gibbs Falls, or a 30-minute hike to the stunning overlook from Crawford Cliff. This cliff is reached by turning left off the Crawford Path, at the sign for Mount Clinton Road, crossing the bridge over Gibbs Brook, then taking an immediate right at the sign for Crawford Cliff. This wonderful little trail of needles and ferns passes a quiet place in Gibbs Brook called The Pool, which serves nicely to cool the feet of a hot hiker. The view from the cliffs at the top looks up and down the valley, and reveals the higher Willey Range rising beyond Mount Willard in the west.

Directions: There are two entrances to the Crawford Path. For shorter hikes, park at the Visitor Center or the AMC Hostel and find the trailhead on the east side of US 302, 0.1 mile north. For longer or overnight hikes, park at the Mount Clinton Road parking area, 0.2 mile north of the Visitor Center, on the east side of US 302. The Crawford Connector Trail leads 0.3 miles from this lot to the Crawford Path.

Trail: Ultimately, the Crawford Path leads 8.5 miles (one-way) to the summit of Mount Washington. Along the way, it is 0.25 mile to Gibbs Falls, 0.5 mile to Crawford Cliffs, 2.7 miles to Mizpah Hut, or 7 miles to Lakes of the Clouds Hut.

Elevation: 1,900 feet to 2,200 feet (Gibbs Falls or Crawford Cliff); 1,900 feet to 3,800 feet (Mizpah Hut); 1,900 feet to 5,200 feet (Lakes of the Clouds Hut); or 1,900 feet to 6,288 feet (Mount Washington summit).

Degree of difficulty: Easy to Gibbs Falls, moderate to Crawford Cliff, strenuous beyond these points.

Surface and blaze: Forest floor to Gibbs Falls and Crawford Cliff. Rocky, open ledges for other destinations. Blazes are blue, but scarce.

CRAWFORD NOTCH STATE PARK AND OLD WILLEY HOUSE SITE

[Fig. 22(6)] Crawford Notch State Park encompasses nearly 6,000 acres and sits within the White Mountain National Forest. It includes an impressive mountain pass, a campground, a visitor center, dramatic cliffs, numerous waterfalls, rivers to swim and fish, and trailheads for many hiking adventures. US 302 runs downhill through the middle of this elongated park, whose entrance begins near the Gate of the Notch. Less than half a mile into the park, two very high and wispy waterfalls bounce lightly down the sheer face of Mount Webster on the east. Flume and Silver Cascades each stairstep their way from ledge to rocky ledge in long thin streamers before disappearing under the highway to join the Saco River. Another 2 miles brings the visitor to the Crawford State Park Headquarters, located at the historic Willey House Site.

A small monument marks this spot where, in 1826, the entire Willey family was wiped out by a landslide that thundered down from Mount Willey. The mountain undoubtedly had a different name then, before tragedy immortalized this family. The irony of this dreadful event was that the Willeys' house—abandoned when they heard the landslide coming—was the only thing left unscathed. A piece of ledge above it caused the onrushing river of rock, trees, and mud to spit into two streams that flowed to either side of the house, burying all nine people.

The site has now become a hub for visitors to the Crawford Notch State Park. A State Park Visitor Center, a store, a gift shop, and a snack bar now sit placidly on the spot from which the Willeys once ran in terror. The sheer and lonesome cliffs of Mount Webster, across the valley, remain unchanged and a small lake, where the Saco River has been dammed, lies at their base. The lake is periodically stocked with fish, and children under 15 years old are invited to try their fishing skills.

The only campground in this state park, the Dry River Campground, lies 3 miles south of the visitor center, on US 30. It offers quiet, wooded tent sites and minimum amenities that tend to foster a more pleasant camping experience.

Directions: From the AMC Crawford Notch Visitor Center, go 2.7 miles south on US 302 to the Willey House site on right.

Activities: Gathering historical or hiking information, viewing educational displays, shopping, snacks, picnicking, camping, fishing for children, hiking.

Facilities: Staffed visitor center, educational displays, maps, store, snack bar, picnic tables, lake, waterfalls, restrooms, trails, campground.

Dates: Mid-May to mid-Oct.

Fees: None for hiking or visitor center. There is a charge to camp.

Closest town: Twin Mountain, 11 miles.

For more information: Crawford Notch State Park, Box 177, Twin Mountain, NH 03595. Phone (603) 374-2272.

TRAILS FROM THE WILLEY HOUSE SITE

[Fig. 22(9)] Across the road from the Willey House Visitor Center, between the lake and the cliffs of Mount Webster, two short hiking loops run through the woods and picnic tables are situated in the shade of some lakeside trees. Behind the visitor center buildings, on the west side of the road, the Kedron Flume Trail leads 1 mile up to an interesting flume and waterfall on Kedron Brook. Situated 3.4 miles south on US 302 is the trail to lovely Arethusa Falls which, at 200 feet high, is the highest year-round fall in New Hampshire.

POND LOOP AND SAM WILLEY TRAILS

[Fig. 22.8] These two easy and well-marked trails begin across the street from the Willey House Site. The Pond Loop bears left, just beyond the bridge, and loops through the woods adjacent to the pond. The Sam Willey Trail bears right and follows the Saco River. Along the way, look for the telltale signs of beaver activity. Conical mounds of sticks in the water might be one of their lodges, and tree stumps cut off in a pyramidal shape indicate a beaver-felled tree.

Trails: Pond Loop runs for 0.5 mile and Sam Willey Trail is 1 mile long.

Elevation: No elevation gain.

Degree of difficulty: Easy.

Surface and blaze: Forest floor. Yellow Blazes.

KEDRON FLUME TRAIL

[Fig. 22(7)] This trail takes off from the back of the picnic area beside the Willey House Site on the west side of US 302. It climbs partway up the eastern flank of Mount Willey to meet Kedron Brook, which has carved a very narrow gorge, or flume, through the rock.

Trail: 2-mile (round-trip) hike to Kedron Flume.

Elevation: 1,300 feet to 1,900 feet.

Degree of difficulty: Moderate.

Surface and blaze: Forest floor, some rocks. Blue blazes

ARETHUSA FALLS TRAIL

[Fig. 22(10)] Tumbling more than 200 feet down the lower slopes of the Willey Range is New Hampshire's tallest waterfall, the lovely Arethusa Falls. A 1.5-mile trail follows Bemis Brook up to the base of this cascade, where, if you arrive in the late afternoon, the sun in the west backlights the water as it comes leaping over the top. The waterfall then slides in a broad veil down the layers of Mount Oceola Granite that stand almost vertical, forming a sheer face. An inviting pool gathers beneath the falls, where the hiker can cool off before the trip back down.

Directions: From the Willey House site in Crawford Notch, go 3.4 miles south on US 302 to a spur road on the right, which has a sign for Arethusa Falls. A lower

Striped Maple

This unusual member of the maple family usually remains part of the understory of New Hampshire's upland forests, seldom growing more than 15 feet high or 8 inches in diameter. It is easy to identify, even in winter, by its bright green bark with vertical white stripes. *Acer pensylvanicum* has several common names in addition to striped maple. Some call it "moosewood" because moose like to chew on its bark in the winter, and others call it "goose foot maple" because of the broad, webbed-foot look of its leaves. In May and June, long clusters of yellow flowers droop from the ends of the branches, a trait that, along with its distinctive bark, helps to separate this tree from a similar species, the mountain maple (*Acer spicatum*). The flowers of mountain maple are upright and its bark is brown.

parking lot on the right sits adjacent to the spectacular Frankenstein Cliffs, while 0.2 mile farther up this unnamed road is another, smaller, lot, with a refreshment stand. The trail to Arethusa Falls begins there.

Trail: 3.0-mile (round-trip) hike up Bemis Brook to Arethusa Falls, the highest in New Hampshire.

Elevation: 1,240 feet to 2,000 feet.

Degree of difficulty: Moderate.

Surface and blaze: Rugged surface with lots of roots and rocks. Blazes are blue.

DAVIS PATH TO MOUNT CRAWFORD

[Fig. 22(11)] The Davis Path, built in 1845 by Nathaniel P. T. Davis, was one of the early bridle paths leading to the summit of Mount Washington. Such was the effort and determination required that one of the mountains along the way was named Mount Resolution. It fell into disuse rather quickly, until 1910, when it was restored as a footpath by the AMC.

Much of the length of this trail lies within the vast Presidential-Dry River Wilderness, where camping shelters are all but nonexistent. Any that remain from the days before the area's wilderness designation are scheduled to be removed, so backpackers here should have proper provisions and maps and be prepared to adhere to backcountry camping rules. Water sources can be few and far between in the Dry River area, but the area is also prone to flash flooding. Hikers should always have one eye on the weather, and the other on higher ground. This roadless area, with lots of room to stretch out, is just the place to get a taste of wilderness solitude.

The Davis Path lies almost completely within the Presidential - Dry River Wilderness. It runs for 15 miles, from US 302 to the summit of Mount Washington, roughly following the ridge of summits that run south from Mount Washington's Boott Spur. After 12.1 miles, this trail runs along ridges that are completely exposed, but before that it skirts in and out of the forests around such scenic peaks as Mount Crawford, Stairs Mountain, and Mount Resolution.

Mount Crawford makes a wonderful destination for a day hike. Accessed by a short spur trail off the Davis Path, it is a pleasant, 2.5-mile walk (one-way) from US 302. The outlook from this summit encompasses about 250 degrees. On the northwest, the view is right into Crawford Notch, between Mount Webster and Mount Willard. To the west stands Mount Carrigain with its observation tower, and to the northeast loom Mounts Eisenhower and Monroe. On all sides, this summit looks down into the green solitude of wilderness.

The summit of Mount Crawford stands at 3,119 feet, and is approached by a spur trail off the Crawford Path. The last 0.3 mile is over open pavement of Mount Oceola Granite. Smooth and whitish, it offers a few tiny pockets of soil that are studded with small spruce and fir. Blueberries, meadowsweet, and the pink blooms of pale laurel (*Kalmia polifolia*), peek out here and there, and, on a summer day, the sun-warmed rock offers a dozen cozy picnic nooks.

Directions: From the Willey House site in Crawford Notch State Park, go 5.6 miles south on US 302 to a large parking area on the left, or east, side of the road. The Crawford Path leaves from the north end of this lot.

Trail: 5.0-mile (round-trip) hike to the summit of Mount Crawford on the historic Davis Path.

Elevation: 1,000 feet to 3,119 feet.

Degree of difficulty: Moderate.

Surface and blaze: Forest floor, some granite ledge. Blazes are blue to Mount Crawford summit cutoff, then yellow.

🏠 LAKES OF THE CLOUDS HUT

[Fig. 19(7)] A favorite destination for hikers along many of the paths that approach Mount Washington is the historic stone hut at Lakes of the Clouds. Here, two tiny glacial tarns glint blue in the sun on the small plateau between Mounts Washington and Monroe. Aptly named Lakes of the Clouds, they lie at elevations of 5,025 and 5,050 feet, and are the uppermost headwaters of the Ammonoosuc River.

In 1915, a stone hut was built here to shelter hikers from the often brutal weather. Since then, the Appalachian Mountain Club has added significantly to the original building that is now its Lakes of the Clouds Hut. Looking down from the summit of Mount Washington, one must peer carefully to see this stone building that seems to blend in with the rocky surface. It appears impossibly tiny from that vantage point, over a mile away, but the hut can accommodate up to 90 people at a time.

Reservations are necessary at the hut, which lies at the junction of many of the trails ascending the Presidentials from all directions. The Crawford Path, which serves as the Appalachian Trail through this section, passes by here. The views are stupendous, and acres of delicate alpine vegetation surround the hut.

Directions: Approach the hut via either the Ammonoosuc Ravine Trail, the Crawford Path, or the Davis Path, or by links from any of the other trails to Mount Washington's summit. The Ammonoosuc Ravine Trail is accessed by driving 5.2 miles east off US 302 on Base Road (the road to the Cog Railway) to a trailhead parking lot on right. (*See* Crawford Path, page 116, and Davis Path, page 120, for directions to those trailheads.)

Activities: Hiking, lodging, viewing alpine vegetation.

Facilities: Lodge, trails.

Dates: June 5 - Sept. 12.

Fees: There is a fee for lodging.

Closest town: Twin Mountain, 14 miles.

For more information: AMC, Box 298, Pinkham Notch, NH 03581. Phone (603) 466-2727 for overnight reservations.

WOOD FROG
(*Rana sylvatica*)

WMNF Franconia Region

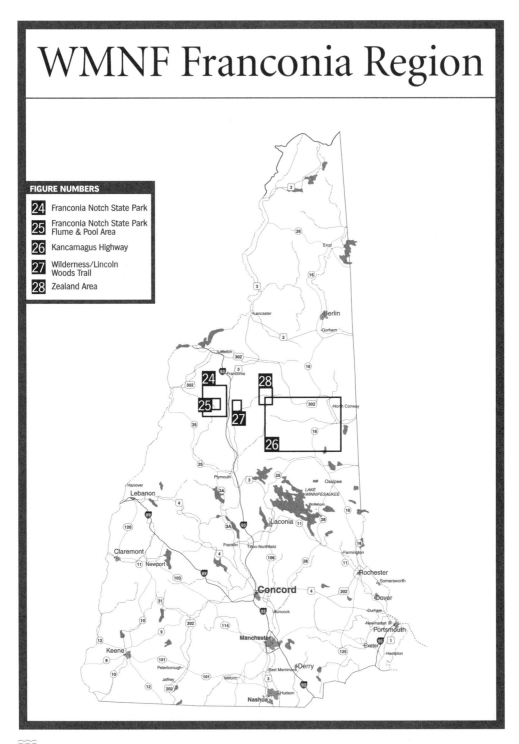

FIGURE NUMBERS

24	Franconia Notch State Park
25	Franconia Notch State Park Flume & Pool Area
26	Kancamagus Highway
27	Wilderness/Lincoln Woods Trail
28	Zealand Area

WMNF Franconia Region

The Franconia Region of the WMNF lies north of the scenic Kancamagus Highway, between Franconia and Crawford Notches—two of New Hampshire's most magnificent glacial valleys. At its heart sits the 45,000-acre Pemigewasset Wilderness. While highways define the perimeter of the Franconia Region, none penetrate this roadless area. Interstate 93 forms the region's western border; US 3 and 302 define the northern and eastern edges; and NH 16 skirts its eastern corner. On the south, NH 112, the Kancamagus Highway, divides the Franconia from the Sandwich Region. Although the Franconia Notch State Park straddles Interstate 93, and lies partly in the Kinsman Region, it will be discussed in this section.

The Franconia Range, second highest in the White Mountains, lies a little over 20 miles southwest of the mighty Presidential Range—but only as the crow flies. As the roads run, it is at least an hour's drive. The peaks of this range, Lafayette, Lincoln,

[*Above:* Franconia Notch is home to New Hampshire landmarks like the Old Man of the Mountain]

Liberty, and others, run north and south along a narrow ridge above tree line, and drop off sharply into Franconia Notch, one of the most spectacular notches in the White Mountains. At more than 5,000 feet in elevation, several of these rocky summits share much of the same alpine habitat and vegetation as the Presidentials.

Two of the most frequently visited areas in the Franconia Region are Franconia Notch and the Kancamagus Highway. Both areas are spectacular, and most enjoyable at times other than their busiest. Franconia Notch tends to be bustling on August weekends and the Kancamagus Highway can be congested with "leaf-peepers" in early October, when the foliage peaks. Most other times find these popular areas free of crowds.

The Kancamagus Highway, locally called "the Kanc," is a 34-mile-long scenic road on the Franconia Region's southern perimeter that runs across the WMNF from Lincoln to Conway. Scattered along its length are national forest campgrounds, scenic vistas, historic sites, and hiking trailheads. Those on the north side of the highway will be discussed as part of this region, while those on the south will be included in the Sandwich Region.

Long before humans built roads, nature had already divided this land with rivers. The roads merely followed nature's pattern. Interstate 93 parallels the Pemigewasset River down through Franconia Notch, while US 302 traverses the valleys of the Ammonoosuc and the Saco rivers. The Kancamagus Highway follows the East Branch of the Pemigewasset up to the divide at Kancamagus Pass, and from there, the Swift River east, down to the Saco.

Rivers define this region in another, more intimate, way. They invite the visitor right into their riverbeds. Rather than deep, raging torrents, for most of the year these are shallow, crystalline streams that run in icy-cool rivulets around immense piles of glacier- and water-rounded boulders. Their beds of pink and beige granite are clean and inviting—to the angler stalking a wary trout, or to a hiker wanting to cool his feet or splash water on her face.

In many places, the waters of these shining streams—the Pemigewasset, the Saco, the Swift, and their countless tributaries—gather in pools deep enough for swimming. Almost anywhere, you can pull off the road, choose your own personal rock in the middle of a shallow riverbed, and commune with the elements for a while, in a place where the moving water brings a stream of cool air. Tucked in this murmuring retreat, the only sounds you hear are those made by bubbling waters rushing around smooth stones, or perhaps the chatter of a resident kingfisher as he skitters about looking for dinner.

The Franconia Region of the WMNF is both surrounded by mountains and filled with mountains. In elevation, they sort of taper off to the southeast. Imagine a giant horseshoe of peaks—the Franconia Range on the west, Mounts Garfield, Galehead, and the Twins across the north, and the Willey Range on the east—all serving to cradle a vast, forested and roadless area at its heart. This is the 45,000-acre Pemigewasset Wilderness.

Looking out over the seemingly endless forests of the Pemigewasset Wilderness from any of the high peaks surrounding this wild expanse, it is difficult to believe that the area was once devastated by timber cuts and fires. Logging railroads criss-crossed the area, and the sparks from coal-driven engines set the remaining slash ablaze. But that was long ago, and nature—as it will when given time—has repaired much of the damage. Amazingly, in a few of the least accessible spots, a few small pockets of old growth have survived among the regenerated forests.

The return of the Pemigewasset Wilderness to pristine quality was assured when it was officially declared a wilderness area in 1984. In accordance with wilderness policies, tracks, bridges and roads have been removed, but a few reminders still peek out of the seemingly endless green. The Wilderness Trail, for example, a sort of central artery from which other trails diverge into the wilderness, lies atop an old railroad bed for much of its 9 miles. The trail is now carpeted with needles and leaves under an arching canopy of trees, but you can still see rotting remains of old railroad ties poking up through the brown earth. Another railroad remnant, the last remaining bridge trestle, lingers suspended over Black Brook, and sits uncomfortably upon the horns of an

The Grand Hotels

During the 1800s in New Hampshire, grand hotels ruled the social scene. At one time, in the White Mountains there were nearly 30 large resort hotels, each hosting hundreds of guests. Railroads brought the wealthy from cities along the East Coast, often to spend the entire summer in the clean and "socially rarefied" air of these luxurious establishments. The reasons the hotels flourished and became a focus for high society are several. Industrialism created a large wealthy class with a substantial disposable income, in the days before income tax. It became *de rigueur* to flaunt one's wealth among one's peers in the cool mountain air. But, even for the rich, mobility was a problem in those days before the automobile. The rich needed to find transportation to a specific destination, and then stay there. The railroads, which had penetrated the mountains early, saw to that need.

Almost as quickly as it had developed, this opulent summer lifestyle came crashing to an end. Two costly World Wars, the Depression, and the graduated income tax chewed inexorably into the excess wealth. The availability of the automobile, even to people of modest means, meant that no longer were the mountains the personal purview of the rich. By 1945, there were only 15 of the grand establishments left, and now, depending on which hotels you count, the White Mountains are down to 5. Some say there is really only 1 left—the Mount Washington Resort Hotel in Bretton Woods—which can still host several hundred people in grand style. George McAvoy's book, *And Then There Was One*, documents the history of the grand hotel social phenomenon.

administrative dilemma. In accordance with wilderness rules, it should be removed, but by another set of regulations, it qualifies for preservation as a historical artifact. The jury is still out on that one.

What is certain is that the mountains, streams and forests of the Pemigewasset Wilderness may now be visited only on foot. Trails approach the wilderness from all the surrounding highways, many of them long enough to weed out crowds and add the icing of solitude to this backcountry experience.

With nature at work, the Pemigewasset Wilderness can only get better over time. Running north and south through its central region is another long ridge of mountains: North and South Twin Mountains, Mounts Guyot and Bond, and finally, the dramatic drop-off of Bondcliff. Looking south from Bondcliff, out over a vast expanse of uncluttered landscape, the hiker is treated to one of the finest views in the White Mountains—unbroken forests, streams, and mountains, as far as the eye can see.

If this wilderness core of the Franconia Region is relatively unpeopled, the area around the edges offers a different story. Holding many of the more famous White Mountain natural attractions, this splendid periphery, especially Franconia Notch and the Kancamagus Highway area, is popular with visitors year-round. Geological formations, lakes and waterfalls, hiking trails, historic sites, skiing, and fall foliage *nonpareil* are all easily seen and traveled to on all-season roads. An astonishing number of these sites are packed into the spectacular Franconia Notch.

Franconia Notch

Franconia Notch is certainly one of the most sensational of New Hampshire's famous notches. Driving north on Interstate 93, this sharp cleft in the mountains first jumps into view about 13 miles south, near exit 31. The silvery, vertical face of Cannon Mountain glints eastward into the morning sun, with a blanket of talus spread gracefully at its feet. Mount Lafayette and Eagle Cliffs stand high on the other side of the valley of the Pemigewasset River. In the middle stretch of the notch, the four-lane interstate highway narrows to a less intrusive, two-lane parkway, with three exits offering parking and access to the more popular features of the notch.

Driving through Franconia Notch is a stirring experience, but a full appreciation of the area requires making the notch a destination, not simply a passage. Scattered along its length, Franconia Notch boasts three picturesque lakes, a scenic tramway, many geological sites, and miles of hikes, ranging from easy half-milers to strenuous backpacking expeditions. The most celebrated resident of the notch is the Old Man of the Mountain. This gigantic visage—an accident of geology created by protruding, horizontal layers of granite—has become New Hampshire's official emblem, found on everything from travel brochures to car license plates. The Old Man peers sternly out of the northern end of Cannon Mountain's cliffs into his own reflection in Profile Lake below.

Geologically, Franconia Notch is made up of several different kinds of granite that welled up under the metamorphic rocks, hundreds of millions of years ago. The notch was initially cut into a V-shape by the flow of rivers, then during the last two and a half million years—the Pleistocene Ice Age—it was sculpted by ice into the classic U-shaped glacial valley. The sheer cliffs of Cannon Mountain form the quintessential *roche moutonnée* or sheepback topography (*see* page 54), created when the mile-high mountain of ice slid up over this massive mountain from the northwest, and plucked away huge blocks of rock from the southeastern face. This silvery face also illustrates the way that granite tends to exfoliate, or peel off in concentric layers. On Cannon's sheer wall, you can look straight up into the edges of several of these layers.

On the eastern side of the notch stands the serrated edge of Eagle Cliff, and towering behind it, Mount Lafayette. This giant of a mountain, with an elevation of 5,260 feet, was renamed to honor the French Marquis de Lafayette, who supported the colonies in their war for independence. Its summit and some others in the Franconia Range reach far enough above the tree line to create an alpine plant habitat similar to that atop the Presidentials. They rise so steeply that they are prone to landslides. Eight times in the last 50 years, major slides have roared down the slopes of Franconia Notch's eastern wall, sometimes burying the road under 20 to 30 feet of debris. Look for these slide scars on Mount Lafayette, across from Profile Lake, or on Mount Flume, behind the Flume Visitor Center.

The numerous attractions in Franconia Notch may be seen in a great variety of ways. The visitor has a choice of driving, hiking, biking, snowmobiling, skiing (alpine or nordic), or riding in a tram car suspended high above the valley on a cable. The Cannon Mountain Tramway is the oldest aerial tramway in North America.

The Franconia Notch Parkway replaces Interstate 93 through the narrowest portion of the notch. This less intrusive, yet more accessible route easily gets you to the attractions and parking that are hidden in the trees. The main footpath along the floor of the notch is the Pemi Trail, a heavily used path for hikers, snowshoers, or cross-country skiers that parallels the Parkway. It leads through most of the valley sites and connects to many of the hiking trails that lead up the slopes. For bicyclists, there is the 9-mile, paved Recreational Trail, which scoots along the notch, in and out of the trees, and around the lakes and streams. This trail is also used by snowmobilers in the winter and pedestrians year-round. For the ultimate, eagle's-eye view of the region, the Cannon Mountain Aerial Tramway runs year-round, to an elevation of 4,000-feet, carrying alpine skiers in the winter and enthusiastic viewers the rest of the year.

LABRADOR TEA
(Ledum groenlandicum)
Growing up to three feet tall, this is an evergreen with white blooms.

Franconia Notch State Park

Franconia Notch State Park occupies more than 6,000 acres of the Pemigewasset River Valley and adjacent mountain slopes.

Ref: Franconia Notch State Park

Bald Mt

Artist's Bluff

Rt 18

ECHO LAKE

93

Eagle Cliff

Greenleaf Trail

Aerial Tramway

Kinsman Ridge Trail

Cannon Mountain

PROFILE LAKE

4

Cannon Cliffs

Old Bridle Path

N

Lonesome Lake Trail

Hi-Cannon Trail

Dodge Cutoff

Lonesome Lake Trail

Falling Waters Trail

LONESOME LAKE

PEMIGEWASSET RIVER

93

Pemi Trail

Basin Cascade Trail

CASCADE BROOK

3

2

Cascade Brook Trail

Liberty Spring Trail

Flume Slide Trail

Service Road

Loop Trail

Mt Pemigewasset Trail

Mt Pemigewasset

Indian Head Trail

1 5

	Key
1	Flume Visitor Center
2	Basin East
3	Basin West
4	The Old Man of the Mountain
5	Roaring River Memorial

- ········ Nature Trail
- – – – – Appalacian Trail
- ········ Trail
- – · – · – Recreational Trail

Franconia Notch State Park

[Fig. 24] Franconia Notch State Park occupies more than 6,000 acres of the Pemigewasset River Valley and adjacent mountain slopes, and is surrounded by the larger White Mountain National Forest. In the 1920s, threatened by further logging, this area was protected in the nick of time by the state and the Society for the Protection of New Hampshire Forests, whose "Save the Notch" campaign elicited the contributions of thousands of citizens to purchase the land that would become this extraordinary state park.

In very few places are so many natural attractions concentrated in one 9-mile stretch. From Indian Head on the south end to Artist's Bluff on the north, and all the paths, lakes, trails, and waterfalls in between, there is enough to see and do to fill an entire vacation.

FLUME VISITOR CENTER

[Fig. 24(1)] Most travelers approach Franconia Notch from the south, on Interstate 93. The attractive new Visitor Center located near the entrance to the Flume Gorge at the south end of the notch is an excellent place to begin. Inside are informative displays on logging history and the geology of the Flume, the Basin, and Franconia Notch itself. A free movie runs every half hour, offering the visitor an overview of the notch and its history, both natural and human.

Sitting quietly in one corner of the visitor center, belying its historic importance, sits an original Concord Coach, that bouncing and heaving carriage that became a symbol of Westerns, but whose origin was right here in New Hampshire. Throughout the 1800s, these classic stage coaches were manufactured by the Abbot-Downing Co. of Concord, New Hampshire. Their delicate appearance makes it hard to believe that these dainty conveyances not only traveled the Wild West, but also pounded regularly up through the rugged notches of the White Mountains, delivering passengers and mail to the north country.

The Flume Visitor Center offers information and maps, ample parking, shaded picnic areas, a cafeteria, and magnificent views of the Franconia Ridge summits which seem to sit directly in its backyard. Several hiking trails take off from or near the center and will be discussed later.

The biggest attraction here, of course, is the Flume Gorge, situated about 1 mile east, behind the visitor center, on a well-marked, 1-mile trail that runs through two covered bridges. A shuttle bus will shave off most of the walk if you prefer. Tickets are required to see this attraction.

Directions: On the Franconia Parkway, which replaces Interstate 93 through Franconia Notch, take Exit 1, which is 2.3 miles north of Interstate 93's Exit 33, to the Flume Gorge Visitor Center on the right.

Activities: Obtaining information, maps, food, and gifts. Viewing educational

Franconia Notch St. Pk. Flume & Pool Area

A 2-mile loop leads through the gorge, where vertical walls tower 80 feet high as the Flume Brook crashes through the chasm, and around a glacial pothole called The Pool.

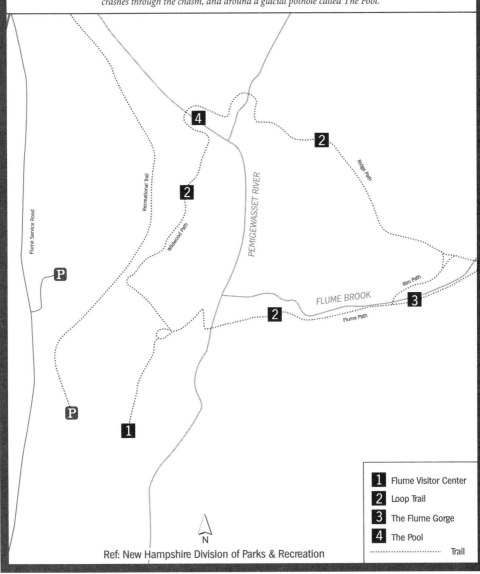

Ref: New Hampshire Division of Parks & Recreation

N

1 Flume Visitor Center
2 Loop Trail
3 The Flume Gorge
4 The Pool
.... Trail

displays and movie. Hiking, picnicking, visiting the Flume Gorge.

Facilities: State park personnel to answer questions, maps and books, gift shop, cafeteria, displays, movie auditorium, trails, parking, restrooms, picnic tables.

Dates: Open May 15 to Oct. 15.

Fees: Visitor Center and trails are free. Items are for sale in shop and cafeteria. There is a charge to visit the Flume.

Closest town: Lincoln, 4.5 miles.

For more information: Flume, Route 3, Franconia NH 03580. Phone (603) 745-8391. Or Franconia Notch State Park, NH Division of Parks and Recreation, 172 Pembroke Road, Box 856, Concord, NH 03302. Phone (603) 271-3254.

THE FLUME GORGE

[Fig. 25(3)] The Flume Gorge is a spectacular narrow cleft in the Conway Granite at the bases of Mounts Liberty and Flume. Vertical walls tower 80 feet high as the powerful Flume Brook crashes through this narrow chasm. This is not a gorge you view from a distance or peek into from above. You actually walk through this dramatic slice in the rock, on boardwalks that run its full 800-foot length. The sheer vertical walls of orange and pink Conway Granite are dripping with ferns, moss and lichens. Once, this deep cleft—only 12 feet wide in places—was filled with molten lava, which hardened to dark basaltic rock. This has been largely worn away by the ferocious force of falling water, but here and there along the gorge, a remnant of this softer black rock may be seen.

Before 1883, a huge boulder hung suspended between the walls of the Flume, but that year, a violent storm washed it downstream. At the upper end of the gorge, where a wide, gravel trail replaces the wooden boardwalk, Avalanche Falls comes pounding over a lip of granite and tumbles into the gorge. From here, the trail continues in a loop around The Pool, a 150-foot wide pothole (*see* page 131) in the Pemigewasset River, one of the largest in the Northeast.

FLUME GORGE AREA TRAILS

Several trails take off from, or near, the Flume Visitor Center. In addition to the 2-mile loop trail that leads to the Flume Gorge, two others, the Mount Pemigewasset Trail and the Indian Head Trail, lead to the summit of Mount Pemigewasset, west of the Parkway. A short, self-guided nature trail called the Roaring River Memorial Trail leads to a view of Mounts Liberty and Flume. Also, the Pemi Trail and the Recreational Trail—each running the length of Franconia Notch—connect the hiker, biker, skier, or snowmobiler to most of the other attractions in the valley.

LOOP TRAIL TO FLUME GORGE

A 2-mile loop of variously named, and easy to follow trails leads through the spectacular Flume Gorge and around a glacial pothole called The Pool. A map is available, and if a shorter walk is desired, a shuttle bus will take the visitor directly to the gorge, cutting off 1.4 miles. From May to October, you may purchase a ticket to see this amazing slot through solid granite where a dike of black lava once intruded.

The trail or the bus departs at the back door of the visitor center, and heads through a beautiful covered bridge over the Pemigewasset River.

This loop hike is a broad, well-signed path with picnic tables, benches, informative signs, and several rain shelters along the way. Before and after its boardwalk through the gorge, it runs through a tall forest of beech, sugar maple, and yellow birch. Several of the birch are perched atop huge boulders, their gnarly, old roots snaking over the rock, grasping for a meager purchase of soil in the cracks. The Pemigewasset River bubbles below the two covered bridges on this loop. It tumbles in clear, green braids through beds of pink granite and forms pools that are home to the square-tailed Eastern brook trout.

Trail: 2-mile loop through Flume Gorge and around The Pool.

Elevation: 1,000 feet to 1,500 feet.

Degree of difficulty: Easy.

Surface and blaze: Wide gravel path with clear signs. No blazes.

MOUNT PEMIGEWASSET TRAIL

[Fig. 24] The cliffs on the southeastern shoulder of Mount Pemigewasset, when seen from the proper angle, form a profile only slightly less celebrated than the Old Man of the Mountains. This one is called Indian Head. It is best viewed from the Indian Head Resort parking lot, on US 3, 1.5 miles north of Exit 33, or 1 mile south of the Flume Visitor Center.

Climbing to the top of these cliffs dissolves the impression of an Indian's head, but does reward the hiker with a splendid view of the Pemigewasset Valley and east to the rugged Franconia Ridge. There are two trails that go to this summit. The Mount Pemigewasset Trail leaves the northernmost parking area at the Flume Visitor Center at the same place as the bike path, or Recreational Trail. It shares the paved bike path for 150 yards before branching off to the left, traveling under US 3 and the parkway, crossing a brook, and heading into the woods. It then climbs another 1.5 miles (one-way) to the cliffs on Mount Pemigewasset that form the Indian Head.

Along this trail you may catch sight—or sound—of a winter wren (*Troglodytes troglodytes*), skulking amid the ground cover. This is a tiny bird with an outrageously big song, its complicated series of chatters and trills so lengthy that it seems the bird would run out of breath. If you are lucky, you will see this plump little songster, bobbing up and down on relatively long legs, its pert little wren tail pointing straight up in the air.

Trail: 3.6-mile (round-trip) hike to the Indian Head Cliffs on Mount Pemigewasset.

Elevation: 1,000 feet to 2,557 feet.

Degree of difficulty: Moderate.

Surface and blaze: Gravel, forest floor, some rocks, paved path at beginning. Rare blue blazes.

INDIAN HEAD TRAIL

[Fig. 24] The Indian Head Cliffs on Mount Pemigewasset can be reached by another, more lightly used trail, the Indian Head Trail. It departs US 3 about 1 mile south of the Flume Visitor Center, on the west side of the road, just south of the Indian Head Resort. Although it is a tiny bit longer, this trail is a pleasant, less populated route to the summit.

Directions: From Interstate 93, take Exit 33 onto US 3. Go 1.3 miles north to "Trailhead Parking" sign on the west side of the road.

Trail: 3.8-mile (round-trip) hike to the Indian Head cliffs on Mount Pemigewasset.

Elevation: 1,000 feet to 2,557 feet.

Degree of difficulty: Moderate.

Surface and blaze: Forest floor, some ledge. Blazes are yellow.

ROARING RIVER MEMORIAL NATURE TRAIL

[Fig. 24(5)] This 0.3-mile, self-guided nature trail takes off from the southern-most parking lot at the Flume Visitor Center and offers a pleasant meander along a flat path cushioned with forest duff. Numbered wooden posts correspond with the trail guide available at the trailhead kiosk, and illustrate interesting points about northern forests. The high point of this short stroll is a lovely gazebo with benches, a perfect spot for a quiet picnic, and an outstanding view. Mounts Liberty and Flume loom high on the opposite side of the Pemigewasset River, which splashes along below.

Trail: 0.6-mile (round-trip) walk through the woods to a gazebo overlook.

Elevation: No elevation gain.

Degree of difficulty: Easy.

Surface and blaze: Forest duff. No blazes.

FRANCONIA NOTCH STATE PARK RECREATIONAL TRAIL

[Fig. 25] This paved bicycle path runs 9 miles through Franconia Notch from the Flume Visitor Center to its northern terminus at the Skookumchuck Trailhead. While primarily used by bikers, pedestrians are welcome, as well as snowmobilers in the winter. Notwithstanding the unavoidable sounds of the Franconia Parkway, which is never far away, this is one of the more pleasant ways to travel the full length of the notch and get to the many points of interest along the way. It weaves in and out of the woods, curves around lakes and waterfalls, and travels through the hubs of activity at the Flume Visitor Center, the Lafayette Place Campground, and the Cannon Mountain Tramway. Side paths lead off the Recreational Trail to all the scenic attractions in the notch, but bicycles must stay on the paved surface. In a few places where the bike path and hiking trails briefly coincide, cyclists may be asked to walk their bikes. Those who plan to ride the trail both ways might want to park at the Flume Visitor Center parking lot, ride north first, and save the downhill for the return trip. Bike rentals and repairs are available at the Cannon Mountain Bike Shop, located at the Peabody Base Lodge, off NH 18 at the northern end of the Recreational Path.

Directions: Access the southern end of the Recreational Trail from the northern-most parking area at the Flume Visitor Center. The northern terminus is found at the

Skookumchuck Trailhead, on US 3, 0.6 mile off Interstate 93, from Exit 35.

Trail: 9-mile, paved bike path through Franconia Notch.

Elevation: 1,000 feet to 1,900 feet at highest point.

Degree of difficulty: Easy cycling.

Surface: Paved.

PEMI TRAIL

[Fig. 24] The Pemi Trail is the pedestrian alternative to the bike path, both of which parallel the road and the river through the notch. It is heavily traveled by hikers, snowshoers, and cross-country skiers, and meanders for 5.6 miles, from the Liberty Springs Trailhead, 0.3 mile north of the Flume Visitor Center, to the Old Man Parking Area, near Profile Lake. It frequently intersects other trails, roads, and the bike path, so the traveler must stay alert to signs to stick to this trail. A free map is available at the Flume Visitor Center that will help sort this trail out from the numerous others it crosses. The Pemi Trail offers a way to get the visitor out of his or her car and links up to quieter trails, farther off the road.

Directions: Start the Pemi Trail from the Liberty Springs Trailhead, 0.3 mile north of the Flume Visitor Center, the Old Man Viewing Area (West) near the Cannon Tramway, or at various attractions throughout Franconia Notch.

Trail: 5.6-mile (one-way) foot path for hikers, snowshoers, or cross-country skiers, running through Franconia Notch.

Elevation: 1,000 feet to 1,960 feet.

Degree of difficulty: Moderate.

Surface and blaze: Gravel, forest floor, wooden bridges. Occasionally shares paved bike path. Blazes are blue, but very infrequent.

▨ THE BASIN

The Basin in Franconia Notch is a glacial pothole carved out of the riverbed during the last 25,000 years. A green jewel in a setting of pink and beige stone, the Basin was scoured out by violently swirling meltwater, filled with abrasive sand and boulders, during the centuries that the Laurentide Glacier was retreating from this area. Now, because the water is largely free of the grit and stone required for such carving, the process proceeds at a much slower pace. A constant waterfall breaks over one high wall and keeps the pool whirling around in its smooth bowl of rock before it finally exits through a narrow slot on the downstream side and returns to the stream. At 30 feet in diameter, this pothole is sizable, but even so, you can look down through 15 feet of clear, green water, and see its boulder-strewn bottom.

The woods surrounding the Basin and nearby trails are a mix of tall hardwoods. Spread out beneath them is an attractive understory of striped maple (*Acer pensylvanicum*), and hobblebush (*Viburnum alnifolium*). These two understory species both have very broad leaves, a strategy that takes advantage of the meager light that filters through the canopy of larger trees overhead.

Directions: From the Flume Visitor Center, go 1.5 miles north on the Franconia Notch Parkway to signs for the Basin. There are two Basin parking areas; this is the east one. Park here and follow the Pemi Trail and signs for the Basin under the highway, a 5-minute walk to the Basin.

LONESOME LAKE

[Fig. 24] This placid mountain lake, situated 1,000 feet above Franconia Notch, has been a natural draw for hikers since the days of the grand hotels in the 1800s. It nestles between tree-lined shores, but still has enough openness to afford great views of the rocky summits

Dwarf Cinquefoil

Named *Potentilla robbinsiana* for nineteenth-century botanist James W. Robbins, this federally protected species is found only in the alpine meadows of Mount Washington and possibly in the nearby Franconia Range. Its tufts of deeply toothed leaves are only about an inch high and the five-petaled yellow flower is a mere 0.25 inch across. Dwarf cinquefoil flowers in June and is so easy to miss that seeing it should be considered a rare privilege.

of the Franconia Range to the east. The AMC's Lonesome Lake Hut, one of the club's eight huts in the White Mountains, sits on the west side of the lake and offers meals and lodging by reservation. A three-quarter-mile Around the Lake Trail connects with several other trails in the region.

The shortest and most popular way to reach the lake is to hike the Lonesome Lake Trail from the Lafayette Place Campground, but this trail is very worn and takes the hiker through the busy campground. For the hiker who isn't staying at Lafayette Place, there is a somewhat less-traveled route that approaches Lonesome Lake from the Basin, via the Basin-Cascade and Cascade Brook trails, the latter a link in the Appalachian Trail. This approach takes off from the Pemi Trail as it winds around the Basin, thereby offering two attractions in one hike.

LONESOME LAKE TRAIL TO LONESOME LAKE

[Fig. 24] **Directions:** From the Flume Visitor Center, go 3.5 miles north on the Franconia Notch Parkway to a sign for "Trailhead Parking" indicating the Falling Waters and the Old Bridle Path trails on the east side of the road. Walk 0.1 mile under the highway to Lafayette Campground and find the Lonesome Lake Trail taking off from the campground's south parking lot.

Trail: 3.2-mile (round-trip) hike to Lonesome Lake. At the lake, there is the 0.8-mile Around the Lake Loop, if you wish to add this on.

Elevation: 1,770 feet to 2,740 feet.

Degree of difficulty: Moderate.

Surface and blaze: Forest floor, some rocks. Blazes are yellow.

PEMI, BASIN-CASCADE, AND CASCADE BROOK TRAILS TO LONESOME LAKE

Directions: From the Flume Visitor Center, go 1.5 miles north to the Basin East

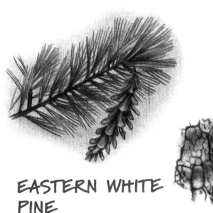

EASTERN WHITE PINE
(Pinus strobus)

parking area [Fig. 24(2)]. A five minute walk on the Pemi Trail, following "To Basin" signs, leads under the parkway to the Basin, and 5 minutes more on the Pemi Trail leads to the junction with the Basin-Cascade Trail. This trail later joins the Cascade Brook Trail to Lonesome lake.

Trail: 4-mile (round-trip) hike to Lonesome lake.

Elevation: 1,400 feet to 2,740 feet

Degree of difficulty: Moderate.

Surface and blaze: Initially paved, then forest floor, some rocks. Blazes are blue on Basin-Cascade and white on Cascade Brook Trail.

HIKING TRAILS TO THE FRANCONIA RIDGE

Life at the bottom of Franconia Notch has its charms, but a walk on the windy, wide-open trail at the top of Franconia Ridge is sublime. The Franconia Ridge Trail, a portion of the Appalachian Trail, follows this north-south ridge over the summits of Mounts Lafayette, Lincoln, Little Haystack, Liberty, and Flume—all members of the 4,000-footer group.

The Franconia Ridge Trail is only one arc of a circular mountaintop route that winds around most of the Pemigewasset Wilderness. To walk here is to be in a realm of wind, rock and delicate alpine plants. From the top of this precipitous ridge, one looks down into the spectacular Franconia Notch in the west, and out over miles of Pemigewasset Wilderness in the east. The sheer Bondcliff and Mount Carrigain with its fire tower loom on the eastern horizon, and to the northeast, you see puffs of smoke from the Cog Railroad engine as it chugs up the side of Mount Washington. Toward the west, you look down at Cannon's vertical cliffs and watch the sun dance off the surface of Lonesome Lake. Walking this ridge, with its 360-degree horizon filled with mountains, is a hard-won, but priceless, mountain experience—one that is difficult to give up when the time comes to head back down to earth again.

As often happens in places of scenic grandeur, this area demands close attention to safety. The ridge is above the tree line and completely exposed to the elements. Strong winds, rain, snow, and lightning are all possibilities. Hikers must be prepared with proper clothing, extra food and water, and the latest in weather information. They also must be ready to head below timberline at the first hint of storm.

All the trails that lead up to the top of this ridge from the west side are relatively long, but the treks are amply rewarded and certainly worth the effort of the fit hiker. Round trips for the three hikes described in the following information range from 9 to 10 miles each and require a full day. An overnight backpacking trip is also an option, with reserved camping at the AMC's Greenleaf Hut, or primitive camping in the national forest. Once outside the state park borders, primitive camping is allowed as long as specific WMNF backcountry camping rules are observed. A brochure with these regulations is available at the Flume Visitor Center or any WMNF ranger station.

FALLING WATERS-OLD BRIDLE PATH LOOP TO FRANCONIA RIDGE AND THE SUMMIT OF MOUNT LAFAYETTE

The Falling Waters Trail is aptly named. It passes by a whole series of waterfalls along Dry Brook, but Cloudland Falls, an 80-foot cascade over a slick granite face, grabs the most attention. In places, the footing on this trail can be rough and steep as it ascends 3.2 miles to the summit of Little Haystack Mountain. Here, you find a high, wind-swept path, edged with small rock borders, running north and south along the Franconia Ridge Trail. It snakes over summits and down into saddles like a miniature Chinese Wall. Turn north here and follow the rock cairns and the white blazes over the 5,000-foot-plus summits of Mounts Lincoln and Lafayette. During this 1.7-mile traverse, any awareness of climbing or fatigue is banished by the sheer magnificence of the view.

Mount Lafayette, elevation 5,260 feet, is the highest point on Franconia Ridge, and if you tuck into the lee of a boulder out of the wind, it's a great place for a picnic lunch. From here, head downhill on the Greenleaf Trail for 1.1 miles to the AMC Greenleaf Hut, and then take the Old Bridle Path Trail for 2.9 miles, back to the trailhead parking. The upper end of this last trail runs dramatically along the rim of Walker Ravine, with close-up views of the mountains you scaled earlier and the many slide tracks coming down their western slopes.

Directions: From Exit 33 on Interstate 93, go 5.9 miles north on the interstate and the Franconia Notch Parkway to a "Trailhead Parking" sign on the east side of the road. The Falling Waters and the Old Bridle Path trails take off here as one. After 0.2 mile, bear right onto the Falling Waters Trail. Follow this to the summit of Little Haystack Mountain, then the Franconia Ridge Trail to Mount Lafayette, then the Greenleaf Trail to Greenleaf Hut, and finally, the Old Bridle Path Trail back to the beginning of the loop.

Trail: 8.9-mile loop hike to the summit of Mount Lafayette.

Elevation: 1,780 feet to 5,260 feet.

Degree of difficulty: Strenuous.

Surface and blaze: Forest floor, rock steps, bald summits with cairns. Watch for icy spots in spring and fall. Blazes are blue on Falling Waters and Greenleaf Trails, white on the Franconia Ridge Trail, and yellow on the Old Bridle Path Trail.

GREENLEAF TRAIL TO FRANCONIA RIDGE AND THE SUMMIT OF MOUNT LAFAYETTE

Directions: From Exit 33 on Interstate 93, go 7.9 miles north on the interstate and the Franconia Notch Parkway to Exit 2. Park in the southernmost Cannon Mountain Tramway lot, at "Hiker Parking" sign. From here, follow the signs for the Greenleaf Trail for 200 yards back along the road you drove in, under the highway overpass. Turn left up the highway's on ramp, for 50 feet, to the trailhead on the right. Follow the Greenleaf Trail 2.7 miles to AMC's Greenleaf Hut, then another 1.1 miles to the summit of Mount Lafayette. This is the shortest route to this summit, and thus is fairly rocky and steep. For the first half-mile, it runs fairly close to the highway, but you can forget the ambient road noise by admiring the prolific wood sorrel and the beautiful rock-top fern gardens.

Trail: 7.6-mile (round-trip) hike to the summit of Mount Lafayette.

Elevation: 1,980 feet to 5,260 feet.

Degree of difficulty: Strenuous.

Surface and blaze: Forest floor, rocks. After Greenleaf Hut, the trail is mostly above treeline. Blazes are blue

SKOOKUMCHUCK TRAIL-GARFIELD RIDGE TRAIL TO FRANCONIA RIDGE AND THE SUMMIT OF MOUNT LAFAYETTE

Directions: From Interstate 93, take Exit 35 onto US 3, just north of the Franconia Notch State Park boundary. Go 0.6 mile to a trailhead parking lot on the right. This is also the northern terminus for the bike path, or Franconia Notch Recreational Trail. The Skookumchuck Trail begins at the north end of the parking lot and climbs 4.3 miles to the Garfield Ridge Trail, the continuation of the Appalachian Trail north of Mount Lafayette. Go 0.8 mile south on the Garfield Ridge Trail to the summit of Mount Lafayette.

Trail: 10.2-mile (round-trip) hike to Franconia Ridge and the summit of Mount Lafayette. At 5.1 miles (one-way), the Skookumchuck Trail is a longer route to the ridge and the summit of Mount Lafayette, but is also quieter, less frequently used, and more attractive.

CANNON MOUNTAIN

[Fig. 24] The sheer, imposing cliffs on the eastern face of Cannon Mountain are the first thing that strikes the visitor who approaches Franconia Notch from the south. Though more than 1,000 feet lower than Mount Lafayette, on the other side of the notch, this dome-shaped mountain is such a massive presence that all eyes are drawn to it, before anything else in the notch.

Cannon Mountain takes its name from a slab of rock resting on a boulder that, from Profile Lake below, resembles a cannon aiming its barrel down the notch. South of here, on Kinsman Ridge, three small, rounded summits are aptly named the Cannon Balls.

Each side of this massive mountain presents a different face. The vertical granite cliffs on the eastern side gleam silver in the morning sun. Below them, a skirt of broken rock, called *talus,* is ample evidence of the irresistible forces of erosion, gravity, and the process of exfoliation, in which granite peels off in thin layers. Much of this rock fall happened soon after the Laurentide Glacier melted 14,000 years ago, when wide fluctuations of temperature caused ice to wedge in the cracks, breaking the rocks. The same process continues today, but at a slower pace. Despite the massive pile of debris at the base of Cannon Cliffs, which demonstrates the tendency for this rock to slough, these cliffs remain an irresistible draw to rock climbers.

On the northern end of this cliff hangs the famous profile called the Old Man of the Mountain, visible from Profile Lake and from a certain angle along the Franconia Notch Parkway. On the northern side of this mountain, Cannon Mountain Ski Area drapes white or green stripes down the mountain, depending on the season. In winter, six lifts and dozens of trails are available for both alpine and nordic skiing. One of them, the Cannon Aerial Tramway, runs most of the year, lifting visitors high above the notch, on a scenic tour *par excellence*. In spring and early summer, despite all the human activity around this mountain, the moving black spots on the ski trails often turn out to be rotund black bears, who come out of the woods to feed on the succulent new plants on these open slopes. On Cannon's northern side, the Peabody Base Lodge is the location of several ski lifts and a shop, which rents ski equipment in the winter and bikes in the summer. On its western side, Cannon Mountain is a massive slope of green forests.

THE OLD MAN OF THE MOUNTAIN

[Fig. 24(4)] Peering intently out from the northern edge of Cannon Mountain's cliffs is the Old Man of the Mountain, New Hampshire's state emblem since 1945. The Old Man is a famous, but fortuitous, geological event, created by the juxtaposition of several layers of granite, stacked one atop the other in just such a way that, from the proper angle, they compose a strikingly realistic face. In 1805, a party of surveyors first looked up from Profile Lake and saw this profile looking somberly down the valley. No doubt, Native Americans saw him earlier, but none of their impressions has made it down through the centuries. Around 1840, Nathaniel Hawthorne wrote a story called *The Great Stone Face* that firmly established the Old Man in White Mountain lore.

The same forces of wind, rain, freezing, and thawing that have created the Old Man of the Mountain are bound to tumble him, bit by bit, or in one seismic shudder, into the valley below. Nonetheless, since 1916, people have been doing their best to push that eventuality farther into the future. Several generations of geologists, quarrymen, and caretakers have installed supportive turnbuckles and rods, seismic measuring devices, and waterproofing, in attempts to keep out the relentless elements. They conduct regular inspections to monitor stresses and movements in the rock. These caretakers fuss and worry over the Old Man, trying to preserve him for the enjoyment of a few more generations. So far, he seems to be hanging together fairly well.

The Old Man of the Mountain may be seen from a viewpoint on the east side of the parkway, 7.6 miles from Exit 33 on Interstate 93, but a better place to see him in his element is the Old Man Viewing Area on the west side of the road. This is located off Exit 2, at 7.9 miles from Interstate 93. Here, a short paved path, the Profile Lake Trail, leads the visitor to the north shore of tiny Profile Lake, where the Old Man is reflected in what has come to be called the "Old Man's Washbowl" or "Old Man's Mirror." Its smooth surface is broken only by surfacing trout and the occasional canoe paddle. Fishing in this quiet, 15-acre mountain tarn is permitted with a New Hampshire fishing license.

This short easy hike is lined with informative plaques, interesting vistas, and the blossoms and berries of meadowsweet, goldenrod, thistles, and mountain ash. The Old Man Viewing Area also has a small museum and an ice cream shop, making this a very pleasant place to spend an hour or two.

Directions: From Exit 33 on Interstate 93, go 7.9 miles north on the interstate and the Franconia Notch Parkway to Exit 2, and follow the signs to the Old Man Viewing Area, located just south of the parking lot for the Cannon Mountain Tramway.

Activities: Viewing the Old Man rock profile, short hike, museum visit.

Facilities: Paved trail, informative plaques, museum, parking, restrooms, ice cream shop.

Dates: Trail open year-round. Shop and museum open late May to mid-Oct.

Fees: None for museum and trail. There is a charge for shop items.

Closest town: Franconia, 6 miles.

For more information: Franconia State Park, Franconia, NH 03580. Phone (603) 745-8391.

CANNON MOUNTAIN AERIAL TRAMWAY

[Fig. 24] The first aerial tramway in North America was built on Cannon Mountain in 1938, and before it was replaced in 1980 by the current "Tram II," it carried seven million passengers to Cannon Mountain's 4,100-foot summit. Today's tram has carried many more, 80 people at a time on a 5-minute ride to the best view in the notch, from an observation tower at the summit. On summer weekends, the visitor may also enjoy a cookout at the top. The tramway's base building houses a cafeteria, a gift shop, and restrooms, and next door is the New England Ski Museum, a place to peek at the history of skiing in the White Mountains.

Directions: From Exit 33 on Interstate 93, go 7.9 miles north on the Franconia Notch Parkway to Exit 2, and follow signs to Cannon Mountain Tramway on the west side of the road.

Activities: Skiing in winter (the tramway is one of six ski lifts included in Cannon Mountain's lift ticket price). In summer, aerial viewing of Franconia Notch and White Mountains. Museum visit, meals, shopping.

Facilities: Aerial Tram, cafeteria, gift shop, restrooms, museum.

Dates: Open year-round, except for a few weeks in spring and late fall.

Fees: Museum is free. There is a charge to ride the tram.

Closest town: Franconia, 6 miles.

For more information: Cannon Mountain, Franconia, NH 03580. Phone (603) 823-5563.

ECHO LAKE

[Fig. 24] This lovely lake, located just north of Cannon Mountain, is one of two

Echo Lakes in New Hampshire, but this one has a real, bona fide echo. Any shout, hoot, or whistle thrown across Echo Lake from its western shore gets thrown right back at you from the rock formations on Eagle Cliff across the notch.

Echo Lake provides a lot of amusement, considering its diminutive size. On the southern end, a free boat launch may be reached from the Cannon Mountain Tramway parking lot. The northern shore provides a smooth, sandy beach where swimmers find the water tingling, even on the hottest summer afternoon. Fishing is permitted from the shore or from a small boat, and camping for a very few RVs is available at the parking area, on the lake's northern shore. Across NH 18, and 0.1 mile east, is the trail to Artist's Bluff, a rocky outcrop from which a breathtaking vista rewards a minimal hiking effort. The 0.5-mile climb up the Bald Mountain-Artist's Bluff Trail is a bit steep, but blessedly short, and the view down the length of Franconia Notch is spectacular.

Directions: From the Franconia Parkway, a continuation of Interstate 93, take Exit 3 onto NH 18. Go 0.3 miles west to Echo Lake Beach parking on the left.

Activities: Swimming, fishing, canoeing, hiking, RV camping.

Facilities: Lake, beach, boat rentals, trail, a few RV campsites.

Dates: Beach, June 20 to Sept. 7. RV park, year-round. Hiking, year-round. Fishing and boating, whenever the lake is free of ice.

Fees: Fishing, boat launch, and trail are free. There is a charge for camping, swimming, and renting boats.

Closest town: Franconia, 5 miles.

For more information: Franconia State Park, Franconia, NH 03580. Phone (603) 745-8391.

RUBY-THROATED HUMMINGBIRD (Archilochus colubris) Hummingbirds have the unique ability among birds to fly backwards or straight up or down.

BALD MOUNTAIN-ARTIST'S BLUFF PATH TO ARTIST'S BLUFF

[Fig. 24] This little trail provides a brief climb to a lofty perch above Echo Lake, and a lovely look down through Franconia Notch. It becomes immediately clear how Artist's Bluff got its name—the curves of mountains, lakes, even the road below beg for a painter's brush. If you are moving north, this spot offers a wonderful last look at Franconia Notch.

Trail: 1-mile (round-trip) hike to the cliffs of Artist's Bluff.

Elevation: 1,900 feet to 2,340 feet.

Degree of difficulty: Moderate.

Surface and blaze: Forest floor, rocks. Blazes are red.

Kancamagus Highway

The Kancamagus Highway, named for the last chief of the Pennacook Indians, runs 34 miles between Lincoln and Conway.

North Conway

Conway

SACO RIVER

302

112

LOON LAKE

West Side Road

North Moat Mt

Middle Moat Mt

South Moat Mt

Moat Mt Trail

Dugway Road

Boulder Loop Trail

Attitash Trail

Middle Sister Trail

Bartlett

302

Bear Notch Road

FALLS POND

3

Lovequist Trail

Bolles Trail

2

Oliverian Brook Trail

SAWYER RIVER

SAWYER POND

Mt Tremont Trail

Sawyer Pond Trail

SWIFT RIVER

Signal Ridge

Sawyer River Trail

Hancock Notch

Hancock Notch Trail

4

Greeley Pond Trail

Scar Ridge Trail

Mt Osceola

Mt Osceola Trail

Wilderness Trail

Black Mt

112

Osseo Trail

1

93

Ref: National Forest Scenic Byway

N

1	Lincoln Woods Visitor Center
2	Passaconaway Historic Site
3	Rocky Gorge Scenic Area
4	Kancamagus Pass
·····	Trail

The Kancamagus Highway-North Side

[Fig. 26] This guide has chosen the Kancamagus Highway as a border to divide the Franconia Region on the north from the Sandwich Region to the south. Therefore, the attractions on the north side of the road will be discussed here and the ones on the south side will be described in the next section.

The Kancamagus Highway, named for the last chief of the Pennacook Indians, runs 34 miles between Lincoln and Conway, and bisects the White Mountain National Forest into the Franconia and Sandwich Regions. From the west, the road climbs its first 8 miles along various branches of the Pemigewasset River, and at its high point—the 2,855-foot Kancamagus Pass—it begins the long downhill run to Conway, following the tumbling course of the Swift River. For sheer scenery, the drive from one end of this road to the other is unbeatable, but there is far too much to explore along the way for the visitor to simply drive through. Dozens of hikes, waterfalls and overlooks compete to pull you out of your car and into the vistas.

The Kancamagus Highway has been designated a National Scenic Byway and is open year-round, except during the worst winter storms. Its winding turns, forested canopy, and breathtaking overlooks are a treat any time of the year, but in early October, this road is truly a bestseller. That's when New Hampshire's fall foliage puts on a show of unparalleled beauty. Everyone seems to know that, though, so the wise traveler will plan to come midweek during peak foliage season, or perhaps a little before the color reaches its brightest. Up-to-the-minute foliage reports may be heard in September and October by calling (800) 258-3608.

A WMNF visitor center is conveniently located in Lincoln, at the end of the exit ramp where the Kancamagus Highway, NH 112, leaves Interstate 93. Inside, you will find brochures about attractions and accommodations, maps, weather information, restrooms, and a telephone. A large table relief map provides orientation for the visitor new to this beautiful region, and friendly staff are available to answer questions. Beyond the visitor center, the Kancamagus Highway runs through Lincoln's 1-mile-long business district, then, within another 3 miles, enters the WMNF.

LINCOLN WOODS VISITOR CENTER

[Fig. 26(1)] The Lincoln Woods Visitor Center appears on the left side of the road, shortly after you enter the WMNF on the Kancamagus Highway, 5.7 miles from Interstate 93. Unlike the visitor center in Lincoln, this one is a trailhead, geared more to the hiker. There is no electricity and no phone, but you will find ample parking, restrooms, information about attractions up the road, and a congenial staff who know the trails in this area well. Maps, camping information, and advice about hiking trails that lie along the rest of the highway are all available here, as well as information about hiking in the Pemigewasset Wilderness that spreads out to the north.

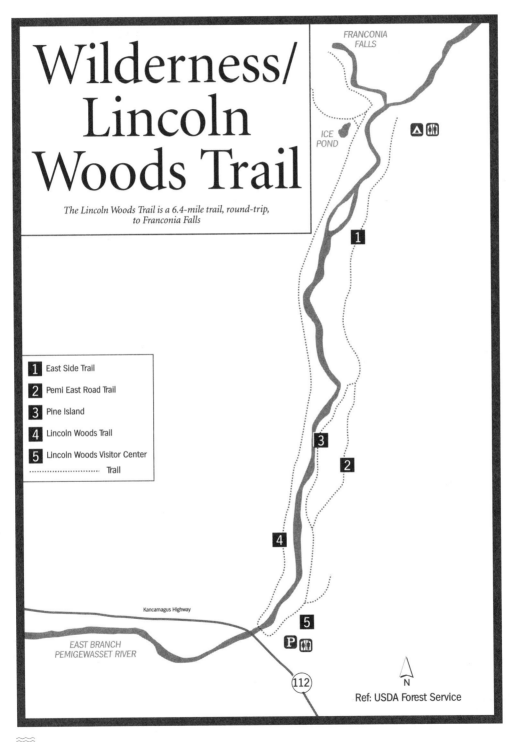

Wilderness/ Lincoln Woods Trail

The Lincoln Woods Trail is a 6.4-mile trail, round-trip, to Franconia Falls

FRANCONIA FALLS

ICE POND

1

1 East Side Trail

2 Pemi East Road Trail

3 Pine Island

4 Lincoln Woods Trail

5 Lincoln Woods Visitor Center

.... Trail

3

2

4

Kancamagus Highway

5

EAST BRANCH PEMIGEWASSET RIVER

112

N

Ref: USDA Forest Service

At this trailhead you find the southern terminus of the Wilderness Trail, an 8.9-mile hiking route that leads into the heart of the Pemi Wilderness, following the East Branch of the Pemigewasset River. Numerous other trails branch off from this central artery, providing a way to explore the many mountains and valleys within the wilderness. A good portion of the Wilderness Trail sits atop an old railroad bed whose tracks are long gone but whose old wooden ties have not quite yet disappeared into the earth. There are several primitive tent sites scattered around the periphery of the 45,000-acre Pemigewasset Wilderness, and ample opportunity for backpackers, using any of the connecting trails, to plan a multiday camping trip.

For the day hiker, this trail provides a 3.2-mile trip, one way, to nearby Franconia Falls. Here the East Branch of the Pemigewasset River slides over smooth granite ledges into inviting green pools, a lovely spot for a picnic or a swim. In an attempt to limit overuse of the Franconia Falls area, the U.S. Forest Service staff at the visitor center issue a limited number of passes to people hiking up the Wilderness Trail (here called the Lincoln Woods Trail) to the falls. The passes are free.

In times of low water, the hiker may ford the river near the falls, and either camp at the primitive tent site on the opposite side, or return to the visitor center via the East Side Trail that runs down the other side of the river. For a longer loop—during high water, this might be necessary—you can hike 5.4 miles up the Wilderness Trail to the 180-foot suspension bridge that crosses the river, then take the East Side Trail back to the visitor center. A small, but potentially confusing detail, is that the first 2.8 miles of the Wilderness Trail, from the visitor center to the Wilderness Boundary, has been renamed the Lincoln Woods Trail, to clarify which part of it actually lies within the wilderness. For practical use, consider the two the same.

Directions: From Interstate 93, take Exit 32 onto NH 112, or the Kancamagus Highway, for 5.5 miles, to the visitor center parking on the left.

Activities: Information gathering, hiking, cross-country skiing in winter.

Facilities: Parking, restrooms, park personnel, maps, trails.

Dates: Open all year, except for a few weeks after Columbus Day and before skiing season.

Fees: None.

Closest town: Lincoln, 5.5 miles.

For more information: Lincoln Woods Visitor Center, Route 112, Lincoln, NH 03251. No phone.

WILDERNESS TRAIL

[Fig. 26] **Trail:** 8.9-mile hiking trail from Kancamagus Highway to Stillwater Junction in the Pemigewasset Wilderness. First 2.8 miles is called the Lincoln Woods Trail.

Elevation: 1,160 feet to 2,050 feet.

Degree of difficulty: Moderate.

Surface and blaze: Primarily old railroad bed covered with forest duff, some rocks, stream crossings on suspension bridges and some wading. Initially, no blazes. Later, yellow.

LINCOLN WOODS TRAIL (WILDERNESS TRAIL) TO FRANCONIA FALLS

[Fig. 27] **Trail:** 6.4-mile trail (round-trip) along the Lincoln Woods Trail to Franconia Falls. The hiker can return the same way or ford the river and come down the East Side Trail on the other side of the East Branch Pemigewasset River.

Elevation: 1,160 feet to 1,440 feet.

Degree of difficulty: Moderate.

Surface and blaze: Forest duff over an old railroad bed. No blazes, but trail is evident.

EAST BRANCH PEMIGEWASSET LOOP

Trail: 10.2-mile (round-trip) loop up Lincoln Woods and Wilderness Trails, crossing the river on a suspension bridge and returning via the East Side Trail.

Elevation: 1,160 feet 1,700 feet.

Degree of difficulty: Moderate grades, but lengthy.

Surface and blaze: Forest duff over an old railroad bed. Blazes absent or yellow.

SAWYER POND TRAIL

[Fig. 26] Sawyer Pond lies not in the official wilderness, but in its own designated Scenic Area near the steeply rising cliffs of Mount Tremont and Owl's Cliff. Its cool, clear water makes a wonderful swimming spot, and brook trout lurk tantalizingly beneath the surface. A WMNF campsite with sheltered tent platforms sits back from the west side of this 56-acre pond, so that you could split up a long day-hike by camping overnight in this beautiful spot.

The hike into this pond has some unique features. Although it is 4.5 miles to the pond, the trail is relatively flat—an unusual blessing in this mountainous territory. The Sawyer Pond Trail wends through a tall, pine forest, its floor a bed of soft pine needles. Even though Sawyer Pond is 700 feet higher than the start of the trail, the climb is modest and is barely noticeable.

Another oddity about this hike becomes evident a mere 50 yards from its begin-

MINK
(Mustela vison)
Like other members of the weasel family, which includes the skunk, the mink emits a pungent odor when provoked.

Camping In The White Mountain National Forest

For many, experiencing the WMNF involves camping. Living out of doors, you are surrounded by the marvelous sights, sounds, and smells that are the essence of the forest. Depending on the level of convenience required, visitors can camp at one of several different levels, each requiring care in order to minimize impacts upon the land. Visitors should use "leave no trace" practices while camping in the WMNF. At the primitive camping level, this includes packing out all trash from primitive sites and using camp stoves in place of campfires. Wood or charcoal fires leave unsightly scars and pose an unnecessary fire risk. A copy of the brochure *Backcountry Camping Rules* is available at any WMNF visitor center.

The WMNF operates over 20 organized campgrounds, some of which take reservations, and more than 50 backcountry tent sites and shelters. Lists and descriptions of these can be obtained from any of the WMNF ranger stations. Reservations at specific sites can be made by calling (800) 280-2267 or TTY (for the hearing impaired) (800) 879-4496.

Throughout most of the WMNF, hikers may camp away from organized campsites as long as they avoid wood and charcoal fires, use "leave no trace" camping practices, and are at least 0.25 mile from trails, roads, and bodies of water. In both Crawford and Franconia state parks, located within the national forest, camping is permitted only in campgrounds. Reservations at these state parks can be made by calling (603) 271-3628.

Several private hiking clubs operate camping facilities in the WMNF. The Appalachian Mountain Club operates several lodges and eight mountain huts for hikers. For reservations call (603) 466-2727. The Randolph Mountain Club also manages two huts in the northern Presidentials. For information call (603) 466-2438.

Scattered around the edges of the WMNF are many private camping facilities that are better suited to larger recreational vehicles.

ning, when the trail abruptly ends at the edge of the Swift River. The hiker must cross here, without the benefit of a bridge, so must be prepared with an extra pair of sneakers. To wade across, stay on the shallower, upstream side of a row of boulders. First, carefully assess the level of the river. If the water is more than knee-high, come back another day.

Trail: 9-mile (round-trip) hike to Sawyer Pond.
Elevation: 1,237 feet to 1,940 feet.
Degree of difficulty: Moderate.
Surface and blaze: Forest floor, some rocks, one river crossing. Blazes are yellow.

PASSACONAWAY HISTORIC SITE

[Fig. 26(2)] About midway along the Kancamagus Highway, there is a clearing on the north side of the road. The Russell-Colbrath house stands here, next to a small cemetery surrounded by a wall of granite slabs. This building is all that remains of the old village of Albany, a farming and logging community that thrived in the mid-1800s. The center-chimney cape, typical of the homes of its day, has been restored to its original look and furnished in the style of the period.

A haunting tale of pain and anguish seems to seep from the rough wooden boards inside this house. One evening, in 1891, Thomas Colbrath stepped outside for "just a little while." Every evening for the next 39 years, his wife, Ruth, lit a lamp in the window for his anticipated return. One day, in 1933, he finally did return to his home in the heart of these mountains—but it was three years too late. Ruth had died in 1930.

The house, even without the sad tale, is an interesting collection of the small common articles of household living in the mid-19th century. The rooms are arranged as though people were still in residence, and a well-informed attendant is on hand to answer questions.

Out behind the house and clearing, the Rail 'n' River Trail is a pleasant 0.5-mile loop though a forest and along the Swift River. Towering over these woods are some very large white pines. Informative plaques along the way tell the history of logging in the area and the significance of these tall straight pines that, in colonial days, were claimed by the King of England for his sailing ships. They were called "mast trees," and some were so large it required 88 oxen to haul each one out of the woods.

Directions: From the Lincoln Woods Visitor Center, go 18 miles east on the Kancamagus Highway (NH 112) to a sign and parking on the north side of the road.

Activities: Tour of historic house and grounds, hiking.

Facilities: Restored nineteenth century, center-chimney house, kitchen garden, cemetery, hiking trail, restrooms.

Dates: Memorial Day to Columbus Day.

Fees: None.

Closest town: Conway, 12.5 miles.

For more information: Saco Ranger Station, 33 Kancamagus Highway, Conway, NH 03818. Phone (603) 447-5448 or TTY 447-1989.

Trail: The Rail 'n' River Trail is an interpretive trail that loops 0.5 mile through a mixed forest and along the Swift River.

Elevation: 1,300 feet. No elevation gain.

Degree of difficulty: Easy.

Surface and blaze: Gravel path, no blazes.

BEAR NOTCH ROAD

[Fig. 26] Bear Notch Road runs 9.2 miles from the Kancamagus Highway (NH 112) to US 302 in Bartlett. It runs through bright young forests and offers several sweeping overlooks where mountains to the east and west may be seen from a fresh angle. This road is paved, but is not plowed in the winter. It is mentioned here primarily for its potential as an escape route from the occasional traffic snarl on the western end of the Kancamagus and on NH 16 in Conway, at the height of a summer or fall foliage weekend. This little stretch is a most pleasant way to cut off the whole Conway-North Conway corridor, if things look busy there.

Directions: Bear Notch Road exits the Kancamagus Highway north toward Bartlett, 21 miles west of Lincoln or 13 miles east of Conway.

ROCKY GORGE SCENIC AREA

[Fig. 26(3)] At the Rocky Gorge Scenic Area, the Swift River comes close to the Kancamagus Highway and invites the visitor to stop and cool off. The water runs cool and clear around granite boulders that have been smoothed by ages of incessant water work. Near the midpoint on this accessible stretch of river, the water dives into a small, straight-sided cleft in the rock called Rocky Gorge. Its slotlike shape hints that a dike of some other, more easily eroded rock has been worn away. The water deepens and swirls through this spot with greater force, and visitors are warned not to swim within 125 feet above or below the gorge.

That still leaves lots of cold river to take the "muggies" out of a warm afternoon, and ample off-road parking near this area offers a place for a tailgate picnic. The soothing sounds of water, running around clean granite boulders, work to smooth out the wrinkles in a troubled mind.

Directions: From the Lincoln Woods Visitor Center, go 21.7 miles east on the Kancamagus Highway to a sign and parking for the Rocky Gorge Natural Area on the north side of the road.

Activities: Swimming, fishing, hiking, viewing the gorge, cross-country skiing in winter.

Facilities: Parking, trail, restrooms.

Dates: Open year-round.

Fees: None.

Closest town: Conway, 12 miles

For more information: Saco Ranger District. 33 Kancamagus Highway, Conway, NH. Phone (603) 447-5448 or TTY 447-1989.

LOVEQUIST TRAIL AROUND FALLS POND

[Fig. 26] A wooden bridge crosses Rocky Gorge and leads to a lovely 0.7-mile loop trail around Falls Pond, where rumors of fish and the quiet of the forest add another dimension to this stop along the Kancamagus. This Lovequist Trail, like so many others along the highway, also serves as a cross-country skiing trail in the winter.

Trail: The Lovequist Trail is a loop running 0.7 mile around Falls Pond to the

NORTHERN PARULA
(Parula americana)
Parula means "little titmouse," which refers to the bird's active foraging through foliage for insects.

north of the Rocky Gorge Scenic Area.

Elevation: 1,100 feet to 1,150 feet.

Degree of difficulty: Easy.

Surface and blaze: Forest floor. Red blazes.

BOULDER LOOP TRAIL

[Fig. 26] The Boulder Loop Trail has been carefully laid out with numbered stops and a printed guide that tells the visitor about the area's glacial history, plant ecology, and forest practices. It winds through fields of giant boulders that have been loosened by frost and have tumbled down the southernmost spurs of the Moat Mountains. One can only wonder at the crashing of trees and the explosions of earth that each of these thunderous descents must have caused. Many types of lichen grow on the sides of these mammoth rocks. One fascinating genus, the *Umbilicaria*, resembles dead leaves or dark sheets of peeling paint. The Boulder Loop climbs nearly 1,000 feet. At two places along the way, there are open views of the valley below and the mountains to the south, including the rugged, rocky crest of Mount Chocorua.

Directions: On the Kancamagus Highway, 30.4 miles east of Interstate 93, or 6.4 miles west of NH 16, Dugway Road turns north off the highway into the Covered Bridge Campground. There is no road sign, but there is a campground sign. Turn north into the campground, then immediately right into the parking lot. The Boulder Loop Trailhead begins just north.

Trail: 3.1-mile loop through boulder fields and forests, to cliffs on the southwestern side of the Moat Mountains.

Elevation: 860 feet to 1,750 feet.

Degree of difficulty: Moderate.

Surface and blaze: Forest floor, to rocky ledges. Blazes are yellow.

MOAT MOUNTAINS

[Fig. 26] It is difficult to imagine, but 200 million years ago, all of New Hampshire was buried under thousands of feet of volcanic material. Pangaea, the supercontinent, was breaking up; the earth's crust was being torn asunder. Great cracks opened, and lava welled up through them and rolled out over the land.

Even more difficult to comprehend is that nearly all of this volcanic material is gone—dissolved by the elements and carried away to the sea. Only a few small deposits of volcanic rock remain to tell the story, and the most famous of these are the Moat Mountains. In fact, this small range of only modest height—about 3,000 feet—has given its name to the rock formation known as the Moat Volcanics.

North, Middle, and South Moat Mountains form a north-south line to the west of the Saco River Valley, near North Conway. The Moat Mountain Trail runs 9 miles over the summits of all three, from West Side Road in North Conway, to Dugway

Road, just off the Kancamagus Highway. The 2.3-mile (one-way) hike included here covers the southern third of this trail and climbs to a magnificent view from the summit of South Moat Mountain. This relatively short hike is steep in spots, gaining 2,150 feet in elevation in a little more than 2 miles.

The Moat Mountain Trail passes through several kinds of forests on the southern flank of South Moat Mountain. Patches of deep, dark hemlock forest alternate with nearly pure stands of red pine, which grows well on these drier, upland slopes.

Red pine (*Pinus resinosa*), is easily recognized by its reddish bark, which flakes off in jigsaw puzzle-like pieces. It bears needles that are distinctively grouped in twos, while those of white pine grow in bunches of five. Pitch pine has three to a cluster.

Another kind of forest—the one where American beech dominates—took a considerable beating from the severe ice storm of the winter of 1998. You'll pass through stands of this smooth-barked species in which many trees are badly broken. Remarkably, although they look thoroughly dead, with their crowns completely snapped off, some of these determined trees sprouted leaves directly out of their broken trunks the following spring.

The trees on this mountainside are interesting, but the truth is that hikers usually spend most of their time watching their feet, and the rocks under them. In this case, most of the rock is a deep gray color with small inclusions of white and pink—Moat Volcanics with tiny feldspar crystals. Layers of this rock spread out in flat sheets in some places, or stand on end in others. These remnants of geological turmoil remain, either because they were deepest here, or were more protected from the forces of erosion. In any case, you won't see them in many other places in New Hampshire.

The view from the summit of South Moat Mountain will more than compensate for any sweat the hiker may have shed in getting there. Mount Chocorua raises its craggy peak immediately to the southwest, Bear Mountain is a little northwest, and the mighty Presidentials dominate the far northeastern horizon. Directly north, the Moat Mountain Trail may be seen winding over the summits of Middle Moat and North Moat Mountain. Down to the east lies the Saco River valley, Whitehorse and Cathedral Ledges, and the towns of Conway and North Conway. The only sounds are the wind and the distant whistle of the Conway Scenic Railroad. On a weekday morning, it is entirely possible to have this whole scene entirely to yourself.

Directions: On the Kancamagus Highway, 30.4 miles east of Interstate 93, or 6.4 miles west of NH 16, Dugway Road turns north off the highway into the Covered Bridge Campground. There is no sign for the road, but there is a sign for the campground. Follow this road, bearing left through the Albany Covered Bridge and across the river, bear right for 4 miles to a small, brown hiker sign at the Moat Mountain Trailhead. Park on the side of the road, but be sensitive to the "No Parking" signs in front of private homes, and park between them. The Albany Covered Bridge is closed to vehicles from November to May, but access to trailhead is possible via West Side Road and Still Road in Conway.

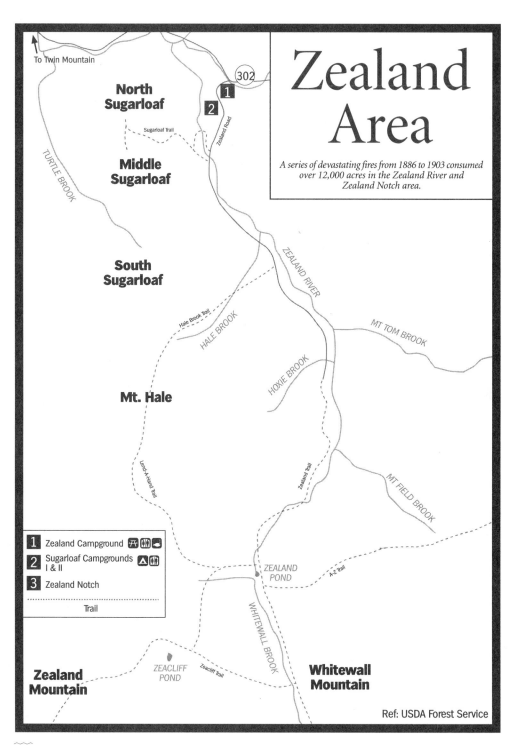

Zealand Area

A series of devastating fires from 1886 to 1903 consumed over 12,000 acres in the Zealand River and Zealand Notch area.

To Twin Mountain

302

North Sugarloaf

Middle Sugarloaf

South Sugarloaf

Mt. Hale

Zealand Mountain

Whitewall Mountain

TURTLE BROOK

Sugarloaf Trail

Zealand Road

ZEALAND RIVER

MT TOM BROOK

HALE BROOK

Hale Brook Trail

HOXIE BROOK

Lend-A-Hand Trail

Zealand Trail

MT FIELD BROOK

ZEALAND POND

A-Z Trail

WHITEWALL BROOK

ZEACLIFF POND

Zeacliff Trail

1 Zealand Campground
2 Sugarloaf Campgrounds I & II
3 Zealand Notch

.... Trail

Ref: USDA Forest Service

MOAT MOUNTAIN TRAIL TO SOUTH MOAT MOUNTAIN

[Fig. 26] This trail begins on a gravel road between two farms. At 0.2 mile, a wooden arrow directs the hiker left onto a smaller, woods road. Head straight through the junction of this and another woods road. Then, clear yellow blazing marks the rest of the hike.

Trail: 4.6-mile (round-trip) hike from Dugway Road to the summit of South Moat Mountain.

Elevation: 620 feet to 2,770 feet.

Degree of difficulty: Strenuous.

Surface and blaze: Forest floor, rugged rocks. blazes are yellow.

Zealand Area

[Fig. 28] The area around the Zealand River and Zealand Notch profoundly illustrates nature's ability to bounce back from nearly total vegetative destruction. A series of devastating fires from 1886 to 1903 consumed over 12,000 acres here. Not only were trees, plants, and animals wiped out, but the flames were so hot they consumed the soil right down to the bare rock. The bare cliffs of Whitewall Mountain stand in mute testimony to these conflagrations.

After 100 years, the area has grown back up with bright and airy forests, filled with birch and red maple, pioneer trees that seek out disturbed areas. Along the watercourses, the fir and spruce that once covered these slopes are springing up in the shade of the hardwood overstory, and clear streams run down the surrounding mountains. The railroad lines that once hauled the fruits of this land to local mills, however, have disappeared into history. Only here and there does an ancient railroad bed remain as the base for a hiking trail.

The Zealand area is now the realm of hikers, campers, and anglers, and is accessed by the Zealand Road off US 302. Along this 3.5-mile stretch of partly paved, partly gravel road, are three campgrounds, a picnic area, numerous hiking and cross-country skiing trails, and ample parking areas. Zealand Road is closed to vehicular traffic from mid-November to mid-May, but certainly accessible to the hardy skier or snowshoer. Where the road ends, at 3.5 miles, begins the Zealand Trail. It leads 2.5 miles in to Zealand Pond and connecting trails to Zealand Falls and the AMC's Zealand Falls Hut. At each trailhead along this road, there is a kiosk and a large, clearly delineated map of the area.

Directions: From the junction of US 3 and US 302 in Twin Mountain, go 2.3 miles east on US 302 to Zealand Road on the right.

Activities: Camping, hiking, fishing, picnicking, cross-country skiing.

Facilities: 3 campgrounds, hiking trails, cross-country ski trails, picnic facilities, restrooms, parking.

Dates: Trails are open year-round and 2 campgrounds are open mid-May to mid-Dec. The third closes in mid-Oct. Zealand Road is closed to vehicles from mid-Nov. to mid-May.

Fees: Hiking and skiing are free. There is a charge to camp, and a WMNF parking pass is required to park for extended periods. A New Hampshire fishing license is required to fish.

Closest town: Twin Mountain, 2.3 miles from Zealand Road entrance.

For more information: WMNF Ammonoosuc Ranger Station, Trudeau Road, Bethlehem, NH 03574. Phone (603) 869-2626 or TDD (603) 869-3104.

ZEALAND CAMPGROUND AND RECREATION AREA

[Fig. 28(1)] Immediately after Zealand Road turns off US 302, the small (11-site) Zealand Campground sits on the left, and to the right, an attractive picnic area lines the edge of the Ammonoosuc River. Close to the highway, these two facilities offer a quickly-accessible picnic area or campsites, in the shade of riverside trees, and places to throw a lure or an inner tube into the Ammonoosuc River. The campground is rustic, clean, and quiet, except for a little road noise. A sign here gives precise distances to further attractions up the road.

Directions: From the junction of US 3 and US 302 in Twin Mountain, go 2.3 miles east on US 302 to Zealand Road and the Zealand Campground.

Activities: Camping, picnicking, fishing, swimming. The river is very shallow here.

Facilities: Campground, toilets, picnic tables, grills, parking.

Dates: Mid-May to mid-Dec.

Fees: There is a charge to camp.

Closest town: Twin Mountain, 2.3 miles.

For more information: WMNF Ammonoosuc Ranger Station, Trudeau Road, Bethlehem, NH 03574. Phone (603) 869-2626 or TDD (603) 869-3104.

SUGARLOAF CAMPGROUNDS I AND II

[Fig. 28(2)] Sugarloaf Campgrounds I and II are located on the Zealand Road, 0.5 mile and 0.6 mile, respectively, from US 302. The entrance to each turns off the road to the right and each has roughly 30 campsites. These campgrounds are wooded, spacious, and far enough from US 302 that they are pleasantly quiet. Either makes a perfect base from which to spend a few days exploring the Zealand area. Sugarloaf I has the advantage of flush toilets, while Sugarloaf II is open a bit later in the season, until mid-December.

Directions: From the junction of US 3 and US 302 in Twin Mountain, go 2.3 miles east on US 302 to Zealand Road. Turn right on Zealand Road and go 0.5 mile to Sugarloaf I and 0.6 mile to Sugarloaf II.

Activities: Camping.

Facilities: Campsites, toilets.

Dates: Sugarloaf I, mid-May to mid-Oct. Sugarloaf II, mid-May to mid-Dec. Reservations can be made 14 days in advance.

Fees: There is a charge to camp.

Closest town: Twin Mountain, 3 miles.

For more information: Ammonoosuc Ranger Station, Trudeau Road, Bethlehem, NH 03574. Phone (603) 869-2626 or TDD (603) 869-3104.

🐾 SUGARLOAF TRAIL

[Fig. 28] North and Middle Sugarloaf Mountains may seem diminutive compared with the 4,000-footers to the south and east, but their bald summits provide excellent views for relatively little effort. The approach to either one is via the Sugarloaf Trail, which leaves the Zealand Road, 1 mile from US 302. The trail initially runs along the banks of the Zealand River which, when seen from above in a certain afternoon light, reflects a gorgeous golden color. At 0.9 mile, this pleasant, wooded trail reaches a col where, if you turn left, you go to Middle Sugarloaf. This mountain, at 2,539 feet, is the taller of the two. The less steep branch turns right and heads to North Sugarloaf, a choice that avoids the use of a small ladder on the Middle Sugarloaf Trail. Either choice—try both, if you are ambitious—offers a clear look at how time and the driving force of nature have restored this once-scorched landscape to a sea of green, rumpled by waves of mountains.

Directions: From the junction of US 302 and US 3 in Twin Mountain, go 2.3

Snowshoe Hare

The snowshoe hare (*Lepus americanus*) takes its name from its oversized rear paws, which can leave a print 5 inches long atop the snow. This trademark is only one of the coping strategies this rabbitlike creature uses to stay alive in a world where hare is on the menu of everyone from hawks to bobcats. The snowshoe hare's splayed, fur-covered feet enable it to leap along on top of deep snow while its less suitably equipped predators tend to bog down. Another way the hare outwits its enemies is to merely sit still in its "form," a small, body-shaped shelter molded into the grass or low branches. A third way that the snowshoe hare—also called the "varying" hare—protects itself from pursuers is by changing color. In summer, its furry coat is a mottled brown, perfect camouflage among leaves and earth, while in the winter, the animal grows hair that is tipped in white, or a cream color, which lets it blend into the winter-white background. Hares are not only larger than their cousins, rabbits, but also differ by bearing young that are fully furred, have open eyes, and literally hit the ground running. Snowshoe hare abound in the northern forests of New Hampshire, especially where young hemlock trees spray their lower branches out over the snow. Look for tracks that show large hind prints coming down in front of smaller fore prints, and a leaping stride as long as 10 or 13 feet.

miles south on US 302 to Zealand Road. Turn right and go 1 mile to the Sugarloaf trailhead, which leaves the road on the right, just south of the bridge over the Zealand River. Limited pull-off parking is located on the north side of this bridge.

Trail: 2.4-mile (round-trip) hike to the summit of North Sugarloaf, or a 2.6-mile (round-trip) hike to the summit of Middle Sugarloaf.

Elevation: North Sugarloaf, 1,644 feet to 2,310 feet. Middle Sugarloaf, 1,644 feet to 2,539 feet.

Degree of difficulty: Moderate.

Surface and blaze: Forest floor, some rocks, open ledges at the summits. Middle Sugarloaf involves climbing one small ladder. Blazes are yellow.

HALE BROOK TRAIL

[Fig. 28] Mount Hale is the highest of the Little River Range, the small group of mountains that includes the Sugarloaves. At 4,054 feet, Hale just squeaks into the 4,000-footer club, but its bare summit rewards the hiker with a fine view. Named for Edward Everett Hale, a nineteenth century minister, author, and explorer of the White Mountains, Mount Hale offers a view that sweeps around the horizon from the Presidentials to Mount Carrigain. Closer is a dramatic look down into Zealand Notch, with its steep, bare walls a result of the fires that raged over the area a hundred years ago.

On its climb to the summit of Mount Hale, the 2.3-mile Hale Brook Trail runs through a forest made up primarily of birch, but a clue to the forest of the future lies at your feet. Knee-high along the edges of the trail is a crowded layer of small sugar maple saplings, waiting to take over as a dominant species in New Hampshire's northern hardwood forests. Sugar maples do not colonize an area as quickly as do birches, but their seeds can sprout in the shade of these pioneers, and after the birch live out their short lives, the sugar maples are waiting in the wings to take over.

From the trees overhead, you will often hear the incessant song of the red-eyed vireo (*Vireo olivaceus*), New Hampshire's most abundant songbird—and certainly its most tireless singer. This vireo's song is somewhat similar to a robin's, but a good clue to identification is that this bird goes on almost continuously, all day, even in the heat of the afternoon, when most other birds are quiet.

Directions: From the junction of US 302 and US 3 in Twin Mountain, go 2.3 miles south on US 302 to Zealand Road. Turn right and go 2.5 miles south to the Hale Brook Trailhead and parking lot on the right.

Trail: 4.6-mile (round-trip) hike to the summit of Mount Hale.

Elevation: 1,770 feet to 4,054 feet.

Degree of difficulty: Moderate.

Surface and blaze: Forest floor, some rocky ledge, a few stream crossings. Blazes are yellow.

ZEALAND TRAIL TO ZEALAND POND

[Fig. 28] This 2.5-mile hike leads from the end of Zealand Road to Zealand Pond. Zealand Trail runs primarily along an old railroad bed, so the modest climb of 450 feet is nicely spread over an easy grade. There are several stream crossings on this trail, and most have bridges. Enough time has elapsed since a railroad ran here that a tall birch and maple forest has grown up. The foliage muffles all sound but the gurgling Zealand River running below.

The AMC's Zealand Falls Hut is only 0.3 mile beyond the pond, and is accessible via the Twinway Trail. The hut is open year-round to accommodate winter hikers and cross-country skiers. There are back-country ski trails in the Zealand Area, both along Zealand Road, and in the area surrounding Zealand Falls Hut. In the summer, the AMC can help the visitor plan a hut-to-hut hike, and arrange for the hiker's shuttle to pick you up at the trailhead. In the winter, you can ski in to Zealand Falls Hut, stay overnight, and explore the cross-country ski trails in that area. Reservations are required for the hut and highly recommended for the shuttle.

Directions: From the junction of US 302 and US 3 in Twin Mountain, go 2.3 miles south on US 302 to Zealand Road. Turn right and go 3.5 miles to the end of the road to the Zealand Trailhead.

For more information: For reservations at Zealand Hut or on the hiker's shuttle, call (603) 466-2727.

Trail: 5-mile hike (round-trip) to Zealand Pond, or 5.6-mile hike (round-trip) to Zealand Falls Hut.

Elevation: 2,000 feet to 2,450 feet.

Degree of difficulty: Moderate.

Surface and blaze: Duff-covered railroad bed. Some rocky detours. Several stream crossings. Blazes are blue.

QUEEN ANNE'S LACE
(Daucus carota)
A very common wildflower found across North America from Alaska to Mexico. Growing to 5 feet tall, the flowers are creamy white with a single dark flower in the center.

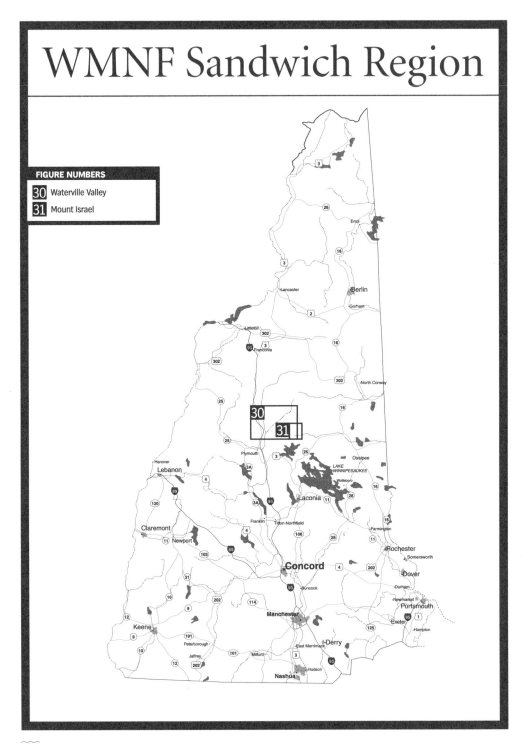

WMNF Sandwich Region

FIGURE NUMBERS

30 Waterville Valley
31 Mount Israel

WMNF Sandwich Region

The Sandwich Region of the White Mountain National Forest is its southern-most section, lying south of the Kancamagus Highway, east of Interstate 93, and west of NH 16. The Sandwich Range of mountains is a meandering string of 3,000- and 4,000-footers, stretching east and west across the center of the region and crowning the remote backcountry of the Sandwich Range Wilderness.

These are beautifully individual peaks, having amazing variety, in both shape and composition. Pink Conway Granite underlies Mounts Potash, Kancamagus, and Welch, while the greenish Mount Osceola Granite composes Mounts Osceola and Chocorua. Mount Israel's ledges are made of Kinsman Quartz Monzonite, and a Quartz Syenite ring dike marks the roots of an ancient volcano around the cones of Mount Tripyramid. Hundreds of millions of years ago, these various igneous rocks rose from below to shoulder aside the older mica schist of the Littleton Formation.

[*Above:* The Sandwich Range as seen from Mount Israel]

Today, this schist is seen primarily on just one peak, Sandwich Dome, which has somehow stood its ground against the invading granitics.

The Sandwich Range Wilderness stretches 12 miles across this region, encompassing most of these high peaks and the intervales between them. These lower lands hold pockets of old-growth forest, pristine mountain ponds, boulder-filled valleys, and wild rivers. Dozens of hiking and cross-country skiing trails traverse the area and are maintained by the WMNF and several private clubs such as the Appalachian Mountain Club, Squam Lakes Association, Waterville Valley Athletic and Improvement Association, and the Wonalancet Out Door Club. Each of these organizations publishes maps or guides to its trails (*see* Appendix B).

Some of these trails approach the Sandwich Range from the north, off the scenic Kancamagus Highway (*see* page 143), while others lead in from more remote trailheads on the south side. Some climb the high peaks, while others—often more rewarding—climb lower summits with panoramic views of the entire range. Mount Israel is an excellent example of the latter. Many trails follow the winding routes of rivers and streams through the wilderness, providing less strenuous wooded walks where trees and birds and falling waters soothe the senses with a calmer ambience than that found atop the breathtaking windblown summits.

Welch and Dickey Mountains

In the southwest corner of the Sandwich Region stand two medium-sized mountains that provide extraordinary views of the surrounding peaks, valleys, and of each other. A moderate loop hike of 4.4 miles runs up the southern slope of Welch Mountain, over its summit and that of its neighbor, and down the western side of Dickey Mountain. These two peaks, at 2,605 and 2,734 feet respectively, are not the highest around, but because each has an enormous exposure of granite ledge, the trek over them is an airy, out-in-the-open experience. For about half the hike, there are views in many directions, encompassing the Valley of the Mad River on the east, the Pemigewasset Valley on the west, the peaks of Tecumseh and Tripyramid on the north, and Mount Cardigan on the distant southern horizon.

The Welch and Dickey Loop Trail offers constant variety. After half an hour in the woods, it breaks out onto great expanses of granite pavement, fringed with small evergreens, including Jack pine (*Pinus banksiana*). This northern species is found in only a few spots in New Hampshire and can be recognized by its distinctly curvaceous cones, which require fire to open them and release their seeds. Scattered elsewhere over the smooth granite are tiny islands of soil where shorter alpine plants have gained a tenuous foothold. The rest of the exposed pink granite is painted with a thin layer of green and black lichens—the rudimentary beginnings of what will, one day, be soil.

Christmas Tree Plantations

One quick look around New Hampshire makes it clear that what grows best in this state are trees. If timber is the product, the grower must wait 80 to 100 years for a crop, but a more immediate satisfaction may be had from growing Christmas trees. In only 8 to 10 years, the fruits of the manager's labor are ready for harvest, and ready to bring joy to someone's Christmas.

Not that growing Christmas trees is without effort. To achieve a full, nicely shaped tree requires regular pruning, shearing, and fertilization. The grass between the rows of trees must be mowed as well, to prevent it from competing for nutrients and from sheltering small rodents, who may kill the trees by chewing the bark off their trunks. An occasional application of pesticide may also be necessary.

New Hampshire has more than 200 Christmas tree plantations, most under 10 acres, which, together, annually produce more than 100,000 trees and add over $1 million to the state's economy. The favorite species among New Hampshire folks is the aromatic balsam fir, but many growers plant a variety of trees—spruce, white pine, and scotch pine—to satisfy all tastes and to protect against pests and diseases that may attack one species and not another.

Growing Christmas trees not only beautifies the landscape and fuels the economy, it also provides a rewarding hobby or vocation, puts otherwise unproductive land to work, helps prevent erosion, and provides cover for certain wildlife, like fox, deer, and nesting songbirds. Many plantations encourage you to come and cut your own tree, and finding a bird's nest in the one you've chosen is an treasured omen, portending good things for the coming year.

As the trail crosses these two mountaintops, it ducks in and out of wooded copses where reindeer lichens (*Cladonia rangiferina*) raise their frosty green growth from the peaty soil. In regions far to the north, this plant provides much of the diet of the caribou. On the descent of the western slopes of Dickey Mountain, it is hard to resist looking back over the route you've just traveled across a curve of bare summits, but look down at your feet as well, to spot a distinct dike of smooth gray basalt that cuts through the granite.

Directions: From Interstate 93, take Exit 28 onto NH 49. Go 5.5 miles east on NH 49 to the second entrance to Upper Mad River Road. Turn left and go 0.7 mile to Orris Road. Turn right and go 0.6 mile to trailhead and parking on the right.

Trail: 4.4-mile loop trail over the summits of Welch and Dickey mountains.

Elevation: 1,060 feet to 2,734 feet.

Degree of difficulty: Moderate, with some steep sections on the upper ledges.

Surface and blaze: Forest floor, stone steps, and large expanses of open granite ledge. Caution is required on this bare rock, which ices over in colder months and may be treacherous from Nov. through Apr. Blazes are yellow.

Waterville Valley

This beautiful valley is also a ski area and mountain resort that offers hiking, skiing, golfing, biking, tennis, skating, swimming, boating, and just relaxing.

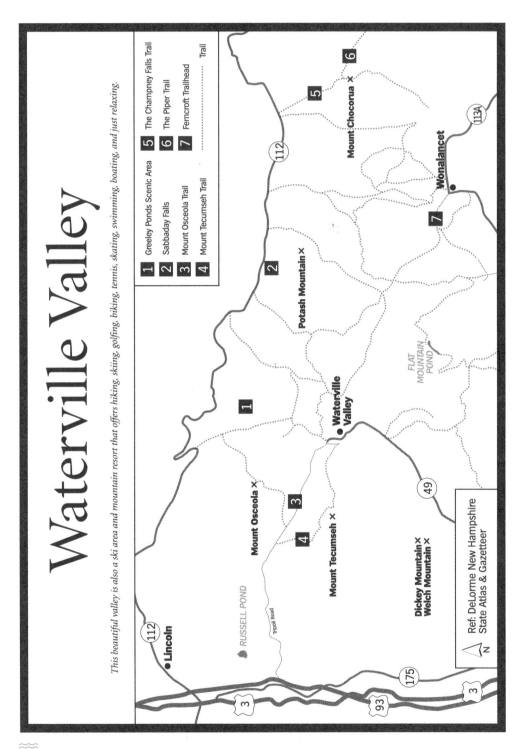

1 Greeley Ponds Scenic Area
2 Sabbaday Falls
3 Mount Osceola Trail
4 Mount Tecumseh Trail
5 The Champney Falls Trail
6 The Piper Trail
7 Ferncroft Trailhead
⋯⋯ Trail

Ref: DeLorme New Hampshire
State Atlas & Gazetteer

N

Waterville Valley

[Fig. 30] The Waterville Valley offers visitors opportunities to enjoy outdoor activities—beginning with the scenic drive up NH 49 into this spectacular valley and including hiking, alpine and nordic skiing, golfing, biking, tennis, skating, swimming, boating, or just relaxing at a comfortable inn or condominium and gazing at the mountain view, with fine food and a health club close at hand.

Waterville Valley is many things. First, it is the breathtakingly beautiful valley where the Mad River flows down from Greeley Ponds, between 4,000-foot Mount Tecumseh on the west and the distinctive cones of Mount Tripyramid on the east. Depending on the season, the Mad River either trickles around, or thunders through, this winding gully full of bleached boulders and driftwood. Driving into the Valley on NH 49 is a delight to the eye, as the view ahead shifts back and forth among the impressive mountains of the Sandwich group—Tecumseh, Tripyramid, Osceola at the head of the valley, and the cliffs of Whiteface Mountain looming to the east. Altogether, there are five 4,000-footers adjacent to this valley.

Second, Waterville Valley is an excellent ski area and mountain resort. It is a self-contained town, actually, that is tastefully arranged to accommodate a large number of visitors in a mountain setting that feels secluded. Hundreds of visitors can be tucked away in the many inns and condominiums that surround the ski slopes on the back side of Mount Tecumseh. Fifty alpine trails equipped for snow-making, 105 kilometers of nordic trails, a golf course, biking and hiking trails, an in-line skate park, as well as rental equipment for all of the above ensure full days leading into nights of fine dining or just browsing in the town square, an area with shops and cafes, and sometimes even fireworks.

Directions: From Interstate 93, take Exit 28 onto NH 49. Go east for 11 miles to the center of the complex.

Activities: Skiing, golfing, tennis, biking, hiking, skating, lodging, camping, dining, shopping.

Facilities: Nordic and alpine ski trails, golf course, health club, skate park, town square, tennis courts, bike trails, hiking trails, conference center, hotel accommodations, and campground.

Dates: Open most of the year, except portions of Apr., Oct., and Nov.

Fees: There is a charge for all but the hiking.

Closest town: Campton, 11 miles.

For more information: Waterville Valley Resort, 1 Ski Area Road, Waterville Valley, NH 03215. Phone (800) 468-2553. Web site: www.waterville.com.

▓ HIKING IN WATERVILLE VALLEY

More than 100 miles of hiking trails weave a lacy web through the forested slopes of Waterville Valley. Some lead to the stunning summits of Mounts Tecumseh,

Tripyramid, and Osceola—all topping 4,000 feet. Others follow brooks or the mighty Mad River along the valley floor. They range in length from less than 0.5 mile to 5 miles, and all are suitable for the average hiker. An excellent map of these trails has been compiled by the Waterville Valley Athletic and Improvement Association (WVAIA).

The Waterville Valley Resort offers access to the Sandwich Wilderness. The blind upper end of the valley, where no roads lead out—except Tripoli Road which is closed in winter—assures that there is no through traffic to disrupt the peace here, and lots of backcountry in which to get away from whatever bustle attends the ski area.

For more information: Waterville Valley Athletic and Improvement Association, Waterville Valley, NH 03215. A map of the valley's hiking trails is available from the resort's Adventure Center, or from the area's only service station on Tripoli Road, near its junction with NH 49.

Tripoli Road

[Fig. 30] Partly paved and partly gravel, Tripoli Road travels 12 miles across the Sandwich Region, from Interstate 93 to Waterville Valley. Closed in winter and in mud season, it is open and well-graded from late spring to late fall. It climbs a winding, forested route along Eastman Brook to its high point, the 2,300-foot pass at Thornton Gap between Mounts Osceola and Tecumseh, then descends to the relatively civilized world of Waterville Valley. Along this otherwise undeveloped road, one organized campground lies 3 miles off the road at Russell Pond, and the rest of the route offers multiple opportunities for hiking, fishing, and primitive camping. The visitor seeking a quiet forest experience for a few days may choose from among many primitive campsites that lie just off this road. Brook trout lurk in the gurgling waters of Eastman Brook, and at night, the forest's wildlife—owls, raccoons, deer, even black bear—may put in an appearance around a quiet campsite. To arrange primitive camping, stop at the trailer building just beyond the Russell Pond Campground to check for site availability and to pay a fee.

Also located along Tripoli Road are several trailheads whose paths lead to ponds and peaks deep in the national forest. The Mount Tecumseh Trail leads up the northwest side of this mountain to a grand view of the Tripyramids and Mount Osceola. The hiker may then descend the east side of the mountain to the Waterville Valley ski area, or retrace the quieter route back to Tripoli Road. A little farther east on this road, the Mount Osceola Trail leads to the summit of this 4,340-foot mountain.

Directions: From Interstate 93, take Exit 31 to Tripoli Road.

Activities: Scenic driving, camping, fishing, hiking.

Facilities: Paved and gravel road, 1 WMNF campground and many primitive campsites, pull-off parking, brook, trails.

Dates: Road closed to vehicles from late Nov. to May.

Fees: None for hiking or driving the road. There is a charge to camp.

Closest town: Woodstock, 3 miles from west end of Tripoli Road.

For more information: WMNF Pemigewasset Ranger District, RFD 3, Box 15, NH Route 175, Plymouth, NH 03264. Phone (603) 536-1315.

BALSAM FIR
(*Abies balsamea*)

🔲 RUSSELL POND-WMNF RECREATION AREA

[Fig. 30] The 2,000-foot ledges of Russell Crag are visible from Interstate 93, just north of the exit for Tripoli Road. No trails climb this distinctive landmark, but nestled in behind it is 39-acre Russell Pond and a WMNF campground of the same name. Here is a way to put some distance between yourself and the highway, without going very far.

Flush toilets, hot water, and showers are the amenities here, but the stillness of the forest, spacious and private campsites, and a deep green pond to swim, canoe, or fish are the real drawing cards. The campground has its own forest ranger and provides access for the handicapped.

Directions: From Interstate 93, take Exit 31 onto Tripoli Road. Go 2 miles to the entrance sign for Russell Pond-WMNF Recreation Area on the left. Turn here and follow this road for about 3 miles to Russell Pond and the campground

Activities: Camping, fishing, swimming, canoeing.

Facilities: Campsites, picnic tables, grills, restrooms, coin-operated showers, flush toilets, pond.

Dates: Open mid-May to mid-Oct.

Fees: There is a fee to camp.

Closest town: Woodstock, 8 miles.

For more information: WMNF Pemigewasset Ranger District, RFD 3, Box 15, NH Route 175, Plymouth, NH 03264. Phone (603) 536-1315. To make reservations, phone (800) 280-2267.

🔲 MOUNT TECUMSEH AND MOUNT OSCEOLA TRAILS OFF TRIPOLI ROAD

The summits of Mounts Tecumseh and Osceola may both be reached on trails that leave Tripoli Road. Each of these trails continues beyond its respective summit and offers access to these mountains from the other end. The opposite end of the Mount Tecumseh Trail [Fig. 30(4)] starts at the Mount Tecumseh Ski Area in Waterville Valley and the other end of the Mount Osceola Trail [Fig. 30(3)] turns off the Greeley Ponds Trail that leaves the Kancamagus Highway. From their Tripoli Road termini, these two trails are longer, quieter woods walks where fewer fellow hikers are encountered.

Mount Tecumseh Trail: 3.1-mile hike (one-way) from Tripoli Road to the summit of Mount Tecumseh. If you continue down to Waterville Valley, the distance is 5.6 miles (one-way). From the summit the view is of Mounts Osceola and Tripyramid.

Elevation: 1,820 feet to 4,003 feet.

Degree of difficulty: Strenuous. Some of the route is steep and there are a few gains and losses of elevation.

Surface and blaze: Forest floor, some rocks, several stream crossings. Blazes are yellow.

Mount Osceola Trail: 3.2-mile hike (one-way) from Tripoli Road to the summit of Mount Osceola. If you follow the trail down the other side of the mountain to the Greeley Ponds Trail, it is 5.7 miles (one-way). The Tripoli Road approach to this summit is the more moderate and pleasant climb, and the view from the top is a grand look down the valley of the Mad River.

Elevation: 2,280 feet to 4,340 feet.

Degree of difficulty: Moderate.

Surface and blaze: Forest floor, some rocks. Blazes are yellow.

Greeley Ponds Scenic Area

[Fig. 30(1)] The Greeley Ponds are two shallow, deep green ponds that lie tucked between the slopes of Mounts Osceola and Kancamagus, just a little south of the Kancamagus Highway. The Greeley Ponds Trail leads 5 miles from this road to Livermore Road in Waterville Valley, but a pleasant and shorter hike is to walk in to the ponds from the north, enjoy lunch in the placid wilderness setting beneath high surrounding cliffs, and hike back out the same way. This hike gains only 200 feet in elevation and offers a scenic walk between soaring cliffs. To walk among mountains and gaze upward can often be as inspiring as climbing to their summits and looking down.

North Pond, which is reached in less than an hour over fairly even terrain, is surrounded by steep slopes clothed in spruce-fir forests, their dark greens accented in the autumn with the bright red berries of mountain ash. The autumn also brings an understory dotted with the large beige "ears" that are the buds of hobblebush, a winter food highly prized by moose and deer. Along the trail, tiny spruce saplings sprout from atop large erratic boulders. It has taken many centuries for lichens, mosses, and forest detritus to make enough soil here for this to occur.

The trail is well-worn and muddy in places, but boardwalks made of logs cover most of the wettest spots. To reach both North and South ponds, the hiker travels 1.9 miles (one-way) through a tall forest of old hemlocks and yellow birch, as well as some old-growth spruce.

Directions: From Interstate 93, take Exit 32 onto NH 112 East, the Kancamagus Highway. Go 10.4 miles to Greeley Ponds trailhead and parking on the right.

Trail: 3.8-mile (round-trip) hike to Greeley Ponds.

Elevation: 1,940 feet to 2,180 feet.

Degree of difficulty: Easy.

Surface and blaze: Forest floor, some rocks, several wet areas covered by boardwalks. Blazes are yellow.

Sabbaday Falls.

Sabbaday Falls

[Fig. 30(2)] Less than 0.5 mile off the Kancamagus Highway is one the most beautiful and accessible waterfalls in the White Mountains. Named Sabbaday because early explorers arrived here on the Sabbath, its straight-walled channel and emerald-green pools are the result of the erosion of a basalt dike. Eons ago, this molten rock invaded a crack in the Conway Granite, and because it was softer than the granite, the smooth, gray basalt was worn away by the raging glacial meltwaters of Sabbaday Brook. You can still see remnants of the dark, once-molten stone along the channel, and, adjacent to it, another narrower dike, remains intact.

A picnic area sits just off the parking lot and a wide gravel path leads you on a 15-minute walk to the falls. For a longer hike into the Sandwich Range Wilderness, the Sabbaday Brook Trail continues beyond the falls, south and west for 5 miles, to a col between North and Middle Tripyramid Mountains.

Directions: From Interstate 93, take Exit 32 to NH 112 E, or Kancamagus Highway. Go east for 21 miles to the Sabbaday Falls sign on the right.

Activities: Hiking, picnicking, viewing falls.

Facilities: Picnic tables, trail, parking, restrooms.

Dates: Trail open year-round. Kancamagus Highway may be closed by severe storms in the winter.

Fees: There is a fee for parking.

Closest town: Conway, 15 miles.

For more information: WMNF, Lincoln Woods Visitor Center, Route 112, Lincoln, NH 03251. WMNF Saco Ranger District Visitor Center, RFD #1, Box 94, Conway, NH 03818. Phone (603) 447-5448.

Potash Mountain

[Fig. 30] The view is panoramic from atop the 2,700-foot granite summit of Potash Mountain. Look south and trace the rocky bed of Downes Brook winding deep into the Sandwich Range Wilderness, passing by Mount Passaconaway with its noticeable slide scar. Or turn north for a grand view of the Swift River valley, or east to see Mount Chocorua's rocky summit piercing the sky. The relatively short hike—2.1 miles (one-way)—to the bare ledges on Potash Mountain begins at a multipath trailhead on the south side of the Kancamagus Highway, 22 miles east of Interstate 93. Here, the Downes Brook Trail combines the beginnings of the Mount Potash Trail, the University of New Hampshire Mount Hedgehog Loop Trail, and a blue-blazed cross-country ski trail. Follow the hiker logo signs and yellow wooden arrows 0.3 mile to the Mount Potash Trail, then another 1.9 miles to the summit.

This trail begins by winding through a tight little forest of shoulder-high spruce and fir and soon makes a crossing over Downes Brook, which could require wading shoes during times of high water. Then the path climbs through a dark hemlock forest until it breaks out onto the rocky slabs and ledges of the summit. For a longer hike, stay on the Downes Brook Trail which leads to Mount Whiteface after 6 miles, or take the University Trail for a loop of 4.8 miles over Hedgehog Mountain.

Directions: From Interstate 93, turn east at Exit 32 onto NH 112, or Kancamagus Highway. Go 22 miles to the Mount Potash and Hedgehog trailhead on the right, across from the entrance to the Passaconaway Campground.

Trail: The Mount Potash Trail turns off of the Downes Brook Trail 0.3 mile from the trailhead and leads to the summit of Potash Mountain, a 4.2-mile (round-trip) hike.

Elevation: 1,250 feet to 2,700 feet.

Degree of difficulty: Moderate.

Surface and blaze: Forest floor, one large stream crossing, rocky ledges near the summit which can be slippery when wet or icy. Blazes are yellow.

Mount Chocorua

[Fig. 30] From any direction, your first glimpse of Mount Chocorua alerts you that this is a very special mountain. At only 3,500 feet, Chocorua fails to make the 4,000-footer club. It isn't even the highest peak in the Sandwich Range. But, this rugged, distinctively shaped cone of rock is one of the most beloved and photographed peaks in the White Mountains.

Its eye-catching dome, composed of greenish Mount Osceola Granite, protrudes above all the forested peaks surrounding it and can be seen from the Lakes Region and the southern White Mountains. From the east, the summit has an almost hooked shape, and from the south, this treeless peak, resembling a jumbled pile of rocks, reflects dramatically in Chocorua Lake.

Besides being exceptionally photogenic and providing pleasant hiking challenges, Chocorua also possesses its own legend. In the late 1600s, there was a Chief Chocorua, of the Pequawket tribe, who was a silent, brooding man, suspicious of the few white folks in the area. But apparently, he allowed himself enough faith in one white person that, when he needed to take a trip north, he entrusted the care of his son to a man named Campbell. In his absence, the boy allegedly accidentally swallowed poison and died. Chocorua took this very badly, blamed the Campbells, and took revenge by killing Campbell's wife and all his children. Cornelius Campbell pursued Chief Chocorua up the mountain, demanding surrender. But, instead, Chief Chocorua threw a curse upon all white men, their homes, families, crops, and livestock. Then, he turned and hurled himself off the rocky summit—a tragic story without any winners, except that the chief won a share of immortality in the names of the mountain, the lake, a river, and the nearby village of Chocorua.

Although this legend adds another dimension to this unusual mountain, most people who know Chocorua love it for its striking beauty and for the alliterative sound of its name. It is pronounced "Chuck-**ore**-oo-wa."

Snow often dusts the rocky gray cone of this mountain as early as October, lending further texture and contrast to its irregular surface. Several processes account for its rugged look. Millennia of frost wedging has pried apart the joints in the granite, sending huge blocks of rock tumbling down the slopes. Glaciers, too, have covered this peak, carving northwest/southeast-trending striations in the rock and chewing blocks out of the southeast face. Add to these forces the unrelenting erosive power of water over the eons and its a wonder there is any mountain left at all.

The cone that remains has an irresistible charisma for hikers, it seems. From every side, a web of trails like the spokes of a wheel trace their way up to the hub at the mountain's summit. Because they all converge on a single destination, you may find yourself in a crowd near the top. It is best to hike this mountain in midweek or sometime other than July and August. The presence of other hikers, however, cannot spoil the stunning 360-degree view from the peak. Mount Washington and the Presidential Range dominate the northern horizon, and the other peaks of the Sandwich Range stretch off to the west. Below, the Kancamagus Highway and the valley of the Swift River wind west across the White Mountain National Forest.

TRAILS TO MOUNT CHOCORUA'S SUMMIT

Two of the most popular, yet pleasant, trails to the summit of Mount Chocorua are the Piper Trail on the eastern slope and the Champney Falls Trail that leaves the Kancamagus Highway on the north. The Piper Trail requires a modest parking fee. The Appalachian Mountain Club's *White Mountain Guide* and its map # 3, *Crawford Notch-Sandwich Range* show several possible loop hikes including the Piper, Hammond, and Weetamoo trails, or the Liberty and Brook trails. All lead to the summit, which, despite its spiky appearance, is actually quite broad with many vantage points. The Champney Falls and the Piper trails are popular because they are more direct and are relatively well graded.

THE CHAMPNEY FALLS TRAIL

[Fig. 30(5)] This trail, though well used, offers a pair of advantages. One is the short loop, 1.4 miles from the trailhead, that passes Pitcher and Champney Falls, two cascades standing side-by-side that are spectacular in the spring or just after a rain. The other is the option to take a pleasant, less traveled path, to the Middle Sister Peaks east of, and a little lower than, Chocorua. The Middle Sister Cutoff leaves the Champney Falls Trail 3 miles from the trailhead and offers a spectacular, up-close view of Chocorua without scaling its somewhat daunting cone. This path also avoids the numerous hikers possible in midsummer on the busier trails.

Directions: From the west end of the Kancamagus Highway (NH 112), go 25.6 miles east of Interstate 93, or from the east end of the highway, go 11.6 miles west on NH 112 from NH 16. Here you will find the trailhead for both the Bolles and the Champney Falls trails on the south side of the road.

Trail: 7.6-mile (round-trip) hike to the summit of Mount Chocorua.

Elevation: 1,260 feet to 3,500 feet.

Degree of difficulty: Strenuous.

Surface and blaze: Forest floor, rocky ledges, stream crossings. Wet and icy rock surfaces may be slippery. Sturdy boots and, in colder weather, crampons are recommended. Blazes are yellow.

THE PIPER TRAIL

[Fig. 30(6)] This 4.5-mile (one-way) hike to the summit of Mount Chocorua is lengthy but gently graded at the bottom where it follows the course of the Chocorua River through a mixed forest of hemlock, birch, and maple, changing to spruce and fir as you gain elevation. On steeper slopes and on the open ledges nearer the top, switchbacks take some of the breathlessness out of the ascent, and at various outlooks along the way, the startling cone of the mountaintop leaps into view between the trees.

Directions: From the junction of NH 113 and NH 16 in Chocorua Village, go 5 miles north on NH 16 to Davies Store on the left. Inside the store, you must pay a modest parking fee to use the private access road and parking area behind the store, adjacent to the trailhead.

Trail: 9-mile (round-trip) hike to the summit of Mount Chocorua.

Elevation: 780 feet to 3,500 feet.

Degree of difficulty: Strenuous.

Surface and blaze: Forest floor with lots of exposed roots, bare granite ledges, stream crossings. Open rock may be slippery when wet or icy. Sturdy hiking boots and, in colder seasons, crampons are recommended. Blazes are yellow.

Ferncroft Trailhead and The Bowl

[Fig. 30(7)] Wonalancet centers around a large meadowland—unusual in this mountainous region—nestled in an amphitheater of rounded mountain peaks. These are the central Sandwich Range peaks of Mounts Whiteface, Wonalancet, and Paugus. This tiny community at their feet lies across the lines where four towns come together and lacks distinct borders of its own. It has a rich history as a retreat for city folk a hundred years ago, when early innkeepers created a bucolic vacation spot here. Little in the way of buildings remains to testify to the thousands who once came to hike, relax, or play croquet in the clean mountain air. Wonalancet does, however, retain a post office, a tiny hilltop cemetery, and a very old and distinguished hiking organization, the Wonalancet Out Door Club (WODC).

For 106 years, the WODC has blazed and maintained more than 50 miles of hiking trails that lead into the Sandwich Range Mountains and Wilderness. The efforts of this and other private hiking clubs add to the richness of backcountry opportunities in New Hampshire. Whenever a storm, like the massive hurricane of 1938 or the crippling ice storm of 1998, hits the forests of the state, the volunteers of WODC and other clubs put hundreds of hours into cleanup, an effort that would otherwise take years, or perhaps never get done.

Ferncroft is the WODC's main trailhead, and it is located just off NH 113 A in Tamworth. The quiet, open meadows around it are all that remain of the bustling tennis and croquet courts, orchards, and gardens of the Ferncroft Inn, the largest of six inns that once clustered here. One by one, they all fell to fire or disuse, and now, the name Ferncroft simply denotes this trailhead, with its ample parking, informative kiosk, and the blue-lettered signs of the WODC. Blue is also the color of the blazes on the many WODC trails that lead from here to the north, east, and west. They run to mountain summits, through wooded notches, and around a large forest research area called The Bowl.

The Bowl is a secluded valley in a high glacial cirque that lies cupped between Mount Whiteface, Mount Passaconaway, and Mount Wonalancet. It is one of the few spots in New Hampshire where the sounds of a logger's axe or chainsaw were never heard. The Rollins Trail from the summit of Mount Whiteface skirts its upper lip and looks down into one of New Hampshire's few remaining stands of virgin spruce and fir.

COMMON RAVEN
(Corvus cryptoleucus)
The raven's wedge-shaped tail and larger size help differentiate it from the American crow.

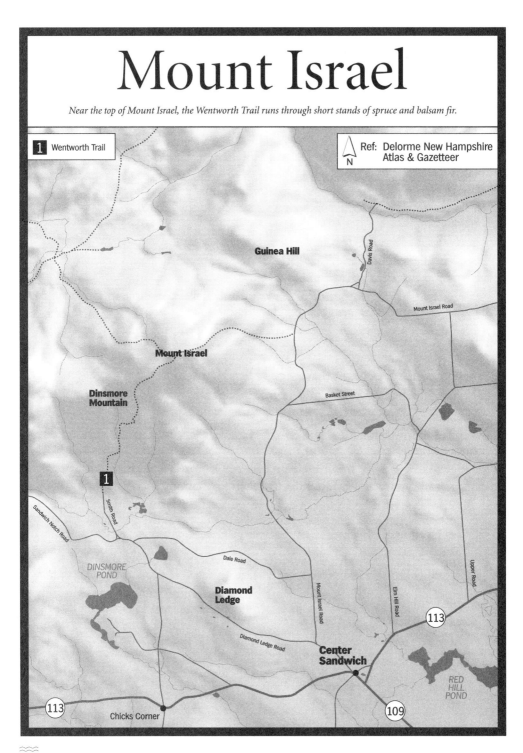

Mount Israel

Near the top of Mount Israel, the Wentworth Trail runs through short stands of spruce and balsam fir.

1 Wentworth Trail

Ref: Delorme New Hampshire Atlas & Gazetteer

N

Guinea Hill

Davis Road

Mount Israel Road

Mount Israel

Dinsmore Mountain

Basket Street

1

Smith Road

Sandwich Notch Road

DINSMORE POND

Dale Road

Diamond Ledge

Mount Israel Road

Elm Hill Road

Upper Road

113

Diamond Ledge Road

Center Sandwich

RED HILL POND

113

109

Chicks Corner

The Wonalancet Out Door Club publishes an excellent map and trail guide, which is available for sale or to consult free at the kiosk in Ferncroft. Using this or the Appalachian Mountain Club's *White Mountain Guide* and its map # 3, *Crawford Notch-Sandwich Range*, the visitor can plan hikes of various lengths and degrees of difficulty to the mountaintops, valleys, ponds, and streams of the Sandwich Range Wilderness. The Blueberry Ridge Trail leads to Mount Whiteface, whose bare southern ledges are visible for miles south of the Sandwich Range. The Blueberry Ridge Trail connects with the Rollins Trail, which affords a look into The Bowl. Dicey's Mill Trail leads to the summit of Mount Passaconaway, or on a multiday trip, you can head all the way east to Mount Chocorua on the Bee Line Trail. Primitive camping is permitted in the wilderness following the WMNF rules, and a few shelters and cabins are available.

Directions: To reach the Ferncroft trailhead in Wonalancet, go east on NH 25 and NH 113 in Tamworth, to where NH 113 turns north. Go 2.4 miles north on NH 113 to NH 113 A, and then 7 miles northwest on NH 113 A to Ferncroft Road. Turn right on Ferncroft, and go 0.5 mile to a gravel road. Turn right and go 0.1 mile to trailhead parking and kiosk.

Activities: Hiking and backcountry camping.

Facilities: Trails, informational kiosk, parking.

Dates: Open year-round.

Fees: None.

Closest town: Tamworth, 8 miles.

For more information: Wonalancet Out Door Club, Member Services, HCR 64, Box 5, Wonalancet, NH 03897. Web site: www.hydrocad.net/wodc. Both WODC and AMC maps and guides can be purchased at the AMC Pinkham Notch Visitor Center or the WMNF's Saco or Pemigewasset ranger stations.

Mount Israel and the Wentworth Trail

[Fig. 31] No easier, more enjoyable hike provides such a magnificent overview of the whole Sandwich Range, stretching east and west across the southern part of the WMNF, than does the 2.1-mile trip to the summit of Mount Israel. The Wentworth Trail [Fig. 31(1)] climbs a comfortable, even grade through a mixed hardwood forest on the mountain's southern slope. Atypically for New Hampshire's long-used forests, many of the trees along the trail are quite old. Red oaks and sugar maples 3 or 4 feet across are not uncommon on the upper slopes. It is obvious that the Mead family, who owned this tract and donated it to the WMNF, made a deliberate decision not to log it heavily.

Low rock walls run back and forth across this southern slope. No doubt they were once tall enough to keep flocks of grazing sheep in place, but the detritus of decades and the tumbling of time have rendered them low enough to step over comfortably

White Pine

The stately white pine (*Pinus strobus*) is ubiquitous throughout most of New Hampshire's medium and low elevations. But the 100-foot giants we see today would have been dwarfed by the towering pines that greeted European colonists in the 1600s. Because those behemoths—some measuring 8 feet in diameter and over 200 feet in height—had such long straight boles, they quickly became reserved solely for the British Royal Navy, as masts for their great tall ships. A "broad arrow" was hewn into the bark of these old giants, marking them as "King's Pines," off limits to anyone else.

Though only a handful of these old-growth pines remain in isolated pockets today, younger white pines may be seen nearly everywhere. This is a pioneer species that quickly colonizes disturbed areas or old fields, where sunlight and exposed mineral soil are available. It also tolerates well the acidic soil resulting from New Hampshire's granite bedrock.

To differentiate a white pine from a red pine or a pitch pine, you need only count the needles. White pine has five slender needles to a bunch, while red pine has two, and pitch pine, three. White pine also has a distinctive shape. Looking along the top of almost any New Hampshire forest, you can spot the white pine protruding above the other trees, extending its upturned branches, like supplicating arms, to the sky.

now. The open canopy created by white birch, American beech, and bigtooth aspen give an airy feel to this sunny southern slope, while an understory of asters, trailing arbutus, and Christmas fern thrives on the light the tall trees let in. *Epigaea repens*, the trailing arbutus, is a low creeper in the heath family that is usually one of the first wildflowers to bloom in the spring. On a sunny slope like this one, it takes advantage of its evergreen—and ever-ready—leaves to put out fragrant pink or white blossoms as early as March.

Mount Israel's bedrock is primarily schist of a rusty variety that makes for a reddish soil. But scattered over the mountain are boulders of various granitic rocks, such as Kinsman Quartz Monzonite, that were dragged here from the north and west by the most recent glacier. Pegmatite dikes add the sparkle of large white crystals to the variety.

Near the top of the mountain, the trail turns flat and runs over rocky ledges through short stands of spruce and balsam fir. There is a wonderful lookout to the southeast, over the shimmering surfaces of Squam Lake and Lake Winnepesaukee. Keep following the yellow blazes on the rock a bit further, to a distinct peak with an obvious cairn of rocks marking the true summit. Here, waits a spectacular view of the entire Sandwich Range, running east and west across the northern horizon. Immediately north, you look straight into the face of Sandwich Dome. Moving east from that are Flat Mountain, two of the conical peaks of Mount Tripyramid, Whiteface Mountain, Mount Passaconaway in the background, Mount Paugus's lumpy profile, and finally, the distinctive rocky dome of Mount Chocorua.

If, instead, you look west of Sandwich Dome, in the distance looms the massive dome of Mount Moosilauke, its 4,802-foot summit obscured as early as October by local snow squalls.

Directions: Near the junction of NH 25 and NH 25 B in Center Harbor, find Bean Road and turn north, going 8 miles to Center Sandwich. Turn north onto Grove Street, which becomes Diamond Ledge Road. At 2.4 miles, follow Diamond Ledge Road into a right turn, and go straight, past another right turn, for 0.4 mile to a big brown sign for the Mead Wilderness Base, a Boy Scout outdoor education center. Park here and find the Wentworth trailhead to the left of the buildings.

Trail: 4.2-mile trail (round-trip) to the summit of Mount Israel.

Elevation: 930 feet to 2,630 feet.

Degree of difficulty: Moderate.

Surface and blaze: Forest floor, some rocks. Open ledge at summit. Blazes are yellow.

Flat Mountain Pond

[Fig. 30] The walk to Flat Mountain Pond in the Sandwich Wilderness gives the visitor enough time and sufficient distance for the concept of wilderness to thoroughly sink in. As defined in the 1964 Wilderness Act, wilderness is "...an area where the earth and its community of life are untrammeled by man, where man himself is a visitor who does not remain....an area protected and managed so as to preserve its natural conditions and which generally appears to have been affected primarily by the forces of nature, with the imprint of man's work substantially unnoticeable."

Flat Mountain Pond, originally a beaver pond with the stumps to prove it, is a 30-acre mountain lake lying at 2,300 feet elevation. Surrounded by mountains and forests of spruce, balsam fir, and birch, the long, narrow lake lies 1,000 feet below the table-top summit of Flat Mountain. While you perch on a rock at the northern end of the pond and scan the shimmering waters and the undeveloped shoreline, the silence is such that you can hear your own heart beat.

The 4.2-mile walk (one-way) through the Sandwich Wilderness to reach this spot is almost better than the destination. For much of the way, the trail follows the Whiteface River, its bed a long winding swath of massive granite boulders, smoothed to a polish by millennia of tumbling waters. The river splashes along beside the trail, alternating between cascades and clear, green pools, presenting a thousand places for hikers to cool their faces or feet on a warm summer day.

Although it isn't short, the Flat Mountain Pond Trail is known for its easy grades, climbing only 1,300 feet in over 4 miles. Besides making this a pleasant hike, the

Nurse Logs

A nurse log is a tree that toppled over years ago and then, in subsequent decades, accumulated a coating of forest debris and moss, which became a rich seedbed for other young trees. Whenever you see a suspiciously straight line of trees in the woods, you may be looking at the product of a nurse log. Look for a slight rise under them, the remains of an old fallen tree, or if the old nurse log has long since rotted away, you may find a line of interlacing surface roots that began life atop the log, then settled once it was gone.

Most nurse logs in the Northeast are conifers—usually hemlock or white pine—because these evergreens decompose more slowly than deciduous trees. A nurse log must endure for decades in order to develop a bed of moss sufficient to nurture young seeds. Birches and maples decay much too fast, while decomposing oaks resist the growth of moss altogether. The nurse log may become a nursery for either conifer or deciduous trees, as long as the seedlings can tolerate the shade of the surrounding forest. In New Hampshire, hemlock and yellow birch—both shade tolerant—are often found growing atop nurse logs.

relatively flat going offers another advantage not found on most mountain trails—the freedom to lift your eyes off your feet and look around for evidence of wildlife. The shadow overhead of a woodland hawk draws your eyes skyward. Perhaps you catch a glimpse of another one of these streamlined birds—a sharp-shinned hawk, a Cooper's hawk, or the larger northern goshawk—as it flashes through the woods on the short rounded wings and long tail that allow these birds to deftly maneuver among the trees.

The observant hiker never lets a muddy spot go unexamined for the tracks of various woodland animals—bobcats, moose, black bear—who all leave their tracks and their droppings regularly along this trail. Look also for upturned trees or sheltered caves under rocks where a black bear might den up for the winter.

Because most human visitors to the wilderness inadvertently advertise their presence with sounds and smells, it is traces of animals that are most often found, not the animals themselves. Aside from the ubiquitous red squirrel who scolds vociferously as you walk by, or the chipmunk who scurries in and out of rocky crevices, wildlife experiences tend to be more a matter of sleuthing around for clues—bear claw marks high up the trunk of a beech tree, or the teeth marks of moose or deer on the bark of small saplings, or the missing buds on a low blueberry bush where a snowshoe hare has dined. It is even possible to detect the resting spot of a bobcat in the winter—a patch of melted snow and the outward-fanning lines the animal's claws made as it reached out for a long, catlike stretch as it got up to leave.

Just as it takes sharp eyes to pick up on these subtle wildlife clues, it also requires close attention to follow all the turns of the Flat Mountain Pond Trail. The trail is marked with both yellow and blue blazes and a few brown and yellow wooden arrows, but there are places, especially at stream crossings, where the blazes are easy to overlook. The Appalachian Mountain Club's *White Mountain Guide* and its map # 3, *Crawford Notch-Sandwich Range*, is highly recommended here.

The 8.4-mile (round-trip) hike to Flat Mountain Pond makes a comfortable day hike because of the easy grades, but a two-day loop is also possible here. Use the primitive shelter at the south end of the pond overnight, and then continue on the Flat Mountain Pond Trail to its other end, where it meets either the Bennett Street Trail or the Gleason Trail, both leading to Bennett Street, 2 miles west of the beginning of the loop.

Directions: From NH 25 in Moultonborough, turn north on NH 109 and go 5 miles north to Center Sandwich. Turn right on NH 113 and 113 A and go 6.9 miles to Whiteface Intervale Road on the left. Turn left and go 0.5 mile to trailhead and parking on the left.

Activities: Hiking, primitive camping.

Facilities: Trail, primitive shelter.

Dates: Open year-round.

Fees: None.

Closest town: Sandwich, 9 miles.

For more information: White Mountain National Forest, Pemigewasset Ranger District, RFD # 3, Box 15, Plymouth NH, 03264. Phone (603) 536-1315. AMC's *White Mountain Guide* and maps are available at most WMNF visitor centers.

MOOSE

(*Alces alces*) The largest member of the deer family, the moose can grow up to 10 feet tall and weigh more than 1,000 pounds. Its habitat is the northern forest, often near fresh water, where it feeds on aquatic plants.

WMNF Kinsman Region

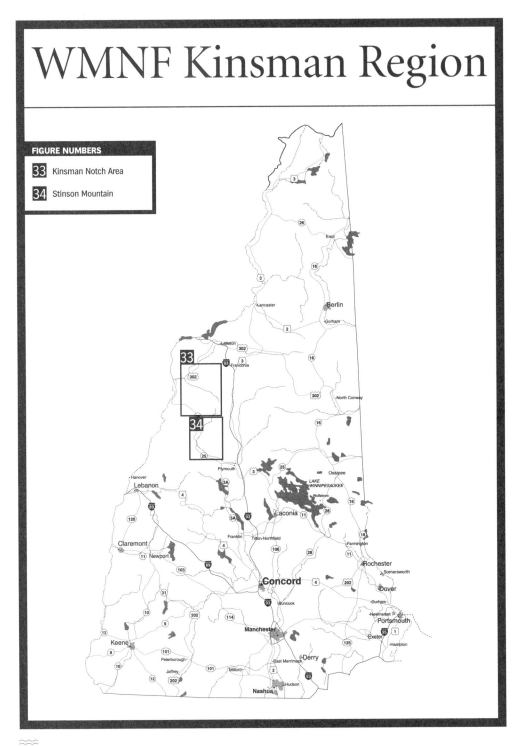

FIGURE NUMBERS

33 Kinsman Notch Area

34 Stinson Mountain

WMNF Kinsman Region

The Kinsman Region is the westernmost section of the White Mountain National Forest, and although it may cast less of a shadow than its sister sections to the east, its low-key ambience offers a welcome change from the relative bustle of Franconia Notch, the Kancamagus Highway, or the Presidential Region. A visitor need only turn west, instead of east, on NH 112 to enter this quiet backyard of the WMNF. Here, the roads are less traveled and the trails, less trodden. The mountains of this region—after a few high-risers in the northeast corner—begin to thin out, and the land, punctuated with farmers' fields and old country towns, slopes gradually to the west, down to the Connecticut River.

Geologically, this area is one of arc-like stripes of differing kinds of rock. There is a little of everything here—granitics, gneiss, schist, old volcanics, and the jumbled conglomerate rock that makes up places like Black Mountain. Even limestone, a real

[*Above:* Hemlock trees bend gracefully under the heavy snow]

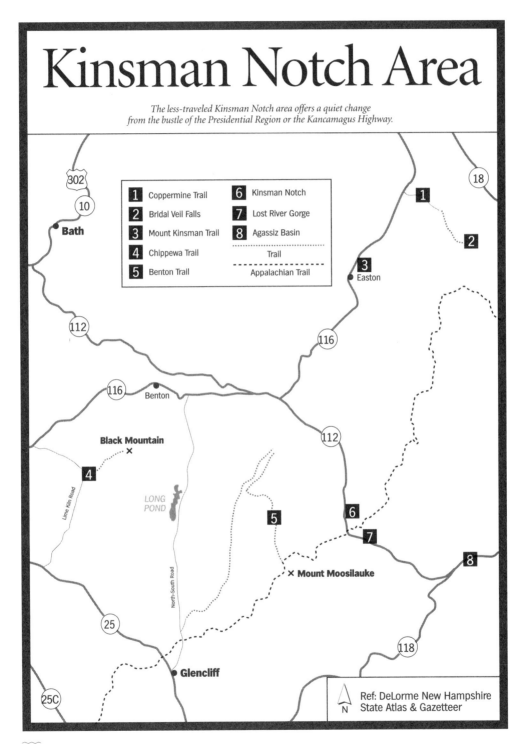

Kinsman Notch Area

*The less-traveled Kinsman Notch area offers a quiet change
from the bustle of the Presidential Region or the Kancamagus Highway.*

302

10

Bath

1 Coppermine Trail
2 Bridal Veil Falls
3 Mount Kinsman Trail
4 Chippewa Trail
5 Benton Trail

6 Kinsman Notch
7 Lost River Gorge
8 Agassiz Basin

·········· Trail
------- Appalachian Trail

18

1

2

3
Easton

112

116

116
Benton

112

Black Mountain
×

4

Lime Kiln Road

LONG POND

6

5

7

8

North-South Road

× **Mount Moosilauke**

25

118

• **Glencliff**

25C

N Ref: DeLorme New Hampshire
State Atlas & Gazetteer

rarity in New Hampshire, puts in an appearance here and there.

The striped and twisted outcrops, visible as you drive through Kinsman Notch, resulted from the squeezing, folding, and intrusion of rock that went on here millions of years ago and miles below the surface of other rock that has since eroded away. Glistening white dikes of quartz and pegmatite slash through darker gray gneiss. In places, whole blocks of ancient schist have dropped into partially molten granitic rock and are still suspended there, like pieces of fruit in a gelatin salad.

Dominating this section are the Kinsman Range, running southwest from Franconia Notch, and Mount Moosilauke, the 4,802-foot centerpiece of the region. Scattered around the edges of the Kinsman Region are some other little jewels in the 3,000-foot category, such as Black Mountain and Stinson Mountain. Others, like the somewhat smaller Rattlesnake Mountain, offer hikers moderate climbs.

Kinsman Notch

[Fig. 33(6)] NH 112, winding west through Kinsman Notch, is the perfect entrance into this quiet corner of the WMNF. This notch—one of the White Mountains' more sparsely visited—cuts between Mount Moosilauke to the southwest and the Kinsman Ridge to the northeast. Like New Hampshire's other notches, this crevice winds through the mountains on a route built eons ago by geological processes. Erosion by rivers and glacial meltwater, combined with faults and weakened rock joints, have deepened this zig-zag path through the mountains, over which millennia of wildlife, ancient humans, and now modern civilization have passed.

The high point in Kinsman Notch is 1,880 feet, a watershed divide where an old beaver pond, now human-dammed, is the source of the Wild Ammonoosuc River, a northwest-bound river with a long history of floating logs down to the mills on its spring flood. Here, the Beaver Pond Scenic Area welcomes visitors to stop for a moment and appreciate how today, this small lake reflects, once again, the forest-clad slopes of surrounding mountains.

Only a little farther west, the notch, the river, and the road all make a dramatic turn to the north. There is always a solid reason for river systems to make an abrupt turn, and here, it is because the softer granitic rock over which this one has been flowing runs head on into the massive swath of Littleton schist that makes up Mount Moosilauke. The notoriously erosion-resistant schist of this tough old mountain is what makes it one of New Hampshire's well-known monadnocks. Several miles along this northward leg the Wild Ammonoosuc finally finds a route through eroded joints on the mountain's lower slopes and is able to turn west again.

🖩 LOST RIVER GORGE

[Fig. 33(7)] The Lost River, which runs southeast, the opposite direction out of

Wild Turkey

The wild turkey (*Maleagris gallipavo sylvestris*) was once prevalent in New Hampshire, then disappeared for 100 years, and now, thanks to reintroduction and reforestation, is making a comeback. The quintessential image of a turkey is seen only in the spring, when the male puts on his impressive courting display. Puffing out his iridescent copper-colored feathers and spreading his striped tail into a gigantic fan, he seems to double in size, strutting around and jiggling his brilliant red head and throat.

The rest of the year, wild turkeys generally travel less flamboyantly, in quiet flocks, gleaning crop leavings and acorns from the fields and forests. Turkeys generally prefer to walk, but when pressed, they can explode into flight. At night, they roost in tall pine trees, safe from their predators and sheltered from the wind.

Benjamin Franklin, who admired both the looks and the grit of the wild turkey, fought valiantly to have this bird named the official national symbol. The bald eagle, apparently perceived as more glamorous, won out. There are now an estimated 9,000 wild turkeys in New Hampshire—enough to allow a limited hunting season—but most people still celebrate Thanksgiving by roasting the much fatter, and far less intelligent, freezer-case variety. This poor, pasty-white, distant cousin of the wild turkey is raised on large domestic farms and lacks the wily survival skills a wild turkey needs to make it through New Hampshire's lean winters.

Kinsman Notch, may now be smaller than the Wild Ammonoosuc, but it was once much larger, and the clues left behind by that ancient torrent tell an intriguing story. The river isn't really "lost" at all, but it has been so named for a couple of reasons. One is that, in many places, it courses along beneath a deep gorge full of gigantic pieces of broken granite, where only its echoing gurgle beneath the rock gives a hint of its presence. Another is that the raging deluge that originally carved this deep gorge is gone forever.

Evident along the walls of this chasm are the unmistakable marks left by a surge of glacial meltwater that flowed for hundreds of years. Large boulders and tons of gravel were carried along by the flood and ground away at the steep rock walls that now tower 50 feet above the floor of the gorge. The water and rock mixture smoothed the walls to a fine polish and carved enormous potholes along the way.

Since the Wild Ammonoosuc looks to be the larger of the two rivers emerging from this notch, why does the smaller Lost River have a gorge with all the earmarks of a raging torrent? The answer lies in the way that the glacier melted back some 12,000 to 14,000 years ago.

The Laurentide glacier melted away very slowly, its snout moving gradually to the north. It is thought that—for a few hundred years, at least—the retreating nose of ice sat stationary, just north of the notch, blocking any flow of meltwater in that direction. So all of what gushed out from under the snout of the glacier tore down the Lost River Gorge, in a violent slurry of boulders, gravel, and glacial flour, which ground and polished the smooth surfaces and rounded depressions we see here today. Another peri-glacial process, frost splitting, accounts for the enormous boulders that broke free from the high northern walls of the gorge and tumbled down into its bottom, under which the "lost" part of the river now flows.

Lost River Gorge is formed of a particular granite called Kinsman Quartz Monzonite, whose large, rectangular crystals of feldspar can be seen beneath the moss and lichen. For about 0.75 mile, a boardwalk winds back and forth over cascades and caverns among the huge, ice-split rocks. It wiggles through caves with exotic names like Sun Alter, Thor's Workshop, Lemon Squeezer, and the Cave of Silence—the only spot in the gorge where the river cannot be heard running below. The visitor passes over huge chunks of moss-covered granite and looks up at others seemingly poised to drop at any moment but which actually have hung in these same precarious positions for thousands of years.

All along the boardwalk, on a pleasant autumn day, the sun spreads dappled light over falling water and colorful leaves and glints off the faces of broken granite chunks the size of trucks. The view from Lookoff Point along the boardwalk spans Mounts Tripyramid, Osceola, and Tecumseh, 15 miles to the southeast.

In 1912, the 148-acre Lost River Reservation was the first property purchased by the Society for the Protection of New Hampshire Forests (SPNHF), beginning its mission to preserve special places in the forest. Though SPNHF still owns the property and maintains a small visitor center and some short hiking trails, Lost River's other facilities are maintained by the White Mountain Attractions Association. It manages an unobtrusive cluster of buildings housing a visitor center, museum, cafeteria, and gift shop, and also conducts guided tours. Educational displays, a nature garden full of labeled native plants, and geological specimens make this a place where learning and enjoyment blend seamlessly. Children of all ages enjoy squeezing through the caverns and crevices among the giant granite blocks down in the gorge, while adults are awed by the hanging moss and fern gardens and the pounding waterfalls of spring.

Directions: From Interstate 93, take Exit 32 and turn west onto NH 112. Go 6.5 miles to a sign on the right marked "Lost River Gorge and Boulder Caves."

Activities: Tour gorge, explore gardens, hike nature trails, view ecology displays, picnic.

Facilities: Glacial meltwater gorge, boardwalk with informative signs, hiking trails, nature garden, picnic tables, cafeteria, gift shop, educational displays.

Dates: Open mid-May to mid-Oct.

Fees: There is a charge to tour the gorge on the boardwalk and for items in the shops. SPNHF displays and trails are free, as are the nature garden and picnic area.

Closest town: North Woodstock, 5.8 miles.

For more information: Lost River, Kinsman Notch, North Woodstock, NH 03262. Phone (603) 745- 8031.

▨ AGASSIZ BASIN

[Fig. 33(8)] Before NH 112 even begins its climb uphill to Lost River Gorge and through Kinsman Notch, it passes by a series of cascades and enormous potholes carved long ago by glacial meltwater roaring down out of the mountains. Today, Moosilauke Brook tumbles down a trough obviously sculpted by a much larger torrent. A short trail crosses the brook on two high bridges, providing a 250-yard observation loop over rock formations.

Directions: From the junction of NH 112 and US 3 in North Woodstock, go 1.8 miles west on NH 112 to Mountain Side Drive and the Gordon Pond trailhead on the right. Agassiz Basin and parking are on the left, directly across the road.

Trail: 250-yard walk around the glacial potholes of Moosilauke Brook.

Elevation: No elevation gain.

Degree of difficulty: Easy.

Surface and blaze: Forest floor, wooden bridges. No blazes.

The Kinsman Range and Trails

The Kinsman Ridge begins where Cannon Mountain backs out of Franconia Notch. Three so-called Cannon Balls line up their rounded profiles on its southwestern ridge, which continues southwestward in a line of granitic peaks including North and South Kinsman mountains. Farther south, beyond Mount Wolf and some lesser luminaries, the ridge ends abruptly as it drops into Kinsman Notch.

The rugged Kinsman Ridge Trail runs nearly 17 miles down this ridge, connecting Franconia Notch with Kinsman Notch, and 11 miles of this trail are a link in the Appalachian Trail (AT) (*see* page 295). Along its length, primitive campsites are available, offering opportunities for multiday treks. The Appalachian Mountain Club's *White Mountain Guide* offers detailed trail maps for making this trip. Shorter day hikes are also possible along this ridge, and two of them—the summit of Mount Kinsman, and Bridal Veil Falls—are described below.

▨ MOUNT KINSMAN TRAIL

[Fig. 33(3)] This trail leads 3.7 miles (one-way) to the Kinsman Ridge Trail, which travels another 0.9 mile to both summits of Mount Kinsman. If this length exceeds your comfort zone, this same trail offers the hiker two shorter alternatives. Two miles from the Mount Kinsman trailhead, just after crossing Flume Brook, a short (150-yard) side trail leads to Kinsman Flume, where a dike of once-molten material that entered a crack in older rock has since been eroded away, leaving a steep-sided gorge. Only 70 yards farther, on the Mount Kinsman Trail, a short (0.2 mile) spur turns right to Bald Peak, where a fine view opens up to the west. Sugar maples cover the lower slopes of the Kinsman Ridge, and an old sugar house stands beside the Mount Kinsman Trail, about 0.25 mile in, a silent witness to a once-lively maple syrup operation.

The Mount Kinsman Trail leaves NH 116 in Eastman. After reaching the Kinsman Ridge Trail at the top of the ridge, it is only 0.4 mile south to the summit of Mount Kinsman's North Peak, and another 0.9 mile farther to its South Peak.

From the partially open summit of North Peak, the eastern horizon is full of Mount Lafayette and the rest of the Franconia Range. This view could be enough for one day, but by pushing on the other 0.9 mile down the Kinsman Ridge Trail to the South Peak, the hiker is rewarded with a full 360-degree view that includes the Green Mountains of Vermont, plus the added benefit of finding alpine tundra plants like mountain cranberry (*Vaccinium cespitosum*) or three-toothed cinquefoil (*Potentilla tridentata*), which spread across this slightly higher, and more exposed summit.

Directions: On NH 116 in Easton, go 2 miles north of the Easton Town Hall (or 7 miles north of the junction of NH 116 and NH 112). Watch for the sign that marks the Easton/Franconia town line. The Mount Kinsman Trail has no sign, but it begins on a dirt road that passes between two stone pillars on the right side of the road, adjacent to the town line sign.

Trail: 10-mile (round-trip) hike, if both North and South Peaks are included, 8.2 miles for North Peak only, or 4.5 miles to Kinsman Flume or Bald Peak.

Elevation: 1,030 to 4,358 feet.

Degree of difficulty: Moderate to strenuous.

Surface and blaze: Woods roads, forest floor, some rocks. Several stream crossings, two small ladders. Some exposure to weather on South Kinsman Peak. Blazes are blue, but very sparsely placed. Look for brown and yellow wooden arrows at road junctions on the lower end of the trail and stone cairns farther up. Note carefully where the Mount Kinsman Trail joins the Kinsman Ridge Trail, so you can easily find the turn on your way back. AMC's map # 4, *Moosilaukee-Kinsman*, is recommended for use here.

COPPERMINE TRAIL TO BRIDAL VEIL FALLS

[Fig. 33(1)] Coppermine Brook runs down a ravine on the back side of Cannon Mountain, where at about 2,000 feet, it jumps over the rocky ledges as Bridal Veil Falls, one of the more beautiful cascades in the White Mountains. This northwestern flank of Cannon Mountain receives far less attention from the hiking public than the busier Franconia Notch area on the other side. Solitude comes easier here.

Directions: From the junction of NH 116 and NH 18 in Franconia, go 3.5 miles south on NH 116 to Coppermine Road, or go 1 mile north of the Easton/Franconia town line. There is no road sign, but there is a sign reading "Coppermine Village." Turn east and park along the edge of this road. The trail begins 0.4 mile farther east on Copper-mine Road and is marked with a brown and yellow hiker logo and yellow paint blazes.

Trail: 5-mile (round-trip) hike up Coppermine Brook to Bridal Veil Falls.

Elevation: 994 feet to 2,100 feet.

Degree of difficulty: Moderate.

Surface and blaze: Forest floor, some rocks. Blazes are yellow. Blue plastic markers indicate a cross-country ski route on the same trail.

Mount Moosilauke

[Fig. 33] Mount Moosilauke, at 4,802 feet, dominates this western section of the White Mountains. From any direction, its long silhouette hangs bluish on one horizon or another, a north/south-trending series of rounded nobs. The mountain looks nothing like a moose, nor was it named for one. *Moosilauke* is a Native American word for "bald place," and the mountain got its name because its elevation brings it close to tree line in many areas and into the realm of alpine tundra on its highest knob, South Peak. There, acres of rock-strewn grasses are home to many of the same delicate plants found on the summit of Mount Washington.

Mount Moosilauke is as high as it is because it is made of tougher rock than the granitics and volcanics that surround it. The dark gray schists that make up the bulk of this massive mountain were laid down as sand and silt in ancient Devonian seas, 400 million years ago. In the eons since, it has better resisted the erosion that has swept away other heights.

The flanks and the summits of Mount Moosilauke are strewn with glacial till and erratics, indicating that it was once—perhaps more than once—completely covered by continental glaciers. Grooves and striations are also evidence that ice moved slowly but inexorably over its surface.

The summit of Mount Moosilauke and much of the land south and east of it are owned by Dartmouth College. Since 1929, the Dartmouth Outing Club (DOC) has maintained a web of trails on the mountain's eastern and southern slopes and has operated the Moosilauke Ravine Lodge near its base. The Dartmouth land is treated as a natural wilderness area, so no fires or camping are allowed outside authorized camping areas. Some of these eastern trails are well used and fairly arduous, but around the mountain, on its northern flank lies another option, the Benton Trail.

For more information: Director of Trails and Shelters, DOC, Robinson Hall, Box 9, Hanover, NH 03755. Phone (603) 646-2428.

BENTON TRAIL TO THE SUMMIT OF MOUNT MOOSILAUKE

[Fig. 33(5)] The Benton Trail approaches Mount Moosilauke from the north and is probably the easiest and least populous way to climb to this treeless summit.

Until it reaches the top, this trail runs totally through White Mountain National Forest land. All the vegetative zones of the Northeast, from hardwood forest through alpine meadow, are seen along the way. Though less strenuous than some of the eastern routes, it does climb 3,000 feet and requires sturdy boots, lots of food and water, warm clothing, and rain gear. But the exhilaration of standing atop the highest mountain in western New Hampshire—taller even than Vermont's Green Mountains visible across the way—is worth the effort. Find a cozy corner out of the wind, have lunch, and enjoy the tiny flowers and leaves of the alpine plants that hug the stony ground on this summit. In spring or fall, you may catch a glimpse of migrating hawks, making use of the rising air currents along the flanks of this lengthy mountain.

Directions: From the entrance to Lost River Gorge, go 5.2 miles west on NH 112 to Tunnel Brook Road. There is no sign here, but there are yellow state road signs indicating its approach. Turn south here, and go 3 miles, bearing right over a bridge, then left, to pull-off parking and the trailhead on the right. A sign here reads "Benton Trail."

Trail: 7.2-mile (round-trip) hike to the summit of Mount Moosilaukee, New Hampshire's westernmost 4,000-footer.

Elevation: 1,700 feet to 4,802 feet.

Degree of difficulty: Strenuous.

Surface and blaze: Forest floor, stream crossings, rocky ledges. Blazes on trees and rocks are blue, but rare near the bottom.

For more information: WMNF Pemigewasset Ranger District, Box 15, Route 175, Plymouth, NH 03264. Phone (603) 536-1310.

Chippewa Trail to the Summit of Black Mountain

[Fig. 33(4)] Along the western edge of the Kinsman Region runs the Benton Range, a string of mountains averaging just under 3,000 feet. One of them, 2,830-foot Black Mountain, offers a splendid view of Mount Moosilauke to the southeast, plus an expansive western vista that encompasses the Connecticut River valley and the Green Mountains of Vermont. The Chippewa Trail, 1.8 miles one-way, is a pretty hike on a trail passing through large stands of red pine and over a fascinating mix of rock types. An added attraction is an old lime kiln.

Black Mountain is made up primarily of granitic conglomerate rock, a swirly mix of white and gray stone frequently cut by veins of pegmatite. The crystals in pegmatite are quite large, and there are many places where you can see that semisolid rock flowed up against solidified stone, its heat blurring the borders of both. There is also plenty of New Hampshire's older schist on Black Mountain, its fine, dark gray layers glinting with mica flakes.

The biggest geological surprise on Black Mountain is limestone. Very little of this type of rock—made up of the skeletal remains of ancient sea creatures—is found anywhere in New Hampshire. When it was discovered here in 1837, large ovens called kilns were built to burn the quarried stone down to pure lime. Lime was used in plaster and as an agricultural product to sweeten the state's acidic soil. Though the quarrying and burning stopped long ago, like other structures built of stone, the kilns will stand for centuries in the silent woods. They remain intact and can be seen a short distance off the Chippewa Trail.

This trail begins among red maple and fir-balsam, which in October make for a carpet of red through a tunnel of green. About 200 yards in, it passes through a low, wet area where the conically chewed stumps of trees testify to the presence of beavers. Soon after climbing out of this sag, the trail meets a dirt road. If you turn left here and follow the kiln signs, you can walk around these old structures and try to imagine the furious heat of the 1,200-degree fires that once converted limestone to pure lime here.

To continue to the summit of Black Mountain, return to the trail, following the road right for 50 yards, then turning left uphill at a wooden arrow. Yellow blazes mark the way through a high and dry red pine forest on these slopes, but you must be alert to spot them in the maze of pine trunks. After open vistas begin to appear, the painted blazes on the rocks are easier to see.

Directions: From the junction of NH 10 and NH 25, go 5.1 miles east on NH 25 to Lime Kiln Road. Go a total of 3.2 miles on this road (bearing left at 1.4 miles) to a small pull-out parking area on right. There is no trail sign, but the trail is clear and has yellow blazes.

Trail: 3.6-mile (round-trip) trail to the summit of Black Mountain.

Elevation: 1,320 feet to 2,830 feet.

Degree of difficulty: Moderate.

Surface and blaze: Forest floor, rocky ledge. Blazes are yellow. Some care needed to follow them through the red pines.

Hubbard Brook Experimental Forest

[Fig. 34] The Hubbard Brook Experimental Forest, set aside for ecosystem research in 1955, occupies 7,800 acres within the WMNF. The work here of scientists from Dartmouth, Yale, Cornell, and other universities, has put together one of the longest continuous databases of ecological information in the world. Over three decades of research has contributed to well over 1,000 scientific publications.

Hubbard Brook Experimental Forest has focused its work on the many small streams that run down from Mounts Kineo, Cushman, and Green into the Hubbard

Brook, studying the effects of various types of forestry practices and the reduction of lead in the air following the phase out of leaded gasoline. Early work here with acid rain in the 1960s greatly influenced acid rain policies, both in this country and abroad. Neotropical migratory bird populations have also been the subject of a long-running study at Hubbard Brook. Access to any of this data is available by contacting the Hubbard Brook Data Manager, Forestry Sciences Laboratory, Box 640, Durham, NH 03824. Phone (603) 646-3237.

Various recreational opportunities are available in this experimental forest. Tiny Mirror Lake is only 0.8 mile from US 3 along Mirror Lake Road and is open to swimmers and nonmotorized boats. Beach and access points are well signed. At 1.2 miles on Mirror Lake Road, Hubbard Brook Road turns left, and here one can travel for miles through the quintessential northern hardwood forest—in summer and fall via car, mountain bike, or on foot, or in winter on snowshoes, snowmobile, or cross-country skis. These activities are permitted along the main USFS-maintained gravel roads that trace a fairly level course through this forest. Winter is ideal for finding the tracks of ruffed grouse (*Bonasa umbellus*), spruce grouse (*Dendragapus canadensis*), and other wildlife. Stop at the research headquarters at the beginning of Hubbard Brook Road for a brochure and map. Group tours are available as well, in summer and fall, if you arrange them in advance.

Directions: From Interstate 93, take Exit 29 to West Thornton. Turn north on US 3 for 4.9 miles to Mirror Lake Road. Turn left and go 0.8 mile to Mirror Lake swimming or boating access, or 1.2 miles to Hubbard Brook Road and the sign for the Hubbard Brook Experimental Forest. The headquarters building is uphill, behind the sign, just after the left turn onto Hubbard Brook Road.

Activities: In summer and fall: hiking, mountain biking, or driving through a quiet northern hardwood forest. In winter: snowshoeing, cross-country skiing, or snowmobiling. Group tours can be arranged in advance. Swimming and nonmotorized boating on Mirror Lake.

Facilities: Well-graded gravel road. Headquarters building with staff, brochures, and restrooms.

Dates: Open year-round. Hubbard Brook Road is not plowed in winter but is accessible by snowshoes, skis, and snowmobile.

Fees: None.

Closest town: West Thornton, 5 miles.

For more information: U.S. Department of Agriculture, Northeast Forest Experimental Station, Hubbard Brook Experimental Forest, West Thornton, NH 03293. Phone (603) 726-8902.

TROUT LILY
(*Erythronium americanum*)

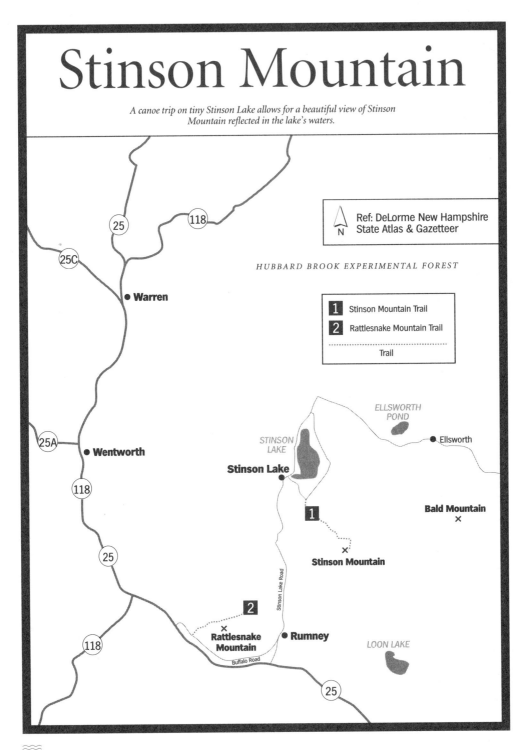

Stinson Mountain

A canoe trip on tiny Stinson Lake allows for a beautiful view of Stinson Mountain reflected in the lake's waters.

25
118
25C
● Warren

▲
N   Ref: DeLorme New Hampshire
     State Atlas & Gazetteer

HUBBARD BROOK EXPERIMENTAL FOREST

1 Stinson Mountain Trail
2 Rattlesnake Mountain Trail
....
Trail

ELLSWORTH POND

STINSON LAKE

● Ellsworth

25A ● Wentworth

Stinson Lake

118

1

Bald Mountain
×

×
Stinson Mountain

25

2

Stinson Lake Road

×
Rattlesnake Mountain

● **Rumney**

LOON LAKE

118

Buffalo Road

25

Stinson Mountain and Stinson Lake

[Fig. 34] From the open ledges atop 2,900-foot Stinson Mountain, the hiker gains a wide view of the picturesque Baker River valley, the river winding among farms and houses and the scars of ancient oxbows cut off from the flow long ago. Stinson Lake and a panorama of mountain ranges lie to the north, east, and west.

For a good deal of the way up the mountain, the Stinson Mountain Trail follows stone walls, an indication of the long-lasting footprint humans have left on this mountain. About 0.5 mile into this hike, the trail turns left around an old cellar hole, its foundations bearing silent witness to the hard-working folks who once carved a living from this rocky slope. The walls and roof have long since dissolved into the forest floor, and sizable trees have sprung from the rocky remains.

The lower end of the trail travels over a slope of hardwoods, and when the sun streams through their bare limbs in spring or fall, it makes for a light and airy place. One is almost grateful for the absence of the leaves. Farther up, when balsam fir and spruce trees take over, they are short and aromatic, so light still manages to bathe the mountainside.

This mountain is made primarily of metamorphic schist, but some boulders have raised aluminous crystals on their surface, resembling tiny fallen fir needles. Here and there lie large chunks of Kinsman Quartz Monzonite, a dark granite filled with white rectangular crystals of feldspar. The latest glacier apparently carried them to Stinson Mountain from northwest of here, where this type of granite forms the bedrock. From Stinson Mountain's summit, notice the lower topography to the northwest, a clear demonstration of the Kinsman Granite eroding more easily than the schist. Filling the hollow of this lowland is tiny Stinson Lake, a shimmering blue jewel surrounded by forested slopes. Though edged with private property, this clear, gravel-bottomed lake has a public boat access and is well worth launching a canoe into, for the ultimate view of Stinson Mountain reflected in its waters. Bass, pickerel, and trout offer anglers an added incentive.

Directions: From NH 25 in Rumney, turn north on Stinson Lake Road. Go 5 miles to Cross Road, and turn right. Go 0.8 mile to Doetown Road, and turn right for 0.3 mile to Stinson Mountain Trailhead on the left. For boat access to Stinson Lake, go 0.1 mile north of the junction of Cross Road and Stinson Lake Road, and turn right.

Activities: Hiking, boating, fishing.

Facilities: Trail, small boat access.

Dates: Trail open all year, but requires extra gear and clothing in winter. Lake accessible from freeze-up to ice-out.

Fees: None.

Closest town: Rumney, 6 miles.

For more information: WMNF, Pemigewasset Ranger District, RFD 3, Box 15, Plymouth, NH. Phone (603) 536-1315.

Trail: The Stinson Mountain Trail runs 2.8 miles (round-trip) to the summit.

Elevation: 1,495 feet to 2,900 feet.
Degree of difficulty: Moderate.
Surface and blaze: Forest floor, rocky ledges. Blazes begin yellow, then disappear, but the trail is clear.

Rattlesnake Mountain and the Rattlesnake Mountain Trail

[Fig. 34] Like the Rattlesnake Hills of Holderness (*see* page 279), Rattlesnake Mountain in Rumney has a large southern exposure of rocky ledge. It is possible both were named Rattlesnake because these warm slopes provided protective nooks for the cold-blooded timber rattlesnake, once prevalent in New Hampshire but now on the state's endangered list. We can only surmise, because *Crotalus horridus horridus,* the timber rattlesnake, has been nearly extirpated in New Hampshire. There are probably fewer than two dozen individuals in the state and only the herpetologists know where they are. One wonders if this was once a place they huddled together in crannies between the sun-warmed rocks.

Other creatures and plants, too, gravitate to such south-facing slopes. The mainly nocturnal bobcat often suns himself on sunny ledges during the daytime, watching through slitted eyes for potential prey. Look in the mud around wet areas on this mountain for his two-inch track, which is rounded and usually lacks claw marks. Certain plants, as well, are drawn to dry, sunny slopes. Atop Rattlesnake Mountain stand hundreds of miniature oak trees, which outcompete many others on warmer, drier slopes. Stunted from the wind, these have also been fire-damaged. See the dark scars on their bark left by the flames.

The rock of this mountain is basically Littleton schist, but scattered around the slopes are boulders bearing those same thready little crystals—perhaps andelusite or sillimanite—that are found on Mount Stinson. Pegmatite dikes also cut through the schist here, bearing large crystals of quartz, mica, and feldspar. These are all products of ancient metamorphism, but the summit of Rattlesnake Mountain also demonstrates a younger geological phenomenon. Here, glacial striations groove a wiggly path across the open ledge, from northwest to southeast, a direction nearly perpendicular to the grain of the rock. The Laurentide glacier, a mere 18,000 years ago, drew these lines by dragging pieces of tough rock , embedded in its underside, across this summit.

The Rattlesnake Mountain Trail [Fig. 34(2)] climbs 1.3 miles to the 1,594-foot summit, then another 0.1 mile out over the exposed ledges. On the northeast horizon sits Stinson Mountain, while the Sandwich Range rises in the distant east. Tucked into a windless nook here, you can feel the warmth coming up through the rock and the meager soil, as you look down below at the pastoral Baker River valley—a tapes-

Sensitive Fern

The delicate sensitive fern (*Onoclea sensibilis*), so-named because it shrivels and turns brown at the first touch of cold weather, is found in most of New Hampshire's low elevation wetlands. It is so closely associated with wet soil that it has become an official indicator of wetlands. *Onoclea sensibilis* lacks the lacy appearance of many local ferns, instead having a broader leaf with a wavy edge. After a shower, droplets of water bead up on these flat leaves like shimmering gemstones.

Identifying ferns is not easy, but the way each species carries its spores is somewhat distinctive. Many ferns arrange their spores in tiny "fruit dots" on the undersides of their leaves, but the sensitive fern encases its spores in brown beads the size of BBs, which cluster atop stiff brown stems of their own. These beads account for this plant's other name, bead fern. Although the sensitive fern withers to brown leaf litter early in the fall, like most ferns, it is a perennial which, again in spring, will hold the wetlands in a bright green embrace.

try of fields and farms and winding river. This is a wonderful little hike that affords a grand view for only moderate effort.

Farther east, the slopes of Rattlesnake Mountain turn abruptly to steep blocks of Concord Granite, visible for a mile or two while driving east along Buffalo Road. Wherever a sheer wall of rock raises its face above the forests of New Hampshire, you are sure to find rock climbers, and this wall is no exception. The Rumney Crags, 1.7 miles east on Buffalo Road, welcome climbers with a WMNF parking area and an information board about the various routes up the cliff faces. This area is overseen by the Rumney Climbers Association.

Directions: To the Rattlesnake Mountain Trail from Interstate 93, take Exit 26 onto NH 25 West. Go 3.9 miles to a traffic circle. Stay on NH 25 West here, and go 6.4 miles farther to Sand Hill Road. Turn right, and go 0.4 mile to Buffalo Road. Turn right, and go 1.2 miles to a trailhead on the left. Trail sign may be missing, but others read "1.0 mile to loop" and "1.4 miles to ledges." By all means, include the loop at the top in your hike to get a view of the ledges.

To reach the Rumney Crags, go 1.7 miles east of this trailhead, on Buffalo Road.

For more information: For information about rock climbing on Rumney Crags see *Rumney*, a book by Ward Smith, one of the Rockfax series of rock climbing guides, available at sports outfitters.

Trail: 2.5-mile (round-trip) loop to the summit ledges of Rattlesnake Mountain.

Elevation: 630 feet to 1,594 feet.

Degree of difficulty: Moderate. Midsection is the steepest part.

Surface and blaze: Forest floor, some rocks, open ledge. Blazes are yellow.

Western Highlands

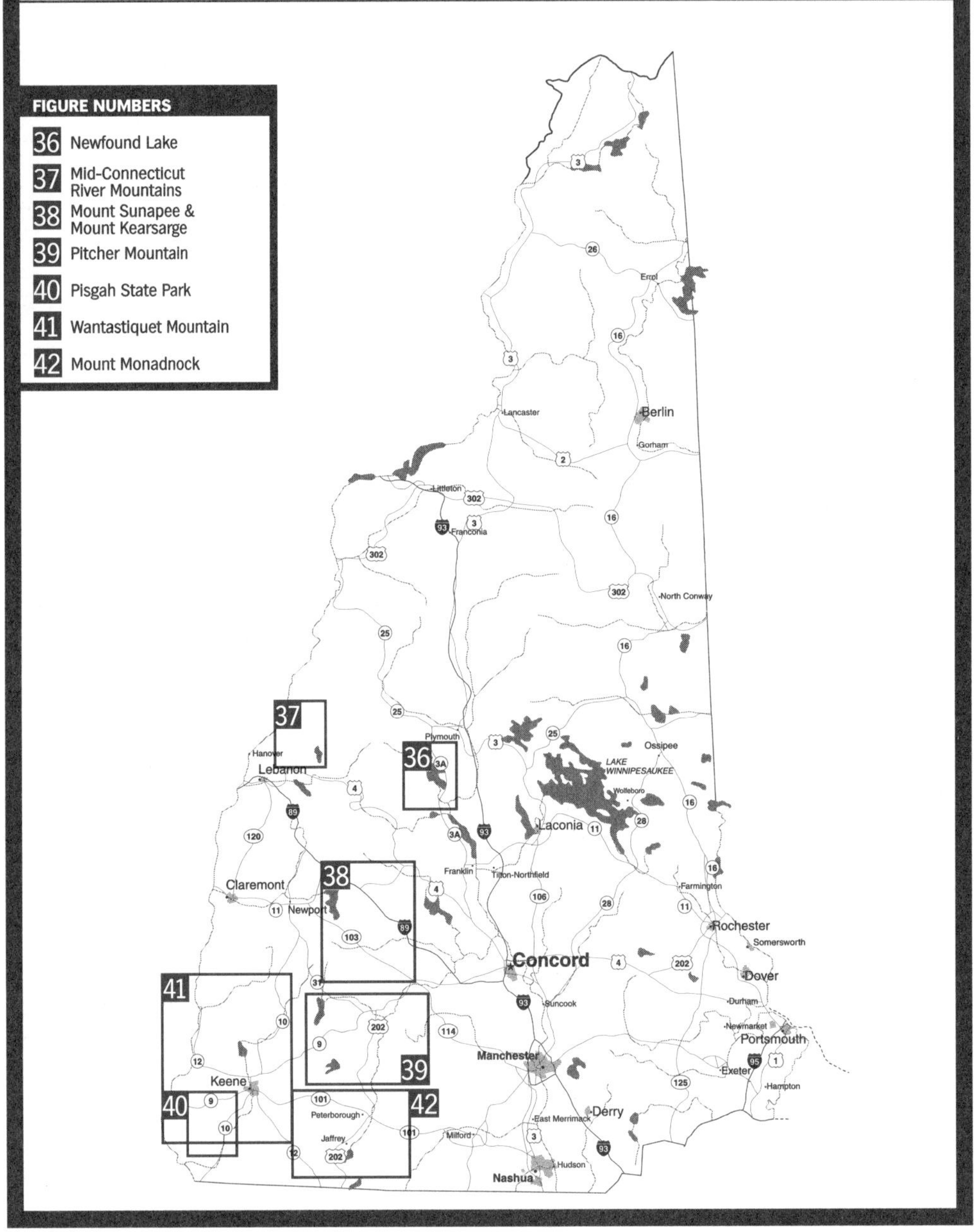

FIGURE NUMBERS

36 Newfound Lake

37 Mid-Connecticut River Mountains

38 Mount Sunapee & Mount Kearsarge

39 Pitcher Mountain

40 Pisgah State Park

41 Wantastiquet Mountain

42 Mount Monadnock

Western Highlands

The Western Highlands of New Hampshire are a rolling carpet of middle-elevation hills and mountains. They peak, generally, at around 2,000 feet with the exception of a distinctive few, like Mount Kearsarge, Mount Cardigan, and Grand Monadnock, which all top 3,000 feet and are counted among the state's rocky balds. Grand Monadnock, at 3,165 feet, is the highest among them.

The higher peaks of the western region are arranged on an irregular sort of spine that runs north and south down the center of this section, and divides the watersheds of the state's two largest rivers, the Connecticut River to the west and the Merrimack River to the east.

Very few truly flat areas can be found in this rolling countryside, but wherever a level area does turn up, as around the small city of Keene, you can bet that the flat spot was once a postglacial lake. As the Laurentide ice sheet melted, the lower ends of

[*Above:* Grand Monadnock, at 3,165 feet, is the highest of southwestern New Hampshire's rocky balds]

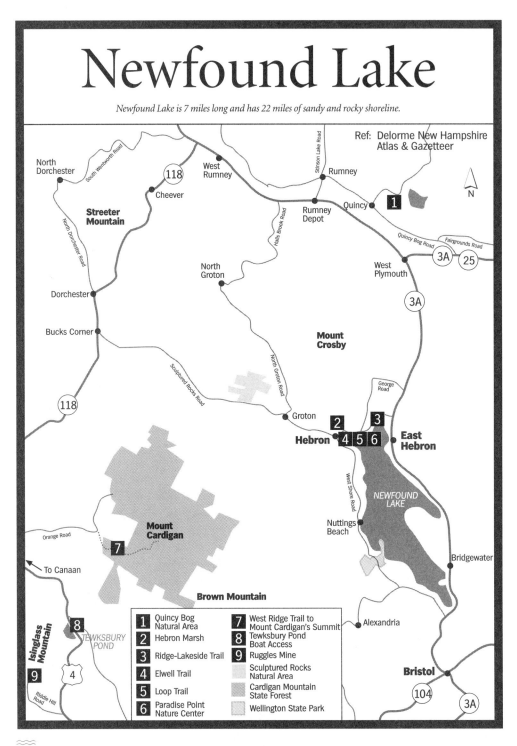

Newfound Lake

Newfound Lake is 7 miles long and has 22 miles of sandy and rocky shoreline.

Ref: Delorme New Hampshire Atlas & Gazetteer

N

North Dorchester

West Rumney

Rumney

118

Cheever

Streeter Mountain

Rumney Depot

Quincy

1

North Groton

West Plymouth

3A 25

Dorchester

3A

Bucks Corner

Mount Crosby

George Road

118

Groton

2

3

Hebron

4 5 6

East Hebron

NEWFOUND LAKE

Nuttings Beach

Mount Cardigan

7

Orange Road

To Canaan

Bridgewater

Brown Mountain

Alexandria

Isinglass Mountain

8

TEWKSBURY POND

4

9

Bristol

104

3A

Riddle Hill Road

1	Quincy Bog Natural Area	7	West Ridge Trail to Mount Cardigan's Summit
2	Hebron Marsh	8	Tewksbury Pond Boat Access
3	Ridge-Lakeside Trail	9	Ruggles Mine
4	Elwell Trail		Sculptured Rocks Natural Area
5	Loop Trail		Cardigan Mountain State Forest
6	Paradise Point Nature Center		Wellington State Park

some valleys were plugged with glacial debris. Behind these debris dams, great lakes of glacial meltwater built up and persisted for centuries, sometimes millennia, until they finally broke through their dams and drained away to the sea. Lake Hitchcock filled the Connecticut Valley, Lake Merrimack, the Merrimack Valley, and Lake Ashuelot, the valley where Keene sits today. Ancient lake beds are flat because water lays down sediment in flat layers. The rivers that now occupy these valleys came later, carving channels and terraces into the sediments and further enhancing the flatness with their own meandering floodplains.

The lakes that dot this region today often lie in beds of granitic gravel or sand, either of which makes for clean, clear water and lovely beaches. Lakes Sunapee and Newfound are two of these blue jewels, in settings eroded both by the glaciers and by the eons of weather before them. Now fed by springs or crystal mountain streams, they lie cool and placid between green and forested hills, reflecting blue sky, white clouds, and serenity.

Connecticut River-Cardigan Mountain-Newfound Lake Region

This northern section of the Western Highlands is a pleasing mixture of rivers, mountains, lakes, and picturesque towns. At fairly regular intervals, a white steeple—that unmistakable signature of small-town New England—rises out of the trees and pierces the clear, blue sky. Rolling farms intersperse with broad swaths of forest and, tucked around every corner, are antique shops, bed and breakfasts, and intriguing and talented artisans practicing various cottage industries out of their eighteenth-century homes.

On the banks of the Connecticut River, venerable Dartmouth College, one of the oldest educational institutions in the country, occupies a goodly portion of the town of Hanover. This private institution, chartered in 1769 for the purpose of educating both Indians and Englishmen, has, in the more than two centuries since, educated people from all corners of the world. Its brick and ivy-covered campus stands in stately serenity around the quintessential quadrangle of green grass and centennial trees. In addition to its educational functions, Dartmouth offers concerts, theater, and art museums, where the visitor can put a cultural finish on a day of outdoor adventure.

Along this western edge of the state, the Connecticut River stitches a wiggly seam between New Hampshire and its neighbor, Vermont. Navigable in places, shallow and rocky in others, the river has long been a route for small boat transportation and a source of hydroelectric power. Its broad, fertile floodplain holds some of the richest farmland in New England, and its setting between the mountains of both New

Hampshire and Vermont makes it a pleasant waterway to explore by canoe or kayak.

Roughly paralleling the river, a chain of widely spaced, medium-sized mountains forms a line running northeast from Hanover to Mount Moosilauke in the White Mountain National Forest. These highlands, with their various rock compositions, form a tantalizing line that simply begs to be climbed. Four of them, Moose Mountain, Holts Ledge, Smarts Mountain, and Mount Cube, long ago became favorite climbing spots for an avid group of outdoor people at the college, the century-old Dartmouth Outing Club. Volunteers from this still-vibrant group now maintain many of the trails in this region.

THE CONNECTICUT RIVER

The Connecticut River arises out of a string of lakes in far northern New Hampshire, named, appropriately, the Connecticut Lakes. The reasons why it runs where it does are ancient and not yet entirely understood. However, geologists do know one thing for sure about this valley: It is a very important division in the bedrock of New England. A recent seismic refraction study of the area shows an abrupt change in the rock types between New Hampshire and Vermont that goes all the way down to the earth's mantle.

Faults and rift valleys play some part in the placement of the Connecticut. The river runs down a series of northeast-southwest faults in the bedrock, and also down an ancient rift valley, a place where the land was almost, but not quite, torn asunder during the breakup of Pangaea 180 million years ago. But, this deeply divided suture is more than your average fault and has origins much older than 180 million years. There is still much to learn about this area, but it is probable that this place was once the edge of North America.

Closer to the surface, the Connecticut Valley is broad, with a relatively flat floodplain in the center created by the river, which has repeatedly changed its course over thousands of years. It has periodically flooded and continuously meandered back and forth, carving away its banks here, depositing silt there, and leaving behind today's floodplain on the floor of the valley.

For the last few thousand years, the 400-mile-long Connecticut River has carved its broad channel into the deep, lake-bottom sediments of old Lake Hitchcock, the long lake that, 10,000 years ago, filled the Connecticut Valley. Today's river has cut down through these sediments, revealing their varved clays, layers laid down in a special way peculiar to lakes. These varves are visible to the curious in many places along the Connecticut's banks and tell the story of seasonal rhythms and the work of flowing water over thousands of years.

Here and there, along the valley walls, you will find other level places situated at a higher elevation. These are river terraces, or pieces of the river's floodplain left behind at a higher elevation when the river meandered elsewhere in the valley and carved further downward.

Farmers valued these terraces, with their river-enriched soil and lack of rocks, which is another reason why settlement of the rocky interior of New Hampshire began along its rivers. Roads, railroads, or highways—often all three——still tend to run along these easily worked benches and occasionally, a whole city, like Brattleboro, Vermont, takes up residence on a river terrace.

CANOEING THE CONNECTICUT RIVER

In many places down its length, the Connecticut broadens out and becomes almost lakelike, with open views of the New Hampshire and Vermont mountains. In other spots, the mountains pinch in from either side, constricting the flow and hastening the river's cut down into the bedrock. Here, you'll find rapids and waterfalls.

Stone Walls

Hundreds of miles of stone walls snake their way through New Hampshire's forests, a mute but enduring testament to a backbreaking agricultural past. Early settlers and their oxen wrenched these glacier-rounded stones from their fields and dragged them to the edges where they served as fences to keep domestic animals from trampling crops. The stones were free, close at hand, and—because more were heaved from the soil by each winter's frost action—a seemingly inexhaustible resource.

One hundred and fifty years ago these structures ran like long strings of beads over the deforested hills, stitching the land together in a neat patchwork of small, cleared plots. It's been said that the toil that assembled them could have erected the pyramids 100 times over. The grand irony of this effort was that just as this "quilt" was being completed, newer farm equipment became available that worked better in larger fields. Moreover, in territories west of New Hampshire, less rocky and heartbreaking lands were opening up for settlement and many of New Hampshire's stony farms were subsequently abandoned.

Today, these enduring, lichen-encrusted walls slowly tumble and weather in the shady silence of a renewed forest. As huge trees grow from them, testifying to their great age, and chipmunks chatter from among their gaps and chinks, they remain as silent reminders of a very different human past.

Access to the Connecticut is available at several public boat launches in towns along the river. One, just below the bridge in Hanover, opens up the possibility of 46 miles of canoeing, floating, or kayaking all the way down to North Walpole. With the exception of a portage around the Wilder Hydroelectric Dam 3 miles below Hanover and one Class IV rapids that should be scouted, this trip offers only tranquility, mountain views, and a passage under the Cornish-Windsor Bridge, the longest covered bridge in the United States.

A detailed source of canoeing and kayaking information is available in *Quiet Water Canoeing Guide,* an Appalachian Mountain Club book by Alex Wilson, or in *The Complete Boating Guide to the Connecticut River,* Embassy Marine Publishing.

Mid-Connecticut River Mountains

The Middle Connecticut River Mountains stretch about 15 miles, roughly parallel to the Connecticut River.

LAKE FAIRLEE

Orford

(25A)

Gilmans Corner

Mount Cube

Old Country Road

1

(244)

(25A)

Post Mills

(91) Ely

Orfordville

Quintown

Five Corners

(10)

(113)

North Thetford

Hardscrabble

(91)

Thetford Center

Smarts Mountain

2

East Thetford

Lyme

Lyme Center

RESERVOIR POND

(10)

CUMMINS POND

Union Village

(91)

3

(132)

CONNECTICUT RIVER

N

Pompanoosuc

Rennie Road

Goose Pond Road

1 Mount Cube Trail

Two Mile Road

Moose Mountain

4

GOOSE POND

2 Lambert Ridge Trail

Etna

3 Holts Ledge

Goose Pond Road

4 Moose Mountain Trail

Canaan Center

- - - Appalachian Trail

Ref: Delorme New Hampshire Atlas and Gazetteer

THE MIDDLE CONNECTICUT RIVER MOUNTAINS

[Fig. 37] Running for about 15 miles, roughly parallel to the Connecticut River, these 2,000-foot to 3,000-foot peaks are grouped together in this book as they are in *The Appalachian Mountain Club White Mountain Guide.* Not really a range of mountains, per se, they lack an official name. For convenience, we will call them the Middle Connecticut River Mountains.

The summits of four of them—Moose Mountain, Holts Ledge, Smarts Mountain, and Mount Cube, are strung out along the Appalachian Trail like beads on a string. The AT climbs up and down over each of them, providing access to each summit from lower elevations. The mountains offer the hiker a variety of terrain, rock types, and vistas and also provide the opportunity to experience hiking on the famous Appalachian Trail.

The hiker can approach these peaks one at a time or, if feeling more ambitious, can hike them all. The routes described below are primarily up-and-back hikes. For longer treks and loop hikes, the reader should refer to the *AMC White Mountain Guide* or the Dartmouth Outing Club Trail Map.

For more information: For maps of these four mountains, write or call the Appalachian Mountain Club (AMC), Box 298, Gorham, NH 03581. Phone (800) 262-4455. Or, Dartmouth Outing Club (DOC), Robinson Hall, Box 9, Hanover, NH 03755. Phone (603) 646-2428.

MOOSE MOUNTAIN AND MOOSE MOUNTAIN TRAIL

[Fig. 37, Fig. 37(4)] Moose Mountain is the southernmost mountain of consequence in this group. Longer than it is wide, Moose stretches southwest-northeast for about 3 miles, and is located just east of Hanover. It is made up of two bands of rock, gneiss and quartzite, that run side by side down the length of the mountain. The mountain is forested all the way to the top with mixed hardwood, so hiking here is pretty much a forest experience without spectacular overlooks.

There are, however, compensations. Occasionally, and always when you least expect it, a heart-stopping ruffed grouse (*Bonasa umbellus*), will burst from its hiding place in the forest litter and fly off in alarm—yours and his. This bird is more often called a partridge in New England, and if you arrive in spring, you may have the privilege of hearing the male grouse's courtship and territorial "drumming," a hollow, repetitive, *voomping* sound he makes by beating his

AMERICAN GOLDFINCH
(*Carduelis tristis*)
During breeding in late summer, the male goldfinch is bright yellow with a black forehead.

Monadnocks

The term *monadnock* comes from the Abenaki Indian word for "mountain that stands alone." Harvard geologist William Morris Davis believed that Mount Monadnock in southwestern New Hampshire so typified the kind of tough rock that remains standing while everything surrounding it is eroded away that he gave the name to all such hills surrounded by relatively flat terrain. By this definition, several other New Hampshire mountains; Kearsarge, Mooselauke, Sunapee, and Cardigan; are also monadnocks. To add to the confusion, there are other peaks whose proper names contain the term: Pack Monadnock, North Monadnock, South Monadnock, and Little Monadnock. In geology, a monadnock is a hill or mountain of resistant rock surrounded by a *peneplain*—an eroded surface of low elevation and relief.

wings. It sounds very much like the revving up of a distant outboard motor.

Moose Mountain has two peaks, North and South, and here the AT passes over the South Peak at 2,290 feet and skirts the North Peak, continuing on through the Middle Connecticut Mountains. As it climbs South Peak, the trail winds over wildflower- and fern-covered forest floor. Spring beauty (*Claytonia virginica*), is particularly abundant in the early spring as is *Erythronium americanum*, the trout lily or dogtooth violet. This pleasant, woodsy trail runs to the summit of Moose Mountain's South Peak and back to Three-mile Road. It passes through primarily mixed hardwoods, ferns, and wildflowers, and takes approximately two hours to hike round-trip.

Directions: From Hanover, take Wheelock Street (which becomes Trescott Road) 5 miles east to its end. Turn left onto Two-mile Road and go 0.7 mile to Rudsboro Road. Turn right and go 1.6 miles to Three-mile Road. Turn left and go 1.3 miles to the AT sign and parking on the left. The trailhead is across the road.

Trail: A 3.8-mile round-trip hike to the south peak of Moose Mountain.

Elevation:

Degree of difficulty: Moderate.

Surface and blaze: Forest floor, a few rocks. Begins with orange and black blazes which turn left to the Fred Harris Trail at 0.4 mile. Do not turn left here. Go straight ahead at this junction, following AT's white blazes to summit.

HOLTS LEDGE AND HOLTS LEDGE TRAIL

[Fig. 37(3)] A short ride north from Moose Mountain to Lyme, alongside the tumbling waters and glistening falls of Grant Brook, brings you to Holts Ledge. This link in the chain of mountains along the Connecticut presents a whole different picture from Moose Mountain even though, at 2,110 feet, its elevation is considerably lower. Here a short stretch of the AT brings you to an abrupt precipice with a sheer drop-off to the northeast. It offers a wonderful view of Smarts Mountain, the next summit in the chain, and far off to the east, the rocky top of Cardigan Mountain blinks white in the sun. To the south Goose Pond glistens in the forest.

Geologically, the ledge is sort of a sandwich of different materials, stood on end. Schists, quartzites, even ancient volcanics all layer together here and tip up on edge to form this northeast-facing cliff.

In recent years, Holts Ledge has become a favored nesting place for the endangered peregrine falcon (*Falco peregrinus*). Signs and fencing atop the cliff denote areas to avoid so that you don't disturb this endangered species, which unfortunately suffered the same fate from DDT poisoning as other large predators.

The now-banned pesticide accumulated in predators at the top of the food chain and caused them to produce such thin egg shells that they broke under the weight of a nesting bird. Reproductive numbers plummeted, and by 1964, peregrines were gone from the eastern United States. Now, with the ban on DDT, and conservation and reintroduction measures, the birds are making a healthy comeback. A close eye is kept on their nesting activities by volunteers below. In the spring, biologists—turned rock climbers—rappel down the cliff, climb into the birds' aeries, and, amid the constant sharp calls of both agitated parents, put identification bands on the young chicks. This helps them know how the birds are doing in the future.

Near the summit of Holts Ledge, fir-balsam make an appearance among the hardwoods. Trickling streams run over moss-covered logs, and in the distance you may hear the exuberant song of *Troglodytes troglodytes,* the winter wren—a textbook example of a tiny bird overburdened by a weighty name. In places the climb to the summit of Holts Ledge is a bit steep, but it is only 1.5 miles to the top, well marked by the white rectangles of the AT, and worth the climb.

Directions: From Hanover, take NH 10 north to Lyme. Turn right around the village green and bear to the right of a white church onto Dorchester Road. Go 3 miles to where the paved road ends at the Dartmouth Skiway. This last little bit of road is called Cummins Pond Road. Park here and walk back 0.1 mile to trailhead on left.

Trail: 3-mile (round-trip) segment of the AT that climbs a forested trail to stunning overlook to the north and east. Allow 1.5 hours.

Elevation: 1,000 feet to 2,110 feet.

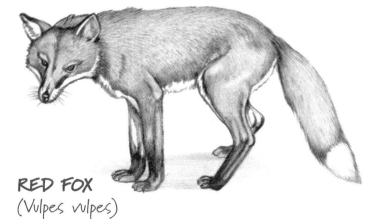

RED FOX
(Vulpes vulpes)
Notorious for preying on chickens, the red fox feeds mainly on small mammals and birds.

Degree of difficulty: Moderate.

Surface and blaze: Forest floor, some rocks. Can be a bit wet. Blazed in AT white rectangles.

SMARTS MOUNTAIN AND THE LAMBERT RIDGE TRAIL

[Fig. 37. Fig. 37(2)] Among other things, Smarts Mountain is composed of the Ammonoosuc Formation. This is volcanic rock that was part of a string of offshore volcanic islands during Ordovician times that were later pushed ashore by tectonic events. Elsewhere, most of these volcanics remain buried under other rocks, but in the case of Smarts Mountain, the overlying rocks have been eroded away, revealing the ancient volcanics.

Smarts Mountain, at 3,238 feet, is the highest of these four Connecticut River peaks. It sits regally to the northeast of Holts Ledge and is reached by the segment of the AT that climbs Lambert Ridge on its southwestern slope. This is another forested mountain, but there are several overlooks along the 3.9-mile (one-way) trail. The hike gains over 2,000 feet of elevation on moderate switchbacks, and the first view is at 0.8 mile. At 3.7 miles, there is a tent platform with a good view as well. A fire tower marks the summit.

Directions: From Hanover, take NH 10 north to Lyme. Turn right around the village green and bear to the right of a white church onto Dorchester Road. Go 3 miles to where the paved road ends at the Dartmouth Skiway. Park here and walk back 0.1 mile to Dorchester Road (dirt road) on the right. Turn right and walk 0.1 mile more to white-blazed post on right. This is Lambert Ridge Trail, the continuation of the AT north from Holts Ledge to Smarts Mountain.

Elevation: 1,000 feet to 3,238 feet.

Trail: 7.8 miles (round-trip) to summit of Smarts Mountain.

Degree of difficulty: Strenuous.

Surface and blaze: Forest floor, some rocky ledge. Trail can be a bit wet at the start but soon climbs to drier forest floor. White AT blazes.

MOUNT CUBE AND MOUNT CUBE TRAIL

[Fig. 37, Fig. 37(1)] South of NH 25A in Orford, Mount Cube's blocky, cube-shaped silhouette rises to an elevation of 2,909 feet. Made of tough metamorphic schist and quartzite, it stands above the surrounding hills and farms. The AT crosses NH 25A near Gilman's Corner and climbs 3.4 miles on various old woods roads to Mount Cube's summit. The trail makes several turns and, near the summit, joins two other trails. Bear right to the North Peak, which is bare of trees, offering fine views to the north and east.

Directions: From Wentworth, go north on NH 25 and 118 to the junction of NH 25A. Turn left and go 4.6 miles west to Mount Cube Trailhead on left.

Trail: 3.4-mile climb (6.8 miles round-trip), to the North Peak of Mount Cube follows old woods roads and forest paths. It makes several turns so watch for the white AT blazes. Near the summit is a junction with two other trails. Bear right to the North Peak Summit

Elevation: 1,200 feet to 2,909 feet.

Degree of difficulty: Moderate.

Surface and blaze: Woods roads, forest floor, some rocks. White AT blazes.

▓▓ MOUNT CARDIGAN

[Fig. 36] At 3,121 feet, Cardigan Mountain may look like just another one of New Hampshire's medium-sized mountains, but unlike some of the other blocky and craggy summits, this "old baldy," as it is sometimes called, is a smooth expanse of undulating, glacier-polished "pavement." The top 300 feet resemble an immense, sloping parking lot, floating on a sea of 6-foot swells. An old fire tower is bolted to the top so that it won't blow away in the worst of the winds that roar unimpeded over the summit.

The most prominent of the rocks forming this mountain is Kinsman Quartz Monzonite, a granitic rock with distinctive crystals of potash. These whitish, rectangular bodies, called phenocrysts, wear slowly and often stand out in relief from the rocks they inhabit. Also crisscrossing the summit are long, white veins of intrusive rock that melted and invaded cracks in the Kinsman.

On a clear day at the summit, a 360-degree view reaches the Presidential Mountains in the north, Massachusetts to the south, and west into Vermont. Newfound Lake is nestled to the east among the smaller peaks of the lakes region.

Cardigan is a much-loved and a much-climbed mountain. Its summit sits in the town of Orange, amid the more than 5,000-acre Cardigan State Forest. The West Ridge Trail (see page 206) takes off from a parking and picnicking area, at the end of the road in, and climbs the western slope of the mountain.

The Appalachian Mountain Club (AMC) maintains several trails up the east side of Mount Cardigan, some of which take off from the AMC's Cardigan Lodge in Alexandria. These trails offer longer hikes and the pleasure of staying at the rustic lodge. Reservations are necessary if you wish to stay at the lodge.

Directions: To reach Mount Cardigan's west side from I-89, take Exit 17 to NH 4. Go east on NH 4 to NH 118 N in Canaan and follow the signs for Mount Cardigan. Road dead-ends at the West Ridge Trailhead and parking lot. In winter and mud season, it ends 0.7 mile sooner, adding 1.4 miles (round-trip) to the climb. Trail maps are available in the box at the trailhead.

Activities: Hiking, picnicking, foliage viewing.

Facilities: Trails, picnic tables, benches, shelter, grills, restrooms, map.

Dates: Open year-round. Last 0.7 mile of road is closed in winter and mud season.

Fees: None.

Closest town: Orange, 4 miles.

For more information: New Hampshire Department of Parks and Recreation,

Box 856, Concord, NH 03302. Phone (603) 271-3254. For maps of eastern slope trails and directions to Cardigan Lodge, contact AMC Cardigan Lodge, RFD Bristol, NH 03222. Phone (603) 744-8011.

WEST RIDGE TRAIL

[Fig. 36(7)] The shortest and easiest route up Mount Cardigan, the West Ridge Trail, makes the 1,220-foot climb at a nice, steady pace. Driving to the trailhead from the west lends wonderful anticipation to the adventure because, for miles, the eastern horizon is totally dominated by Cardigan's rocky summit. In winter and spring, the road stops 0.7 mile short of the trailhead, adding another 1.4 miles (round-trip) to the walk, but this short hike on a woods road, through mixed hardwood forest, provides a nice warm-up and, in the spring, lots of birdsong. The trailhead and its parking area might be enough of a destination for some, as they offer a good view off to the southwest and benches and picnic tables to enjoy it from. Restrooms and a picnic shelter make this a good spot even on a rainy day.

The Cardigan Highlanders, a volunteer group, maintains the West Ridge Trail that takes off from this parking lot and climbs 1.5 miles to the summit. Hiking boots treading on spruce and balsam-fir needles send up such an overwhelming scent that you might well think you have been transported to the Canadian north woods. In the spring, small yellow violets and trout lilies sprout right from the middle of the path, and wet areas full of springy sphagnum moss line the edges of the trail. On the way, look for signs of moose droppings or moose tooth marks scarring the bark of hardwood saplings. As you gain elevation, the trees get noticeably shorter until they finally disappear altogether and you find the horizon full of clean, wind-blown rock.

Trail: 3 miles (round-trip) from trailhead or 4.4 miles (round-trip) from the end of the winter road.

Elevation: 1901 feet to 3, 121 feet.

Degree of difficulty: Moderate.

Surface and blaze: Forest floor, rocky steps, and bald rock at summit. Orange blazes.

TEWKSBURY POND BOAT ACCESS

[Fig. 36(8)] Tewksbury Pond in Grafton, at 46 acres, makes up in tranquility what it lacks in size. A brand new New Hampshire Fish and Game boat launch, with ample parking and proximity to NH 4, makes this surprising little pond a must-stop for those with canoes, kayaks, or nonpetrol powered boats. Anglers will find brook, brown, and rainbow trout, and paddlers will find cool, clear water with picturesque walls of rock flanking the shoreline.

Directions: From Grafton Center, take NH 4 2.5 miles north to New Hampshire Fish and Game sign on the left. Access road proceeds through posted land to a public ramp.

Activities: Fishing, boating, canoeing, kayaking.

Facilities: Parking, boat ramp, restrooms.

Dates: Year-round.

Fees: None. A New Hampshire fishing license is required to fish.

Closest town: Grafton, 2.5 miles.

For more information: New Hampshire Fish and Game Department, 2 Hazen Drive, Concord, NH 03301. Phone (603) 271-3422.

A Word About Towns

In New Hampshire, the term "town" does not mean downtown or urban in the usual sense. The fact that Gap Mountain is in the town of Troy only means that it is within that town's borders. With the exception of a very few unincorporated areas, every inch of the state is divided into towns that abut one another without county or township spaces in between. Each has its own individual character and plenty of trees and hills and country to share with visitors.

MINING IN NEW HAMPSHIRE

New Hampshire's long mining history and the obvious proximity of its rocks to the surface, make this state a mecca for rock hounds. Several active mineral clubs meet around the state, and every August, the New Hampshire Gem and Mineral Festival celebrates the wonders of rocks and minerals at Mount Sunapee State Park.

From an industrial standpoint, New Hampshire's chief mineral resources are its fine granites and the abundance of sand and gravel left behind by the glaciers. The granites—differentiated from the broad class of rocks loosely called granitics by their precise proportions of quartz and feldspar—are of two distinctive varieties. The fine, gray, sugary-textured Concord Granite was intruded into New Hampshire's metamorphics around 385 million years ago, whereas Conway Granite, the second variety, is only a youngster by comparison, intruded under the White Mountains and elsewhere a mere 180 million years ago. Conway Granite also looks very different, with reddish or pink tones; a lumpy, "oatmeal" texture; and large, conspicuous flakes of black mica.

Both varieties are highly prized. They endure as tombstones and famous buildings in every state in the union. The beautiful Concord Granite, still quarried from Rattlesnake Hill in Concord, adorns the Library of Congress in Washington, D.C., while Conway Granite accounts for the rosy color and lumpy texture of the New Hampshire State Library.

The second product of commercial mining in New Hampshire, sand and gravel, is gathered from the vast piles of rock debris left behind by the glaciers thousands of years ago. Distinctive and layered landforms, such as eskers, deltas, and kame terraces found on the Ossipee outwash plain and down the valley of the Merrimack River, have provided building materials and roadbeds for hundreds of years. We are now beginning to appreciate that some of these distinctive landforms support particular ecosystems, too. Pine barrens, for instance, seem to thrive on the rocky, well-drained soils of eskers and deltas. Conservation groups, The Nature Conservancy in particular, are working to preserve some of these distinctive landforms and their particular ecosystems before they are all gone.

On a smaller scale, many other minerals and gemstones have been found in veins of pegmatite—a coarse-grained igneous, or melted, rock that was forced in the form of dikes into cracks in other kinds of rock. At one large pegmatite mine in Grafton, garnet, amethyst, mica, and over 50 other gems and minerals have been found. The mine once was a commercial source for beryl, the New Hampshire state mineral, sought for its industrial and atomic energy uses. Now, at Ruggles Mine, the oldest pegmatite mine in the state, instead of commercial interests, it is individual rock hounds and tourists who work the mine, on a smaller, more personal scale, just for the love of rocks that shine.

RUGGLES MINE

[Fig. 36(9)] At the top of Isinglass Mountain, the open caves and arches of Ruggles Mine shine like alabaster in the sun. After nearly 200 years of commercial mining, the Ruggles Mine is now open to the public for touring and rock collecting. Quartz, feldspar, beryl, and mica are only a few of the 60 or more minerals to be found in this location.

Beryl is a greenish mineral, the mother rock of emerald, and mica used to be sought for use in lamp chimneys and stove windows. Now, its layered and flaky leaves glint like diamonds from the road surface leading to the top of the mountain. A stunning panorama of the surrounding highlands—Cardigan, Kearsarge, and Ragged mountains—awaits the visitor to Isinglass Mountain, whose dazzling geologic character dramatically proclaims that all of New Hampshire's western highlands are not the same.

Directions: From NH 4 in Grafton Center, turn west onto Riddle Hill Road. Go 1.4 miles, following orange Ruggles Mine signs to entrance on right. Entrance road goes another 2 miles to the mine at the summit of Isinglass Mountain.

Activities: Mine touring, rock collecting.

Facilities: Mine, snack bar, gift shop, restrooms.

Dates: Daily, June 15 - October 15. Weekends, May 17 - June 15.

Fees: Entrance fee is charged.

Closest town: Grafton Center, 3.5 miles.

For more information: Ruggles Mine, Grafton, NH 03240. Phone (603) 523-4275.

NEWFOUND LAKE

[Fig. 36] This jewel of a mountain lake, one of the clearest lakes in the country, sits crystalline in a bed of clean, granitic sand. Fed by underground springs and by several tumbling streams, it makes a happy home for swimmers and sailors, and for fish and fishermen. From the sandy shore or a quiet canoe, you can watch the early morning mist rise and reveal forested islands that seem to float like dollops of green meringue on the still water.

Newfound Lake is 7 miles long and has 22 miles of sandy and rocky shoreline, accommodating residents and tourists and even a few loons. A local lake association works hard to balance the needs and desires of people with the critical needs of wildlife and the need to preserve the natural qualities of the lake. Though homes and condos hug the southern end of the lake, the public has access to the lake on the western shore at Wellington State Park. The quiet northern end is home to the Sculptured Rocks geological site and two wildlife sanctuaries managed by the Audubon Society of New Hampshire. Several coves around the lake are no-wake zones to protect loons whose nests are built right at water level and can easily be swamped.

GRAY JAY
(Perisoreus canadensis)
Found in coniferous forests, this bold jay may be seen around forest camps, exploring campsites for food.

Rising east of the lake are humpy hills and an undulating road, NH 3A, that runs along this less-developed shoreline and offers intermittent views of the sparkling lake below. To the west swells Cardigan Mountain, with a few lesser summits in the foreground. Residents of the Newfound area are particularly proud of the spectacular views of fall foliage their area offers.

For more information: In the summer, the Newfound Region Chamber of Commerce runs an information booth on NH 3A, near the south end of the Lake. Or, write or call Newfound Region Chamber of Commerce, Box 454, Bristol, NH 03222. Phone (603) 744-2150.

WELLINGTON STATE PARK

[Fig. 36] Wellington State Park and Beach stretch 0.5 mile along the western shore of Newfound Lake and offer public swimming, boating, and fishing access to its cool, clear waters. There is no camping here, but there is lots of picnic space located either among the tall, shady pines or right at the water's edge. In the summer, a beach store and bathhouse open up and lifeguards are on duty, but at any time of the year, the park is open for picnicking, walking, or quiet contemplation of placid waters and forested hills. Within the park, the New Hampshire Fish and Game Department has recently constructed a beautiful new boat access facility with ample parking, ramps, a dock, and restrooms. Fishing regulations are listed on an information board there.

Directions: From Bristol, take NH 3A north to West Shore Road and turn left. Go 1.9 miles on West Shore Road until it turns right. Go another 1.1 miles to state park sign on the right.

Activities: Swimming, boating, canoeing, fishing, picnicking. Cross-country skiing and snowshoeing in winter.

Facilities: Beach, bathhouse, restrooms, and lifeguards in season, picnic tables, boat access.

Dates: Park is open all year but some facilities are seasonal.

Fees: Day-use fee in season. None out of season.

Closest town: Bristol, 7 miles.

For more information: New Hampshire Department of Parks and Recreation, Box 856, Concord, NH 03302. Phone (603) 271-3254. New Hampshire Fish and Game Department, 2 Hazen Drive, Concord, NH 03301. Phone (603) 271-3421.

PARADISE POINT NATURE CENTER

[Fig. 36(6)] A different world, one more in tune with the rhythms of nature, exists at the north end of Newfound Lake. At the Paradise Point Nature Center, the main attraction is a tall, evergreen forest, home to 300-year-old hemlocks and 100-year-old white pines. Three well-blazed trails of various lengths offer opportunities for year-round rambling, even when the visitor center is closed for the season. In some ways, it is more rewarding to come here when no one else is around and listen to the forest echo with the song of a robin or a hermit thrush.

The Audubon Society of New Hampshire owns and manages this 43-acre property that serves as both a wildlife sanctuary and a center for public education. During the summer, a visitor center houses staff to answer questions, offers an environmental day camp, and gives evening programs for children and adults. Inside the center, educational exhibits, a library, and a nature store provide further learning opportunities.

The trails, under 100-foot pines, hemlocks, and spruce, traverse a spongy forest duff, springy with countless years of fallen evergreen needles. It is the tall, dark hemlock trees that dominate here. Amazingly, each one of these giants has sprung from one of the tiny, 0.5-inch cones that lie underfoot by the thousands.

A sizeable pile of fresh wood chips and a newly excavated, rectangular hole in a tree signal the presence of the pileated woodpecker, while middens of dissected pine cones indicate another denizen of the evergreen forest, the red squirrel. Decorating the trees, rocks, and forest floor are a dozen varieties of mosses and lichens that thrive in the clean, moist air.

Woodsy though they are, the trails at Paradise Point are never far out of touch with the lake. It glistens through the trees at the foot of the sloping hillside, its waters lapping at granite boulders smoothed and rounded by its constant caress. One is reluctant to leave this cool, quiet refuge that offers sanctuary, not just to plants and animals, but to civilization-weary people as well.

Directions: From Bristol, go north on NH 3A for 9 miles toward East Hebron. Turn left onto North Shore Road and go 1 mile to Paradise Point sign and parking lot on the left.

Activities: Hiking, birdwatching, guided tours, and programs.

Facilities: Trails, map and guide, visitor center, handicap access.

Dates: Trails open year-round. Visitor center open in summer and on spring and fall weekends.

Fees: None.

Closest town: Hebron, 2.4 miles.

For more information: Audubon Society of New Hampshire, Box 528-B, Concord, NH 03302. Phone (603) 224-9909.

ELWELL TRAIL AT PARADISE POINT NATURE CENTER

[Fig. 36(4)] Midway along the Elwell Trail, the path is flanked on either side by two gigantic white pine trees, named in honor of Alcott and Helen Elwell, the couple who once owned this land and gave it over to conservation 40 years ago. The axe of progress somehow spared these venerable old trees who have silently witnessed a lot of wind, weather, and whimsical human nature, while standing their ground on this hillside overlooking the lake.

Trail: 0.75-mile loop.

Elevation: No elevation gain.

Degree of difficulty: Easy.

Surface and blaze: Forest floor. Red blazes.

LOOP TRAIL AT PARADISE POINT NATURE CENTER

[Fig. 36(5)] This is a short loop hike down the slope from the visitor center to the lakeshore through a cathedral-like forest of tall and stately pines. It offers a nice view of the undeveloped end of the lake.

Trail: 0.33-mile loop.

Elevation: 1,000 feet to 1,100 feet

Degree of difficulty: Easy.

Surface and blaze: Forest floor. Red blazes.

RIDGE-LAKESIDE TRAIL AT PARADISE POINT NATURE CENTER

[Fig. 36(3)] This is the longest of the trails at Paradise Point. It traverses a mixed pine and hardwood forest, moves through a small wetland, and scrambles around a few boulders. The trail also leads out to the point for a long view of the lake.

Trail: 1-mile loop.

Elevation: 1,000 feet to 1,100 feet.

Degree of difficulty: Moderate.

Surface and blaze: Forest floor, a few rocks. Yellow blazes.

WILD LEEK (*Allium tricoccum*) A leafless stem grows up to 18 inches tall and holds a cluster of white, starlike flowers that bloom in mid-summer.

HEBRON MARSH

[Fig. 36(2)] Birds and other wildlife require different things from a lake than people do. While people tend to like their shorelines neat, weedless, and bug-free, with concrete breakwaters and pure sand beaches, birds and animals are better served by a less tidy arrangement—one with marshy plants, nutritious insects and algae, and lots of slimy invertebrates.

Fortunately, Newfound Lake is both big enough and rich enough to provide both kinds of habitat. The northern end of the lake has something of a blurred margin. Instead of water ending abruptly at the shoreline, here the aquatic habitat sort of eases into terra firma by gradations. Open water becomes a secluded cove which changes over to marshy grasses, shrubs, and hardwood swamp before rising to open fields.

Thirty-six acres of these fields and wetlands make up New Hampshire Audubon's Hebron Marsh, a sister sanctuary to Paradise Point, 1 mile east. Here, in a quiet corner of Newfound Lake, is a refuge for waterfowl, a place for them to nest or simply to feed quietly in the shallows among the reeds. If you are careful in your approach, the ducks, geese, and herons go on about their business, hardly noticing you or your binoculars.

A small, red cottage and an Audubon sign front the road. During the summer, Audubon runs a small store and some educational programs here. Behind the cottage, at the bottom of the right-hand field, is a path leading down to the marsh and a wooden viewing stand, where closer looks at waterfowl can be had. On the way across the field, take a moment to notice the wildflowers, mosses, and reindeer lichen. Wild plants, as well as wild birds and animals, find sanctuary here.

Directions: From Bristol, take NH 3A north to North Shore Road. Turn left toward Hebron and go 2.2 miles to Audubon sign and red cottage on the left.

Activities: Bird watching and wildflower viewing.

Facilities: Trail, seasonal store and staff, viewing stand.

Dates: Wildlife viewing available year-round. Staff and store, seasonal.

Fees: None.

Closest town: Hebron, 0.2 mile.

For more information: Audubon Society of New Hampshire, Box 528-B, Concord, NH 03302. Phone (603) 224-9909.

SCULPTURED ROCKS NATURAL AREA

[Fig. 36] The power of tumbling water has etched its signature onto many of New Hampshire's rocks, but when the foaming current carries stones and gravel along with it, they add their abrasive power to the carving process too. The Sculptured Rocks Natural Area is a living example of water-carved "potholes,"—rounded, bowl-like excavations into the solid bedrock along the course of a river.

The Cockermouth River, impatiently rushing east to Newfound Lake, has carved this 30-foot-deep canyon right through the bedrock. Stand on the high bridge over the surging waters and your ears will confirm that the work is still in progress. Booming and grinding sounds issue continuously from beneath the bridge as small boulders and gravel caught up in the torrent are spun around inside a pothole currently under construction. Each day the basin is excavated a tiny bit bigger until, like its neighbors visible all along the canyon, one side is worn through and the erosive forces move on to another spot.

Thousands of years ago, when the great continental ice sheet was melting, the amount of water coming through this small defile must have been enormous, and the noise and tumult much louder than it is today. But, even now, this prodigious water sculpture goes inexorably on, and the evidence here is more than a little impressive.

Directions: From Bristol, take NH 3A north to North Shore Road and turn left. Go 2.4 miles west to Hebron and bear right onto Groton Road. Go 2.9 miles to Sculptured Rocks sign and parking area.

Activities: Pothole viewing, picnicking.

Facilities: Parking across the road, picnic tables in woods.

Dates: Open year-round.

Fees: None.

Closest town: Hebron, 2.9 miles.

For more information: Newfound Region Chamber of Commerce, Box 454, Bristol, NH 03222. Phone (603) 744-2150.

QUINCY BOG NATURAL AREA

[Fig. 36(1)] It would be difficult to find 40 acres with more varieties of life than this amazing natural area. Animals as small as invertebrates and as big as moose, plants ranging from microcsopic phytoplankton to a 150-year-old red oak, numerous ferns, clubmosses, wildflowers, sedges, and over 115 varieties of birds are here because of an glacial accident 14,000 years ago.

This bog originated from a *kettle*, a roundish depression in the ground created when a large chunk of ice broke off the retreating glacier and became buried in glacial debris. Eventually, the ice melted and the debris slumped, creating a depression that filled with water. Sphagnum moss grew around the edges and formed floating masses on the surface. As plants died over the years, they sank to the bottom and were compacted into the 30 feet of peat that lies on the bottom of this bog.

This remarkable wetland has elements of a pond, a bog, a swamp, a marsh, and an upland forest. Beavers move in and out of the pond, insectivorous plants grow in the acidic bog water, water-tolerant swamp maples and tamarack trees wet their "feet" at the edges of the swamp, and sedge grasses inhabit the marshy areas. All around the edges is an oak and pine forest, growing among granitic outcrops. Where plants lead, animals will follow, so the variety of animal life here is just as amazing.

Mount Sunapee & Mount Kearsarge

Mount Sunapee's peak is 2,743 feet, and Mount Kearsarge's peak is 2,937 feet.

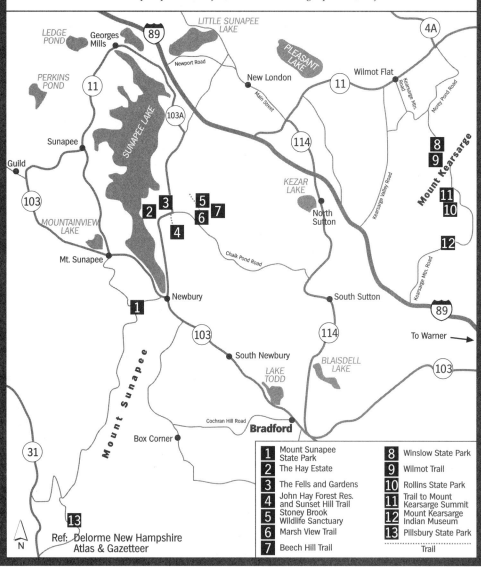

1	Mount Sunapee State Park	**8**	Winslow State Park
2	The Hay Estate	**9**	Wilmot Trail
3	The Fells and Gardens	**10**	Rollins State Park
4	John Hay Forest Res. and Sunset Hill Trail	**11**	Trail to Mount Kearsarge Summit
5	Stoney Brook Wildlife Sanctuary	**12**	Mount Kearsarge Indian Museum
6	Marsh View Trail	**13**	Pillsbury State Park
7	Beech Hill Trail		Trail

Ref: Delorme New Hampshire Atlas & Gazetteer

Credit for seeing that this area was set aside in 1978 as a conservation and education area goes to two biologists, George Kent and Hobart VanDeusen, who understood its value to both humans and wildlife. They are both gone now, but their legacy remains with the bog, the nature center, and the well-laid out and meticulously maintained ecological trail.

Directions: From I-93 in Plymouth, take Exit 26. Go 2.7 miles west on NH 25 to brown Quincy Bog sign. Turn right onto Quincy Road and go 2.9 miles to Quincy Bog Road. Turn right and go 0.3 mile, following signs to parking lot, information board, and visitor center.

Activities: Hiking, wildlife and plant viewing. In winter, cross-country skiing and snowshoeing. No camping, fires, or vehicles.

Facilities: Trail, trail guides, visitor center with library, displays, guided walks, and programs.

Dates: Self-guided trail is open all year with maps available at information board. Visitor center has special hours and scheduled tours in summer months. Call for times.

Fees: None.

Closest town: Quincy.

For more information: Rumney Ecological Systems, Box 90, Rumney, NH 03266. Phone (603) 786-9812.

Sunapee-Kearsarge Region

The spine of mountains that separates the watersheds of the Connecticut and Merrimack rivers rears up in this region as the highly visible, 2,743-foot Mount Sunapee. The south end of this long mountain rises from a ridge in Pillsbury State Park and the northern end terminates abruptly on the south shore of Sunapee Lake. The contrasts between mountains and lakes, between forests and rocky summits, make for grand scenery and wonderful recreation.

Farther east, Mount Kearsarge rises to 2,937 feet as another of New Hampshire's monadnocks. Protected by two state parks without camping facilities, Kearsarge is a quiet mountain for hikers and picnickers. On its southern slopes, the Mount Kearsarge Indian Museum is a place to see high-quality Native American artifacts from all over the country and to begin to appreciate the way Indians view their relationship with the earth.

Mount Sunapee is a bit busier, home to a state-run ski area in the winter and a chairlift, hiking trails, and various events in the other seasons. Stretching north from the base of the mountain is a beautiful, long lake of the same name. Mount Sunapee State Park manages a public beach on its southwestern shore. The quieter east side of Sunapee Lake is home to several privately owned nature reserves, where wildlife gets its share of the space and the public is welcome to share the trails and vistas. Good roads run all the way around the lake, their hilly routes offering intermittent views of both mountains and water.

The Sunapee-Kearsarge region is rich with both recreational and cultural activity. Opera houses in Claremont and Newport and a playhouse in New London provide summer entertainment. The area is also an antiquer's heaven with shops in almost every town and along many roadways.

🏵 MOUNT SUNAPEE

[Fig. 38] Mount Sunapee's massive prominence sits at the southern end of Sunapee Lake, presenting as beautiful an aspect when seen from the lake as the lake does when viewed from atop the mountain. Its highest peak at 2,743 feet is only one of three on this substantial mountain that runs 6 miles from north to south in the town of Newbury. Its structure is primarily Kinsman Quartz Monzonite, a granitic rock that, 385 million years ago, intruded into New Hampshire's Littleton Formation from below. Most of the Littleton metamorphics have eroded away, but a few long and narrow belts of it run along the flanks of the mountain.

Mount Sunapee is the northern terminus of one of New Hampshire's long trails, the 52-mile Monadnock-Sunapee Greenway (*see* page 299). This trail links the two mountains for which it is named and travels through some of the least-populated territory in southern New Hampshire. Perched at 2,400 feet on Sunapee's southeastern shoulder is Lake Solitude, unique for its remote location and high elevation. To the west of the lake, White Ledge rises 300 feet and through it runs a dike, or intrusive band, of granite that is over 1 mile long. A perfect hiking destination, it can be reached via the Solitude Trail from the summit and affords excellent views off to the east.

Recently, a pleasant surprise emerged from the eastern slopes of this, one of the busiest, most developed mountains in the state. Biologists have discovered several sizeable patches of old growth forest containing birches, maples and red spruce that have held their ground here unmolested for nearly 300 years.

MOUNT SUNAPEE STATE PARK AND STATE BEACH

[Fig. 38(1)] This 2,900-acre park offers something to do in every season. In the winter, the park runs a fully equipped ski area with snowmaking, ski patrol, dozens of trails, and seven lifts. Rentals, lessons, and child care are offered along with first aid, restaurants, and a lounge.

One chair lift operates in nonsnow seasons, too, taking hikers, sightseers, and mountain bikers to the top of the mountain. From June through August, you can even enjoy a barbecue on the summit, and the base lodges are open as well as a smaller one on the top of the mountain. Headquartered at Mount Sunapee's base is the New England Handicapped Sports Association which offers skiing and other recreational help for the handicapped.

For the hiker, Mount Sunapee is something of a novelty: It is one mountain where you can start hiking at the top. Take the chairlift up and pick up one of several blazed trails that take off there on its way to Lake Solitude or to join the Monadnock-Sunapee Greenway which runs through the park. The chairlift runs every day from June through August, and it runs on weekends in May, September, and October. You can ride both ways, or hike up and ride down, or ride up and bike down—whatever suits your needs. The Summit Trail takes off from the base near the Lower Ridge Ski Trail and runs 2 miles to the summit.

If you prefer to avoid the busy scene at the state park parking lot and come up the east side of the mountain, the Andrew Brook Trail runs 1.8 miles from NH 103 to Lake Solitude. The trailhead is 0.75 mile south of the junction with NH 103A. The Newbury Trail also comes 2 miles up the mountain from NH 103, with a trailhead in Newbury, 0.25 mile west of the junction with NH 103A. All trails are color blazed, moderate in difficulty, and gain about 1,500 feet in elevation. Trail maps are available at the Mount Sunapee base lodge or contact Mount Sunapee State Park.

A number of special events take place on Mount Sunapee throughout the year. The League of New Hampshire Craftsmen holds its annual Craft Fair, usually in August, and the Audubon Society of New Hampshire sponsors a Naturefest in September. There are foot and bicycle races, a Gem and Mineral Show, and other events that all make the mountain a popular destination. On weekends from June through September, barbecue is served at the summit from 1 p.m. to 5 p.m. A chairlift ride to the top and a barbecue supper is a great way to wind up a busy day outdoors.

At the bottom of the mountain and across the road, is the entrance to the other part of the state park, the State Beach at Sunapee Lake. This beautiful lake is a prime spot for swimming, boating, fishing, and sailboarding all summer long. The view across the lake is of Sunset Hill and the John Hay Estate and Wildlife Management Area.

Directions: From Newbury, take NH 103 west for 2.6 miles from its junction with NH 103A. At state park signs turn right for the state beach or left for the mountain.

Activities: At the mountain: skiing, snowshoeing in winter; in summer, hiking, chairlift, lift-served mountain biking, barbecue, and events. At the lake: swimming, boating, fishing, picnicking.

Facilities: Fully equipped ski area, hiking trails, chairlift, restaurants. Beach, picnic area, bathhouse,

CHIMNEY SWIFT (Chaetura pelagica)

Hawk Migration

Hawks are fully capable of making their long migrations under their own steam but, like any other well-adapted species, they take wise advantage of ways to conserve energy. Mountains and valleys offer two such ways. When normal air currents meet a mountain or ridge, they rise, providing lift under a bird's outstretched wings. Additionally, on sunny days, a valley's dark, flat surfaces—open fields or pavement—absorb heat from the sun and generate a rising pocket of air known as a thermal which provides yet another lift. There is little need for the birds to flap their wings. They soar round and round, up into the rising air mass, then simply sail off the top and down the wind until they find another.

canoe rentals. Boat tour of lake on the cruise boat *Mount Sunapee.*

Dates: State park is open all year. Activities and facilities vary by season. Lifts open for skiing in season and again after May for rides.

Fees: There is a charge for skiing, chairlifts, beach, and use of the boat ramp.

Closest town: Newbury, 3 miles.

For more information: Mount Sunapee State Park, Box 2021, Mount Sunapee, NH 03255. Phone (603) 763-2356. New England Handicapped Sports Association, Box 2135, Mount Sunapee, NH 03772. Phone (800)-628-4484.

THE HAY ESTATE

[Fig. 38(2)] While more and more of the land along Sunapee Lake's shoreline is occupied by private homes, there is one grand section of nearly 1,000 acres that will forever remain open to the preservation of wildlife and the enjoyment and edification of the public. John Hay was once a secretary to Abraham Lincoln and later, a writer and a diplomat in Europe. In 1888, he began buying abandoned farmland on the shores of Sunapee Lake, and soon he had created a working farm and a summer home he named The Fells, a term used in his ancestral Scottish Highlands. In the 1920s, his son Clarence greatly expanded the house and formalized the gardens, allowing the bulk of the acreage to return to forests. In 1960, the Hay family put 675 acres of the property into the hands of the Society for the Protection of New Hampshire Forests (SPNHF) and later donated another 300 acres, with 1 mile of Sunapee Lake shoreline, to the U.S. Fish and Wildlife Service.

The New Hampshire Division of Parks and Recreation also helps to manage the property so that, today, the Hay Estate, which includes The Fells, the John Hay National Wildlife Refuge, the Land Studies Center, and the John Hay Forest Reservation, has almost as many managers as the property has names.

The managers are nonetheless clear and unanimous in their mission. The Hay family wishes the land to be used for education and conservation, and to those ends, all parties work together. Contemporary naturalist and writer John Hay, the grandson of the original assembler of this tract, puts the goal this way: "A society disengaged from the land on which it is ultimately dependent, cannot be assured of a healthy future... Our fundamental association with the land needs to be rediscovered."

BIRDFOOT VIOLET
(Viola pedata)
This violet is identified by its bird's-foot shaped leaves.

The Hay Estate provides the visitor a quiet respite from the busier life on the other side of the lake. Park in the lot near "The Fells" sign and choose either to walk down the road toward the lake to see The Fells estate house and the gardens, or to cross the road and take the hiking trail up through the John Hay Forest Reservation on Sunset Hill.

Directions: In Newbury, go 2.2 miles north on NH 103A from its junction with NH 103. At sign reading The Fells, turn left into parking area. A gate house there houses Hay Estate offices. To visit the Wildlife Refuge, The Fells, and the gardens, walk west down the dirt road from the parking lot toward the lake. To hike to the top of Sunset Hill, cross 103A and follow signs to the top of the hill.

Activities: Hiking, wildlife viewing, visiting the historic house and gardens,

Facilities: Hiking trail up Sunset Hill. Paths, estate house, and gardens toward the lake.

Dates: Trails open all year. House and gardens open weekends and holidays from May-Oct.

Fees: There is a charge to visit the house. None for trails.

Closest town: Newbury, 2.2 miles.

For more information: Society for the Protection of New Hampshire Forests, 54 Portsmouth Street, Concord, NH 03301. Phone (603) 224-9945. New Hampshire Division of Parks and Recreation, Box 856, Concord, NH 03302. Phone (603) 271-3254.

THE FELLS AND GARDENS

[Fig. 38(3)] The Fells is not a home for touring and marveling at the past lives of the well-to-do. Now housing the Land Studies Center, it is, instead, very much a working space in the Hay family's vision of conservation education. It is home to a natural history library and a place for workshops and classes to help people understand the concept of living and working with nature and the land. Naturalists, resource managers, and teachers come here for seminars and conferences.

Surrounding the stately old house are ornate fountains and colorful, terraced flower gardens, now maintained by volunteers. Beyond the green lawns are forest-framed views of Sunapee Lake along whose shores lies a 300-acre wildlife refuge. It's a fine place to wander in the afternoon when the sun slants over the trees and lights up the gardens.

THE JOHN HAY FOREST RESERVATION AND SUNSET HILL TRAIL

[Fig. 38(4)] The John Hay Forest Reservation, directly across NH 103A from the parking area, is accessed by the Sunset Hill Trail. Maps and a trail guide are in a box at the trailhead. This trail leads first through a bright hardwood forest but the trees quickly turn to hemlock and red spruce. Notice the way the forest darkens and the understory plants get scarce when evergreens become dominant.

At the summit, where the Hay family loved to picnic in the days when they lived at The Fells, there is open ledge and a view out to the west of Mount Sunapee and Sunapee Lake. The top of this hill is clear of forest, not because of timbering or fire, but because of sheep. Decades ago, these domestic animals nibbled down the vegetation until there was nothing to hold the soil and it eroded or blew away. Now this hill is open to the rosy hues of sunset.

Trail: 3-mile hike (round-trip) to the top of Sunset Hill.

Elevation: 1,100 feet to 1,800 feet.

Degree of difficulty: Easy.

Surface and blaze: Woods road with periodic signs, yellow blazes.

STONEY BROOK WILDLIFE SANCTUARY

[Fig. 38(5)] The press of development seems always to head for woods and water. People want to live there because it is pleasant and quiet, and there is often lots of wildlife around. But, in the process trying to escape each other, we tend to break up wildlife habitat into tiny, less effective pieces and to diminish the very thing that attracted us in the first place.

It has become increasingly evident to wildlife biologists that, while preserving small pieces of habitat is good, preserving large pieces is better. Saving small pieces adjacent to one another is the next best thing. A pileated woodpecker or a moose cares little for property lines, as long as there is enough green space without houses and people in it.

Behind the 1,000-acre Hay Reservation on the eastern shore of Sunapee Lake, sits Chalk Pond, a small but blessedly undeveloped body of water. On the eastern side of this pond, a few far-sighted citizens and the Audubon Society of New Hampshire have set aside acreage near the Hay Reservation. By setting aside these 362 acres, they have actually increased the open space to nearly 1,300 acres and provided travel corridors for birds and animals. The Stoney Brook Wildlife Sanctuary has the added advantage to wildlife of hosting at least two kinds of habitat.

Stoney Brook Sanctuary lies in two parts along Chalk Pond Road, with undeveloped land between them. The western piece is lower and wetter, covered with a young forest of red maple, oak, and fir-balsam. Here, moisture-loving species like sphagnum moss and club mosses lend a spongy feel to the ground. Deer, partridge, and beaver love this kind of habitat and an easy, half-hour walk through this sanctuary can be filled with surprises. Perhaps a deer has left its tracks in the soft mud, or a partridge might explode from the shrubby understory as you walk by. At the far end of the loop trail, a brown, wooden viewing stand provides a look out over an old pond, well on its way to becoming a beaver meadow, a great place to spot migrant and resident birds.

The eastern parcel, located less than 1 mile east on the same road, is a whole different kind of habitat, a good illustration of what a tiny bit of elevation can do. The trees here, with more beech and oak in the mix, stand taller, on steeper, drier slopes, and the trail through this segment leads visitors on about an hour-and-a-half hike over fairly hilly terrain. As you pass through a bright stand of smooth-barked beech trees, be sure to look closely for healed-over bear-claw marks. Bear often climb beech trees to get at the nutritious nuts that are the fruit of this tree.

Wetlands

"Wetland" is the broad term that includes lakes, streams, swamps, marshes, and bogs. These special areas serve a number of valuable purposes—as flood storage areas, as water filters, and as wildlife habitat. The United States has lost over half of the wetlands it once possessed, but thanks to a number of factors—a low population, a naturally wet climate, and the industrious beaver—New Hampshire has retained almost 90 percent of its original amount. There is always something to see in a wetland—a beaver lodge, a great blue heron, a moose, a flock of ducks, or perhaps just an open expanse to rest the eye from continuous forests.

Directions: From Newbury, go 3 miles north on NH 103A and turn right onto Chalk Pond Road (at Sunapee Hills sign). Go 1.3 miles to the western segment of the sanctuary and another 0.9 mile to the eastern parcel. Look for the Audubon sign and parking at each stop. The trailheads are at the small parking areas.

Activities: Hiking, wildlife viewing.

Facilities: Trails, parking, map, and trail guides.

Dates: Open year-round.

Fees: None.

Closest town: Newbury, 5 miles.

For more information: Audubon Society of New Hampshire, Box 528-B, Concord, NH 03302. Phone (603) 224-9909.

MARSH VIEW TRAIL AT STONEY BROOK WILDLIFE SANCTUARY

[Fig. 38(6)] **Trail:** 0.5-mile loop.

Elevation: 1,150 feet

Degree of difficulty: Easy.

Surface and blaze: Forest floor and marshy edge. Can be wet at times. Red blazes.

BEECH HILL TRAIL AT STONEY BROOK WILDLIFE SANCTUARY

[Fig. 38(7)] **Trail:** 1.5-mile loop.

Elevation: 1,200 feet to 1,300 feet.

Degree of difficulty: Moderate.

Surface and blaze: Forest floor, some rockiness. Yellow blazes.

MOUNT KEARSARGE

[Fig. 38] Visible for miles, Mount Kearsarge's double hump stands high and alone, surveying the surrounding smaller mountains. The name is derived from *Carasarga,* a Native American word meaning "notch-pointed mountain of pines." It's another one of New Hampshire's monadnocks—mountains of tough, erosion-resistant, metamorphic rocks that have held up longer than the surrounding terrain. In this case, the rock is Littleton Schist.

Winslow State Park lies on the north side of this 2,937-foot mountain, and Rollins State Park occupies the southern slopes. The summit offers 360-degree views—on a clear day, all the way to the Boston skyline, the White Mountains, and the Atlantic Ocean. It is easily accessible by roads that travel nearly to the top on either side.

The summit of Kearsarge is an excellent place to watch hawks, climb the fire tower, or look for glacial striations, those great northwest-southeast grooves cut into the bald peak by even harder rocks that were embedded in the bottom of the most recent glacier, the Laurentide ice sheet. Thousands of years ago, this glacier buried all of New Hampshire under ice 1 mile thick. Many erratic boulders appear along the roads and trails, further evidence of the passage of massive ice sheets over the region. Geologists believe that Mount Kearsarge is one of the best summits in the state to study the erosional effect of glaciers. A hike to the summit of Kearsarge from either side runs through fragrant spruce and fir and offers stunning overlooks along the way.

When climbing this mountain, either on foot or in a car, it is fun to watch the tree species change from hardwoods, like maple and birch, to the boreal species of spruce and balsam-fir. Whenever New England mountains get higher than 2,500 feet, the next 1,000-foot gain is akin to traveling several hundred miles north. Rainfall increases and temperature decreases as you enter the subalpine, spruce-fir zone where an altogether different community of plants dominates.

WINSLOW STATE PARK

[Fig. 38(8)] This park, on the northwestern shoulder of the mountain, sports a picnic area with a million-dollar view. The road up from Wilmot ends at a parking lot located on a small plateau that seems to leap right off into the scenery. A lovely picnic area and restrooms are situated here and the Winslow Trail to the summit takes off just to the left of a maintenance garage. In the winter, the last 0.5 mile of this road is unplowed, but it's almost worth a hike up in the snow for the close-in views of Mount Sunapee to the southwest, Ragged Mountain to the north, and the snow-streaked ski areas of Vermont.

Directions: From NH 11 in Wilmot, turn south on Kearsarge Valley Road and follow Winslow State Park signs 3.6 miles to the parking and picnic area.

Activities: Hiking, picnicking.

Facilities: Restrooms, picnic tables, trails.

Dates: Trails open all year. Last 0.5 mile of road not plowed in winter.

Fees: There is an admission charge, in season.

Closest town: Wilmot, 3.6 miles.

Trail: The Wilmot Trail leads 1 mile through forest to open summit with 360-degree view.

Elevation: 1,750 to 2,937 feet.

Degree of difficulty: Moderate.

Surface and blaze: Forest floor and boulders. Red and orange blazes.

For more information: Winslow State Park, Box 295, Newbury, NH 03255. Phone (603) 526-6168.

WHITE BIRCH
(Betula papyrifera)
This birch has chalky white bark that peels in strips, adding decorative texture to the winter landscape. It grows by water and on moist hillsides.

ROLLINS STATE PARK

[Fig. 38(10)] This state park blankets the southern slopes of Mount Kearsarge, in the town of Warner. It includes a 3.5-mile scenic auto road with parking lots at either end. At the upper end, a picnic area with views off to the south and east is a fine destination in itself. But with just a little more effort and a short, 0.6-mile hike to the summit, the panorama opens up to 360 degrees. Acres of rocky nooks offer protection from the wind and a place to contemplate the world below. Look around for glacial striations carved into the bald summit by the last glacier. The auto road has been here since 1866 and was rebuilt by the Civilian Conservation Corps in 1935.

Directions: From I-89, take Exit 8 in Warner onto NH 103W. Turn north on Kearsarge Mountain Road and follow this road to the park's lower parking area.

Activities: Hiking, picnicking.

Facilities: Auto road, trail, picnic tables, pit toilets.

Dates: Road closed in winter. Hiking up road permitted anytime.

Fees: Seasonal.

Closest town: Warner, 4 miles.

Trail: A 0.6-mile trail leads to the summit. Short, but steep in places.

Degree of difficulty: Moderate.

Surface and blaze: Rocky. Silver blazes present where necessary.

For more information: Rollins State Park, Box 219, Warner, NH 03278. Phone (603) 456-3808.

MOUNT KEARSARGE INDIAN MUSEUM

[Fig. 38(12)] The Mount Kearsarge Indian Museum sits on the southern flank of

Mount Kearsarge and is a secret that has been too well kept. Since 1991, this museum, residing in a big red barn, has been a showcase for the vast collection of Native American artifacts gathered over a lifetime by Charles Thompson. Large, airy rooms display hand-crafted tools, clothing, and ceremonial objects of many Native American tribes. Particularly well represented are the Plains and Southwest tribes and Eastern Woodland Indians, such as New Hampshire's own Penacooks.

Glass cases of bead work, jewelry, and finely woven baskets stand beside dug-out canoes, bone fishhooks, stone war clubs, and disassembled peace pipes. The visitor learns that displaying a peace pipe with the mouthpiece attached would violate ceremonial custom. And this is only one piece of information you come away with, because this is not a museum where you simply file through and look at things. Each visitor is, instead, led through on tours starting every hour, by a guide who knows the stories and the customs that accompany the artifacts.

Like the Native Americans, who seem not to draw lines between art and utility, the beauty of these exhibits carries seamlessly over from decorative items, to tools, to objects of religious significance.

In the children's room, kids can touch a pair of moose antlers, some porcupine needles, and a beaver pelt, and outdoors, there are re-creations of various kinds of Indian homes. Visitors are also welcome to take a walk through Medicine Woods, a 2-acre, self-guided tour of wild plants that Indians used for medicine, dyes, and food.

The Kearsarge Indian Museum is a nonprofit Educational and Cultural Center that reaches out to the community with programs for children and adults. The center's mission is to raise awareness of Native American traditions, philosophy, and art and to foster an understanding of the conservation and land stewardship that Indians have practiced for thousands of years.

Directions: From I-89, take Exit 8 to Warner. Go 1.4 miles along Main Street to Kearsarge Mountain Road. Turn right and go 1.2 miles to museum sign and parking.

Activities: Guided museum tour, walk through Medicine Woods, souvenir shopping.

Facilities: Museum, Medicine Woods, restrooms, handicap access, Dreamcatcher Store.

Dates: May-October.

Fees: There is a charge for the museum tour.

Closest town: Warner, 1.2 miles.

For more information: Mount Kearsarge Indian Museum, Box 142, Warner, NH 03278. Phone (603) 456-2600.

PILLSBURY STATE PARK

[Fig. 38(13)] This 5,000-acre park, just north of the picturesque village of Washington, is one of the state's least developed parks and, consequently, one of its wildest. The silence can be nearly complete—unless you consider the eerie cry of a loon noise. This relatively low-lying area boasts many wetlands and nine ponds.

Forty primitive camping sites are scattered around May Pond, including remote sites where you either walk or canoe in. The rest of the wetlands are left for quiet paddling, fishing, and use by wildlife.

In general, wherever you find water, you find wildlife, so Pillsbury is home to black bear, moose, fisher, beaver, and otter. A rich variety of bird life is attracted to all these wetlands—herons, osprey, loons, and songbirds aplenty. Necessities to bring here include binoculars, a fishing pole, a canoe, and ample time to unwind.

The 52-mile Monadnock-Sunapee Greenway Trail (*see* page 299) runs through Pillsbury State Park on its way to its terminus at Mount Sunapee, a few miles north of here. Several of Pillsbury's trails connect to this long trail while others provide access to the many hills that ring the park's ponds. To the south, between Pillsbury State Park and Pitcher Mountain, the Monadnock-Sunapee Greenway runs through one of its most remote and beautiful sections.

The park manager's residence and office is just inside the gate and the campsites are at May Pond, a little beyond that. Half the campsites are available by reservation and half on a first-come, first-serve basis. About 1 mile farther on the park road, several trails take off, leading to the more remote sections of the park or connecting with the Monadnock-Sunapee Greenway. A trail map is available at the manager's office.

Directions: From NH 9 in Hillsborough, turn north on NH 31. Go 13.9 miles, through the village of Washington, on to the state park entrance on the right.

Activities: Hiking, camping, fishing, canoeing, kayaking, mountain biking, wildlife watching, skiing, and snowshoeing.

Facilities: Trails, long and short, 40 primitive campsites, pit toilets, small boat access, manager in residence.

Dates: Camping May-Sept. Hiking year-round.

Fees: Fee to camp.

Closest town: Washington, 3.5 miles.

For more information: Pillsbury State Park, Box 1008, Washington, NH 03280. Phone (603) 863-2860.

Monadnock Region

Monadnock is an old Abenaki Indian word meaning "rock mountain rising alone above the plains." This region takes its name from just such a peak. Mount Monadnock, sometimes called Grand Monadnock, sits so prominently above the "plain" that it is visible from 50 miles away. It dominates everything else in the region.

Although at 3,165 feet it is far from the highest mountain in the state, Grand Monadnock is composed of hard, metamorphic rocks, so time and weather have eroded away less of its surface than that of the surrounding hills. As you drive along

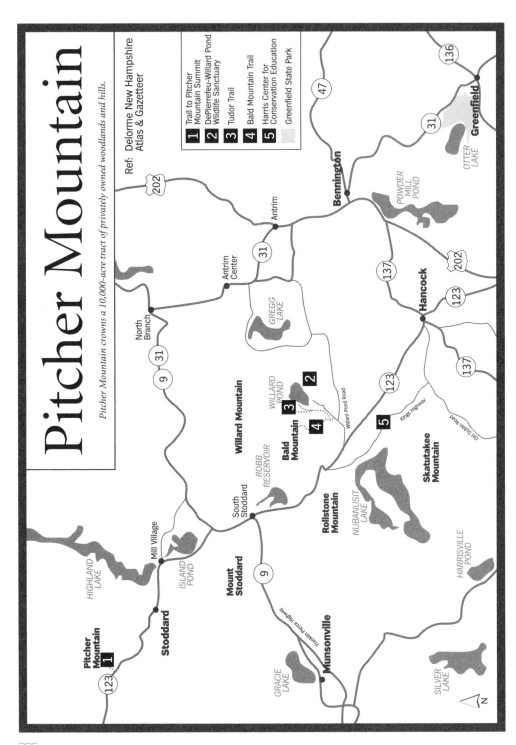

Pitcher Mountain

Pitcher Mountain crowns a 10,000-acre tract of privately owned woodlands and hills.

Ref: Delorme New Hampshire Atlas & Gazetteer

1 Trail to Pitcher Mountain Summit
2 DePierrefeu-Willard Pond Wildlife Sanctuary
3 Tudor Trail
4 Bald Mountain Trail
5 Harris Center for Conservation Education
Greenfield State Park

the winding curves and back roads of southwestern New Hampshire, glimpses of this rocky peak seem to jump out surprisingly from openings in the trees.

The lightly populated area around the mountain is sometimes called the quiet corner of New Hampshire—quiet only in the sense that it often gets bypassed by the throngs heading for the larger White Mountains up north. In terms of scenic vistas and outdoor recreational opportunities, the region is far from lifeless. There may be fewer people here, but there are more moose and bear and bobcats, and more opportunity to explore the out-of-doors in relative peace.

The unique appeal of this area is that, after spending a day outdoors—hiking, fishing, canoeing, or skiing—in the evening, the visitor can take in a concert, a summer theater production, or even a performance of marionettes. Lodging and dining can be as simple and private as a quiet campfire at a state park or as elegant and comfortable as a cozy bed and breakfast.

PITCHER MOUNTAIN

[Fig. 39] Pitcher Mountain crowns a 10,000-acre tract of woodland and hills that is privately owned, but thankfully, it is under conservation easement never to be developed. Its 2,153-foot summit is easily accessible, a pleasant 20-minute hike up a piece of the Monadnock-Sunapee Greenway Trail right off of NH 123. A small, rocky summit with a 360-degree view lets you look south to Mount Monadnock, north to Mount Sunapee, and, on a clear day, west to the mountains of Vermont. Bird life is rampant among the low trees on the way up, in the shrubbery at the top, and in the fields that cover the slopes below.

Directions: From NH 9 in Stoddard, go 4.8 miles north on NH 123. Parking and kiosk are near the road.

TRAIL TO PITCHER MOUNTAIN SUMMIT

[Fig. 39(1)] **Trail:** A 30-minute hike climbs 350 feet over 0.4 mile on a short stretch of the longer Monadnock-Sunapee Greenway.

Elevation: 1,803 feet to 2,153 feet.

Degree of difficulty: Easy.

Surface and blazes: Forest floor and grassy fields. Bare rock at summit. Trail is clearly tracked.

DEPIERREFEU-WILLARD POND WILDLIFE SANCTUARY

[Fig. 39(2)] Spanning over 1,000 acres, Willard Pond is New Hampshire Audubon's (ASNH) largest wildlife sanctuary. It offers an array of habitats, from the unspoiled 100-acre natural pond, to 2,037-foot-high Bald Mountain, to the forest and rocks in between. Willard is a pond with a mountain, literally, in its back yard. There can be no doubt as to the location of this rocky knob; it looms immediately to your left from the moment you enter the Sanctuary.

Along most of the trails lie numerous, large glacial erratics—boulders dropped when the most recent glacier melted. Left behind, they have become footholds for a number of interesting lichens. The papery-looking rock tripe, genus *Umbilicara*, curls like paint peeling off an old barn. Though they look dead, these lichens are very much alive, an efficient composite organism composed of a fungus and an alga that have evolved a workable lifestyle together. The fungus provides the supporting structure while the alga manufactures food through photosynthesis.

Audubon maintains several hiking trails here with terrain varying from wetlands, to rocks on the pond shoreline, to Bald Mountain. Maps are available on site. For quiet canoes or other nonpetrol boats, the New Hampshire Fish and Game Department (NHF&G) has furnished a boat launch into Willard Pond.

Directions: From Hancock, drive 3.7 miles west on NH 123. Turn right onto Willard Pond Road. Go 1.6 miles on this dirt road, bearing left at the fork, to a parking lot. Maps are available at the ASNH kiosk across from the caretaker's cabin. The New Hampshire Fish and Game Department kiosk and boat ramp are ahead at pond edge.

Activities: Hiking, canoeing, boating, fly-fishing.

Facilities: Hiking trails, 100-acre pond.

Dates: Open year-round. In winter, pond is frozen and in spring, road is rough.

Fees: None.

Closest town: Hancock 5 miles east.

For more information: Audubon Society of New Hampshire, Box 528-B, Concord, NH 03302. Phone (603) 224-9909.

TUDOR TRAIL

[Fig. 39(3)] This 20-minute hike loops close to the pond and returns through the woods. The going is mostly flat with some scrambling around boulders. There are great views over quiet, undeveloped Willard Pond and plenty of places to stop for bird-watching or a brown bag lunch. At the far end of the loop, before the trail turns back, look for boulders covered with rock tripe.

Trail: 0.25-mile loop.

Elevation: No elevation change.

Degree of difficulty: Easy.

Surface and blaze: Can be wet in spring, a few boulders to work around. Blazes are yellow.

BALD MOUNTAIN TRAIL

[Fig. 39(4)] The climb up this steep little mountain is a bit more challenging than the Tudor Trail, but the hiker is rewarded at the top with good views of the Monadnock region. Gaining Bald Mountain's summit of 2,037 feet requires a short but steep climb and takes about two hours. The red blazes of this trail veer right at the far end of the Tudor Trail Loop and continue for a way along the pond's edge before turning sharply left and uphill.

Trail: 3.0-mile (round-trip) hike to Bald Mountain's summit.

Elevation: 1,200 feet to 2,037 feet.

Degree of difficulty: Moderate along pond; strenuous up the mountain.
Surface and blaze: Pond edge, boulders, forest floor. Blazes are red.

HARRIS CENTER FOR CONSERVATION EDUCATION

[Fig. 39(5)] The Harris Center in Hancock is surrounded by more than 8,000 acres of conservation land, half of which the center owns, manages, or monitors. These green acres serve as an outdoor laboratory for educating schoolchildren, their parents, graduate students, and visitors about almost anything to do with the out-of-doors.

The picture window of the center's office, once an elegant summer home, looks out over the forest toward Pack Monadnock and its neighbor, North Pack. Eleanor Briggs, who donated this family estate and founded the Harris Center in 1970, named it for her cat, Harris, formerly a New York City stray who loved to follow her on walks in the woods.

A key Harris Center mission has been to become the nucleus of something much bigger, a large "supersanctuary" in the Monadnock Region, an area big enough to serve the needs of wide-ranging species like moose and bear and bobcat, and a place for people to enjoy and learn more about natural history. Thanks to New Hampshire Audubon, the Society for Protection of New Hampshire Forests, and New Hampshire Fish and Game, and several other public and private conservation groups, this supersanctuary has already grown to include over 8,500 acres.

The emphasis at the Harris Center is to get people outdoors to see, feel, and smell the things that live there. It is through this hands-on approach that we really begin to connect with things natural. Thousands of schoolchildren have "connected" here in ways they'll remember all of their lives.

As for grownups, hardly a weekend goes by that the center isn't bustling with free programs or workshops or hikes. You can learn about wood frogs, peepers, and spotted salamanders while standing at the edge of a vernal pool, or take a canoe trip down the Ashuelot River to see what lives along the banks. In the winter, you can snowshoe through a workshop on tracking the animals who live in these parts, or in June, you can meet Clyde the Glide, a flying squirrel and his researcher at one of the center's evening programs. The Harris Center publishes a quarterly calendar of activities. Write or call for a copy.

Several hiking trails traverse the center's land, and they range from easy to moderate. One leads you through a classic boulder train of scattered glacial erratics. Others take you to one of several ponds, or to the top of Thumb Mountain or 2,002-foot Skatutakee Mountain. The trails are open to the public and a map and interpretive booklet are available at the office.

Directions: From Hancock, go 2 miles west on NH 123. Turn left on Hunt's Pond Road and follow this to the end. Turn left on King's Highway Road and go 0.5 mile to Harris Center driveway.

Activities: Hiking, field trips, programs, and workshops. Nature Day Camp in summer.

Facilities: Trails, parking.

Dates: Trails open year-round, dawn to dusk. Weekend programs year-round except August.

Fees: None for programs. There is a charge for summer camp.

Closest town: Hancock, 3 miles.

For more information: Harris Center, 341 King's Highway, Hancock, NH 03449. Phone. (603) 525-3394.

GREENFIELD STATE PARK AND CANOEING POWDER MILL POND AND THE CONTOOCOOK RIVER

[Fig. 39] This 400-acre park is located on the shores of 61-acre Otter Lake in Greenfield and offers bass fishing and some other nearby opportunities for canoeing and kayaking. Nestled in the pine-scented woods are some 250 tent sites, restrooms, and showers. The park has a boat launch and separate beaches for camping and day use. If boating is all you wish, there is free access to Otter Lake without entering the park.

Two and a half miles west of Greenfield State Park, the north-flowing Contoocook River spreads out behind a small dam at Bennington and backs up into the placid, 220-acre Powder Mill Pond. There, it surrounds a few small islands at the base of a particularly pretty mountain, and bass and pickerel swim beneath its quiet surface. In the early morning, the ripples from your paddle are the only things that break up the raggedy profile of Crotched Mountain, reflected in the waters of the northern end of the pond.

Directions to Greenfield State Park: From junction of NH 101 and US 202 in Peterborough, go 6.5 miles north on NH 202 to signs for Greenfield State Park. Turn east on Forest Road. Go 3.8 miles to park entrance.

For canoeing access to Otter Lake: Follow directions to Greenfield State Park, but go only 3.2 miles on Forest Road and turn left into the free boating access to Otter Lake. New Hampshire fishing license required to fish.

For canoeing access to Powder Mill Pond and Contoocook River: Follow directions to Greenfield State Park, but go only 1.3 miles on Forest Road and turn right immediately after crossing the covered bridge for New Hampshire Fish and Game Boating and Fishing access. No camping, swimming, or fires are permitted at these boating access points, and a New Hampshire fishing license is required to fish.

Activities: At Greenfield State Park, camping, hiking, fishing, swimming, boating, and picnicking. Snowmobiling and cross-country skiing in winter.

Facilities: At the park: campsites, picnic tables, trails for hiking or cross-country skiing, boat rentals, and park store. Showers and restrooms. Separate camping and day-use areas.

Dates: Trails open year-round. Camping and beach facilities, Memorial Day-Labor Day.

Fees: There is a charge for state park use, in season. None for New Hampshire Fish and Game boat launch or Otter Lake access.

Closest town: Greenfield, 2 miles.

For more information: Greenfield State Park, Box 203, Greenfield, NH 03047. Phone (603) 547-3497. For fishing license information, New Hampshire Fish and Game Department, 2 Hazen Drive, Concord, NH 03301. Phone (603) 271-3422.

WARWICK PRESERVE

[Fig. 41(2)] At Warwick Preserve in the spring, Partridge Brook comes foaming down the southwestern side of Butterfield Hill, cuts under the road, and leaps in a waterfall down the other side. It drains this 36-acre gem of a preserve that is owned by The Nature Conservancy and is open to the public.

The entrance path runs through a virtual carpet of periwinkle (*Vinca minor*). This family of plants with pinkish or purplish flowers is more than just pretty. It has long been a source of anticancer therapy, with the drugs vincristine and vinblastine being vinca alkaloids.

A well-marked, but steep trail ascends the hill through a forest of beech, hickory, and hemlock. The rock here is relatively rich in calcium and provides a richer diversity of plants and some unusual wildflowers such as showy orchis (*Orchis spectabilis*), squawroot (*Conopholis americana*), and Dutchman's breeches (*Dicentra cucullaria*). Look also for the delicate maidenhair fern (*Adiantum pedatum L.*), which only grows in calcium-rich soil, a commodity New Hampshire is very short on because the state has very little limestone. The preserve abuts NH 63 and trail maps are available in a box at the entrance.

Directions: From NH 9 in Chesterfield, go north on NH 63 for 5.5 miles. Look for yellow Nature Conservancy signs and limited, pull-off parking near Partridge Brook.

Activities: Hiking.

Facilities: Trail.

Dates: Open year-round.

Fees: None.

Closest town: Westmoreland, 1 mile.

For more information: The Nature Conservancy, 2 ½ Beacon Street, Concord, NH 03301. Phone. (603) 224-5853.

WARWICK ACCESS TRAIL

[Fig. 41(1)] This relatively short trail climbs 400 feet in a distance of 2,000 feet, so it is, of necessity, a bit steep. Leaves on the ground can be slippery. It passes over a small ravine, by a cave, and near some open ledges that provide views of the Connecticut River valley.

BOREAL CHICKADEE
(Parus hudsonicus)
This brown-capped bird sings its "chick-a-dee" in a buzzy voice.

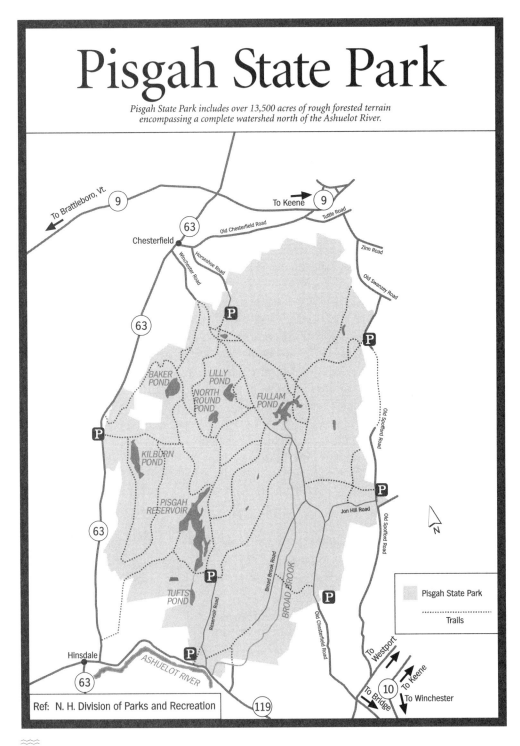

Pisgah State Park

Pisgah State Park includes over 13,500 acres of rough forested terrain encompassing a complete watershed north of the Ashuelot River.

To Brattleboro, Vt.

9

To Keene 9

63

Chesterfield

Old Chesterfield Road

Tuttle Road

Zinn Road

Winchester Road

Horseshoe Road

Old Swanzey Road

63

P

P

BAKER POND

LILLY POND

NORTH ROUND POND

FULLAM POND

Old Spofford Road

P

KILBURN POND

P

PISGAH RESERVOIR

Jon Hill Road

Old Spofford Road

N

P

Broad Brook Road

BROAD BROOK

P

Pisgah State Park

Trails

TUFTS POND

Reservoir Road

Old Chesterfield Road

To Westport

Hinsdale

ASHUELOT RIVER

To Bridge

10

To Keene

To Winchester

63

119

Ref: N. H. Division of Parks and Recreation

Trail: Less than 0.5 mile long.
Elevation: 400 feet to 800 feet.
Degree of difficulty: Short, but strenuous.
Surface and blaze: Forest floor, leaves and duff, some rocky ledges. Very well marked with yellow arrows. Sturdy walking shoes and a walking stick are recommended.

CHESTERFIELD GORGE

[Fig. 41(3)] This cool, hemlock-shaded gorge lets the sun in only on its own terms—as long, slanting shafts that barely glint off the tumbling water and wet rocks, even at midday. Cut deep into the slanted bedding of ancient metamorphic rock, this V-shaped cleft illustrates in miniature the way that rivers and faulting carve a valley, as opposed to the typical U-shaped valley carved by a glacier. Beech and black and yellow birch trees make an appearance here, but the high, old hemlocks tend to shade out all but the most shade-tolerant plants.

As Wilde Brook cascades through the gorge, its mists are held in by the coolness and the high, steep walls, creating a perfect habitat for mosses and ferns. A well-trodden trail loops down into the gorge for 0.7 mile, providing a cool respite on a hot summer day. Five minutes into the loop, any road noise from above has completely disappeared.

Directions: Adjacent to NH 9, 5.5 miles west of Keene. Look for Chesterfield Gorge Natural Area sign and parking lot on right.
Activities: Picnicking, hiking.
Facilities: Restrooms, visitor center, picnic tables, grills, hiking trail.
Dates: Trail and restrooms open year-round. Visitor center, seasonal.
Fees: None.
Closest town: Spofford, 1 mile.
For more information: Pisgah State park, Box 242, Winchester, NH 03470. Phone (603) 239-8153.

CHESTERFIELD GORGE TRAIL
Trail: Wide, well-trodden trail. 0.7 mile.
Elevation: 700 feet to 550 feet.
Degree of difficulty: Easy.
Surface and blaze: Forest duff. No blazes.

PISGAH STATE PARK

[Fig. 41] Pisgah State Park is the largest and the wildest of New Hampshire's state parks, straddling the borders of three towns: Chesterfield, Hinsdale, and Winchester. Topographically, this 13,500-acre park lies in the shape of a giant bowl, surrounded by a horseshoe of ridges and mountains, with its open end to the south. Running through this opening are the two major brooks that provide drainage for the park's seven major ponds. They join the swiftly flowing Ashuelot River in Winchester a little west of the picturesque Ashuelot Covered Bridge.

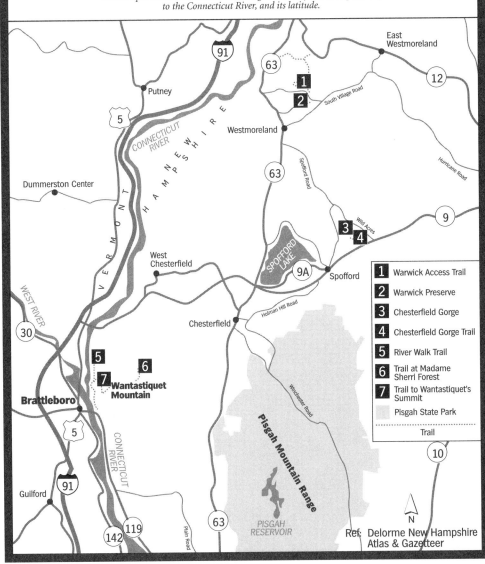

Wantastiquet Mountain

Wantastiquet Mountain has unusual ecological diversity due to its proximity to the Connecticut River, and its latitude.

Legend:

1 Warwick Access Trail
2 Warwick Preserve
3 Chesterfield Gorge
4 Chesterfield Gorge Trail
5 River Walk Trail
6 Trail at Madame Sherri Forest
7 Trail to Wantastiquet's Summit
  Pisgah State Park
  Trail

Ref: Delorme New Hampshire Atlas & Gazetteer

Pisgah is accessed by six trailheads which surround the park on all sides, preserving the tranquility at its heart. Each trailhead has parking and a kiosk with maps and information about Pisgah's many trails, which are all either old roads or clear paths and are well-blazed in a color specific to each. Excellent views of the Connecticut River valley to the southwest and Mount Monadnock to the east reward the hiker who climbs to the top of 1,300-foot Mount Pisgah.

The park is strictly a carry-in carry-out area and, currently, no fires or camping are allowed. Canoeing and kayaking with a wilderness feel can be had at Fullam, Kilburn, and Reservoir ponds. Fullam has nearby parking and the other two require a short portage. A new visitor center, where rangers and more information are available, is located on Old Chesterfield Road just inside the southeastern entrance to the park. Each month, the park and a support organization called Friends of Pisgah run a guided informational hike on various natural history topics at the park. A list of these is posted at each trailhead.

Directions: Pisgah is most easily approached from NH 63, either in Chesterfield or Hinsdale, where you can stop at either the Horseshoe Road or Kilburn Road trailhead and pick up a detailed map that shows the location of the other trailheads and the visitor center. All trailheads are clearly marked. The Horseshoe Road entrance is higher and offers a nice initial overview of this immense park.

Activities: Hiking, picnicking, canoeing, kayaking, biking, cross-country skiing.

Facilities: Trails, boat ramps, seasonal visitor center.

Dates: Trails open year-round. Dirt roads closed during spring mud season.

Fees: None.

Closest town: Winchester, Hinsdale, and Chesterfield, 2-4 miles.

For more information: Pisgah State Park, Box 242, Winchester, NH 03470. Phone (603) 239-8153.

WANTASTIQUET MOUNTAIN

[Fig. 41] In New Hampshire's southwesternmost corner, Wantastiquet Mountain abruptly rears its impressive wall of dark gray schist alongside the Connecticut River. Next to the river, a dirt road, the River Walk, hugs the mountain's western shoulder, and here, the bedding planes of this metamorphic schist, formerly a sedimentary rock, are clearly visible, protruding vertically through the soil and standing practically on end. It is almost impossible to comprehend the forces that were necessary to drive horizontal layers of rock upright like this. Wantastiquet's summit is only 1,335 feet, but its sudden rise next to the river provides such good views of the surrounding towns and the Connecticut River valley that it has become a popular hiking spot.

Ecologically speaking, Wantastiquet boasts an unusual diversity. Its latitude makes it a natural for the transitional forest of southern New Hampshire, so we find lots of white pine and oak. Its proximity to the slight climate-moderating influence of the Connecticut River brings in some normally southern plants as well, such as shagbark hickory and mountain laurel, and even the occasional sassafras tree. Add to these factors the mountain's modest elevation, which is just high enough to nurture northern hardwoods—white birch and maple—and you begin to see how accidents of latitude, elevation, and the course of a river can cause an interesting mix of plants that would normally inhabit three different biomes.

Wherever there is a variation in plant life, a wider diversity of wildlife will naturally follow. Different birds, insects, and mammals make their homes in and around different plants. Add the aquatic habitat of the Connecticut River, and this spot becomes a magnet for wildlife, despite its proximity to the city of Brattleboro, Vermont. Watch for "storms" of warblers in the spring, migrating up the river valley and stopping to glean insects from the riparian foliage, and keep an eye out for two kinds of squirrels, the red squirrel who thrives on evergreen cones and the gray, who prefers the oak's acorns. Aquatic mammals—beaver, otter, and muskrat—are very likely to be seen along the river bank. Once, the rocky ledges of Wantastiquet were a last refuge for the endangered timber rattlesnake, but there have been no documented sightings of this species here for many years.

A thousand acres of state-owned forest and natural area cover Wantastiquet Mountain and lie along the river. There are three ways to enjoy it. The River Walk runs 1.5 miles along the river from Hinsdale to Chesterfield and makes for a pleasant, woodsy ramble. This walk overlooks the river to the west and affords opportunities to witness the variety of wildlife associated with riparian habitats—shorebirds, migrating warblers, otter, and mink. Access to this road is possible from either end, but the Chesterfield end is quieter and boasts a splendid, sheer wall of schist, rising right up out of the parking lot, where the rock's vertical bedding is strikingly apparent.

At the southern, or Hinsdale end of this road, the 45-minute hike to the summit presents an option to the River Walk. Once at the top, the hiker overlooks the meandering Connecticut River below and can see, but not hear, the Lilliputian activities of the city of Brattleboro, Vermont across the way.

The third alternative is to approach this mountain from the back, or east side, through the Madame Sherri Forest. This 488-acre reserve is managed by the Society for the Protection of New Hampshire Forests. Here, an open and airy hardwood forest surrounds the tumbling stone ruins of Madame Sherri's country "castle," where she once lavishly entertained her theatrical friends from New York. An information board at the entrance to the property tells the story of this flamboyant French costume designer, whose former estate is now returning to a genteel wildness and has been set aside for conservation purposes.

An easy 0.5-mile walk along the old woods road that bears left in front of the "castle" leads to Indian Pond, a quiet refuge for moose and aquatic wildlife like beaver, otter, and mink. In the spring, this sanctuary puts on a spectacular display of pink lady's slippers (*Cypripedium acaule*). In New Hampshire, it is illegal to pick them or dig them up, but admiration is permitted. The other woods road that heads uphill from the castle is a pleasant hike for a while but then fades out in a morass of mountain laurel. There are no maps here, but the trail to Indian Pond is fairly clear.

Directions: To reach the Chesterfield River Walk access from NH 9 in Chesterfield, turn south onto Mountain Road just to the east of the bridge that crosses the Connecticut River. Go 1.1 miles to the end where the River Walk begins. To reach the Hinsdale River Walk or summit access from NH 9 in Chesterfield, go across the bridge to Vermont and turn south on VT 30 which becomes VT 5, 9, and Main Street, as well. Go 2.7 miles through Brattleboro to 119 E. Turn east onto NH 119 and go 0.5 mile across two green bridges to Mountain Road. Turn left. Parking and trailhead are 0.2 mile ahead. Here, you have a choice of taking the River Walk or hiking to the summit of Mount Wantastiquet. To reach the Madame Sherri Forest from NH 9 in Chesterfield, turn south onto Mountain Road just before the bridge to Vermont. Go 0.1 mile and turn left onto Gulf Road (dirt). Go 2.3 miles to red gate, information board, and parking on the right.

Bobcat

The only wild feline to breed in New Hampshire, the bobcat (*Lynx rufus*), is especially fond of rocky, south-facing ledges and caves. Seldom seen because it hunts at night, this solitary animal preys on snowshoe hare and other small animals. Bobcats are brown, have short ear tufts and a short tail with a black spot on the top. They weigh 15 to 35 pounds and are about 30 inches long. Their growls and hisses are similar to, but deeper and louder than, those of the familiar house cat. Bobcats roam up to 20 square miles of territory, so preserving large tracts of open space is important to this species.

Activities: Hiking, snowshoeing, wildlife viewing, and plant viewing.

Facilities: Trails.

Dates: Open year-round.

Fees: None.

Closest town: Brattleboro, Vermont, 0.7 mile.

For more information: New Hampshire Division of Forests and Lands, Box 1856, Concord, NH 03302. Phone (603) 271-3456. For Madame Sherri Forest, Society for Protection of New Hampshire Forests, 54 Portsmouth Street, Concord, NH 03301. Phone (603) 224-9945.

RIVER WALK TRAIL

[Fig. 41(5)] **Trail:** A flat, 1.5-mile, wooded, dirt road (3 miles round-trip). Follows the Connecticut River along the western edge of Wantastiquet Mountain.

Elevation: No elevation gain.

Degree of difficulty: Easy.

Surface and blaze: Flat, dirt road. No blazes. Be aware that there are several roads and trails that lead off upslope and tend to fade out without reaching the summit. So, stick to this road.

Mount Monadnock

Mount Monadnock is a National Natural Landmark and is protected by the Society for the Protection of New Hampshire Forests, the Town of Jaffrey, and the State of New Hampshire.

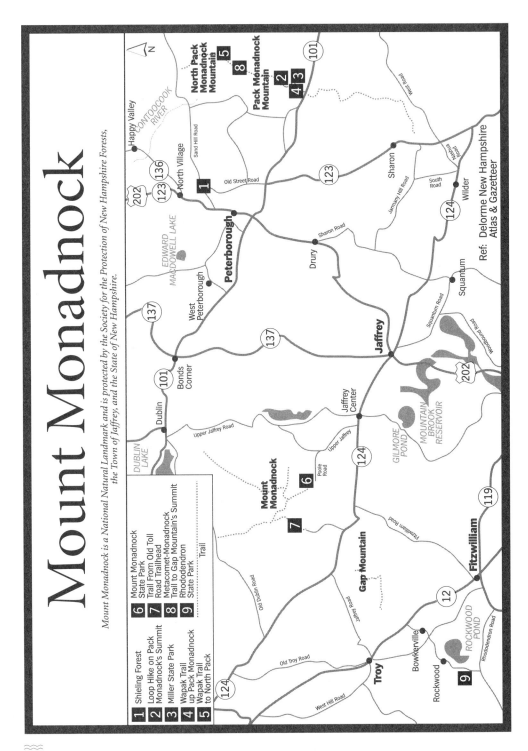

1	Shieling Forest	
2	Loop Hike on Pack Monadnock's Summit	
3	Miller State Park	
4	Wapak Trail up Pack Monadnock	
5	Wapak Trail to North Pack	
6	Mount Monadnock State Park	
7	Trail From Old Toll Road Trailhead	
8	Metacomet-Monadnock Trail to Gap Mountain's Summit	
9	Rhododendron State Park	
⋯⋯	Trail	

Ref: Delorme New Hampshire Atlas & Gazetteer

TRAIL TO WANTASTIQUET'S SUMMIT

[Fig. 41(7)] This 45-minute hike is at the Hinsdale end of the River Walk Trail and climbs steadily and comfortably to the top. It is a clearly discernible woods road that sweeps in wide switchbacks across the western face of the mountain and remains in the trees until it reaches the top. At the summit, there are magnificent views to the west over the broad Connecticut Valley and the Green Mountains of Vermont.

Trail: 3.0-mile round-trip hike to Mount Wantastiquet's summit.

Elevation: 350-feet to 1,335 feet.

Degree of difficulty: Moderate. Allow 1.5 hours round-trip.

Surface and blaze: Woods road, rocky and damp in places. No blazes, but route is clear.

TRAIL AT MADAM SHERRI FOREST

This quiet, wooded trail goes through hardwood forest and along the edge of a pond.

Trail: 0.5-mile to a pond.

Elevation: No elevation gain.

Degree of difficulty: Easy.

Surface and blaze: Forest floor and woods road. No blazes.

▓ MOUNT MONADNOCK

[Fig. 42] Occupying a good portion of this quiet corner of New Hampshire is 3,165-foot Mount Monadnock which, after Mount Fuji in Japan, is said to be the second most climbed mountain in the world. Geologically it is composed of tough metamorphic schists and quartzites, intruded here and there with veins of coarse, granitic rocks. Those who climb Monadnock can hardly miss the distinctive, raised crystals on many of the rock faces. Resembling bird tracks or little crosses, these crystals are sillimanite, a rock produced by the heat and pressure of metamorphism. Because they are harder than the rock they inhabit, they have eroded less and now stand out in relief. At the summit, the visitor may also notice that tiny garnet crystals, like droplets of currant jelly, decorate the surface as well.

Monadnock overshadows all of its 2,000-foot neighbors. On New Hampshire's eroded surface, a mountain's elevation is entirely dependent on how tough the rocks are, and Monadnock's rocks are very tough. The mountain is actually the remains of a syncline—the bottom, or bowl portion, of a massive rock fold. These bottom folds are subject to a higher degree of metamorphosis, thus become harder. Over hundreds of millions of years, miles of overlying rock have been eroded away so that now only the shallow bowl at the bottom of the fold remains, with Monadnock's summit as one "lip" and Pumpelly Ridge as the other.

Though its rugged terrain may be uninhabited now, the mountain has a long history of human occupation. Since the 1700s, its forests have been repeatedly cut and burned, and thousands of sheep have grazed on its high slopes. Even a hotel, now gone, once did business here. Monadnock's summit is well below tree line, so if its trees had not been burned and its soil destroyed and blown away by the wind, its

Beech

Fagus grandifolia, the American beech, is a dominant tree in the New Hampshire highlands. This tall, graceful tree has unusually smooth, gray bark, and its fruit, the beech nut, is a favorite of ruffed grouse, black bear, and wild turkey. Look for the telltale claw marks of bear who have climbed the tree to get at these nutritious nuts. Young beech trees will often hang on to their leaves long after other leaves have fallen. The remaining leaves rustle and flutter lightly in the winter woods. The extremely pointed buds of beech trees are so sharp that early woodsmen used them as toothpicks. Beech trees are lovely, but they do have enemies. Beech bark scale disease is the combined assault of an insect and a fungus which slowly kills the infected tree by causing cracks in its bark, opening the tree to attack from other parasitic fungi and insects. Interestingly, trees at higher elevations and colder temperatures seem more resistant. Beech also send up many root sprouts to ensure the next generation, but whether beech will remain a dominant, overstory species in the future is still open to question.

summit would not be the rocky, windblown peak we see today.

Monadnock will undoubtedly remain a bald for the foreseeable future. Even without the thousands of hiking feet that scramble over its summit, this high, exposed rock would require millennia to form enough soil to sustain a forested cap once again. The good news is that the mountain will continue to provide the breathtaking 360-degree vistas for the thousands of intrepid hikers who ascend each year.

Grand Monadnock, as it is sometimes called, is now a National Natural Landmark lying amid more than 5,000 acres of land protected by the Society for the Protection of New Hampshire Forests, the Town of Jaffrey, and the State of New Hampshire. Home to more than 40 miles of hiking trails, a state park, and a year-round campground, the mountain with its exposed summit is a mecca for outdoor enthusiasts. At the main entrance of Mount Monadnock State Park, a visitor center offers trail maps, displays, and other information. The top 300 feet of the climb to its summit is exposed rock, making for great geological observations and a 360-degree vista but also for occasionally high winds. Go armed with a coat, water, and a hiking companion.

MOUNT MONADNOCK STATE PARK

[Fig. 42(6)] Mount Monadnock State Park is part of the Monadnock Reservation owned by the Society for the Protection of New Hampshire Forests and leased to the state. The park manages the trails, a visitor center, and a year-round campground at the base of the mountain. Trailheads are scattered around all sides of the mountain, but the more popular trails take off from park headquarters. Several less traveled and more peaceful routes up this well-trod mountain take off from the Old Toll Road Trailhead. One of these quieter trails ascends by way of another small peak, Monta Rosa. Following this route, just below Monadnock's summit, there is an excellent

The Covered Bridges of New Hampshire

Covered bridges are not simply romantic symbols of the past. They are still very much a part of New Hampshire's landscape. Traditionally, bridges were built with covers to protect their wooden materials from destruction by the elements—to make them last longer, not to keep the rain and snow off the people who used them. The fact that they also kept horses from spooking as they crossed a rushing stream or provided shelter from a sudden squall were only secondary benefits. New Englanders were most concerned with frugality. The term "kissing bridges" alludes to some other scandalous purpose that covered bridges may have served.

About 50 covered bridges grace the rivers and streams of New Hampshire, but the total number varies from year to year, depending on how many have burned down, washed away, or been rebuilt— as they still are, with some regularity. No two of them are exactly alike, and the older ones are held together by wooden pegs called "tree nails," pronounced "trunnels." The Cornish-Windsor Bridge spans the Connecticut River and is the longest covered bridge in the United States. The oldest, in Haverill, crosses the Ammonoosuc River to Bath, Maine.

A complete list of New Hampshire's covered bridges is available from the New Hampshire Bureau of Travel and Tourism, 172 Pembroke Road, Concord, NH 03301. Phone (603) 271-2343.

view of the dramatic Billings Fold in the metamorphic rock, named for geologist Katharine Fowler-Billings.

Directions: To reach park headquarters from NH 202 in Jaffrey, go 2.5 miles west on NH 124. Turn right onto Dublin Road and follow the signs to Monadnock State Park. To reach Old Toll Road Trailhead go 3 miles farther west of Dublin Road on NH 124 to a state park parking area and kiosk.

Activities: Hiking, picnicking, cross-country skiing, camping.

Facilities: Campground and 40 miles of trails. In summer, visitor center, park store, flush toilets.

Dates: Year-round camping, hiking, skiing. In winter, pit toilets and no water.

Fees: There is a fee charged for camping and hiking.

Closest town: Jaffrey, 3 miles east.

For more information: Monadnock State Park, PO Box 181, Jaffrey, NH 03452. Phone (603) 532-8862.

TRAIL FROM OLD TOLL ROAD TRAILHEAD

[Fig. 42(7)] This 2.2-mile trail (one-way) runs through forest and over open rocky summit as it climbs 1,665 feet. This less-traveled route to the summit of Mount Monadnock gets the hiker away from the crowds and affords a view of the Billings Fold. It takes off from the Old Toll Road Trailhead, first as the Old Halfway House

Porcupines (Erethizon dorsatum) *are large nocturnal rodents and have approximately 30,000 barbed quills.*

Trail, then turns left onto the Monta Rosa Trail to that summit. From there, follow the Smith Summit Trail to the summit of Monadnock. The Billings Fold is visible on a sheer wall to the right just below the summit. Pick up a detailed trail map at the kiosk and start on the Old Halfway House Trail just beyond the gate.

Elevation: 1,500 feet to 3,165 feet.

Degree of difficulty: Strenuous.

Surface and blaze: Forest floor and bare rock outcrops. White blazes over rocky surfaces.

GAP MOUNTAIN

[Fig. 42] Sitting unobtrusively to the south of Grand Monadnock is 1,862-foot Gap Mountain, another part of Monadnock State Park. A 1-mile hike up a short stretch of the Metacomet-Monadnock Trail brings you to its summit where the horizon is full of Mount Monadnock to the north. This friendly mountain provides a hike that is easier, shorter, and less crowded than those ascending Gap Mountain's northern neighbor. The presence of juniper bushes and stone walls strung through the woods attest to the area's pastureland past. Look closely at Gap Mountain's metamorphic rocks and see the bedding, or layering, that speaks of their sedimentary origins.

Directions: To hike up the south side of Gap Mountain, go 7 miles west of Jaffrey on NH 124 to Troy Road. Turn left for 3 miles to NH 12, then turn left onto NH 12 for 1.4 miles to Gap Mountain Road. Turn left. At each fork, stay on paved road until you reach a sign that reads "No parking beyond here." Pull off near the wetland and walk 0.25 mile farther up road to a gate and state park kiosk.

METACOMET-MONADNOCK TRAIL

[Fig. 42(8)] To reach the summit of Gap Mountain, hike 45 minutes (one-way) on a short segment of this longer trail, through a young pine forest and rocky ledges.

Trail: 1-mile (one-way) hike to summit.

Elevation: 1250 feet to 1862 feet.

Degree of difficulty: Moderate.

Surface and blaze: Forest floor, grass, rock ledge. White blazes.

RHODODENDRON STATE PARK

[Fig. 42(9)] Designated as both a State Botanic Site and a National Natural Landmark, 500-acre Rhododendron State Park is unique in every sense of the word. *Rhododendron maximum* is at the northern limits of its range here, and some of the clusters on this 16-acre site stand 20 feet tall. Normally a southern species, this is the largest stand of rhododendron in the East, north of the Alleghenies. They bloom in mid-July but are impressive at any time of the year, standing with their feet in wet, boggy soil and their tops towering over the shaded, well-maintained trails.

Because the rhododendron are overshadowed by immense, old hemlocks, this grove provides a shady respite on a hot summer day. Even when the rhododendron are not blooming, there are ferns, mountain laurel, and many other plants to see. The Fitzwilliam Garden Club maintains an informative Wildflower Trail where, from April to freeze-up, something is always in leaf or flower. Keep a lookout for signs of rabbits and enjoy the birdsong along the flat, easy trails that run about 1 mile under an arch of shiny, evergreen leaves. If you need a bigger challenge, a 1.1-mile trail to Little Monadnock Mountain (1,883 feet) takes off from one of the loops. There is a map at the kiosk in the parking area.

Directions: From Troy, go 4 miles south on NH 12. Turn right on NH 119, going left, then right around the square, following Rhododendron State Park signs for 3.1 miles to state park on right.

Activities: Hiking, wildflower viewing, picnicking.

Facilities: Trails, pit toilets, picnic tables.

Dates: Open year-round.

Fees: Day-use fee in season.

Closest town: Troy, 7 miles.

For more information: Monadnock State Park, Box 181, Jaffrey, NH 03452. Phone (603) 532-8862.

SHIELING FOREST

[Fig. 42(1)] The New Hampshire Division of Forests and Lands manages this

Erratics

Sprinkled liberally over most of New Hampshire are boulders that differ in rock composition from the bedrock on which they rest. There is good reason for this. They have come from somewhere else. These boulders, ranging in size from watermelons to the phenomenal Madison Boulder that looks like a freighter docked in the woods, have been picked up or plucked off of mountains and ledges by the great ice sheets that covered New Hampshire thousands of years ago. The glaciers flowed slowly southward until a mere 14,000 years ago when a warming climate caused them to melt in place. When the ice melted, stones of all sizes that had been part of the icy colossus were dropped. These boulders are a part of every field and forest, and some have even been incorporated into houses and basements when they were too big to move. Glacial erratics remain an intriguing part of the landscape, a legacy of New Hampshire's dynamic past.

48-acre property for both public education and enjoyment. A pleasant, shady spot for a family walk or a picnic, this little forest also offers programs and demonstrates how to manage small woodlots.

A few minutes into a hike down the Boulder Trail, you would never guess that you are within 3 miles of Peterborough. A glacial erratic boulder the size of a small house sits quietly among the pine needles, as it has for all the thousands of years since the glacier dropped it there. Sometime in that period, enough ice crept into a crack in this boulder to split it apart so that one half sits precariously balanced next to the other.

At the back side of the forest, near an old woods road, a forest of silvery beech trees stands next to a granite outcrop that is also fractured by frost and time into a jumble of angular pieces. The difference is that this outcrop is bedrock—rock that is anchored here—whereas erratic boulders were transported here by the ice sheet.

Throughout the forest, old decomposing trees lie where they fell decades ago, slowly becoming part of the soil again and helping to nourish their descendants. Birds sing and flit through the branches and a bubbly brook runs under a bridge, inviting you to sit a spell and let the quiet of the woods wash over you as the falling water washes over the rocks.

Directions: In Peterborough, from NH 202 N, go 0.9 mile east on NH 101. Turn left on Old Street Road and go 2 miles to Shieling Forest sign and parking on the right.

Activities: Hiking, picnicking, wildflower trail, educational programs.

Facilities: Trails, picnic tables, trail guide and map at kiosk in parking area.

Fees: None.

Closest town: Peterborough, 3 miles.

For more information: New Hampshire Division of Forests and Lands, Box 1856, Concord, NH 03302. Phone (603) 271-3456.

Eastern Hemlock

Tsuga canadensis, or Eastern hemlock, is a prominent member of New Hampshire's forests. Hemlocks frequently grow to be 3 feet thick and 70 feet tall, and all that begins in a tiny cone half an inch long.

From a distance, hemlock is easy to distinguish from other evergreens. Its tiny needles make it fuller and lacier than pine, and its rounded shape distinguishes it from the slim spires of spruce or fir-balsam. Also, unlike the others, hemlock's leader, or topmost twig, is limp and droops over, some say, always to the east. There's a certain logic to this belief when you consider that local prevailing winds are generally from the west.

Hemlock has several advantages over the deciduous trees it often accompanies. Like other evergreens, it doesn't have to replace all of its needles annually, and thus it gets a jump on spring photosynthesis, before the hardwoods leaf out. Hemlock also has shade-tolerance on its side. Seedlings can survive many years in the shady understory, whereas most hardwoods need more direct sunlight. In winter, pliable hemlock fronds will bow and shed heavy snow and ice while hardwoods are more likely to break under the load.

While hemlocks lend a soft, lacy contrast to a mixed forest, a pure stand of this species can be a bit dreary. Because hemlock tends to shade out everything else, it leaves the forest floor a dim dark place clothed only in its own needles.

PACK MONADNOCK AND NORTH PACK

[Fig. 42] *Pack* means "little" in the language of the Native Americans who named these peaks. This pleasant little pair of mountains, at 2,290 and 2,278 feet respectively, are a popular getaway for families. A scenic auto road runs to the summit of Pack Monadnock where picnic tables invite you to stay a while. From the fire tower on a clear day, a 360-degree panorama includes the Presidential Range to the north and the Boston skyline to the southeast, while the western horizon is dominated by Grand Monadnock, 12 miles away.

MILLER STATE PARK

[Fig. 42(3)] Miller State Park, which includes Pack Monadnock's summit, hiking trails, and the auto road, is the oldest state park in New Hampshire and is named for General James Miller, a local hero of the War of 1812.

There are two moderate hiking trails that climb Pack Monadnock from the lower parking lot if you would rather hike than drive. One of them, a piece of the longer Wapak Trail, comes up from Massachusetts and then continues on over to the less-peopled summit of North Pack. A third short trail loops the summit of Pack Monadnock. A map of all the trails is available at the state park kiosk in the lower parking lot.

In the fall, these peaks are prime spots to witness the annual hawk migration. As many species of raptors wend their way south, they follow north-south river valleys and mountain chains. On a warm September day, it is not uncommon to count a thousand or more hawks, spiraling up in kettle formations, then soaring off the top and downwind to catch the next thermal.

Directions: Go 4 miles east of Peterborough on NH 101. Sign for Miller State Park is on the left, opposite Temple Mountain Ski Area. Parking and kiosk are just off NH 101.

Activities: Picnicking, hiking, hawk-watching, scenic drive.

Dates: Road open May-Nov.

Fees: There is a charge to use the seasonal road.

Closest town: Peterborough, 4 miles west.

For more information: New Hampshire Division of Parks and Recreation, 172 Pembroke Road, Box 856, Concord, NH 03302. Phone (603) 271-3254.

LOOP HIKE ON PACK MONADNOCK'S SUMMIT

[Fig. 42(2)] This trail is a 0.7-mile loop around the top of the mountain through boreal forest of spruce, fir, and shrubs of the heath family. Bare outcrops of rock and stunning vistas compete with the local and migrating bird life for your attention.

Trail: 0.7-mile loop.

Elevation: No elevation gain.

Degree of difficulty: Moderate.

Surface and blaze: Rocky ledge and red blazes.

WAPAK TRAIL UP PACK MONADNOCK

[Fig. 42(4)] This is a piece of a much longer trail that comes 21 miles up from Watatic Mountain in Massachusetts and ends just beyond North Pack. Pick it up to the right of the lower parking lot in Miller State Park and climb 1.3 miles through the woods to emerge at the upper parking lot on the bare, rocky summit of Pack Monadnock.

Trail: 1.3 miles one-way.

Elevation: 1,400 feet to 2,290 feet.

Degree of difficulty: Moderate.

Surface and blaze: Forest floor and rocky spots. Blazed in yellow.

WAPAK TRAIL TO NORTH PACK

[Fig. 42(5)] The Wapak Trail continues on for 2.3 miles to North Pack, winding through the Wapak National Wildlife Refuge, which occupies the saddle between the two mountains. The trail offers a peaceful, forested hike with fewer people than may be on Pack Monadnock's summit. It takes off from the trail junction near the upper parking area on top of Pack Monadnock.

Trail: 2.3 miles (one-way) beyond Pack Monadnock.

Elevation: 2,290 feet to 1800 feet to 2,278 feet.

Degree of difficulty: Moderate.

Surface and blaze: Forest floor and rocky ledges. Blazed in yellow.

EDWARD MACDOWELL LAKE

[Fig. 42] Nearly 1,200 acres of land and lake make up this Corps of Engineers flood-control recreation area. Nubanusit Brook was dammed in 1950 to protect the towns downstream from disastrous floods. The resulting lake was named for composer and concert pianist Edward MacDowell, who, around the turn of the last century, escaped the urban clamor of New York to spend summers here, composing music in the quiet countryside.

At this lake and recreation area, the U.S. Army Corps of Engineers is on a mission to avail the public of the many

---

The MacDowell Colony

Since 1907, the MacDowell Colony of Peterborough has provided talented artists a temporary refuge of peace and tranquility in which to work. This early and unique artists' colony was founded by concert pianist Edward MacDowell and his wife Marian. Since its founding, over 1,500 writers, composers, sculptors, and other artists have resided here, freed for a time from the cares and distractions of everyday life. From these private cabins amid 450 acres of woodland solitude, they have issued works like Thornton Wilder's *Our Town* and Aaron Copland's *Appalachian Spring*.

---

benefits of the dam and lake besides flood control. Corps rangers manage the area for forestry, fishing, and wildlife habitat and also conduct interpretive programs for the public. There are trails for hiking or skiing, boating and fishing access, lots of picnic areas, and a covered pavilion beside the lake available for group picnics.

Directions: From NH 202 in Peterborough, go 2.3 miles west on NH 101 to Union Street. Turn north on Union Street and follow signs to the dam. Turn left on Wilder Street to the project office and parking.

Activities: Hiking, fishing, boating, picnicking, ranger programs, cross-country skiing, volleyball, boat launch, horseback riding.

Facilities: Picnic tables, grills, restrooms, water, trails, boat launch, handicap-accessible.

Dates: Open year-round.

Fees: None, except a charge to reserve picnic pavilion.

Closest town: Peterborough, 3 miles.

For more information: Project Office, Edward MacDowell Lake, 75 Wilder Street, Peterborough, NH 03458. Phone (603) 924-3431.

Lakes Region Lowlands

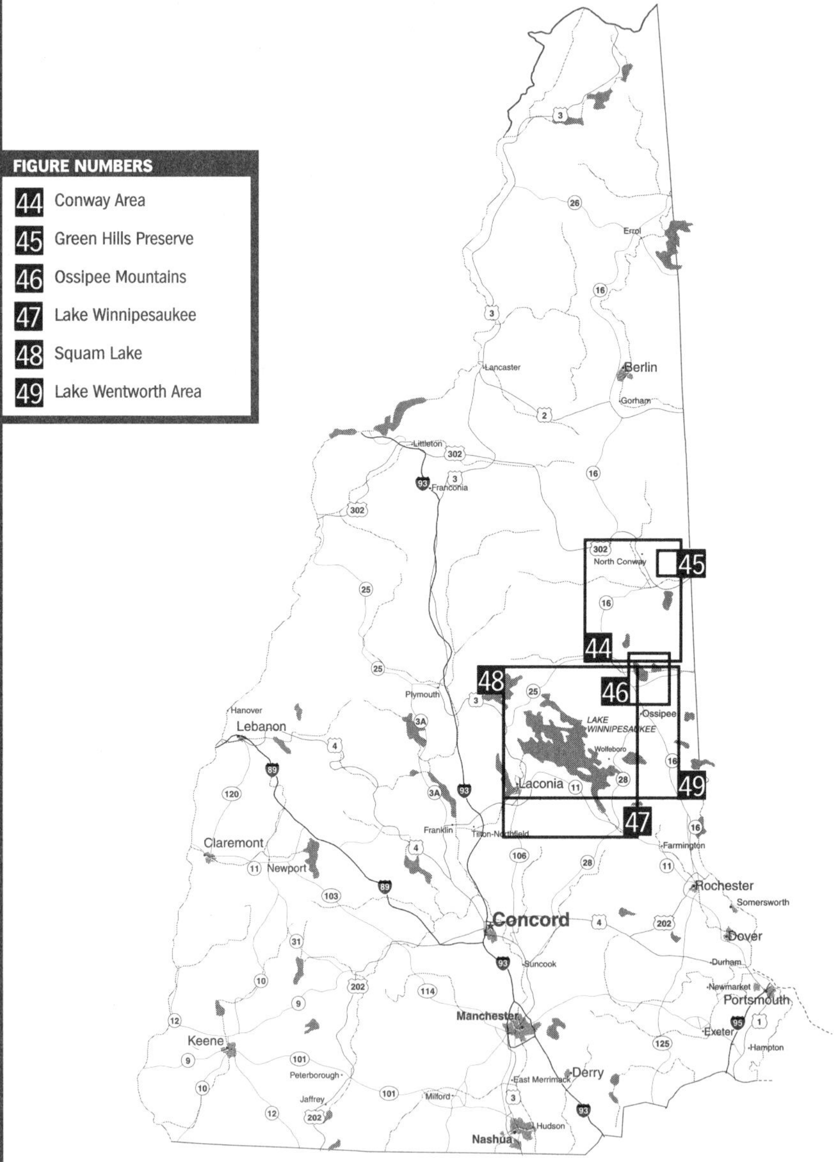

FIGURE NUMBERS

44 Conway Area

45 Green Hills Preserve

46 Ossipee Mountains

47 Lake Winnipesaukee

48 Squam Lake

49 Lake Wentworth Area

Lakes Region Lowlands

Т he Lakes Region Lowlands area of New Hampshire is a premier vacation
spot—with reasons that are ample and readily apparent. Deep green forests,
picturesque mountains, and more than 200 sparkling lakes offer a variety of
scenery, recreation, and wildlife habitat unequaled anywhere else in the state.

The region abounds with both tourist attractions and conservation lands—lots of
chances to mingle, or opportunities to get off on your own. Even the bigger, busier
lakes hold quiet coves to paddle and are surrounded by mountains with lonesome
trails to climb. The area's roads tend to wind over the hills and around the bends in
such a way that lake and mountain vistas are always popping into view.

Groups of small mountains ring the area, standing conspicuously above what is
otherwise an immense glacial outwash plain. Behind them, to the north and west, the
larger White Mountains begin to poke above the horizon, in vistas made more

[*Above:* Heath Pond Bog is a National Natural Landmark]

dramatic by contrast with the lakes and intervales.

Here in the mid-1800s, the White Mountain School of art sprang up as artists tried to capture the magic of the place on canvas. So numerous were they in the summer that Winslow Homer made the artists, themselves, the subject of a painting. His *Artists Sketching in the White Mountains* shows these White Mountain painters at their easels, scattered across the green fields like colorful wildflowers against a backdrop of mountains. Their work tended toward gauzy, romantic images of the region, first depicted as a fearsome and rugged wilderness, then later envisioned in more pastoral scenes of a wilderness tamed. Benjamin Champney, one of the White Mountain Group, later documented this creative and prolific period in his *Sixty Years of Art and Artists.*

The variety of topography found in the Lakes Region—mountains, lakes, broad intervales—results from a tumultuous geological past. Many of the nearby groups of small mountains mark the spots where, 180 million years ago, ancient volcanoes poured great sheets of lava out over the land. These volcanoes erupted during that prolonged episode of pulling apart that accompanied the break-up of Pangaea, the ancient supercontinent.

When the eruptions were over, great cylindrical chunks of overlying rock collapsed into the empty volcanic calderas, forcing some of the molten rock below them to squeeze up around the edges, in a circular arrangement. These *ring dikes,* composed of quartz syenite, hardened into circular rings, and today the remnants of these rings make up both the Ossipee and the Belknap mountain groups.

Far beneath these spent volcanoes, massive intrusions of molten rock remained in the magma chambers, slowly cooling and crystallizing into New Hampshire's youngest granites. The pinkish-colored Conway Granite is one example. Once buried deeply beneath the volcanic rock, these granites now crop out nearly everywhere that the softer volcanics been have eroded away.

In addition to the Ossipee and Belknap mountain groups, the Green Hills, the Moose Mountains, and Red Hill are also products of these same volcanic processes. In these hills, three kinds of rock form outcrops—syenite, granite, and here and there, a smattering of basaltic lava. Scattered in a wide circle around Lake Winnipesaukee, all these mountain groups stand well above the outwash plains of the most recent Pleistocene glacier.

Without the glacial onslaught that peaked about 18,000 years ago, there would be far fewer lakes in the Lakes Region. Many of the lakes, including the largest, Lake Winnipesaukee, fill basins that were carved by the glacier from softer, older granitic rocks in the region. Others are the result of glacial *kettle holes.* All of them are surrounded by an immense outwash plain of sand and gravel—in places, hundreds of feet thick—and by the characteristic landforms left behind by a great continental ice sheet.

Eskers are one type of landform peculiar to glaciers. These long, sinuous ridges of sand and gravel wiggle over today's landscape, tracing the course of ancient tunnels that once ran beneath the mile-high sheet of ice. Great torrents of meltwater gushed through these tunnels and eventually flowed out from under the leading edge, or nose, of the glacier. These subglacial rivers carried vast amounts of sand and gravel which eventually settled out of the water, filling in the tunnels. Now, like the castings of a worm, these winding ridges of debris where the streams once flowed.

The biggest of them all, the Pine River esker, runs roughly parallel with NH 16 through Conway and Ossipee, but its immense size and its history of commercial sand and gravel excavation make it difficult to pick out. Smaller and more easily seen eskers run alongside Route 153 from Conway through Freedom.

Other landforms left behind by the glacier are the elongated hills called *drumlins*. These prodigious piles of glacial till occur when the ice sheet passes over an unusually hard outcrop. Debris accumulates against this hard core and the resulting hill trends in the direction of the glacier's movement. In the Wolfeboro area, nearly a hundred drumlins dot the outwash plain.

Glacial erratics are another hallmark of the previous passage of a glacier. These large boulders were picked up and incorporated into the glacier's ice. Later, as the ice melted, they were dropped in a new location. Madison Boulder, the largest known glacial erratic in the Northeast, sits ponderously in its own 17-acre woods in Madison, New Hampshire (*see* page 261). In other places around the Lakes Region, large groups of erratics radiate out in the shape of a fan where they were dropped by the melting ice. These are called *boulder trains* and are another indication of the glacier's direction of movement.

Most of the lakes in the Lakes Region of New Hampshire occupy low basins scoured both by the glaciers of the Pleistocene and by the eons of relentless weathering before that. Lake Winnipesaukee, the largest, lies in a bowl of 370-million-year-old granitic rock that proved to be softer than the more durable metamorphics that surround it. This and the other low areas are now filled with crystalline lakes that twinkle blue in the sun when seen from the top of any of the surrounding hills.

Lake Winnipesaukee's wildly irregular shape covers nearly 70 square miles. Its many arms and tentacles stretch over the land in a northwest to southeast trend, an

Tamarack Trees

When is a conifer tree not an evergreen? When it's a tamarack or American larch, the only northern conifer that drops its needles annually. The tamarack (*Larix laricina*) loves cool, wet soils and you'll find its slim spires poking out of many of New Hampshire's wetlands. In autumn, the tamarack's short needles turn a golden brown before they fall and in the spring the new needles sprout a brilliant yellow-green. During the cold months, this tree looks a little skeletal, its bare brown twigs covered with warty little bumps where the needles will be. Like its cousin, the bald cypress, a tree of southern swamps, the tamarack thrives in wet areas where other trees would be killed by having their "feet" constantly wet.

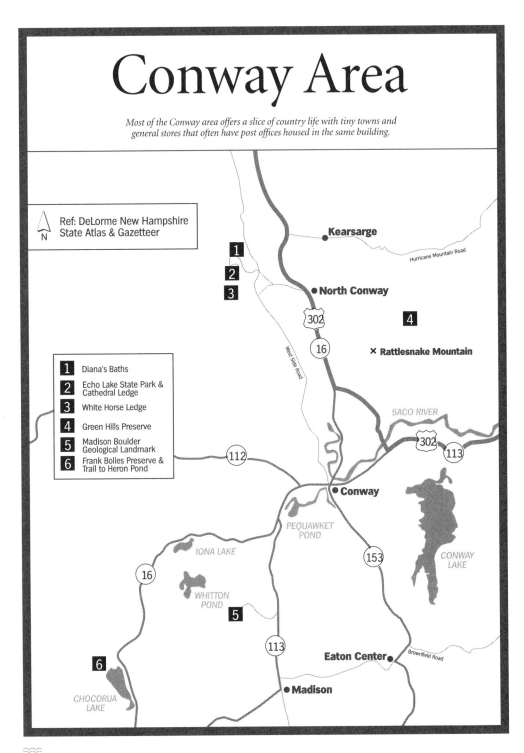

Conway Area

Most of the Conway area offers a slice of country life with tiny towns and general stores that often have post offices housed in the same building.

Ref: DeLorme New Hampshire
State Atlas & Gazetteer
N

Kearsarge

Hurricane Mountain Road

1

2

3

North Conway

302

4

16

× **Rattlesnake Mountain**

West Side Road

SACO RIVER

302   113

1   Diana's Baths

2   Echo Lake State Park &
    Cathedral Ledge

3   White Horse Ledge

4   Green Hills Preserve

5   Madison Boulder
    Geological Landmark

6   Frank Bolles Preserve &
    Trail to Heron Pond

112

● **Conway**

PEQUAWKET
POND

IONA LAKE

153

CONWAY
LAKE

16

WHITTON
POND

5

113

6

Eaton Center ●

Brownfield Road

CHOCORUA
LAKE

● **Madison**

undeniable testimony to the direction in which the ice once grated over the land. Other sizable and equally lovely lakes in the area are Squam, Winnesquam, Wentworth, Merrymeeting, and Ossipee. Most have granitic bottoms, making for exceptionally clear water and clean, sandy beaches.

Long vistas of lakes and mountains await around nearly every corner. Many of these mountains are climber-friendly and a hike up Belmont Mountain, south of Lake Winnipesaukee, rewards the hiker with an instructive look at the whole Ossipee *ring dike* across the lake, to the northeast.

Abenaki Indians were the Lakes Region's first known human inhabitants. Indian artifacts have been found near the place called The Weirs, a name derived from the word *weir,* a fencelike device that early Native-Americans used to ensnare fish. Europeans explored the area in the 1630s and built their first settlements in the 1750s.

Conway-Ossipee Region

This quiet region of small lakes, pine barrens, and sandy hills stretches north of Lake Winnipesaukee to the White Mountain National Forest and east to the border of Maine. With the exception of the Conway-North Conway area, and its emphasis on tax-free shopping and tourism, the rest of this region is a slice of country life dotted with tiny towns having only general stores and post offices—often housed in the same building.

🦑 DIANA'S BATHS

[Fig. 44(1)] Diana's Baths is the intriguing name of a dramatic series of waterfalls located 2 miles west of North Conway Village. Here, Lucy Brook tumbles down from Little Attitash Mountain, swirling around corners and over chunks and slabs of granite the size of pickup trucks, creating a series of impressive cataracts and pools that offer a cool respite on a hot day. Not a well-publicized attraction, these falls are impossible to see from the road. But, once you find the short, easy trail in, you can just follow your ears toward the sound of cascading water that gets louder and louder as you approach.

Visible along the surging stream are the stone remains of an old sluiceway where once the energy of this rushing water was used to power a mill. The water pools gently in several spots, inviting you in for an invigorating dip, and the cool woods that flank the brook hold many little nooks in which to sit and enjoy a picnic lunch. This out-of-the-way spot has no formal facilities and thus, attracts few people. On a slow day, you could have the place all to yourself.

Directions: From NH 16 in North Conway, turn west on River Road. Go a total of 2.2 miles, bearing right past the turn for Cathedral Ledge. Pull off the road just before a small white sign on the left that reads "Lucy Farm." Between the fields of this farm, an unmarked driveway leads 50 yards to the beginning of the Moat Mountain Trail. Walk another 0.5 mile on this trail to Lucy Brook and bear right, following its bank along the multiple falls.

Activities: Swimming, hiking, snowshoeing.

Facilities: Brook, trail.

Dates: Open year-round.

Fees: None.

Closest town: North Conway, 3 miles.

For more information: Mount Washington Valley Chamber of Commerce, Box 2300-G, North Conway, NH 03860. Phone 1-800-367-3364.

ECHO LAKE STATE PARK AND CATHEDRAL AND WHITE HORSE LEDGES

[Fig. 44(2)] This relatively small state park sits wedged between the White Mountain National Forest and the bustling town of North Conway. Despite its diminutive size, it holds three beautiful natural treasures—Echo Lake, White Horse Ledge, and Cathedral Ledge.

Echo Lake is a quiet, green jewel that, on a still morning, holds little except the awesome reflection of White Horse Ledge rising vertically from its western edge.

On the eastern shore, a nice sandy beach and spacious picnic grounds sit under a tall pine and hemlock forest. A 0.5-mile hiking trail loops around the lake through tall red and white pines. The low shoreline is home to such wetland indicator plants as sensitive fern (*Onoclea sensibilis* L.) and sphagnum moss (*Sphagnum* spp.).

Both White Horse Ledge and Cathedral Ledge to its north are dramatic, vertical rock faces that seem to leap up out of the Saco River valley to elevations of 1,470 and 1,150 feet, respectively. White Horse, the smoother of the two, lies directly across Echo Lake from the beach and picnic area, and Cathedral is just to the north. Though it is difficult to get close to White Horse Ledge because private property intervenes, an auto road lets you drive all the way to the top of Cathedral Ledge.

The smooth granite faces of these two ledges beguilingly catch the morning sun and have long been an irresistible draw to rock climbers. For an even longer time, these cliffs have been equally attractive to peregrine falcons, who build their nests high on such rocky ledges. Before the ecological disaster of DDT, these raptors nested here regularly, and now that the use of this pesticide has been banned, they have begun to return. Volunteer spotters below keep an eye on active

BLACK-THROATED BLUE WARBLER
(Dendroica caerulescens)
A black face and white spot on the wing over a blue body identify this warbler.

nests and rock climbers plan their routes so as to avoid disturbing the birds during the spring nesting season.

Geologically, White Horse and Cathedral ledges were sculpted by the same processes. They are classic *roches moutonnée,* French for sheeplike rocks. Their lovely granite cliffs face roughly southeast, the direction in which the Pleistocene glaciers flowed. The ice sheet steepened these rock faces by plucking pieces of rock off their southeastern sides and planing them off to a relatively smooth finish.

If climbing vertically up the sheer face of a cliff is not in your plans, there is a 1-mile auto·road that leads to the top of Cathedral Ledge. An overlook offering breathtaking views of Echo Lake and White Horse Ledge is just 50 yards from the parking lot at the top. To the east, beyond the bustle of North Conway, lie the Green Hills. Notice the pinkish granite outcrops on the southern end of this ridge where the old Redstone Quarry once pulled Conway Granite from the hillside. To the west, the vast White Mountain National Forest begins its westward march up the slopes of the Moat Mountains and, as far as you can see in this direction, the vista is uninterrupted trees. Because peregrine falcons nest on the face of the cliff below this overlook, an occasional gusty thermal can lift one of these pointed-winged raptors right up over your head.

Directions: To reach Echo Lake State Park from NH 16 in North Conway, go 1 mile west on River Road. Turn left at the Echo Lake State Park sign. To reach the Cathedral Ledge Auto Road, follow the directions for Echo Lake State Park, but turn left at the Cathedral Ledge sign instead of the state park sign. (These two signs are very close together.) Follow signs to the auto road which runs 1 mile up to the parking lot at the top of the ledge. The overlook is 50 yards south from the parking area via any of several well-worn trails. Use caution near edges!

Activities: Swimming, picnicking, hiking, drive to scenic view, rock-climbing.

Facilities: Beach, bathhouse, restrooms, picnic tables, 0.5-mile loop trail around the lake, auto road, scenic overview.

Dates: Beach facilities and auto road, open summer and early fall. Hiking trail open year-round.

Cirques

Cirques are great semicircular bowls excavated by valley glaciers out of the side of a mountain. These smaller, riverlike glaciers occupied some valleys long before the massive Laurentide ice sheet rolled over the whole region. As ice accumulated at the head of a valley, the frost action of the valley glacier slowly plucked chunks of rock out of the mountain, carving an amphitheater with a very steep headwall and a rounded bottom. On the eastern slope of Mount Washington, both Tuckerman and Huntington ravines are excellent examples of cirques, and Tuckerman—famous for containing winter snows well into June—has long been a magnet for adventuresome skiers.

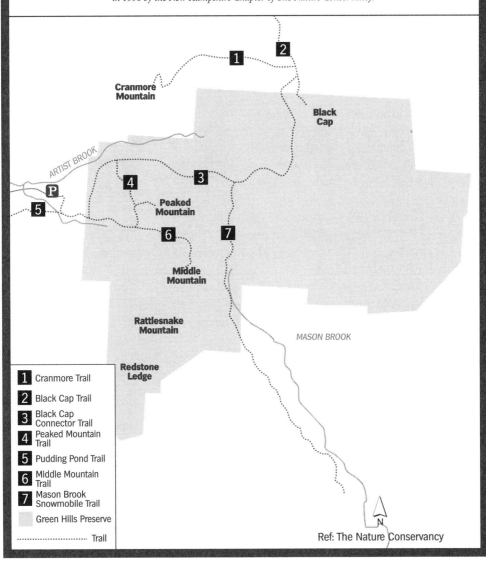

Green Hills Preserve

The Green Hills Preserve, 2,822 acres of mountain and hilltop, was established in 1990 by the New Hampshire Chapter of The Nature Conservancy.

Cranmore Mountain

Black Cap

ARTIST BROOK

P

1 Cranmore Trail

2 Black Cap Trail

3 Black Cap Connector Trail

4 Peaked Mountain Trail

5 Pudding Pond Trail

6 Middle Mountain Trail

7 Mason Brook Snowmobile Trail

Green Hills Preserve

.... Trail

Peaked Mountain

Middle Mountain

Rattlesnake Mountain

Redstone Ledge

MASON BROOK

N

Ref: The Nature Conservancy

Fees: There is a charge for entrance, June through Labor Day.

Closest town: North Conway, 1 mile.

For more information: Echo Lake State Park, Box 565, North Conway, NH 03860. Phone (603) 356-2672. For details about rock climbing, see *Cathedral and White Horse Ledges*, a book by Jerry Hendren.

GREEN HILLS PRESERVE

[Fig. 45], [Fig. 44(4)] The Nature Conservancy's Green Hills Preserve covers 2,822 forested acres of hills and mountains just east of the busy North Conway area. Drive less than 1 mile from NH 16 and you are well within this realm of red pine and pink granite. The preserve has several hiking trails to the tops of three mountains, and maps are available on the property. From the summit of Peaked Mountain, the stunning view stretching west includes Mount Chocorua and the Moat Mountain Range.

Scenery has long been a commodity in the North Conway region. Even before photography became the way we see the world, the painters of the White Mountain School carried away the first images of this pleasing juxtaposition of mountains and intervales. Tourists responded then just as they do now. Considering the area's popularity, it is a point of pride and amazement that this mountain refuge in the Green Hills, so close to an area of high tourism, has been saved from development. It stands in testimony to what the determination and work of a few conservation-minded individuals can do.

The Green Hills are underlain by New Hampshire's youngest igneous rock, Conway Granite, a pluton of which intruded the area around 180 million years ago. At the south end of this 2-mile-long ridge of small mountains sits Redstone Ledge where, from the 1880s to the 1930s, quarries yielded beautiful pink and green stone to adorn buildings all over the country.

The Green Hills Preserve shelters several rare and endangered plants under its mixed forests. Mountain sandwort and White Mountain silverling are tucked into crevices atop Peaked Mountain, which is also home to three kinds of pines: white, pitch, and some very old red pines. Follow the Peaked Mountain trail first through shady forests and then over granite outcrops to the rocky summit where glacial striations mark the passage of the Laurentide ice sheet.

Directions: From the junction of River Road and NH 16 in North Conway, go south on NH 16 for 0.8 mile. Turn left onto Artist Falls Road for 0.5 mile. Bear right onto Thompson Road for 0.3 mile to Pudding Pond sign and pull-off parking. The Nature Conservancy information kiosk with maps is 0.2 mile into the woods on a broad path. All trails begin at this kiosk.

Activities: Hiking, bird-watching, plant viewing, cross-country skiing.

Facilities: Trails, maps, information kiosk.

Dates: Open year-round.

Fees: None.

Pink Lady's Slipper

It is more or less appropriate that New Hampshire calls the pink lady's slipper (*Cypripedium acaule*), its state wildflower. It all depends on the time and the status of the local vegetation. Now, for instance, is a good time for lady's slippers, which prefer a forest understory as habitat, but 150 years ago when much of the state's land was cleared for agriculture, this lovely wildflower would have been scarce indeed. This delicate, orchidlike perennial does best in drier soils, often under a pine forest. Its roots can live 100 years, waiting patiently for just the right conditions of light and moisture to send up its broad, flat leaves and stunning pink blossom. Depending on location and weather, the pink lady's slipper can bloom anytime from April to July, producing only one flower. But, such a flower! Like a beautiful pink balloon, this oddly shaped pouch of a blossom has been called "squirrel shoes" or "moccasin flower," and its genus name, *Cypripedium*, is Latin for Venus slipper. It seems people just can't find the right words to describe this unusual orchid. When its outrageous bloom does appear, its one goal in life is to attract a bumblebee to pollinate it, an important event because, though the plant may live for decades, it may only bloom half a dozen times in its life. Pink lady's slippers are nearly impossible to propagate and as a plant of special concern in New Hampshire, they should be warmly appreciated but never picked.

Closest town: North Conway, 1 mile.

For more information: Green Hills Preserve, Box 310, North Conway, NH 03860. Phone (603) 356-8833.

PUDDING POND TRAIL

[Fig. 45(5)] This popular trail traverses several different habitats, from a dim evergreen forest to the edge along a stream, to a wetland pond where beaver build dams and mink skitter in and out of a brook. A colony of great blue heron nests at Pudding Pond. Look for their large nests of twigs and branches high in the trees. The Pudding Pond Trail turns right at the information kiosk and follows yellow blazes over footbridges and wetlands and around Pudding Pond.

Trail: 2-mile loop through forests and around a pond.

Elevation: 630 feet to 430 feet to 630 feet.

Degree of difficulty: Easy.

Surface and blaze: Woods roads, forest floor, some wet areas. Blazed in yellow.

PEAKED MOUNTAIN TRAIL

[Fig. 45(4)] After a pleasant hike through mixed evergreen and hardwood forest, this trail offers excellent views to the north, west, and south from the summit of Peaked Mountain. Near the top is a stand of rare, old growth red pines, some of which are believed to be nearly 200 years old. Sheltered in crevices on the granite ledges lives *Paronychia argyrocoma,* the White Mountain silverling, or whitlowwort, one of several rare or endangered plants known to exist in the Green Hills Preserve. Mountain sandwort (*Arenaria groenlandica*), whose tufted clumps grow as far north as Greenland, is unlike other alpine plants in that it continues to flower throughout the summer.

To reach this summit, turn left at the information kiosk and hike under the power lines to re-enter the woods. Follow yellow blazes to another kiosk in 0.5 mile. Bear left here for 1 mile to a third kiosk where you turn right and follow blue blazes to the summit.

Trail: 2.1-mile trail (one-way) to the summit of Peaked Mountain.

Elevation: 630 feet to 1,739 feet.

Degree of difficulty: Moderate.

Surface and blaze: Forest floor and exposed rock ledges. Blazes yellow, then blue.

FRANK BOLLES PRESERVE

[Fig. 44(6)] On the way into this nature preserve, you drive by the southern end of quiet Chocorua Lake where, on a spring day, a migrating loon might stop to rest for a few moments on the placid water. A small picnic and swimming spot is maintained here by the Chocorua Lake Conservation Foundation (CLCF) which asks only that there be no motorboat traffic on the lake. Stop for a bit or keep going another 1.25 miles to the Bolles Reserve, which is also maintained by the CLCF for The Nature Conservancy.

Hidden in the heart of this sanctuary is Heron Pond, a deep-green jewel that is wonderfully still, surrounded by forested slopes and the scent of warm pine needles. Peeking above the trees on its north side is the pointed and rocky summit of Mount Chocorua. The pond fills an eight-acre *kettle hole* left behind when a chunk of glacial ice became buried and later melted away, leaving a depression. For reasons not clearly understood, the water level varies considerably in this pond not necessarily in synchrony with the levels of the groundwater.

Frank Bolles was a noted naturalist and writer who nearly 100 years ago recognized that diversity in habitat translates to diversity in plants and animals. In 1969, his daughter gave this 250-acre parcel of land fronting on Lake Chocorua into the care of The Nature Conservancy so that it would remain the sanctuary that he had so carefully studied.

This piece of land boasts several characteristics that conservation groups consider important criteria for protected land. One is its diversity of habitat, everything from lakeshore, to forested uplands, to clearings, to a kettle-hole pond. Just as important is its adjacency to other wild lands. On the west is the 268-acre Clark Reserve while to the north is the vast White Mountain National Forest. Contiguous lands like these protect valuable wildlife corridors and also provide more internal forest that protects nesting birds from the predation associated with edge habitat.

Bear, moose, fox, beaver, otter, and many nesting and migrating birds inhabit or pass through this reserve and so can the hiker, on trails marked with yellow wooden signs and The Nature Conservancy's yellow and green markers. One trail loops Heron Pond while another bears left along the way to go to Bickford Heights, elevation 1,080 feet. Another short spur leads down to Chocorua Lake. Pick up a map provided by the Chocorua Lake Conservation Association in a box about 0.5 mile in from the trailhead.

As in any wildlife area, the visitor is more apt to see traces of animals than the animals themselves. Look for a beaver lodge that is attached to one wall of Heron Pond and the chewed tree stumps associated with beaver activity on the banks. There could be otter, mink, or raccoon tracks around the edge of the pond or at the lakeshore, and discrete piles of droppings in the woods indicate the presence of deer, moose, fox, fisher, or coyote. It may seem quiet here but over 160 species each of plants and animals have been recorded within this preserve.

Directions: From Chocorua Village, go 2 miles north on NH 16. Turn west on Chocorua Lake Road. Go a total of 1.3 miles, continuing to bear right on a dirt road. Go slightly beyond the Dead End sign to a small, yellow Bolles Reserve sign on left with pull-out parking.

Activities: Hiking, plant and wildlife study. Cross-country skiing in winter. Swimming or picnicking at Chocorua Lake entrance.

Facilities: Trails, trail map (available 0.5 mile into Heron Pond Trail), limited parking.

Dates: Open year-round.

Fees: None.

Closest town: Chocorua Village, 3.3 miles.

For more information: The Nature Conservancy, 2 ½ Beacon Street, Concord, NH 03301. Phone (603) 224-5853. Or Chocorua Lake Conservation Foundation, Chocorua, NH 03817.

TRAIL TO HERON POND

[Fig. 44(6)] This trail takes the visitor to the heart of this

PITCHER PLANT
(Sarracenia sp.)
This insect-eating plant grows in boggy soil and uses its leafstalks or "pitchers" to hold pools of water. Insects are attracted by the odor of decay inside, then are forced downward by a hairy lining to the water where they drown and are digested.

preserve where often there are no other visitors. The forested slopes around the pond are an excellent place for a contemplative picnic lunch.

Directions: From the Frank Bolles parking pull-out, follow the red blazes and green and yellow tags of The Nature Conservancy into the preserve and then, more tags and wooden signs to Heron Pond. Trail passes briefly over a wet spot, then quickly rises to drier, upland forest.

Trail: 2-mile loop around Heron Pond.

Elevation: 600 feet to 700 feet.

Degree of difficulty: Easy.

Surface and blaze: Forest floor. Blazes begin red, then turn to yellow wooden signs and yellow and green tags of The Nature Conservancy.

MADISON BOULDER GEOLOGICAL LANDMARK

[Fig. 44(5)] Like a steamship docked permanently in the woods, Madison Boulder lies immobile where it was dropped out of a melting glacier 14,000 years ago. Hard as it is to conceive, geologists have proven that this enormous chunk of Conway Granite was plucked by the ice sheet from its parent ridge about 2 miles north of here and carried south until the ice melted around it. At over 5,000 tons, Madison Boulder is the largest known glacial erratic in the region and has been designated a National Natural Landmark.

This ponderous behemoth of solid rock stands nearly four stories high and 83 feet long, but to a mile-high glacier, it was only a pebble to be carted along with the rest of the debris. The quiet woods surrounding the landmark make for a short, pleasant walk from the parking area. No matter how carefully you read about the boulder's dimensions, there is something about the rock's sheer mass, in combination with the dim, silent woods, that cannot fail to impress.

Directions: From Conway, go south on NH 16 to the junction of NH 113. Turn south on NH 113 for 2.4 miles to a brown Geological Landmark sign on the right. Turn west off NH 113 and follow the signs to the parking area. The boulder is 100 yards into woods. Last 0.5 mile of road not plowed in winter.

Activities: Boulder viewing.

Facilities: None.

Dates: Open year-round.

Fees: None.

Closest town: Madison, 2 miles.

For more information: New Hampshire Department of Economic and Resource Development, 172 Pembroke Road, Concord, NH 03302. Phone (603) 271-3456.

HOYT WILDLIFE SANCTUARY

[Fig. 46(1)] Purity Lake is the southernmost of a long string of lakes that occupy this rural valley winding its way between Eaton Center and East Madison. On the southeastern shore of this lake lie 135 acres of unique wildlife sanctuary named for the Hoyt family who once owned much of the valley's land. This New Hampshire Audubon Sanctuary is unique for its variety of habitats, its glacial features, its country feel, and its two centuries of human history.

The valley's complex history began thousands of years ago when the glacier ground through here, then melted back, depositing massive amounts of sand and gravel and dropping an icy chunk here and there to later become a kettle hole. Later, *Castor canadensis,* that master of landscape design also known as the beaver, moved in to dam the streams into lakes and cut some of the forest down for food and building materials. Lastly, humans added a veneer of mills and fields and farmsteads to the valley. Lumber and grist mills thrived here as humans built dams over old beaver dam sites, but farmers did not fare so well in the gravelly soil. Those who tried to scratch a living in this way moved on 100 years ago, leaving their stone cellar foundations behind in the forest.

The area gave over to a lake resort and two children's summer camps, where nature education became a guiding principle. Continuing this theme, in 1989, Ellen Hoyt Gillard donated these acres to New Hampshire Audubon, to manage as a wildlife sanctuary.

Shortly after entering this reserve, obvious differences begin to emerge between the vegetation in the wet, acidic bog and that atop the dry, gravelly esker where the path is. Sphagnum mosses and various heath plants occupy the wetland below, while bracken fern and white pine thrive on the dry, gravelly ridge. Even on the esker itself, there are differences between the trees and plants growing on the north and south sides. Hemlock hug the cooler, wetter north sides of the esker, while oak and birch grow on the southern side. More subtle still are the variations in plant and animal species between various kinds of wetlands—in this case, a bog and a heath.

Two well-marked hiking trails provide access to the sanctuary's natural features and human artifacts. One trail runs along the top of an esker and looks down into No Bottom Pond, a kettle-hole bog that is slowly filling in with a thick mat of sphagnum moss—as bogs do, over time. Bogs are special places holding a whole array of special plants, and they often form in glacial kettle holes.

The sanctuary's second trail, the Heath View Trail, takes off from the Esker Trail and leads to a different sort of wetland, this one a heath. Though somewhat acidic and therefore home to many of the same species as the bog, there are just enough nutrients here—supplied by the heath's connection to Purity Lake—for small shrubs and delicate wild orchids to spring from the mats of floating moss around the edges. Frogs and small invertebrates, too, can survive here, as well as the birds and mammals that feed on them. The bog in the center of the Esker Trail loop, on the other hand, is an energy-poor place with no nutrient input except rain, insects, and decaying vegetation.

Along the Heath Trail are a few artifacts of the area's human history. Two or three cellar holes and an old graveyard offer mute testimony to the Durgin family who, for a few decades, pitted their farming efforts against this sandy land that wants to be forest.

Directions: From NH 25 in Effingham Falls, go north on NH 153 for 5.3 miles to the sanctuary at the southeastern corner of Purity Lake. A New Hampshire Audubon sign and pull-off parking are on the right. Informative trail guides are available in a box at the trailhead.

Activities: Hiking, cross-country skiing, plant study.

Facilities: Trails, trail guides, limited parking.

Dates: Open year-round.

Fees: None.

Closest town: Eaton Center, 3 miles.

For more information: Audubon Society of New Hampshire, 3 Silk Farm Road, Concord, NH 03301. Phone (603) 224-9909.

ESKER TRAIL

[Fig. 46(2)] This 45-minute walk travels in a loop atop of one of the valley's many eskers and looks down upon the kettle-hole bog below. It is forested with young pine, hemlock, and hardwoods and connects with the second trail system that leads down to the heath and Purity Lake.

Trail: 0.75-mile loop atop an esker and around a kettle-hole bog.

Elevation: 500 feet to 550 feet.

Degree of difficulty: Easy.

Surface and blaze: Forest floor. Yellow blazes.

LITTLE BROOK TRAIL TO HEATH BROOK TRAIL

[Fig. 46(3)] The Little Brook Trail takes off from the northeastern corner of the Esker Trail, connects to the Heath Brook Trail, and offers, roughly, a 1.5-hour loop through forest and heath lands and alongside Purity Lake. There are opportunities for wildlife and plant viewing and a look at the remnants of human history in the sanctuary.

Trail: 2-mile loop walk through bog, heath, and lake habitat.

Elevation: 500 feet to 550 feet.

Degree of difficulty: Easy.

Surface and blaze: Forest and open heath lands. Can be wet at times. Blazes are yellow, then red, then yellow. See trail map at entrance.

OSSIPEE PINE BARRENS AND WEST BRANCH PINE BARRENS PRESERVE

[Fig. 46(8)] Pine barrens are a unique and diminishing plant and animal community made up of species with a healthy measure of fire resistance. In fact, the major plants of this ecosystem actually depend upon periodic fires as a necessary tool to weed out their competitors. Historically, nature provided the fires needed to maintain this habitat, but in the last century, human fire suppression has allowed other trees to edge into and take over the pine barrens.

Karner Blue Butterfly

Lycaeides melissa samuelis, the Karner blue, is a tiny slip of a butterfly that exists in only one place: Concord, New Hampshire. Of the once-extensive pine barrens that used to drape the Merrimack Valley, only a small remnant hangs on atop an ancient, glacial delta now known as Concord Heights.

These delicate blue wings have fluttered there for thousands of years but they are now painted into a tight corner, so to speak. The Karner blue's caterpillars will only feed on wild lupine, which lives only on dry, sandy soil, which is kept open only by periodic fires—conditions that exist only in a shrinking number of pine barrens.

A valiant fight is being fought to save the butterfly from extinction by The Nature Conservancy, U.S. Fish and Wildlife Service, and the New Hampshire Fish and Game Department. Sadly, it is an uphill struggle that this beautiful creature may not win.

The dominant plants of the pine barrens are pitch pine, scrub oak, and early low blueberry. The pitch pine (*Pinus rigida*) has a thick bark which serves as insulation while the scrub oak (*Quercus ilicifolia*) and the blueberry (*Vaccinium augustifolium*) are both able to sprout new growth from their roots after their crowns have burned. Many of the rare insects of the pine barrens spend much of their lives underground, away from potential flames, and the birds can fly off and return when the brief conflagration is over. Though pine barrens appear short in stature and a little dry and scraggly around the edges, several rare butterflies and songbirds find them a perfect habitat and depend on these special woodlands to survive.

Where once the 7,000-acre Ossipee Pine Barrens stretched across the east-central part of the state, now only 3,000 acres remain intact. In addition to fire suppression, humans have further diminished this habitat by mining the aggregates—the sand and gravel—that lie under the pine barrens. Development has also hit this habitat hard because these are flat, dry, and workable lands—a scarce commodity in a rock-bound state like New Hampshire. In the Merrimack Valley farther west, most of the pine barrens atop the eskers, and dunes, and deltas left by the glacier have been excavated, built upon, or paved over. The endangered Karner blue butterfly exists only within a tiny fragment of pine barrens that remain in Concord.

The Nature Conservancy, recognizing the value of these lands, has begun a program of protection which so far has set aside a total of 573 acres in the West Branch Pine Barrens Preserve. The preserve is in two sections at the present, one of which fronts on Ossipee Lake. The plan is to eventually acquire the land between them and unite the two.

A 1-mile loop trail traverses the northern section and affords the visitor a look at this interesting ecosystem. Note that pitch pines have three needles per bunch, as opposed to two for red pine and five for white pine, and that they often sprout needles right out of their twisted trunks. Unlike other pines, pitch pines tend to hold on tightly to their cones for years. In times past, the high resin content in pitch pines made the knots in this wood useful as the heads of torches.

The understory of small oaks found in pine barrens wear leathery leaves that often hang on all winter. Wherever there is an opening among the trees, sweet fern (*Comptonia peregrina*)—not really a fern at all, but a shrub that thrives in dry, sandy soil—adds a fresh tang to the air. Low blueberry (*Vaccinium augustifolium*) covers the ground with its delicate green leaves and twigs. In the spring and early summer, its bell-shaped, pink-tinged flowers portend the luscious fruit to come in August, and in the winter, blueberry's green twigs are a clue to its identification.

Directions: From NH 16 in West Ossipee, go 2 miles north on NH 41 to a small sign for The Nature Conservancy on the right. The loop trail begins at the sign, is not blazed, but is cleared and fairly obvious.

Activities: Hiking, plant study.

Facilities: Trail.

Dates: Open year-round.

Fees: None.

Closest town: West Ossipee, 2 miles.

For more information: New Hampshire Chapter of The Nature Conservancy, 2 1/2 Beacon Street, Concord, NH 03301. Phone (603) 224-5853.

WEST BRANCH PINE BARRENS TRAIL

[Fig. 46(9)] **Trail:** 1-mile loop through pine barrens.

Elevation: No elevation change.

Degree of difficulty: Easy.

Surface and blaze: Flat, dry forest floor. No blazes.

WHITE LAKE STATE PARK

[Fig. 46] Pitch pines, the kind found in pine barrens, seldom grow over 50 feet tall, and consequently, they don't get very big in diameter. That is why the 72-acre stand of unusually large pitch pines in White Lake State Park is unique, and why the National Park Service has declared this stand a National Natural Landmark. These old trees stand uncharacteristically straight, and some have diameters of over 2 feet.

These stately old pines are only one of the attractive features of this park. The thing that jumps up and hits the visitor broadside is the stunning view across the lake. From left to right on the northwestern horizon stand Mounts Whiteface, Passaconaway, Paugus, and Chocorua, all in the White Mountain National Forest. The beach and picnic area are on the southeastern side of the lake so visitors who are swimming or picnicking have this backdrop to gaze upon all day.

Even without the vista, White Lake would be attractive in its own right. Breezes coming down off the mountains ripple its blue-gray, 123-acre surface and an uncluttered shoreline stretches around its perimeter. White Lake is another example of a kettle hole, but in this case, the kettle is large enough, and has enough freshwater inflow, that it is occupied by a lake instead of a bog. It is a pleasant lake for swimming and boating but fishing, reportedly, is not so great. Though some fish are stocked, this kettle hole lake does not receive enough nutrients to sustain many fish.

Two other smaller kettle holes to the west are filled with bogs and all the special plant species associated with that habitat. They are contained within the 35-acre Tamworth Black Spruce Ponds Preserve that abuts the state park. A flat loop trail circles the lake with side trails through this preserve and through the National Natural Landmark stand of pitch pines. Information about these trails is available from the entrance booth during the summer camping season.

White Lake State Park also offers 200 wooded camping sites with restrooms, showers, and a camp store in season. The sites are large and some have lake views. Firewood and canoe rentals are available and there is a boat launch at the southwestern corner of the lake. This is a pleasant, spacious park with lots to do and look at, and room to spread out and relax.

Directions: From NH 25 in Ossipee, go 1 mile north on NH 16 to state park sign on left.

Activities: Camping, swimming, boating, picnicking, hiking.

Facilities: Campsites, restrooms, showers, firewood, boat launch, canoe rentals, picnic tables, all in season. Trails, year-round.

Dates: Seasonal facilities available mid-May to mid-Oct. Trails open year-round.

Fees: There is a charge for camping and day use in season.

Closest town: West Ossipee, 1 mile.

For more information: White Lake State Park, Box 41, West Ossipee, NH 03890. Phone (603) 323-7350.

WHITE LAKE AND TAMWORTH BLACK SPRUCE PONDS PRESERVE TRAILS

[Fig. 46(7)] A 2-mile loop trail circles White Lake. It connects on its northwest corner to another 1-mile loop that goes through the Pitch Pine National Natural Landmark and the Tamworth Black Spruce Ponds Preserve.

Trail: 3-mile loop, total.

Elevation: No elevation gain.

Degree of difficulty: Moderate.

Surface and blaze: Woods roads and broad paths. No blazes.

THOMPSON WILDLIFE SANCTUARY

[Fig. 46(5)] Perhaps the only drawback about a beautifully forested and mountainous place like New Hampshire is that, without climbing a mountain or sailing out to sea, you can rarely look out and see for many miles. But there are a few spots where this is possible, such as New Hampshire Audubon's Alice Bemis Thompson Wildlife Sanctuary, located in the center of the Bearcamp Valley in Sandwich.

The trail into this protected area takes the visitor over a footbridge in the middle of an open wetland where a 360-degree view takes in the Sandwich Mountain Range to the northwest and the Ossipee ring dike to the southeast. Between them, thanks to the beavers who dammed up Atwood Brook, are acres of open meadow and beaver wetland—a prime spot for birds and other wildlife. This is a good place to stop awhile and look for great blue herons, kingfishers, wood ducks, and dozens of other wetland species.

The trail continues across the wetland and into an upland hardwood forest. Signs of deer, moose, or fox often turn up here, and in the early summer, listen for the songs of nesting songbirds who call this reserve their home for the season.

Marking the edges of the sanctuary's central pond—or meadow, depending upon the season and the current whereabouts of the beavers—are some of New Hampshire's more interesting trees. The pointed spires of tamaracks, also known as larch trees, punctuate the perimeter of the wet area. In the fall, their short green needles turn a golden brown color and fall off, leaving behind what looks like a dying tree. This, however, is not the case at all. This evergreen look-alike drops its needles every year, just like its deciduous cousins, the oak and the maple. Before they fall, the golden needles create a feathery, golden spire amid the gorgeous melange of autumn color. A pleasant surprise in the spring is to note the new and brilliantly green needles tufted all over the tamarack's bare branches.

This place offers a lot of different habitats to attract birds and animals, and the practice of patience can pay off here with a sighting or a "sounding" of something wild. Atwood Brook, where otters play and beavers work, runs underneath the footbridge in the open center of the sanctuary. Along its edges lurk shy ducks and kingfishers and even the occasional bittern, and from the tall grasses sometimes comes the sweet, clear song of a water thrush or the harsh croak of a rail.

Wildlife is always here, even if we don't meet it face to face. Often, it is just as thrilling to find the traces. Look for hoof or paw prints in the mud along the edges where a moose or a deer or a fox has come for a drink. In the upland woods, check out the hemlock saplings for the characteristic three-toothed marks of a hungry deer eating bark in the winter. Black bear, too, have been known to frequent the area.

Directions: From South Tamworth, go west on NH 25 for 1.2 miles. Turn north on NH 113 for 2.9 miles to the New Hampshire Audubon sign and a small parking place on the left.

Activities: Hiking, bird- and other wildlife-watching.

Facilities: Trail, which is handicap accessible for first 350 yards. Trail maps available.

Dates: Open year-round.

Fees: None.

Closest town: North Sandwich, 1 mile.

For more information: Audubon Society of New Hampshire, 3 Silk Farm Road, Concord, NH 03301. Phone (603) 224-9909.

THOMPSON WILDLIFE SANCTUARY TRAIL

[Fig. 46(6)] **Trail:** 1.25-mile loop across the wetland and into the forest.

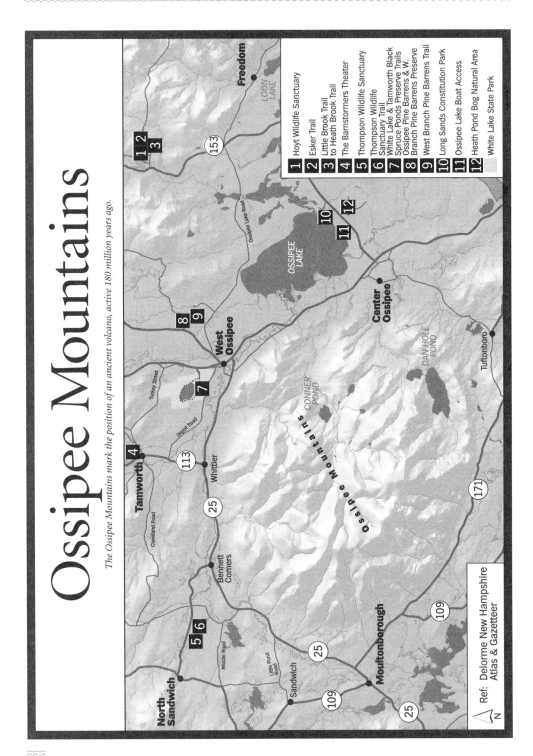

Ossipee Mountains

The Ossipee Mountains mark the position of an ancient volcano, active 180 million years ago.

1	Hoyt Wildlife Sanctuary
2	Esker Trail
3	Little Brook Trail to Heath Brook Trail
4	The Barnstormers Theater
5	Thompson Wildlife Sanctuary
6	Thompson Wildlife Sanctuary Trail
7	White Lake & Tamworth Black
8	Spruce Ponds Preserve Trails
9	Ossipee Pine Barrens & W. Branch Pine Barrens Preserve
10	West Branch Pine Barrens Trail
11	Long Sands Constitution Park
12	Ossipee Lake Boat Access
	Heath Pond Bog Natural Area
	White Lake State Park

Ref: Delorme New Hampshire
Atlas & Gazetteer

Elevation: 550 feet to 600 feet.

Degree of difficulty: Easy.

Surface and blaze: Woods road, forest floor, some boardwalk. Red and yellow blazes.

THE BARNSTORMERS THEATER

[Fig. 46(4)] Tiny Tamworth, New Hampshire, is home to the oldest summer theater in America. Formed in 1931, the Barnstormers Theater is still very much alive and in full operation. In fact, it has recently undergone a major renovation in order to become a year-round cultural center for the community.

In 1931, Francis Grover Cleveland, youngest son of President Grover Cleveland, together with his wife, Alice, and their friend, Edward Goodnow, conceived the idea of bringing live theater to this region, where people from Boston and New York spent their summers. For the next 64 years, until his death in 1995, Francis was the glue that held the operation together. He was an accomplished actor as well as a director, a producer, a painter, and a set builder. He even drove the old truck in which the cast and all their sets and costumes toured the region, "barnstorming" communities as far as 40 miles away with traveling summer entertainment.

The founders are gone now, but not their inspiration. The theater has, for many years, been permanently located on Main Street in Tamworth, a local landmark with an official historical marker, and usually one or two stray cats occupying the front porch. It offers a full summer season of plays that vary from classics, like *Death of a Salesman*, to new plays by aspiring playwrights. This is professional theater performed by gifted actors from all over the country. Throughout July and August, there are evening performances, and if you wish, the theater will arrange dinner for you at a nearby restaurant. An evening of live theater in a small country town provides yet another perspective on life in New Hampshire.

Directions: From NH 16 in Chocorua Village, go 3 miles west on NH 113 to intersection with NH 113 A. Go straight through this intersection on Main Street for 0.2 mile to the large, white Barnstormers building on the right.

Activities: Live theater, dinner if arranged.

Facilities: Theater, restaurant nearby.

Dates: June 30 to Aug. 31.

Fees: There is a charge for admittance.

Closest town: Theater is in Tamworth.

For more information: The Barnstormers, Box 434, Tamworth, NH 03886. Phone (603) 323-8500.

THE OSSIPEE MOUNTAINS

[Fig. 46] The Ossipee Mountains make an almost perfect topographic circle. This group of peaks, of which Mount Shaw, at 2,990 feet, is the highest, are the eroded remnants of a *ring dike*. They mark the position of an ancient volcano, active 180 million years ago. During Jurassic times, the Atlantic Ocean was opening up, and northeastern North American was rifting apart much as East Africa is today. Volcanoes, every bit as imposing as today's Mount Kilimanjaro, were then spewing lava and ash out over what is now the placid Lakes Region.

The very best view of this unusual group of mountains would be from high up in a satellite. Failing that, a look at a topographical map shows the distinctive circular aspect of this 9-mile-wide massive. On the map, this clump of abruptly rising mountains is outlined by NH highways 16, 25, and 171 but there are virtually no roads that go through them and also no regularly maintained hiking trails.

The best overall look, from the ground, at the Ossipee ring dike is gained by climbing Belknap Mountain, one of a similar, ring dike group of mountains on the other side of Lake Winnipesaukee. The Ossipees do bear mentioning here, however, because when you are in the Lakes Region, they are a constant blue and brooding presence on the horizon, reflected in lakes, filling valley views, peeking up over other hills, and dominating the northern shoreline of Lake Winnipesaukee.

For more information: See *The Geology of the Ossipee Lake Quadrangle* by James Robert Wilson.

OSSIPEE LAKE

[Fig. 46] On the eastern side of the Ossipee Mountains, a lake of the same name fills a 3,000-acre, glacial basin with reflections of blue skies and the surrounding hills. This lake is quieter than Winnipesaukee, its larger cousin to the southeast, but has little in the way of public access. However, Long Sands Conservation Park does provides some short hiking trails along the south end of the lake and there is boat access to the lake by launching at the Pine River boat launch.

LONG SANDS CONSTITUTION PARK

[Fig. 46(10)] This is a nice little hiking park with ample parking and five well-marked, easy trails suitable for families and the handicapped. One is a boardwalk through a wet area to views of the lake. Others traverse small examples of eskers and drumlins, and from one high point, you look out over an occupied beaver pond and wetland heath. Mature pitch pine forest covers the whole area, consistent with the larger, overall Ossipee Pine Barrens, and in low spots are such wetland indicator plants as rhodora and sphagnum moss.

Directions: From Center Ossipee, travel 2.8 miles east on NH 25 to Long Sands Road. Turn north and go 0.2 mile. Bear right on Conservation Trail to parking and a posted map of trails.

Activities: Hiking, plant study.

Facilities: Trails.

Dates: Open year-round.

Fees: None.

Closest town: Center Ossipee, 3 miles.

For more information: Ossipee Lake Beach Committee, Ossipee, NH or New Hampshire Division of Forests and Lands, 172 Pembroke Road, Concord, NH 03302. Phone (603) 271-3456.

OSSIPEE LAKE BOAT ACCESS

[Fig. 46(11)] This boat launch connects to Ossipee Lake via the Pine River, involving about 0.5 mile of paddling or slow motoring along the Pine River to the south end of the lake. There are six floating docks for day use and plenty of parking.

Directions: From NH 16 in Center Ossipee, turn east on NH 25. Go 0.6 mile to the launch and parking area on the right.

Activities: Boat launch and parking.

Facilities: Concrete launch ramp and floating wooden docks.

Dates: Boating season.

Fees: None.

Closest town: Center Ossipee, 0.6 mile.

For more information: New Hampshire Parks and Recreation Department, Box 856, Concord, NH 03302. Phone (603) 271-3556.

HEATH POND BOG NATURAL AREA

[Fig. 46(12)] Bogs exist in all corners of the boreal world. Much of Canada, Russia, and Scandinavia is covered with bogs in various stages of succession, from open ponds to bouncy tundra. Heath Pond Bog is such a striking example of this distinctive kind of community that it has been designated a National Natural Landmark.

Bogs were never much use to the farmer so those that were not filled in were pretty much left alone. A few examples like Heath Pond Bog have remained long enough for people to begin to appreciate their unique character. Imagine moss growing so thick, for so long, that it extends out over an open pond and actually supports trees and shrubs and even the odd hiker that ventures out onto its fringe. When you step out onto the bog, what you thought was solid ground under your feet begins to bounce and the trees and bushes all around begin to tremble.

In the center of this tremulous circle of vegetation lies an inky, black pond. Who knows how many feet of decomposing plants have settled onto its bottom, where they are slowly transforming into peat, a partially oxidized kind of organic matter we work into our gardens and historically have even used for fuel.

Bog plants are a world unto themselves—species that have, over time, evolved ways to cope with the acidic environment that builds up in a bog because of its lack of nutrient-bearing fresh water. These are plants such as tamarack, black spruce, rhodora, skunk cabbage, and the basic carpet under them all, sphagnum moss. This moss is soft and spongy and so absorbent that native peoples dried it out and used it for diaper material, among other things.

Cotton grass (*Eriphorium* spp.) is an almost mystical plant in the low light of

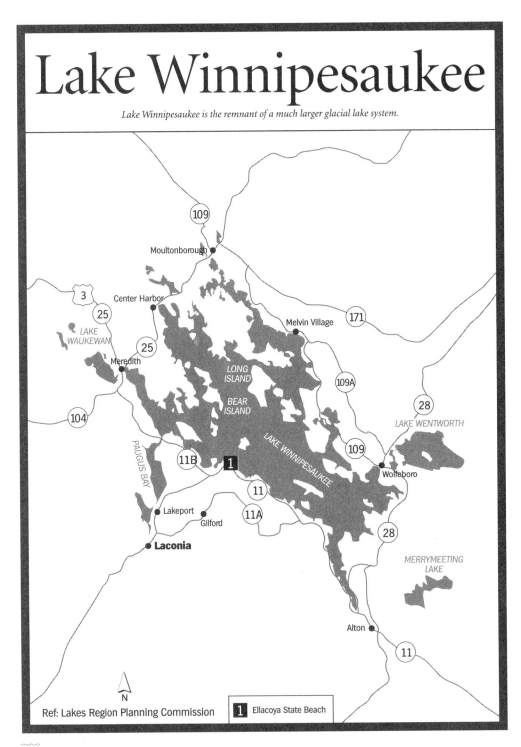

Lake Winnipesaukee

Lake Winnipesaukee is the remnant of a much larger glacial lake system.

109

Moultonborough

3

25

Center Harbor

171

Melvin Village

LAKE WAUKEWAN

25

Meredith

LONG ISLAND

109A

BEAR ISLAND

28

LAKE WENTWORTH

104

PAUGUS BAY

LAKE WINNIPESAUKEE

109

11B

1

Wolfeboro

11

Lakeport

11A

Gilford

Laconia

28

MERRYMEETING LAKE

Alton

11

N

Ref: Lakes Region Planning Commission

1 Ellacoya State Beach

evening, when you can no longer see its stems. It appears as a layer of disembodied white tufts suspended 18 inches over the wet and spongy surface. One tier higher in this picture is the lovely rhodora (*Rhododendron canadense*), which in the spring sprays its outrageous lavender blooms over the tips of spindly branches well before they open their leaves.

These plants somehow manage to eke out a living atop the thick floating mat of vegetation, most obtaining their meager nutrients from the decomposition beneath their feet. But some, like the sundew and pitcher plant, have evolved more ominous ways of filling their nutritional needs—they actually prey on insects.

The quiet and somewhat carnivorous world of the bog has always fared best without the interference of humans, but if we tread carefully around the edges, we can enjoy its peculiar beauty without upsetting the magic. Take a few minutes to walk out to the edge of this very different world.

Directions: From NH 16 in Center Ossipee, go east on NH 25 for 1.6 miles. There is no sign, but there is pull-off parking and a small boulder with a bronze plaque marking the beginning of a short path.

Activities: Walking and plant study.

Facilities: Path.

Dates: Open all year but frozen in winter.

Fees: None.

Closest town: Center Ossipee, 1.6 miles.

For more information: New Hampshire Division of Forests and Lands, 172 Pembroke Road, Concord, NH 03302. Phone (603) 271-3456.

Squam Lake-Lake Winnipesaukee Region

This east-central area of New Hampshire is almost more water than land. Lake Winnipesaukee alone covers nearly 45,000 acres, its sprawling tentacles of water invading the land in so many places that it boasts 283 miles of shoreline.

Long bays and sheltered coves give this lake a thousand faces and dozens of different ways to be enjoyed.

▨ LAKE WINNIPESAUKEE

[Fig. 47] Winnipesaukee's Indian name means "Smile of the Great Spirit." Legend has it that the lake got her name from Wonaton, a great chief who found himself and his canoe out on the lake under dark and threatening skies. He was so taken by the way the sun suddenly came slanting in under the storm clouds and glinted off her shimmering surface that he saw it as a great spiritual omen and gave the lake this beguiling name. She remains a lake that smiles upon many thousands of vacationers as well as the several small towns that gather around her shores.

Eastern Brook Trout

Eastern Brook trout (*Salvelinus fontinalis*) is the most widely distributed species of trout found in the White Mountain National Forest waters. Brook trout vary in size, depending on the availability of food and the size of the body of water in which they live. Smaller fish eat insects, both larval and adult, and larger ones eat mostly other fish. These trout have red spots ringed in blue on their sides, a squared tail, and white margins on their lower fins. They require pure, cold water in which to live, and are a favorite with fishermen because of their good taste and their spunky behavior when hooked.

Sprinkled around Lake Winnipesaukee are hundreds of coves and inlets and islands. Depending on who is counting, the islands number somewhere between 274 to 360 in all, and the hundreds of miles of shoreline this creates makes Winnipesaukee a hub for swimming, fishing, boating, entertainment, and dozens of vacation resorts.

For more information: Regarding Lake Winnipesaukee vacations or lodging, contact the New Hampshire Office of Travel and Tourism Development, Box 1856, Concord, NH 03302. Phone (603) 271-2343. Online: www.visitnh.gov.

SWIMMING AND BOATING AT LAKE WINNIPESAUKEE

On this big and busy lake, many resorts have their own beach and boating access. Most towns have a beach, a dock, and a boat access for their residents, and some, like Meredith and Weirs Beach, have beach and boating access for the public as well.

ELLACOYA STATE BEACH

[Fig. 47(1)] Ellacoya State Beach in Gilford is part of the state park system and is open to everyone. It offers swimming, picnicking, and RV camping, along with a beautiful view of the Ossipee Mountains across the lake.

A 600-foot sandy beach and a grand mountain view draw visitors to this popular beach on Lake Winnipesaukee, New Hampshire's largest lake.

Directions: From the junction of NH 11 and NH 28 in Alton, go north on NH 11 for 11 miles. Look for the Ellacoya State Beach sign and parking on the right.

Activities: Swimming, picnicking, RV camping.

Facilities: Beach, bathhouse, lifeguard in season. Campground with hookups. Picnic grounds.

Dates: Mid-June to Labor Day.

Fees: There is a charge for admission.

Closest town: West Alton, 3 miles.

For more information: New Hampshire Division of Parks and Recreation, 172 Pembroke Road, Concord, NH 03302. For

COMMON LOON
(Gavia immer)

Kettle Holes and Bogs

Many of New England's bogs exist in kettle holes. A kettle hole is a bowl-like depression created when a chunk of glacier broke off and was left behind and subsequently covered over with outwash sediment. The block remained frozen long enough to mold the earth around it into solid banks, and when the ice finally did melt, the sediment on top slumped, creating a round hole. If the hole was deep enough to extend below the water table, it became a pond.

Not every kettle hole pond became a bog. If streams developed, running into and out of the pond, then it evolved into a viable body of fresh water. But, if the pond remained without a source of fresh water other than precipitation, the resulting low-nutrient, high acid environment set the stage for this special kind of wetland called a bog.

Bogs often develop over granitic soils or rocks. Because these contain little lime or phosphorous—alkaline nutrients needed by many plants—this limits the kinds of plants that will grow here. A few plants, such as sphagnum moss, sedge, spruce, tamarack, and certain members of the heath family, can tolerate these acidic, low-nutrient conditions. They manage to eke out a living here, obtaining what they need from the decomposing mat beneath their feet. Other species, like carnivorous plants, have evolved more creative ways to find sustenance. They trap and digest insects.

In a bog's low-oxygen environment, decomposition becomes anaerobic, acidic, and excruciatingly slow. Great depths of partially decomposed vegetation called peat accumulate on the bottom of the pond. Thus bogs evolve, eventually filling in completely. Heath Pond Bog is an example of one stage of this succession, with a floating mat of vegetation encircling the inky black pond at its heart.

information, phone (603) 271-3556. For reservations, phone (603) 271 3628.

CRUISING LAKE WINNIPESAUKEE

Several tour boats cruise Winnipesaukee's sparkling waters. The most famous is the *Mount Washington*, a 230-foot-long vessel that sails between four ports on the lake. This vessel offers narrated day cruises, dinner-dance cruises, and live entertainment. Shorter, more casual rides can be had on the *Judge Sewall* out of Wolfeboro Bay, or if you want real basic, show up at the Weirs Beach harbor Monday through Saturday and catch a ride on the mailboat. The *Sophie C.* is the only official U.S. Post Office afloat.

For more information:

Regarding both the mailboat and the *Mount Washington*: Mount Washington Cruises, Lakeside Avenue, Weirs Beach, NH 03247. Phone (603) 366-BOAT. Regarding the *Judge Sewall*: *Judge Sewall*, c/o The Wolfeboro Inn, 44 North Main Street, Wolfeboro, NH 03894. Phone (603) 569-3016.

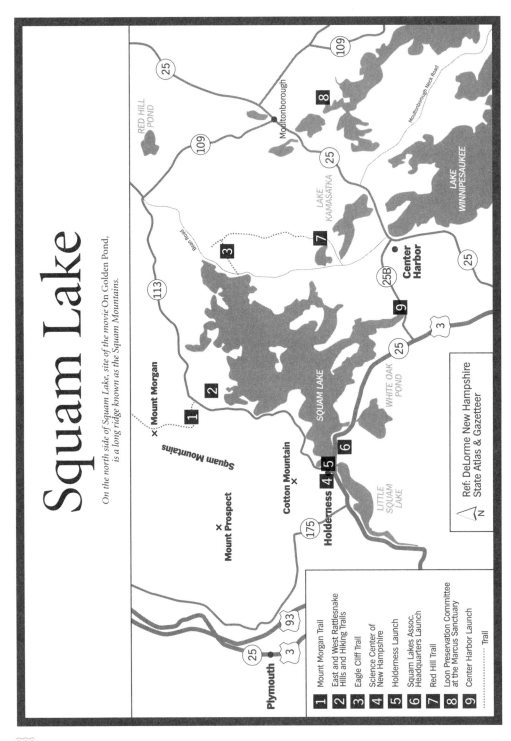

Squam Lake

On the north side of Squam Lake, site of the movie On Golden Pond, is a long ridge known as the Squam Mountains.

Ref: DeLorme New Hampshire State Atlas & Gazetteer

1 Mount Morgan Trail
2 East and West Rattlesnake Hills and Hiking Trails
3 Eagle Cliff Trail
4 Science Center of New Hampshire
5 Holderness Launch
6 Squam Lakes Assoc. Headquarters Launch
7 Red Hill Trail
8 Loon Preservation Committee at the Marcus Sanctuary
9 Center Harbor Launch
·········· Trail

▒ SQUAM LAKE

[Fig. 48] Squam Lake spreads out like a sparkling blue china plate to the northwest of its bigger and busier sister, Lake Winnipesaukee. Crystal clear water laps at its clean, sandy shores just as it has since the glacier carved out this basin thousands of years ago. An ancient Native-American language called it *Kees-ee-nunk-nip-ee,* or "Goose-Lake-in-the-Highlands." A few centuries later, Hollywood called it Golden Pond.

It is not surprising that this lake was chosen as the backdrop for that well-known movie; one look at its wooded and largely undeveloped shoreline, lined with hills and mountains so close that in places you can touch their walls, puts it in a whole different league from other, more commercialized lakes.

An enchanting way to get an overview of the lake, and also learn some its lore, is to take the Golden Pond Tour out of Holderness. The captain of a covered pontoon boat provides anecdotes about subjects as disparate as the making of the movie, *On Golden Pond,* and the status of the local nesting loons. For a stricter focus on natural history, try the specialized cruises offered by the Science Center of New Hampshire in Holderness.

For more information: Squam Lake Tours on Golden Pond, Box 185, Route 3, Holderness, NH. Phone (603) 968-7577. Science Center of New Hampshire, Box 173, Route 113, Holderness, NH 03245. Phone (603) 968-7194.

SQUAM LAKES ASSOCIATION

Both the look and the feel of Squam Lake are largely due to 95 years of work by the Squam Lakes Association (SLA). For nearly a century, SLA's broad vision has promoted low impact, yet staunchly public, use of Squam and several other nearby lakes. The organization helps to knit together the fabric of this special area by extending its mission to the care and protection of much of the mountainous terrain that surrounds the lake

SLA maintains 40 miles of hiking trails in the nearby mountains, monitors water quality and traffic on the lakes, and serves as a regional advocate for responsible land use. In July and August, SLA runs a children's day camp, focusing on outdoor education, in the belief that teaching the next generation respect for nature will continue its mission. SLA also participates in scientific studies and public education about such exotic threats to water quality as Eurasian milfoil and the zebra mussel. So far, Squam Lake remains free of both.

SLA owns two small islands on the lake and manages several group camping areas, which are available by reservation. It rents canoes, kayaks, and sailing boats, teaches water safety, and encourages low-impact enjoyment of the water. Its headquarters in Holderness is a warm and welcoming place with plenty of free information, lake and hiking maps, and a free boat launch into peaceful Piper's Cove, for boats under 25 horsepower. The SLA keeps vigilant watch on any abuse of Squam and surrounding lakes and an equally vigilant eye on any attempt to exclude it from public enjoyment.

Directions: Squam Lakes Association Headquarters is on US 3 and NH 25, 1.6 miles east of NH 113 in Holderness.

Activities: Boat launching, parking, kayak, canoe, and sailboat rentals (weekends only during day camp sessions), programs, visitor center, and store.

Facilities: Boat launch, parking, restrooms, canoes, staff, lake information, and hiking maps.

Dates: June to Labor Day.

Fees: None.

Closest town: Holderness, 1.6 miles.

For more information: Squam Lakes Association, Box 204, Holderness, NH 03245. Phone (603) 968-7336.

SMALL BOAT ACCESSES TO SQUAM LAKE

SLA provides access to small boats at three places on Squam Lake. It asks that your boat be clean of milfoil or mussels and that you pack out your trash.

THE SLA HEADQUARTERS LAUNCH

[Fig. 48(6)] This launch is for nonmotorized boats or those with less than 25 horsepower.

Directions: From NH 113 in Holderness, go 1.6 miles east on US 3 and NH 25. Turn left into Piper's Cove launch area next to the SLA Headquarters building.

THE HOLDERNESS LAUNCH

[Fig. 48(5)] This launch is for all watercraft except Jet Skis.

Directions: At junction of US 3 and NH 25 with NH 113 in Holderness, turn north for 50 yards to boat launch on right. No overnight parking here.

THE CENTER HARBOR LAUNCH

[Fig. 48(9)] This launch is for hand-carried boats only.

Directions: Take NH 25B about 1 mile west from Center Harbor until you see the Dog Cove inlet of Squam Lake on the right. Park along the highway and carry your boat into this SLA-owned property.

SWIMMING AT SQUAM LAKE

Although there is no state beach at Squam Lake, there are several swimming areas either owned or managed by the Squam Lakes Association. The most accessible is Chamberlain-Reynolds Forest in Center Harbor. This wooded peninsula juts out into the lake beside Dog Cove and has water on three sides. The beaches are in the north-western corner. Short, well-marked trails lead to other outlooks from this forest-covered peninsula.

Directions: From NH 113 in Holderness, go southeast on US 3 and NH 25 for 3.8 miles to College Road. Turn left for 0.5 mile to a parking area. To the left of the restroom is a 0.33-mile trail to beaches.

Activities: Swimming, hiking.

Facilities: Beach, restrooms, hiking trails around the rest of the forest.

Dates: June to Labor Day for swimming. Hiking, year-round.

Fees: None.

Closest town: Holderness, 4.3 miles.

For more information: Squam Lakes Association, Box 204, Holderness, NH 03245. Phone (603) 968-7336.

SQUAM LAKES ASSOCIATION HIKING TRAILS

Several small groups of mountains lie northwest of Squam Lake and just outside the White Mountain National Forest. Many of the trails that climb these scenic hills are maintained by the SLA and a map is available at the SLA Headquarters in Holderness. These are generally well maintained but their trailheads can be a little tricky to locate. The striking views from atop these heights, however, make locating the trailheads worth the modest effort. Many trails traverse private lands whose owners' forbearance is earned by hikers' courtesy.

For more information: Squam Lakes Association, Box 204, Holderness, NH 03245. Phone (603) 968-7336.

EAGLE CLIFF AND RED HILL TRAIL

[Fig. 48(3), Fig. 48(7)] The bare, brooding rocks of Eagle Cliff jutting out of the northwestern side of Red Hill are visible from Bean Road below. At 1,430 feet elevation, they offer a fine view out over Squam Lake and the Sandwich Mountains. The short but steep climb up from the road is well worth the effort for the look at the shimmering lake below and the rows of blue hills receding into the distance. After 0.6 mile, you can stop on the cliff to enjoy the view, or continue on this same trail for another 2.5 miles to the fire tower on top of Red Hill.

Directions: At the junction of NH 25 and NH 25B in Center Harbor, look for Bean Road and turn north. Go precisely 5.2 miles, then pull off the road on the lake side by a yellow sign reading "Traffic Entering." Walk back south for 200 yards to another sign reading "Traffic Entering and Turning 200 Feet." The entrance to the Eagle Cliff Trail is directly opposite this sign. You cannot see it from the road, but peak inside the greenery and there it is.

Trail: 0.6-mile trail (one-way) to Eagle Cliff.

Elevation: 500 feet to 1,430 feet.

Degree of difficulty: Strenuous.

Surface and blaze: Blazes are yellow. Surface is variable from forest floor, to old fields, to steep rock which can be slippery with ice in early spring. If the rocks are icy, turn back.

EAST AND WEST RATTLESNAKE HILLS AND HIKING TRAILS

[Fig. 48(2)] Close on the northwestern shore of Squam Lake, two small, knobby hills stand like sentinels, guarding the larger Squam Mountain Ridge behind them. The visitor who arrives on a weekday morning in May or June could have them all to him or herself. A tall and lovely mixed forest blankets these gentle slopes, and at the top of each hill, is a stunning overlook of the lake.

Rattlesnake Hills overlooking Squam Lake.

The lilting songs of both wood and hermit thrushes echo through the woods, competing with a dozen wood warblers. Atop West Rattlesnake Hill, the Armstrong Natural Area, named for the benefactors who donated the land to the University of New Hampshire, is home to wild columbine (*Aquilegia canadensis*) and smooth solomon's seal, (*Polygonatum biflorum*) and a surprising little stand of red pine. Open ledges of deep pink granite undulate around the twisted pines, creating great little places to tuck in and eat a sandwich while surveying the world below.

Signposts at the top of West Rattlesnake indicate several trails. To make a 2.2-mile loop over to East Rattlesnake and back down that hill to your car, follow the Ridge Trail to East Rattlesnake. This hill overlooks the lake as well, but gives a more northerly view that includes a look at Eagle Cliff on Red Hill across the lake.

Directions: From US 3 and NH 25 in Holderness, turn north on NH 113. Go 5.1 miles to Pinehurst Road and turn right. Go 0.9 mile, through a children's camp, bearing left at one fork along the way, and park on the edge of the road before the stone wall and the sign reading, "Pinehurst Private Road." Walk 100 yards farther on this road to the trailhead on the left. The loop tour of both hills follows the Pasture Trail to West Rattlesnake, the Ridge Trail to East Rattlesnake, and the East Rattlesnake Trail back down.

Trail: 2.2-mile loop over both Rattlesnake Hills.

Elevation: 800 feet to 1,250 feet.

Degree of difficulty: Moderate.

Surface and blaze: Forest floor. Yellow blazes are few, but trail is well tracked and signs appear at turns.

THE SQUAM MOUNTAINS AND MOUNT MORGAN TRAIL

[Fig. 48(1)] The Squam Range of mountains is a long ridge that curves around the north side of Squam Lake a little farther west than the Rattlesnake Hills. All of the mountains in this ridge are roughly 2,220 feet high, so they look out over the tops of the Rattlesnake Hills and Squam Lake and all of its myriad islands. From this height, you can also clearly discern the "fingers" of an unusual protrusion into the lake called Five Finger Point. Situated on this point is a remote nature preserve owned by the University of New Hampshire and managed by the Squam Lakes Association.

Mount Morgan's eastward-facing cliff lights up white in the morning sun, begging the hiker to come on up for a look. From its summit, Mount Morgan has a 180-degree view, well worth the moderately strenuous climb. The rocky outcrop at the top is 2.1 miles up and requires about three hours round-trip. Following an old woods road for half the distance, the route then turns sharply uphill on a steep and, in places, some-what eroded trail. The trail is rocky in spots and hiking boots are recommended.

Besides the breathtaking view at the top, other features along the way make this climb worth undertaking. The rock types undergo some interesting changes as you ascend. Near the base of the mountain, the rocks under your feet are mostly granitic, but as you get higher, the character and color of the rock changes to layered and finely textured metamorphics. Predictably, the soil changes as well because the gray or beige granites break down to light-colored, coarser soils, while the darker brown metamorphics erode to finer, darker soils.

Seeps of water emerge from the hillside in several places creating some muddy spots—great opportunities to search for moose and deer tracks. Boardwalks are thoughtfully placed for the hiker, but moose apparently prefer to walk in the mud.

Look for trees that show long, vertical splits in their bark. One of two things caused this injury. These trees either served as lightning rods or they were split by the expansion of their own inner frost. Either trauma would have made a deafening sound in the otherwise silent woods. It's not always possible to tell which process was responsible, but if the tree is a white pine, you can be fairly sure the cause was lightning. White pines do not develop frost cracks and they also stand up higher than most everything else in the forest, thus attracting and conducting more lightning.

Because of the dramatic ice storm of 1998, there are noticeable stands of broken beech trees. Beech are particularly prone to damage from severe winters; their smooth, gray branches seem to break off more easily from a load of ice. This species also falls victim to "beech snap," where the tree's trunk snaps in two, halfway be-tween the forest floor and the canopy. This generally follows a long progression of prior weakening by beech bark disease and carpenter ants.

Directions: From US 3 and NH 25 in Holderness, turn north on NH 113. Go 5.6 miles to a parking lot on the left. Mount Morgan Trail takes off from this lot.

Trail: 4.2-mile (round-trip) to the summit of Mount Morgan.

Elevation: 800 feet to 2,220 feet.

Degree of difficulty: Strenuous.

Surface and blaze: Forest floor, rocks, some erosion of trail. Yellow blazes and signs.

LOON PRESERVATION COMMITTEE AT THE MARKUS SANCTUARY

[Fig. 48(8)] The common loon shatters the morning stillness surrounding many of New Hampshire's lakes with an anything but a common cry. This cascade of loud and mournful laments has come to symbolize wilderness to many, and is a sound that, once heard, is never forgotten.

In 1975, a group of volunteer loon watchers became alarmed by the declining numbers of this ancient bird species. They formed the Loon Preservation Committee, or LPC, an organization under the auspices of New Hampshire Audubon, that is committed to protection of this winsome creature from excessive human impingement on their habitat.

Loons build their nests right at the edge of a lake because their legs are positioned so far back on their bodies that they cannot walk on land. They sort of slide up onto their nests directly from the water, which is their more natural habitat. It is critical during nesting season that the water stay quiet and the level stay reasonably constant so as not to swamp these vulnerable nests.

There is, of course, a natural, seasonal fluctuation of lake levels, but over and above that, many of New Hampshire's lakes are dammed, and their water levels are artificially altered to prevent flooding. Add to this the thrashing wakes produced by boating on these lakes, and it all spells bad news for nesting loons.

As if this weren't enough trouble for the loons, a new and more ominous problem has surfaced. It is thought now that more than half the deaths of adult loons are caused by lead poisoning. Along with the stones they need to pulverize food in their gizzards, loons ingest discarded or lost lead fishing sinkers from the bottoms of lakes. The lead accumulates to lethal levels in their bodies and soon the loon is found dead, washed up on shore.

With all this bad news, the LPC has had its work cut out for it. The group, first of all, had to lobby and educate the rest of us about the ways in which we were unthinkingly harming the loons. Then, with both volunteer and professional help, the LPC has amassed a 22-year database of common loon information unequaled anywhere else. It has banded chicks, treated injuries, and floated hundreds of nesting rafts on lakes around the state. These are floating frames, covered in natural materials, that allow the loon's nest to move up and down with the oscillating water levels. In addition, many of the quiet coves and inlets on the larger lakes are now posted as no wake zones.

The latest education thrust by the LPC targets the lead sinker problem. A traveling biologist and an educational display about the dangers of lead goes out from the Loon Center to schools and clubs around the state. The LPC also runs a lead sinker exchange program, distributing nonlead sinkers free to anglers who turn in their old lead sinkers. Awareness has definitely been raised. In June of 1998 New Hampshire's Legislature, the first in the nation to do so, passed a law outlawing the use of lead sinkers on the state's lakes.

Over the years, the work of the LPC has shown real progress on the front lines— where the actual loons are. This is amply demonstrated by the fact that there are now about twice as many loons on New Hampshire lakes than there were in 1975. A 1997 count estimated 576 birds.

The Loon Preservation Committee is housed in a beautiful new visitor center on the grounds of New Hampshire Audubon's Markus Wildlife Sanctuary in Moultonborough. This 200-acre sanctuary on the northeastern shore of Lake Winnipesaukee is an extraordinary pocket of tranquility on a lake known for its well-developed shoreline.

There aren't always loons nesting within the sanctuary—the LPC's scope is far broader than that—but other surprises await the visitor who hikes the Loon Nest Trail, an approximately 2-mile loop along the lakeshore. In the spring, a carpet of wildflowers covers the forest floor, and the "kip, kip kip, kip" of an osprey often echoes over this quiet cove on the big lake. Next to the trail, wetland indicator plants such as sphagnum moss, rhodora, and sensitive fern line the shore.

Wild minigardens—the kind only time can fashion—top the many erratic boulders. Here, star moss and partridgeberries intermingle with several kinds of lichens: British soldiers, pixie cups, and reindeer lichen. The Markus Sanctuary seems to have more than its share of these erratic boulders, and these seem more angular than others found farther south. Perhaps it is because these boulders came to rest sooner, closer to the mountains and ledges from which they were plucked, and before all their corners had time to be tumbled and rolled off.

In addition to the Loon Nest Trail, an approximately 45-minute walk, the Loon Center also offers a shorter, 15-minute hike called the Forest Walk. All trails begin at the visitor center and a map is available there.

Directions: From NH 25 in Moultonborough, turn east on Blake Road. Go 1 mile to Lee's Mill Road and turn right. Loon Center parking is 0.2 mile on the left.

Activities: Hiking, plant study, bird-watching, shopping.

Facilities: Trails, visitor center, displays, nature store, restrooms, trail maps.

Dates: Trails open year-round. Visitor center open daily, year-round.

Fees: None.

Closest town: Moultonborough, 1.2 miles.

For more information: Loon Preservation Committee, Audubon Society of New Hampshire, Lees Mills Road, Box 604, Moultonborough, NH 03254. Phone (603) 476-LOON.

THE SCIENCE CENTER OF NEW HAMPSHIRE

[Fig. 48(4)] The natural history of the Lakes Region is nowhere better distilled to its essence than at the Science Center of New Hampshire in Holderness. Since 1966, this nonprofit, educational organization has made its mission the advancement of understanding of New Hampshire's wild heritage.

Two hundred acres of rolling farm and forest land, on the northern shore of Squam Lake, are home to the center's indoor and outdoor wildlife exhibits and its hands-on learning tools. Bald eagles and barred owls, black bear and red fox, river otters and little brown bats are all situated comfortably in their natural habitats and

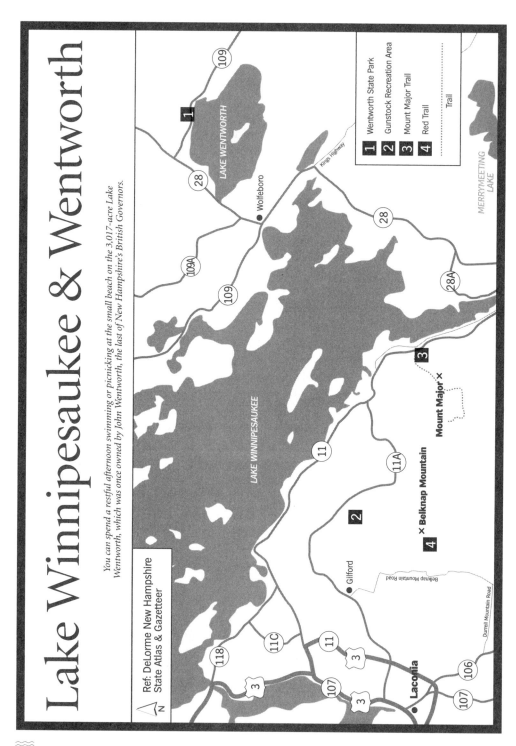

Lake Winnipesaukee & Wentworth

You can spend a restful afternoon swimming or picnicking at the small beach on the 3,017-acre Lake Wentworth, which was once owned by John Wentworth, the last of New Hampshire's British Governors.

Ref: DeLorme New Hampshire
State Atlas & Gazetteer

N

Legend:
1. Wentworth State Park
2. Gunstock Recreation Area
3. Mount Major Trail
4. Red Trail
····· Trail

LAKE WENTWORTH

Wolfeboro

Kings Highway

MERRYMEETING LAKE

109

28

109A

109

28

28A

LAKE WINNIPESAUKEE

Mount Major ×

× Belknap Mountain

11

11A

Gilford

Belknap Mountain Road

Durrell Mountain Road

118

11C

11

3

107

3

3

106

107

Laconia

feed on their normal foods. Most of the exhibited animals are orphaned or injured, and unable to survive in the wild, they serve as ambassadors to the human community to help us understand the needs of their wild brethren.

Lots of interesting information is packed into the small, walk-through buildings near the animals' outdoor living spaces. Or the visitor can simply sit on the benches nearby and observe the behavior of earth's wild creatures. The black bear's rippling coat glistens in patches of dappled sunlight and the puffy red tail of the fox seems almost as thick as its body. An otter's luxuriant fur, when viewed through the glass of its underwater habitat, is bathed in silvery air bubbles that trail behind as it rolls and tumbles and plays in the water. When it comes up for air, this rich brown coat sheds water like the proverbial duck's back.

The science center's exhibit trails are open May through October but workshops and programs are available year-round. From July through October, the center also runs two pontoon boats on Squam Lake, with naturalist captains leading ecology tours. These natural history tours focus on subjects varying from loons, to lake ecology, to fall foliage. They even have a few moonlight cruises.

Under the mature forests at the center are two nature stores, a bat house, flower gardens, forestry exhibits, and buildings full of interactive games and educational displays on everything from deer ticks and Lyme disease, to soil ecology. For those who need to stretch their legs a little more strenuously, there is a steep, 1-mile hiking loop to the 1,067-foot summit of Mount Fayal, next to the center.

The Science Center is handicap accessible and offers plenty to learn at every level of inquiry. Bring a lunch to enjoy in the shady picnic area, for this is a place to spend the whole day.

Directions: From US 3 and NH 25 in Holderness, go 0.2 mile east on NH 113 to the Science Center sign on the left. Parking is at the end of a long drive.

Activities: Wildlife viewing, interactive natural history displays, hiking, picnicking, plant study, programs, cruises, shopping.

Facilities: Live animals and birds, trails, visitor center, nature store, gardens, cruise boats, interactive exhibits, staff naturalists.

Dates: Wildlife exhibits open May through Oct. Lake cruises July through Oct. Events and workshops year-round.

Fees: There is a charge for admission and cruises.

Closest town: Holderness, 0.2 mile.

For more information: Science Center of New Hampshire, Box 173, Route 113, Holderness, NH 03245. Phone (603) 968-7194.

THE NEW HAMPSHIRE MUSIC FESTIVAL

For the past 45 years, the New Hampshire Music Festival has been adding its rich and refined finish to the summer ambience of the Lakes Region. This award-winning orchestra offers six concerts through July and August, with venues both in Plymouth, at Plymouth State College, and in Gilford, at the school's auditorium. Professional musicians from across the country gather together each summer in this, the oldest professional orchestra in the state. What could be a better wrap-up to a day spent outdoors than an evening spent listening to Mozart or Mendelssohn, the strains of the music wafting away on a warm summer breeze?

For more information: New Hampshire Music Festival, 88 Belknap Mountain Road, Gilford, NH 03246. Phone (603) 524-1000.

GUNSTOCK RECREATION AREA

[Fig. 49(2)] In the summer, the winter-frosted slopes of Gunstock Ski Area turn a lush green, and the activity here turns from skiing and snowboarding to hiking, biking, and camping. A popular camping spot for over 60 years, Gunstock also offers cabins, mountain bike rentals, hiking trails, and guided horseback trail rides. A swimming pool, restaurant, and hot showers make this a more civilized outdoor experience than some.

Free trail maps for hiking and biking are available at Gunstock's base lodge or campground store. Three of the hiking trails go from the base to the summit where an eastern outlook affords fine views of Lake Winnipesaukee and the White Mountains. Two others follow the ridge that connects Gunstock to two other peaks in the Belknap group—Mount Belknap to the south and Mount Rowe to the north.

Gunstock's campground and cabins make an excellent base from which to branch out and enjoy the natural attractions of the Lakes Region. Be sure to call for reservations.

Directions: From I-93, take Exit 20 in Tilton and turn left onto US 3. After 6.5 miles, turn right onto US 3 and NH 11, to bypass Laconia. In 3.5 miles, turn right onto NH 11A in Gilford, and go 5.5 miles, following the Gunstock signs, to an entrance on the right.

Activities: Summer: camping, swimming, hiking, biking, special events, dining, and horseback riding. Winter: downhill and cross-country skiing, dining, and camping.

Facilities: Campground, camp store, pool, base lodge, hiking and biking trails, bike and horse rentals, showers, ski trails, and lifts.

Dates: Summer camping, May 15 through Oct. 12. Winter camping, Dec. 4 through Mar. 14. Skiing, Dec. to Mar. Hiking, Mar. to Dec.

Fees: There is a charge for skiing, camping, and equipment, horse, and bike rentals. Hiking is free.

Closest town: Gilford, 3 miles.

For more information: Gunstock , Box 1307, Laconia, NH 03247. Phone (800) 486-7862.

BELKNAP MOUNTAIN AND THE RED TRAIL

[Fig. 49] Here's a mountain that offers a big view for a relatively small hike. You do have to climb the fire tower at the summit in order to see out over the trees, but the fire warden there is friendly, and it's only three little flights of stairs. For your efforts, you get to look out over Lake Winnipesaukee's island-studded expanse and gain a sense of why this lake attracts so many visitors.

Except in the winter, the visitor can drive most of the way up this 2,384-foot forested peak and have only 700 vertical feet left to climb to the summit. Or, if an abbreviated view of Laconia and Lake Winnesquam to the west are sufficient, the western shoulder of Belknap Mountain offers an informal picnic area on a rocky ledge, a mere 100 feet from the parking area, via a red-blazed footpath.

Go to the summit, though, and you can look straight into the face of the Ossipee ring dike, across the lake. It actually looks more like a pile of mountains than a distinct ring. A rounded mound of 3,000-foot peaks hulks there on the northern edge of the lake, in a circle 9 miles wide. This is probably the best view of the ring dike phenomenon.

Directly to the north of Belknap is Gunstock Mountain, a popular ski area and summer campground, and off to the southeast sits the rocky top of Mount Major. Though it is hard to imagine, these peaks, plus the one you are standing on, make up part of another ring dike. An ancient volcano once rumbled right underneath your feet.

Directions: From NH 11A in Gilford, turn east on Belknap Mountain Road. Go 1.4 miles to where this road turns right. Go 1.1 miles farther and turn left where a sign reads, "Belknap Mountain" and "Carriage Road." Go 1.6 miles (road turns to gravel) to parking area on left. In winter, a gate blocks the last 1.3 miles of this road.

Activities: Hiking, picnicking.

Facilities: Trails, fire tower viewing platform, parking.

Dates: Road is open from May until snow season.

Fees: None.

Closest town: Gilford, 4 miles.

For more information: New Hampshire Division of Forests and Lands, 172 Pembroke Road, Concord, NH 03302. Phone (603) 271-2214.

RED TRAIL TO BELKNAP MOUNTAIN'S SUMMIT

[Fig. 49(4)] Four color-blazed trails to the summit take off from the service road to the right of the parking lot. The Red Trail is an attractive choice and makes a 30-minute climb through the forest, under a maple and spruce overstory, along a blueberry- and bunchberry-lined path. In June, clintonia (*Clintonia borealis*) and sarsaparilla (*Aralia nudicaulis*) are in bloom. You can descend the same trail or shorten your trip down by 10 minutes by hiking back to the parking area on the serviceable, but less scenic, Green Trail. This makes a 1.5-mile loop.

Trail: 1.5-mile loop to Belknap Mountain's summit.

Elevation: 1,684 feet to 2,384 feet.

Degree of difficulty: Moderate.

Surface and blaze: Forest floor, some rocks. Red blazes, green if you come down the Green Trail.

🏔 MOUNT MAJOR AND THE MOUNT MAJOR TRAIL

[Fig. 49] Mount Major, at 1,784 feet, is a shorter mountain than its neighbor, Belknap Mountain, but it proves to be a bigger challenge for the hiker. Here, there is no auto road to take you two-thirds the way up. The climb begins right where this rugged little mountain jumps directly up out of Lake Winnipesaukee.

Nonetheless, this popular mountain gets a lot of foot traffic and the trails are well-worn and blazed. The vegetation on the mountain grades from white pine, birch, and hemlock at the base to spruce and subalpine growth in the rocky crevices at the top. In the spring, the lower slopes are full of songbirds. The rocky substance of this mountain crops out in considerable variety. Pink Conway Granite mingles with Kinsman Quartz Monzonite with its distinctive white, rectangular crystals, and a stunning basaltic dike runs right over the summit.

From the top, the view is 360 degrees of lakes and mountains. Looking south from here, you can begin to see the ring shape of the ancient volcano, of which this mountain and the others around it are a remnant. Many of the Lakes Region's mountains have these ancient volcanic origins, and across the lake to the north, the Ossipee ring dike, an even more impressive example, fills the horizon. One hundred eighty million years ago, these ancient volcanoes doused the land with lava and ash, which has since mostly eroded away. All that remains are these mountains—the castings of once-molten rock that mark their massive calderas.

Scenery and geology notwithstanding, probably the first thing that catches the eye of the hiker on the summit of Mount Major is the small stone building that stands there, roofless but determined in its testimony to the workings of the hand of man. Built in 1925 by an Alton summer resident, it has outlasted several roofs and, doubtless by now, its original builder. On a windy day, it serves to keep your lunch from blowing away while you sit with your back braced against its sun-warmed stones.

Turkey vultures lift and hang on the thermals, and far below, the *Mount Washington* travels soundlessly across the lake, offering sightseers a different and equally enchanting perspective on the lakes and mountains.

Directions: From the junction (traffic circle) of NH 28 and NH 11 in Alton, go 6.2 miles north on NH 11 to a brown "Mt. Major Hiking Trail" sign and parking area on the left. The trail takes off from the northwestern corner of this parking lot.

Activities: Hiking, lake viewing.

Facilities: Trail.

Dates: Open year-round. Rocks will be icy in winter.

Fees: None.

Closest town: Alton Bay, 4.2 miles.

For more information: New Hampshire Division of Forests and Lands, 172 Pembroke Road, Concord, NH 03302. Phone (603) 271-2214.

MOUNT MAJOR TRAIL

[Fig. 49(3)] This 3-mile (round-trip) trail leaves the northwestern corner of the parking lot and travels about half of its distance on an old woods road. Follow the blue blazes that initially fork left, then right. Then stay on this road with its blue blazes until you come to a tree with a blue and orange blaze where an obvious trail veers sharply left and uphill. This second half of the trail gets steep, and near the summit, involves some scrambling and the use of hands over rocky ledges. Hiking boots are in order.

Trail: 3-mile (round-trip) climb to the summit of Mount Major.

Elevation: 604 feet to 1,784 feet.

Degree of difficulty: Strenuous.

Surface and blaze: Woods road, forest floor, rocks. Trail is somewhat eroded in spots. Blue blazes.

WENTWORTH STATE PARK

[Fig. 49(1)] Lake Wentworth and its small state beach are only a tiny part of what once was the 4,000-acre estate granted to John Wentworth, the last of New Hampshire's British governors. He was a man of such privilege and power that in 1772 he had a road laid from here all the way to Hanover on the Connecticut River so that he could attend the first graduation at Dartmouth College. Governor Wentworth was in charge around here from 1767 until 1775 until a little fracas called the American Revolution ended his tenure. New Hampshire, by the way, was the first state to declare its independence and the first to adopt a state constitution. There is a historical plaque at the entrance to this park telling more about the man for whom this lake and many other New Hampshire places are named.

These days, Wentworth Lake, northeast of Wolfeboro, provides a restful spot to spend an afternoon. On the north shore of this quiet, 3,017-acre lake there is a small beach and bathhouse for swimming, and tables for picnicking. Visitors are welcome to slip a canoe into the water and explore the lake's quiet coves or paddle among the several islands that seem almost to float here, atop Lake Wentworth's placid waters.

Directions: From Wolfeboro, go 3.3 miles northeast on NH 28 and NH 109. Turn southeast on NH 109 and go 1.4 miles to the state park sign on the right.

Activities: Swimming, canoeing, picnicking.

Facilities: Beach, bathhouse, lifeguard in season. Restrooms, parking, picnic tables, fireplaces.

Dates: May through Sept.

Fees: There is a charge for entrance.

Closest town: Wolfeboro, 4.7 miles.

For more information: New Hampshire Division of Parks and Recreation, 172 Pembroke Road, Concord, NH 03302. Phone (603) 271-3254.

Long Trails

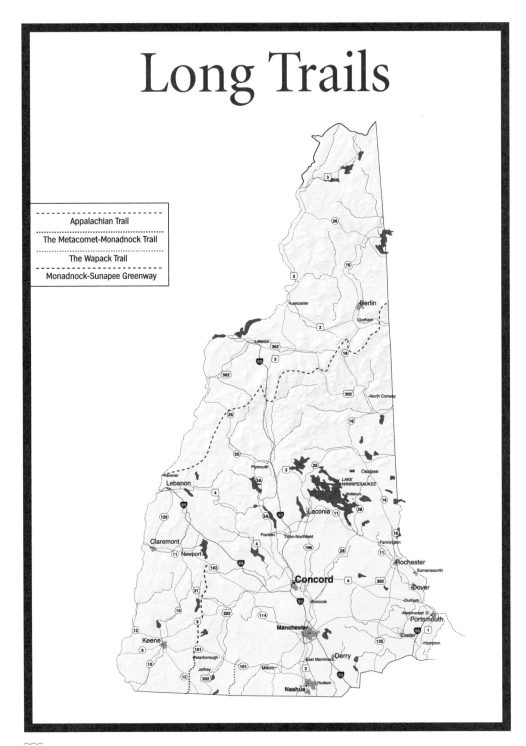

- - - - - Appalachian Trail
········· The Metacomet-Monadnock Trail
········· The Wapack Trail
- - - - - Monadnock-Sunapee Greenway

Long Trails and
Scenic Drives

The best way to appreciate the natural beauty of New Hampshire is to walk or drive slowly through its landscape. A few venerable old walking trails offer opportunities for multiday trips on which hikers may immerse themselves in the backcountry, intimately experiencing the textures, the smells, and the history of the land. The trails described in this chapter are not limited to one area of the state, in fact, several cross New Hampshire's borders to pass through several states. For the automobile traveler, dozens of scenic roads, ranging from broad interstates to winding, backwoods shunpikes, offer panoramic vistas of lakes, valleys, and rows of hills. The drives described here traverse different areas of the countryside and offer visitors the opportunity to enjoy nature's grandeur without leaving the comfort of the car.

[*Above:* Some of New Hampshire's long trails and scenic drives feature the Sandwich Range]

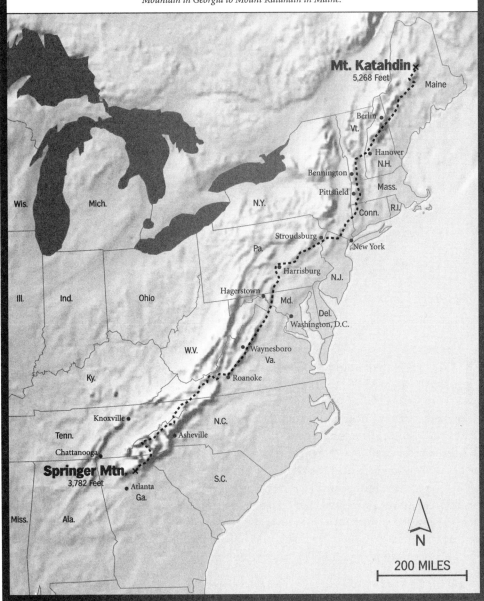

Appalachian Trail

The Appalachian Trail is over 2,100 miles long and stretches from Springer Mountain in Georgia to Mount Katahdin in Maine.

Mt. Katahdin ✕
5,268 Feet

Maine

Berlin
Vt.

Hanover
N.H.

Bennington

Pittsfield

Mass.

Wis.

Mich.

N.Y.

Conn.

R.I.

Stroudsburg

Pa.

New York

Harrisburg

N.J.

Hagerstown

Md.

Ill.

Ind.

Ohio

Del.
Washington, D.C.

W.V.

Waynesboro
Va.

Ky.

Roanoke

Knoxville

N.C.

Tenn.

Asheville

Chattanooga

Springer Mtn. ✕
3,782 Feet

S.C.

Atlanta
Ga.

Miss.

Ala.

N

200 MILES

Long Trails

New Hampshire, despite its diminutive size, is amply endowed with mountains that are crisscrossed by hundreds of miles of hiking trails. In the White Mountain National Forest alone, more than 1,200 miles of trails lace the backcountry. A few of the trails that cross the region are unusually long, some covering several states, enabling the hiker to trek dozens, hundreds, or, in one case, over 2,000 miles, without once touching a tire to pavement.

Most notable among these long trails is the 2,160-mile Appalachian Trail, which runs one of its last legs through New Hampshire, covering 170 miles over ridges, valleys, and mountain peaks, on the way to its northern terminus at Mount Katahdin, Maine. The much shorter but equally venerable Wapack Trail runs north and south, from Mount Watatic in Ashburnham, Massachusetts, to North Pack Monadnock in Greenfield, New Hampshire. This 21-mile trail was completed in 1923, making it the oldest continuously used interstate hiking trail in the Northeast.

Blueberries

No oversized, cultivated, greenhouse blueberry could ever match the sweet taste of the smaller natural variety that grows all over on the drier slopes of New Hampshire's mountains. To be fair, and avoid interstate rivalry, Maine has an equally good crop.

Vaccinium augustifolium, called variously "low sweet" or "early low" or "low bush" blueberry, is a member of the heath family, along with other edibles like cranberries, bilberries, and huckleberries. Blueberries bear tiny, bell-shaped pink and white flowers in the spring, and by August, the dry hillsides—and sandy lowlands, too—are carpeted with these minishrubs laden with frosty blueberries about 0.25 inch in diameter. They can be made into wonderful pies and cobblers, or jellies and juices, but on a hot August afternoon, a handful eaten right off the bush tastes best of all and provides an unexpected bonus to the summer hiker.

Another interstate trail, the Metacomet-Monadnock Trail, travels from Connecticut, through Massachusetts, and into New Hampshire. On the summit of Mount Monadnock, it meets the southern end of the Monadnock-Sunapee Greenway, a long trail lying totally within New Hampshire. The greenway continues north another 50 miles, from Mount Monadnock in Jaffrey, north to Mount Sunapee in Newbury. It follows the spine of mountains that separate the watersheds of the Connecticut and Merrimack rivers and passes through three state parks.

Lastly, and still a work in progress, the New Hampshire Heritage Trail will eventually run the length of the state from Massachusetts to the Canadian border. Unlike the other long trails, this one is a valley trail that will follow the Merrimack and Connecticut rivers for over 200 miles, focusing more upon the history of human settlement than on wild country. Access will be available from some of the state's larger cities, and this trail will be well suited to the average walker. Construction of

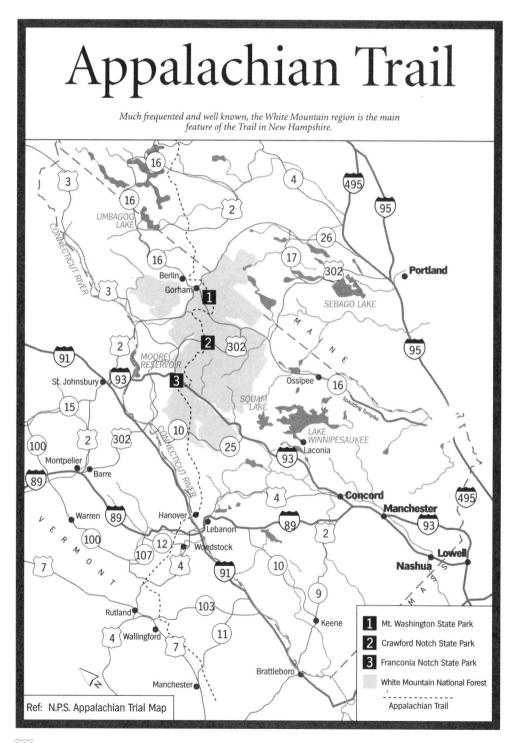

Appalachian Trail

*Much frequented and well known, the White Mountain region is the main
feature of the Trail in New Hampshire.*

1 Mt. Washington State Park
2 Crawford Notch State Park
3 Franconia Notch State Park
White Mountain National Forest
Appalachian Trail

Ref: N.P.S. Appalachian Trial Map

the New Hampshire Heritage Trail has been left to each of the towns that it runs through, and it is about 25 percent completed.

THE APPALACHIAN TRAIL

[Figs. 51, 52] The Appalachian Trail—known as the AT—stretches 2,160 miles up the eastern seaboard, nearly the full length of the Appalachian Mountain chain. From Springer Mountain in Georgia to Mount Katahdin in the heart of Maine's Baxter State Park, this grandfather of all long trails passes through parts of 14 states. Entering New Hampshire at Hanover, the AT meanders to the northeast, mostly within the White Mountain National Forest. It traverses the alpine crests of the Presidential, the Carter, and the Mahoosuc ranges, then exits the state near Grafton Notch, Maine.

Today, thousands of hikers walk sections of the AT, and every year, around 200 hardy souls hike the whole length of it, earning the proud designation of "thru-hiker." This arduous trek generally requires about six months to complete. Most folks begin in April, from the southern end, at Springer Mountain in Georgia. Those who opt to hike the trail from north to south usually depart from Mount Katahdin in June. Needless to say, not everyone can get away for six months, so about a third of the people who accomplish the full length of the Appalachian Trail do so in smaller trail increments, spaced over several years.

Following the Appalachian Trail across New Hampshire leads the hiker through a vast variety of terrain. In places, the AT skirts boggy lowlands where carnivorous plants and low shrubs grab for a foothold on a bouncy, floating mat of sphagnum moss. At maximum elevation, it winds around mountain tarns cradled high in glacial cirques. The trail also squeezes through chasms torn into the rock by the power of glacial runoff and tiptoes over alpine meadows above tree line. The hiker will be in populous spots like Franconia and Crawford notches one day, and alone with the forest and its creatures the next. The 170 miles that the AT travels through New Hampshire include some of the trail's toughest ups and downs, but thru-hikers are rugged by this point in their journey and can almost taste the triumph at the end. Mount Katahdin looms just one state, and less than 200 miles, away.

New Hampshire's leg of the AT begins at Hanover, near the stately, central quad

EASTERN BOX TURTLE
(Terrapene carolina)
A box turtle can withdraw almost completely because of a hinged lower shell that allows the front and rear sections to bend upward to meet the top shell.

Black-Capped Chickadee

This sassy little bird (*Parus atricapillus*) could be an emblem of New Hampshire, because it is so widely distributed and numerous. Its "chick-a-dee-dee-dee" can be heard in all seasons in backyards and forests of all kinds, up to about 3,000 feet elevation where its cousin, the boreal chickadee (*Parus hudsonicus*) fills its niche.

Wherever you see or hear one chickadee, no doubt you'll find a dozen, as they usually travel in small flocks, often together with tufted titmice and white- and red-breasted nuthatches. The perky chickadee never sits still. You'll find it hanging upside down from a twig or standing on a branch pounding ferociously on a seed clenched in its tiny feet. The perky acrobatics of the black-capped chickadee, as well as its dressy black, gray, and white tuxedo-like plumage, make this one of the first birds a new bird watcher can identify. Older hands, too, seldom tire of watching this tough, energetic little bird, and their respect and admiration grow with every year that they witness chickadees hanging on through New Hampshire's fierce winters, while other, less adaptable birds fly south.

of Dartmouth College. The trail crosses the bridge over the Connecticut River from Norwich, Vermont, and its traditional 2-by-6-inch white blazes are painted on utility poles instead of trees. The blazes direct the walker to the corner of Wheelock and Main streets where a plaque embedded in the sidewalk honors the Appalachian Trail. Here, the trail turns south for two blocks, where it picks up Lebanon Street and heads east out of town. Generally, the AT warns of turns, junctions, or other places hikers should be alert with two white blazes, one above the other. Any AT side trails, usually leading to shelters, a water supply or viewpoints, are marked by blue paint blazes.

At Dartmouth, outdoor sports have a long history. In 1909, the Dartmouth Outing Club (DOC), the oldest college outing club in the country, was organized to promote skiing, snowshoeing, and, later, hiking. The early trails blazed by the DOC predate the Appalachian Trail, and many were modified and incorporated into the AT when it

COYOTE
(Canis latrans)
Easily adapting to the presence of man, the coyote often preys on rodents, small animals, and livestock. It is a member of the dog family and has been known to mate with domestic dogs.

came into being in 1926. The DOC is still very much alive and continues to maintain 70 miles of the AT, from Hanover east to Kinsman Notch. This work is done largely by volunteers, called adopters, who each care for 2 or 3 miles of trail. Occasionally, nature throws the volunteers a nasty curve, like the ice storm of 1998, which broke thousands of tree limbs and that landed on the trails, making spring maintenance work much more arduous than usual.

The DOC, headquartered in Robinson Hall, not far from the plaque, provides hiker information and a place for thru-hikers to leave their heavy packs while they explore charming downtown Hanover. The Dartmouth Outing Club manages several AT shelters across the state and maintains about 120 miles of trails altogether, some of which are spur paths to the AT and others that lie on or around Mount Moosilauke, 35 miles north of Hanover.

The AT was the brainchild of Benton MacKaye, a writer and U.S. Forest

Springtails

Hikers are often surprised on a sunny winter day to find the snow speckled with fine black dots. Bending over to look at them closely reveals something even more amazing—they jump! These dots are primitive insects of the order Collembola that have evolved a way to "fly" without wings. A pair of abdominal appendages are held coiled up and braced against another pair until, like a spring, they release and propel this tiny speck of life several inches away from its original location.

Springtails spend most of their short lives under the leaf litter on the forest floor, but on sunny winter days, they work their way up through the snow to bounce around like grains of black pepper in the sunshine. On spring days, they collect by the millions, at the edges of puddles and vernal pools, forming a blue-gray skin over the water.

Service planner who, in 1921, first conceived the notion of setting aside a remote trail along the ridges of the eastern mountains as a place for urban people to reconnect with nature. The idea struck a resonant chord with thousands of other outdoor enthusiasts, and over the next 16 years, the Appalachian Trail became a reality, both by construction of new trail and by knitting together of pieces of preexisting trail along the ridges of the Appalachian Mountains. By 1937, the AT was essentially complete, but its very nature dictates that it remain a constant work in progress. The battering of the elements and the wear and tear of human use make considerable maintenance and occasional re-routing of badly worn sections necessary.

The entity responsible for coordinating the care of the AT is the Appalachian Trail Conference, or ATC. The ATC was formed in 1925 to maintain the trail and to secure its protection from development. In 1968, the AT became the first federally protected footpath and was designated the Appalachian National Scenic Trail. The ATC is headquartered in Harpers Ferry, West Virginia, and accomplishes this gargantuan task of maintenance in partnership with 31 volunteer hiking clubs that stretch up the Atlantic seaboard, from Georgia to Maine.

For more information: Guides and maps for the AT are available from the Appalachian Trail Conference, Box 236, Harpers Ferry, WV 25425. Phone (304) 535-6331. The ATC also has a specific *Guide to the Appalachian Trail in New Hampshire and Vermont.* The Dartmouth Outing Club may be contacted at Box 9, Robinson Hall, Hanover, NH 03755. Phone (603) 646-2428.

THE WAPACK TRAIL

[Fig. 50] The 21-mile Wapack Trail is a much shorter path than the AT, but it is included here because it carries other distinctions. In 1923, the Wapack became the first interstate footpath in the Northeast. It straddles the border between Massachusetts and New Hampshire, winding along the ridgetops of the Wapack Range that trends north and south from Mount Watatic in Ashburnham, Massachusetts, to North Pack Monadnock in Greenfield, New Hampshire. Among its superb overlooks are the summits of Pratt Mountain, the Temple Mountain Ridge, and North Pack Monadnock.

Variety is what this trail offers. Its ridgetop segments dip occasionally into cols and saddles between the heights, passing through a variety of forest types, from predominantly hardwoods on the southern end and on south-facing slopes, to hemlock in the wet northern valleys, to the beginnings of spruce and fir at the tops of the highest peaks. In other areas, the trail passes through old farms and pasture land, where stone walls and cellar holes testify to the region's land-use history. Spattered over the landscape are other clues to the past—low-growing juniper, sumac, and meadowsweet, some of the pioneers that tend to invade old fields.

The Wapack Trail has endured so long despite two little-known facts. First, most of the trail passes through private, not public, land. Credit for the trail's survival goes to both generous landowners and courteous hikers, who know that continued access rests heavily on their thoughtful use of the trail. Second, the Wapack Trail is maintained entirely by a volunteer organization, called the Friends of the Wapack (FOW). This group organizes trail maintenance and publishes a newsletter, a map, and a guidebook called *Wapack Trail Guide: Hikes, History, and Nature* by John Flanders.

For more information: Friends of the Wapack, PO Box 115, W. Peterborough, NH 03468. Web site: www.mv.com/ipusers/blanchette/fow.

METACOMET-MONADNOCK TRAIL

[Fig. 50] The Metacomet-Monadnock Trail is another interstate footpath, this one heading north from the Hanging Hills of Meriden, Connecticut, and ending 117 miles later on the summit of New Hampshire's Mount Monadnock. Less than 20 miles of this trail lie in New Hampshire, but the M & M, as it is called, climbs over some outstanding viewpoints, such as Gap Mountain. At its northern terminus atop Mount Monadnock, this trail also connects with the southern end of the Monadnock-Sunapee Greenway, extending its reach another 50 miles north.

The Metacomet-Monadnock Trail was named for Pometacom, a chief of the Wampanoag tribe, the same people that helped the Pilgrims through their first winter. The trail was conceived and laid out by Professor Walter M. Banfield of the University of Massachusetts and is now maintained by the Berkshire Chapter of the Appalachian Mountain Club.

For more information: Berkshire Chapter—AMC, Box 9369, North Amherst, MA 01095.

THE MONADNOCK-SUNAPEE GREENWAY

[Fig. 50] One long trail that New Hampshire can call totally its own is the Monadnock-Sunapee Greenway. Stretching for nearly 50 miles between the summits of Mount Monadnock in Jaffrey and Mount Sunapee in Newbury, it is the longest trail in the state. Running generally north and south, its route travels over a beautifully varied, and relatively unpopulated, landscape, tracing the spine of highlands that divide the waters running into the Merrimack River from those draining into the Connecticut River.

The Monadnock-Sunapee Greenway moves over rocky summits, through open meadows, and along river valleys. It passes through three large state-owned properties—Monadnock, Pillsbury, and Mount Sunapee state parks—but like the Wapack Trail, the majority of this path lies on private land. To encourage the continued forbearance of landowners, hikers are asked to avoid using wood and charcoal fires, camp and park only at designated sites, and work to maintain a quiet and unlittered trail.

The Monadnock-Sunapee Greenway makes for a great multiday hike, offering five or six days away from traffic, phones, and computers. Five campsites and shelters along the way provide primitive accommodations on a first-come, first-serve basis. Located in New Hampshire's quiet, southwestern corner, the route gives the stealthy and observant hiker an opportunity to spy on moose, fisher, deer, and black bear, or at least to find their tracks in the mud surrounding wet spots or their teeth or claw marks in the bark of trees. The wily bobcat dwells here too, dozing during the day where the sun hits rocky outcrops, then emerging to hunt for snowshoe hare at night.

The greenway was originally laid out in the 1920s by the Society for the Protection of New Hampshire Forests. In those days, hikers were known as "trampers" and came from all walks of life, many from the large cities to the south. Over the years,

GREAT BLUE HERON
(Ardea herodias)
Often spotted standing or stalking in water, this heron catches fish by using its bill, like scissors. It grows to 4 feet tall and has a wingspan of 6 feet.

Bats

Of the world's 1,000 bat species, 8 live at least part of the year in New Hampshire. The most common here, as elsewhere in North America, is the little brown bat (*Myotis lucifugus*). Bats are the only mammals that truly fly.

In the daylight hours of the warmer seasons, bats roost in dark places—in barns or trees, under bridges, sometimes even in attics. Come dusk, they emerge to fly around and devour insects. Each year female bats bear one live young, called a pup, which clings to its mother's fur as she goes out on her nightly forays. Bats are not blind, although they do rely more heavily on echolocation than on sight to avoid obstacles and to locate prey.

Human folklore has given bats a thoroughly scary, but undeserved reputation, and we are only beginning to appreciate some of the benefits they bring. Along with helping to control insect pests more safely than pesticides, some bats pollinate plants and disperse their seeds. It is true that a couple of tropical species live off the blood of livestock or wild animals, but all of New Hampshire's bats avoid other creatures, especially humans, and bite only in self defense. As for the rabies threat, fewer bats have the disease than do foxes, raccoons, dogs, or cats.

In the depth of winter, think what a stroke of luck it is that, in a few abandoned mine shafts around the state, thousands of insect-eating bats hang quietly upside down from the ceiling, their heart and respiratory rates reduced to a minimum to conserve energy. There, they ride out the winter, waiting for the bugs of spring to return.

the trail has known periods of disuse and rediscovery, and has undergone considerable rearrangement, moving generally higher up the hillsides into less occupied lands. Although the greenway is blazed with white, like the Appalachian Trail, confusion is not a problem because the two do not come within 35 miles of each other.

The Greenway is now maintained by volunteers of the Monadnock Sunapee Greenway Trail Club (MSGTC), who welcome prospective new members or trail adopters to contact the group. They also have for sale an excellent trail guide, complete with maps.

For more information: Monadnock Sunapee Greenway Trail Club, PO Box 164, Marlow, NH 03456.

Scenic Drives

The areas of New Hampshire covered in this guide are so replete with natural beauty it is difficult to choose among the roads that run through them, arbitrarily pronouncing some of them "scenic." But some of the more outstanding drives are listed below. Though all of these roads are paved, they run the gamut from interstates to two-laners, from wide-open roads to long green tunnels overarched by forest. Each has its own charm.

DRIVES IN THE NORTH COUNTRY

a) US 3, from Pittsburg to the Canadian border. Runs by all the Connecticut Lakes to the source of the Connecticut River.

b) NH 145, from Pittsburg to Colebrook. Passes by Beaver Brook Falls.

c) NH 26, from Colebrook to the Maine border. Winds through Dixville Notch and later, offers a high view of Umbagog Lake.

d) Mount Prospect Auto Road, off US 3 in Lancaster. Climbs to the Weeks Estate on the summit of Mount Prospect in Weeks State Park, giving splendid views of the northern White Mountains.

e) NH 135, from Woodsville to Lancaster. Follows the Connecticut River north, with long views over its broad and fertile valley.

DRIVES IN THE WHITE MOUNTAIN NATIONAL FOREST

a) US 2, from Lancaster to Gorham. Passes through the wide-open valley between the Crescent and Pliny ranges on the north and the awesome Presidentials to the south.

b) NH 116, from Jefferson to Whitefield. Open farm country with views of Cherry Mountain and the Presidentials to the southeast.

c) NH 115, or 115 A and 115, from US 2 to US 3. Splendid, open views of the meadows of Jefferson, surrounded by the highest of the White Mountains.

d) US 3, from Exit 36 off Interstate 93 to Twin Mountain. Offers views of the Gale River and the Presidentials, and a wayside park.

e) US 302, from Twin Mountain to Bartlett. Offers sublime views of the Presidentials and access to the Cog Railway, then threads between the high cliffs of

WHITE-TAILED DEER
(Odocoileus virginianus)
The white-tailed deer may be the most popular wild animal in the U.S. When alarmed, the whitetail raises its tail, alerting other deer to possible danger.

Crawford Notch, passing wayside parks and several high waterfalls along the way.

f) Interstate 93 and the Franconia Parkway through Franconia Notch, from Lincoln to Franconia. Passes many scenic attractions, including Cannon Mountain, the Flume Gorge, and the Old Man of the Mountain.

g) NH 16, from Franconia south to NH 112. Winds along the quiet valley on the back side of Cannon Mountain, with the Kinsman Ridge to the east.

h) Kancamagus Highway (NH 112 E), from Lincoln to Conway. This is New Hampshire's premier scenic drive, traversing a broad and spectacular section of the White Mountain National Forest, through Kancamagus Pass and along several whitewater rivers. Many roadside overlooks offer views of both the northern mountains and the Sandwich Range to the south.

i) Bear Notch Road, from the Kancamagus Highway to Bartlett. Offers a different set of overlooks into the White Mountains and a shortcut to US 302, avoiding the Conway area, which can be busy in summer and fall.

j) NH 112 W, from North Woodstock to Bath. Compared with 112 E (Kancamagus Highway) this is the quiet road less traveled, which winds up through Kinsman Notch, past the Lost River Gorge, and along the Wild Ammonoosuc River.

k) NH 175, from Woodstock to Plymouth. A quiet alternative to Interstate 93, traveling close to the Pemigewasset River with access to several covered bridges.

l) Tripoli Road, from Exit 31 off Interstate 93 to Waterville Valley. A woodsy back way into the Waterville Valley that offers primitive campsites and fishing along Eastman Brook. The road is partially gravel and closed in winter and mud season.

m) NH 49, from Exit 28 off Interstate 93 to Waterville Valley. Twists through the mountain-flanked valley of the mighty Mad River, ending at the Waterville Valley Resort.

n) NH 16, from Glen to Gorham. A sweeping approach to the Presidentials along the eastern flank of Mount Washington and through Pinkham Notch, with views of Tuckerman and Huntington ravines and the Great Gulf Wilderness. Offers access to the Mount Washington Auto Road and many hiking trails.

o) NH 16 B Loop through Jackson Village. This short drive through this quiet resort community begins where the road runs through a red covered bridge.

DRIVES IN THE LAKES REGION LOWLANDS

a) West Side Road, from NH 16 in Conway to US 302 in Bartlett. Bypasses the busy business districts of Conway and North Conway and runs through the intervale farmland of the Saco River valley. Runs close by the spectacular Whitehorse and Cathedral ledges.

b) NH 113, from Whittier to Chocorua and NH 16, from Chocorua to Conway. Passes through a quiet corner of the upper Lakes Region, with stunning views of Mount Chocorua.

c) NH 153, from Conway to Effingham. A quiet country road that winds among many north/south-trending eskers, which were left behind by the last glacier.

d) US 3 and NH 113, from Ashland to Center Sandwich. A curvaceous and interesting little road that travels around the northern edge of Squam Lake, made Hollywood-famous as Golden Pond.

e) NH 109, from Moultonborough to Center Sandwich. Offers great views of the eastern Sandwich Range.

f) NH 25 B, from NH 25 to US 3, in Center Harbor. A scenic, 3-mile shortcut over a highland north of Lake Winnipesaukee.

DRIVES IN THE WESTERN HIGHLANDS

a) Interstate 89, from Concord to the Vermont border. A pleasant, 60-mile drive over the Western Highlands of the state and then down to the Connecticut River valley. Traffic is seldom heavy on this highway, which offers wide-open vistas and dozens of road cuts, where the complex geology of New Hampshire is visible in sheer, vertical walls of rock.

b) NH 10, from Orford to Woodsville. Follows the Connecticut River valley, some of the richest farmland in the state. Offers picnic areas, covered bridges, and fine views of the Vermont Hills across the river.

c) NH 3 A, from Bristol to East Hebron. Travels down the quiet eastern shore of Newfound Lake, offering high views of the lake and access to nature centers at the north end.

d) NH 31, Newport to Washington. This road offers a wonderful look at rural western New Hampshire as it skirts along the western edge of Pillsbury State Park, one of the state's wildest.

e) Kearsarge Mountain Road, from Warner to the southern flank of Mount Kearsarge. A toll road that leads to phenomenal views east and south, on a clear day, all the way to Boston.

f) Kearsarge Valley Road and Kearsarge Mountain Road, from Wilmot Flat to the northern flank of Mount Kearsarge. This road offers views to the north and west, at Ragged Mountain and the Green Mountains of Vermont.

g) NH 123, from Hancock to Marlow. A meandering trip through the quiet corner of the state, passing high over the flanks of Pitcher Mountain and skirting the Pierce Reservation, a large reserve of conservation land owned by the Society for the Protection of New Hampshire Forests.

h) Pack Monadnock Summit Road, from NH 101 to the summit of Pack Monadnock. A toll road into Miller State Park, where the top of the mountain offers 360-degree views, stretching, on a clear day, north to Mount Washington and southeast to Boston.

Appendices

A. Books and References

Alpine Zone of the Mount Washington Range by Ernst Antevs, Merrill and Webber Company, Auburn, ME 1932.

A Guide to Animal Tracking and Behavior by Donald and Lillian Stokes, Little, Brown and Company, Boston, MA 1986.

A Field Guide to Animal Tracks by Olaus J. Murie, Houghton Mifflin Company, Boston, MA 1982.

Atlas of Breeding Birds in New Hampshire edited by Carol R. Foss, Chadford Publishing, Dover, NH 1994.

The Audubon Society Field Guide to North American Trees—Eastern Region by Elbert L. Little, Alfred A. Knopf, New York, NY 1980.

The Audubon Society Field Guide to North American Wildflowers—Eastern Region by William A. Niering and Nancy C. Olmstead, Alfred A. Knopf, New York, NY 1979.

30 Bicycle Tours in New Hampshire—Third Edition by Adolphe Bernotas and Tom and Susan Heavey, The Countryman Press, Woodstock, VT 1991.

Eastern Trees—A Peterson Field Guide by George A. Petrides, Houghton Mifflin Company, Boston, MA 1988.

Ferns—A Peterson Field Guide by Boughton Cobb, Houghton Mifflin Company, Boston, MA 1984.

Field Guide to New England Alpine Summits by Nancy G. Slack and Allison W. Bell, Appalachian Mountain Club Books, Boston, MA 1995.

Fifty Hikes in the White Mountains by Daniel Doan, The Countryman Press, Woodstock, VT 1990.

Forest and Crag by Laura and Guy Waterman, Appalachian Mountain Club Books, Boston, MA 1989.

Franconia Notch and the Old Man by Brian K. Fowler, Windswept Magazine, Winter 1997.

Franconia Notch: An In-depth Guide edited by Diane M. Kostecke, Society for the Protection of New Hampshire Forests, Concord, NH 1975.

Great Rail-Trails in New York and New England by Karen-Lee Ryan, Rails-to-Trails Conservancy, Washington, DC 1996.

Great Rail-Trails of the Northeast by Craig Della Penna, New England Cartographics, North Amherst, MA 1995.

Hiker's Guide to the Mountains of New Hampshire by Jared Gange, Huntington Graphics, Huntington, VT 1997.

Indian Stream Republic: Setting a New England Frontier by Daniel Doan and Jere R. Danielle, University Press of New England, Hanover, NH 1997.

Lives of North American Birds by Kenn Kaufman, Houghton Mifflin Company, Boston, MA 1996.

Mammals—A Peterson Field Guide by William H. Burt and Richard P. Grossenheider, Houghton Mifflin Company, New York, NY 1980.

Monadnock Guide by Henry I. Baldwin, Society for the Protection of New Hampshire Forests, Concord, NH 1980.

Mount Washington: A Guide and Short History by Peter Randall, University Press of New England, Hanover, NH 1974.

Mountain Biking New Hampshire's State Parks and Forests by Linda Chestney, Nicolin Fields Publishing, Hampton, NH 1996.

Natural Wonders of New Hampshire by Suki Casanve, Country Roads Press, Castine, ME 1994.

New England Hiking: The Complete Guide to More Than 350 of the Best Hikes in New England by Michael Lanza, Foghorn Press, San Francisco, CA 1997.

New England's Landscape by Neil Jorgenson, Globe Pequot Press, Old Saybrook, CT 1977.

New Hampshire Atlas and Gazetteer, Delorme Mapping Company, Freeport, ME 1996.

New Hampshire Nature Notes by Hilbert R. Siegler, Equity Publishing, Orford, NH 1962.

New Hampshire's Landscape by Donald H. Chapman, New Hampshire Profiles Magazine, January, 1974.

New Hampshire's Living Legacy: The Biodiversity of the Granite State edited by James Taylor et. al., New Hampshire Fish and Game Department, Concord, NH 1996.

New Hampshire Wildlife Viewing by Judy Silverberg, Falcon Press, Helena, MT 1997.

Newcomb's Wildflower Guide by Lawrence Newcomb, Little, Brown and Company, Boston, MA 1977.

The North Woods by Peter Marchand, Appalachian Mountain Club Books, Boston, MA 1987.

The Northern Forest by David Dobbs and Richard Ober, Chelsea Green Publishing, White River Junction, VT 1995.

Old and New Poems by Donald Hall, Ticknor and Fields, New York, NY 1990.

Outdoor Explorations in Mount Washington Valley by Ned Beecher, Tin Mountain Conservation Center, Jackson, NH 1989.

Ossipee Pine Barrens by The Nature Conservancy—New Hampshire Chapter, Concord, NH 1997.

Reading the Forested Landscape by Tom Wessels, The Countryman Press, Woodstock, VT 1997.

Roadside Geology of Vermont and New Hampshire by Bradford B. Van Diver, Mountain Press Publishing, Missoula, MT 1987.

Seasons at Eagle Pond by Donald Hall, Ticknor and Fields Publishing, New York, NY 1987.

At Timberline: A Nature Guide to the Mountains of New England by Frederick L. Steele, Appalachian Mountain Club Books, Boston, MA 1982.

White Mountain Guide 26th Edition edited by Gene Daniell and Jon Burroughs, Appalachian Mountain Club Books, Boston, MA 1998.

The White Mountains: Names, Places, and Legends by John T. B. Mudge, Durand Press, Etna, NH 1995.

Written in Stone by Chet and Maureen E. Raymo, Globe Pequot Press, Old Saybrook, CT 1989.

B. Conservation Organizations

Amoskeag Fishway. 1000 Elm Street, Box 330, Manchester, NH 03105. Phone (603) 634-2336. Seasonal fish ladder around the Manchester's Amoskeag Dam on the Merrimack River. Promotes conservation and education about migrating fish. Managed by Public Service Company of New Hampshire.

Appalachian Mountain Club. Box 298, Gorham, NH 03581. Phone (603) 466-2727. Oldest nonprofit conservation, education, and recreation organization in the United States, with over 70,000 members in 11 regional chapters, from Maine to Washington, DC.

Audubon Society of New Hampshire. 3 Silk Farm Road, Concord, NH 03301. Phone (603) 224-9909. Nonprofit organization dedicated to the conservation of wildlife and natural resources statewide, through education, advocacy, and land protection.

Dartmouth Outing Club. Robinson Hall, Box 9, Hanover, NH 03755. Phone (603) 646-2428. College outing club that maintains 75 miles of the Appalachian Trail in New Hampshire.

Friends of the Wapack. Box 115, W. Peterborough, NH 03468. Nonprofit, volunteer organization dedicated to maintaining and preserving the 21-mile Wapack Trail.

Granite State Wheelmen. 9 Veterans Road, Amherst, NH 03031. Recreational bicycling club affiliated with the League of American Wheelmen. Offers group rides, educational programs, and a newsletter. Lobbies for bike-friendly legislation.

Harris Center for Conservation Education. King's Highway, Hancock, NH 03449. Phone (603) 525-3394. Conservation, land protection, and education center for schools throughout the Monadnock Region.

The Hay Estate. NH 103 A, Newbury, NH 03255. Phone (603) 763-5958. The former estate of the John Hay family is now home to a conservation and education organization. The estate occupies 1,000 acres on Sunapee lake.

The Loon Preservation Committee. Box 604, Moultonborough, NH 03254. Phone (603) 476-5666. A nonprofit loon restoration project of the Audubon Society of New Hampshire.

Merrimack River Watershed Council. Box 1377, Lawrence, MA 01842. Phone (978) 681-5777. Nonprofit organization with a mission to protect the Merrimack River watershed through education and advocacy.

The Monadnock-Sunapee Greenway Trail Club. Box 164, Marlow, NH 03456. Maintains and promotes awareness of the 50-mile Monadnock-Sunapee Greenway.

The Nature Conservancy—New Hampshire Chapter. 2 ½ Beacon Street, Suite 6, Concord, NH 03301. Phone (603) 224-5853. International nonprofit conservation organization with a mission to preserve plants and animals by protecting land.

New Hampshire Department of Resources and Economic Development. 172 Pembroke Road, Concord, NH 03301.

Forest and Land Division. Phone (603) 271-2214. Oversees forest protection and the management of state lands and wildlife.

Bureau of Travel and Tourism. Phone (603) 271-2343. Promotes travel and tourism. Provides maps, guides, and brochures free of charge.

Parks and Recreation Division. Phone (603) 271-3556. Protects and manages state parks, historic sites, beaches, campgrounds, and recreational areas.

Bureau of Trails. Phone (603) 271-3254. Administers hiking, snowmobiling, and multiuse trails on state and federal lands.

New Hampshire Fish and Game Department. 2 Hazen Drive, Concord, NH 03301. Phone (603) 271-3421. Manages the state's fisheries and game as well as nongame wildlife.

New Hampshire Natural Heritage Inventory. Box 856, Concord, NH 03301. Phone (603) 271-3623. Documents and monitors species diversity in New Hampshire.

New Hampshire Snowmobile Association. 722 NH 3 A, Bow, NH 03304. Phone (603) 224-8906. Coordinates local clubs, promotes safety, and disseminates trail information.

Randolph Mountain Club. Randolph, NH 03570. Volunteer trail club that maintains 100 miles of trails in the Presidential and Crescent ranges.

Science Center of New Hampshire. Box 173, Holderness, NH 03245. Phone (603) 968-7194. Nonprofit educational organization dedicated to the advancement of ecological understanding.

Seacoast Science Center. 570 Ocean Boulevard, Rye, NH 03870. Phone (603) 436-8043. Offers educational programs and marine and cultural exhibits at Odiorne State Park on the Atlantic Ocean.

Sierra Club—New Hampshire Chapter. 3 Bicentennial Square, Concord, NH 03301. Phone (603) 224-8222. National environmental advocacy organization.

SKI New Hampshire. Box 10, North Woodstock, NH 03262. Phone (800) 887-5464. Organization of 35 nordic and alpine ski areas with 24-hour information about trail conditions and availability of lodging.

Society for the Protection of New Hampshire Forests. 54 Portsmouth Street, Concord, NH 03301. Phone (603) 224-9945. New Hampshire's oldest and largest conservation organization. Dedicated to land protection, education, advocacy, and promoting the responsible practice of forestry.

Squam Lakes Association. Box 104, Holderness, NH 03245. Phone (603) 968-7336. Private, nonprofit association dedicated to conserving the natural beauty and water quality of the Squam Lakes Region. Offers hiking, lake access, camping, and educational programs.

Wonalancet Out Door Club. Wonalancet, NH 03897. Maintains a network of trails in the central and eastern Sandwich Region.

C. Special Events, Fairs, and Festivals

For more information about these and other special events, contact the New Hampshire Bureau of Travel and Tourism's Web site: www.visitnh.gov

JANUARY

Blue Mountain Snowdusters Annual Radar Run—Grantham. Snowmobile safety inspection and public cookout. Phone (603) 224-8906.

Great Glen After Dark—Pinkham Notch. An evening of cross-country skiing and snowshoeing followed by live entertainment. Phone (603) 466-2333.

Historic Logging Program—Tamworth. Experience the golden days of the logging industry. Try the tools and sample lumberjack cuisine. Phone (603) 323-7591.

Ice Day—North Sutton. Old fashioned ice harvesting and stacking in the ice house, for use at summer events. Phone (603) 927-4276.

Winterfest—Berlin, Gorham, and Milan. Ski and snowshoe races, exhibitions, concert, snow sculpture, dog sled demos, and snowmobile activities. Phone (603) 752-6060.

FEBRUARY

Children's Museum of Portsmouth Winter Carnival—Portsmouth. Celebrate winter with activities and special performances at the children's museum. Phone (603) 436-3853.

Ice Harvesting—Tamworth. Cut ice from the pond using the tools of the days before refrigerators. Phone (603) 323-7591.

New Hampshire Music Festival Mostly Music Series—Laconia. Free family concert series. Phone (603) 524-1000.

New Hampshire Special Olympics—Waterville Valley. More than 400 special athletes participate in alpine and cross-country skiing, ice skating, snowboarding, and snowshoeing. Phone (603) 236-8311.

Newport Winter Carnvival—Newport. Carnival queen contest, parade, kids fair, ski jumping, and skating. Phone (603) 863-1510.

Sandwich Notch Sled Dog Races—Center Sandwich. International sled dog distance racing, featuring a 30- and 60-mile race over historic sled dog trails. Phone (603) 929-3508.

Ski For Yourself Cross-Country Camp for Women—Waterville Valley. Women of all ages/abilities stretch body and spirit at the unforgettable four-day camp. Phone (603) 499-0436.

Square and Contra Dancing—Tamworth. Professional callers, live English and Scottish music, all dances taught, beginners welcome. Phone (603) 323-8687.

Winter Carnival at King Pine Ski Area—Madison. Games and activities for the family. Take part in a silly slalom or try your luck in the nordic race. Phone (603) 367-8896.

MARCH

Children's Museum of Portsmouth Music Series—Portsmouth. Bring the family and enjoy toe-tapping music on Sunday afternoons. Phone (603) 436-3853.

Family Nature Series—Bethlehem. Enjoy evening presentations on wildlife, astronomy, wildflowers, and more. Phone (603) 444-6228.

Maple Sugaring—Tamworth. Find out how maple sugaring has changed over time. Participate in a traditional sugaring off party. Phone (603) 323-7591.

New Hampshire Barbershop Festival—Gilford. A concert of barbershop choruses from all over the state. Phone (603) 863-1492.

New Hampshire Boat Show—Manchester. Consumer show featuring new models. Phone (207) 865-1196.

New Hampshire Maple Weekend—Statewide. Visit 1 of 50 participating sugar-houses and learn how maple syrup is made. Free samples and demonstrations. Phone (603) 267-7070.

Portsmouth Community Forum—Portsmouth. Explore the arts of Portsmouth and their impact on the community, and explore the Strawberry Banke Museum. Phone (603) 433-1106.

Seacoast Flower, Home, and Garden Show—Durham. Landscape displays, flower-related businesses, home and garden products, open house at the University of New Hampshire greenhouse. Phone (603) 356-7750.

Ski to the Clouds Cross-Country Ski Race—Pinkham Notch. A 4-mile race, for cross-country skiers and snowshoers, up the historic Mount Washington Auto Road. Phone (603) 466-2333.

Slackers Cup 5km Race and St. Patrick's Day Party—Pinkham Notch. A fun 5 kilometer race for those with waxless skies. This race benefits a disabled skier program. Phone (603) 466-2333.

Spring Fever Barbecue—Pinkham Notch. A trail-side barbecue at Great Glen Trails. Phone (603) 466-2333.

APRIL

Easter Sunday—Waterville Valley. Sunrise service at the summit. Free skiing from 6:30 a.m. to 8:00 a.m. An Easter egg hunt where those who find a golden egg win a season pass. Phone (603) 236-8311.

New Hampshire Music Festival Mostly Music Series—Meredith. Free family concerts. Phone (603) 524-1000.

Pruning and Grafting of Antique Apple Trees—Portsmouth. Learn from the landscape department of the Strawberry Banke Museum. Phone (603) 433-1106.

Springtime Doll Show and Sale—Alton. Displays and sale of antique and modern dolls. Phone (603) 875-6750.

Stark Full Moon Festival—Stark. Night skiing and bonfire under a full moon-rise. Phone (800) TRAILS-8.

MAY

Astronomy Day—Concord. Astronomical, science, and educational activities in a fair-like setting at the Christa McAuliffe Planetarium. Phone (603) 271-7831.

Children and the Arts Festival—Peterborough. Celebrates children's artistic, musical, theatrical, and dance accomplishments. Includes food, entertainment, and a parade of giant puppets. Phone (603) 924-6498.

Children's Fishing Derby—Tamworth. For children 15 and under. Trophies awarded. Phone (603) 323-7591.

Farm Festival—Tamworth. Come see farmers demonstrate early and modern practices for preparing land for summer production. Plowing, sheep sheering, and sheep dogs. Phone (603) 323-7591.

The Little Nature Museum Annual Open House—Weare. Free guided trail walks, museum tours, and special exhibits. Phone (603) 529-7180.

Mother's Day at the Conway Scenic Railroad—North Conway. Mom rides free with one or more of her children. Phone (603) 356-5251.

New Hampshire Day—Canterbury. A celebration of the state's rich heritage. Phone (603) 783-9511.

New Hampshire Annual Lilac Festival—Lisbon. Parades, flea market, golf tournament, carnival, and fireworks. Phone (603) 828-6336.

New Hampshire Sheep and Wool Festival—New Boston. Sheep dog trials, lamb barbecue, sheep competition, and fiber exhibits. Phone (603) 352-4550.

North Lights Quilt Guild Show—Lebanon. Exhibits of new and antique quilts, quilt raffle, demonstrations, vendors, and door prizes. Phone (603) 675-2414.

Rockingham Craftsmen Fair—Hampton. Tole painting, quilting, knitting, dried flower arrangements, carved birds, and pottery. Phone (603) 382-6018.

Townsend's Training Farm Open Horse Show—Pembroke. Open horse show for Walk Trot riders of all ages. Phone (603) 224-9141.

Winni Derby—Weirs Beach. Three-day, family-oriented, landlocked salmon and lake trout derby on Lake Winnipesaukee. Phone (603) 253-8689.

JUNE

Fiddlers Contest—Lincoln. Music fills the valley as fiddlers from all over New England compete. Phone (603) 745-3563.

Herb Day—Canterbury. Celebrate the rites of spring with herb demonstrations and sales, soil testing, and tours of the Shaker Village. Phone (603) 783-9511.

High Hopes Balloon Festival—Milford. Charity event to grant wishes to critically ill children. Balloons, crafts, and bands. Phone (603) 673-7005.

Keepers of the Lore/The Joseph Campbell Festival—Milford. Storytelling festival under several tents around Milford. Phone (603) 654-5944.

Littleton Trout Tournament—Littleton. Three-day fishing tournament on Moore Dam Lake. Phone (603) 444-6561.

Monadnock Valley Indian Festival and Pow Wow—Keene. Native American dancing, singing, and arts and crafts. Phone (603) 647-5374.

Motorcycle Week—Laconia. Parades, fireworks, and races. Attracts thousands of motorcycle enthusiasts from all over the country. Phone (603) 366-2000.

New Hampshire Rose Society Rose Show—Nashua. Competitive display of roses by growers from throughout New England. Phone (603) 673-0754.

Wood Days—Canterbury. Woodworking fair and folk music festival. Furniture makers, boat builders, carvers, and instrument makers. Phone (603) 783-9511.

JULY

Blueberry Culture—Milton. New Hampshire Farm Museum. Phone (603) 652-7840.

Bow Street Fair—Portsmouth. Craft festival along the waterfront. Outdoor music and theater. Phone (603) 431-5709.

Canterbury Fair—Canterbury. Arts, crafts, antiques, chicken barbecue. Phone (603) 783-0335.

Circus—Littleton. Glitter, glamour, and nostalgia under the big top. Phone (603) 444-6561.

Daniel Webster Golf Classic—Tilton. Golf tournament to benefit Boy Scouts. Phone (603) 285-3400.

Gold Panning Special—Lincoln. Learn the art of gold panning at river stops along this all-day train ride from Lincoln to Plymouth. Phone (603) 745-2135.

Hebron Fair—Hebron. Crafts, food, books, plants, auction, and pony rides. Phone (603) 744-5700.

Hillsborough Balloon Festival and Fair—Hillsborough. Balloon and carnival rides, live entertainment, and pancake breakfast. Phone (603) 464-5858.

Lakes Region Open Water-Ski Tournament—Wolfeboro. Water-ski competition for all age groups. Phone (603) 569-6263.

Traditional Tea and Summer Fun Lawn Party—Tamworth. Free presentation on the history of tea at the Remick Country Doctors Museum. Phone (603) 323-7591.

Wolfeboro Antiques Fair—Wolfeboro. Furniture, oriental rugs, jewelry, glass, and books. Phone (603) 569-0000.

AUGUST

Andover Lions Club Lobster Bake and Penny Sale—Danbury. Steamed lobster and rib eye steak dinners at Ragged Mountain Ski Area. Phone (603) 735-5462.

Apple Pie Craft Fair—Newport. Crafts, entertainment, and pie eating contest on the common. Phone (603) 863-3040.

Bee Keeping Day—Milton. Learn about bee keeping at the New Hampshire Farm Museum. Phone (603) 652-7840.

Fruits of Summer—Tamworth. Watch the traditional harvest time food preparation, or try your hand at grinding corn or making corn husk dolls. Phone (603) 323-7591.

Gem and Mineral Show—Newbury. At this annual event at Mount Sunapee State Park, geologists and rock hounds share their knowledge about gems and minerals.

Phone (603) 763-2495.

Granite Man Triathlon—Wolfeboro. Annual swimming, biking, and running competition. Phone (603) 569-5639.

League of New Hampshire Craftsmen Fair—Newbury. America's oldest craft fair. Mount Sunapee State Park. Phone (603) 322-3375.

Native American Weekend—Colebrook. Native Americans meet to share social and cultural traditions. Phone (603) 237-5511.

Nineteenth Century Fair—Andover. Railroad Station Museum, calliope music, crafts auction, and Concord Coach rides. Phone (603) 735-5694.

Pemi Valley Bluegrass Festival—Campton. Acoustic bluegrass, old-time country bands, and workshops. Phone (603) 726-3471.

Shaker Classic Car Show—Canterbury. Vintage automobiles chronicle Canterbury's long relationship with the car. Phone (603) 783-9511.

SEPTEMBER

Concord Kiwanis Antique and Classic Car Show—Concord. Trophies in 25 classes. Phone (603) 226-8016.

Deerfield Fair—Deerfield. Large agricultural fair with exhibits, horse show, and horse pulling. Phone (603) 463-7421.

Fall Festival and Scarecrow Display—North Conway. Runs two weeks and features pumpkin carving, hay rides, cider, cookies, and more than 100 scarecrows on display. Phone (603) 356-7031.

Francestown Labor Day Festival—Francestown. Juried arts and crafts, parade, antique cars, and food. Phone (603)588-2540.

Grand Old Portsmouth Brewers Festival—Portsmouth. Celebrate the rich brewing history of Portsmouth by sampling some of New England's finest microbrews. Phone (603) 433-1106.

Hopkinton State Fair—Hopkinton. One of several state fairs, with traditional agricultural features and tractor pulls. Phone (603) 746-4191.

Lancaster State Fair—Lancaster. Situated in the North Country, this is one of New Hampshire's larger state fairs. Phone (603) 788-4531.

New Hampshire Highland Games—Lincoln. Held at Loon Mountain Park, this is the largest Scottish festival in the Northeast. Four days of celebrating Scottish culture, music, dance, and genealogy. Phone (800) 358-SCOT.

Wool Day—Canterbury. Exhibition of sheep, llamas, goats, and rabbits, with wool demonstrations and wool products for sale. Phone (603) 783-9511.

OCTOBER

Apple Harvest Day—Dover. Arts, crafts, food, and activities. Phone (603) 742-2218.

Harvest Moon Festival—Warner. Native American drumming, playing flutes, and storytelling. Food, games, and crafts. Phone (603) 456-2600.

Keene Bottle Show—Keene. Participants from 16 states and Canada exhibiting and selling collectors' bottles. Phone (603) 352-2959.

Keene Pumpkin Fest—Keene. Enter your carved pumpkin and participate in the world's biggest display of lighted pumpkins, lining the streets and square of downtown Keene. Phone (603) 358-5344.

Leaf Peepers' Dinner—Center Harbor. Family-style meal of ham and scalloped potatoes for locals and tourists. Phone (603) 253-7698.

New Hampshire Marathon at Newfound Lake—Bristol. This 26-mile run circles Newfound Lake. Qualifier for Boston Marathon. Phone (603) 744-2150.

Quilting Exhibit and Blacksmith Demonstrations—Milton. At New Hampshire Farm Museum. Phone (603) 652-7840.

Sandwich Fair—Sandwich. This rural New Hampshire fair supports agriculture through education and entertainment. Phone (603) 284-7062.

Winnipesaukee Scenic Railroad Fall Foliage Festival—Lincoln. Three-hour train ride along lakes and rivers, from Meredith to Livermore Falls. Phone (603) 745-2135.

NOVEMBER

Butcher, Baker, Candlestick Maker—Tamworth. Learn about preserving food for the winter and making sausage, soap, and candles. Phone (603) 323-7591.

Canterbury Shaker Christmas—Canterbury. Entertainment and sleigh/hay rides amid a brightly decorated Shaker Village. Phone (603) 783-9511.

Santa Express—Lincoln. Ride with Santa on this annual family train excursion. Gifts for the kids. Phone (603) 745-2135.

DECEMBER

Candlelight Stroll—Portsmouth. Walk through the candlelit neighborhood of Strawberry Banke, visiting winter festivities along the way. Phone (603) 433-1106.

The Christmas Revels—Hanover. Celebrate the winter solstice with Scandinavian dancers, singers, and musicians. Phone (603) 646-2422.

Lebanon Community Chorus Holiday Concert—Lebanon. Lebanon Opera House. Phone (603) 448-5121.

Victorian Christmas—Tamworth. Tour the Remick Museum and the decorated Remick House and take a sleigh ride. Phone (603) 323-7591.

D. Outfitters, Guides, and Suppliers

NORTH COUNTRY

Sportsman's Lodge. Lodging and fishing on Diamond Pond. Canoe and snow-mobile rentals. Box 167, Colebrook, NH 03576. Phone (603) 237-5211.

Angwin's Camp Driftwood. Cottages, fishing, and hunting on Back Lake. Tackle shop, rental boats and motors. Box 112, Pittsburg, NH 03592. Phone (603) 538-6684.

Lopstick Lodge and Cabins. Mountain view over First Connecticut Lake. Lodging, hiking, swimming, biking, and boating. Fly fishing and bird hunting guide service. First Connecticut Lake, Pittsburg, NH 03592. Phone (800) 538-6659.

The Glen. Log cabins and dining on First Connecticut Lake. Hiking, fishing, and guides. Boat and motor rentals. First Connecticut Lake, Pittsburg, NH 03592. Phone (800) 445-4536.

Tall Timber Lodge. Cabins and Dining on Back Lake. Moose watching, hiking, biking, and snowmobiling. Rentals, guides, and fly fishing school. Back Lake, Pittsburg, NH 03592. Phone (800) 835-6343.

Balsams Grand Resort Mountain Bike and Nature Center. Rentals for biking, skiing, tennis, and snowshoeing. Guided tours. Dixville Notch, NH 03576. Phone (800) 225-0600.

WHITE MOUNTAINS

Appalachian Mountain Club Outdoor Adventures. Outdoor workshops on skiing, snowshoeing, backpacking, and ice-climbing. Lodging in Pinkham Notch or Crawford Notch hostels, and guided hiking and ski tours. Box 298, Gorham, NH 03581. Phone (603) 466-2727.

Appalachian Mountain Club Hiker's Shuttle. Service to 13 trailheads and lodges in Franconia Notch and the Presidentials. Phone for reservations: (603) 466-2727.

Great Glen Trails. Scenic setting along the Peabody River with with close views of Mount Washington. Lessons and rentals for skiing, snowshoeing, tubing, biking, and canoeing. Fishing clinics and guided backpacks. Pinkham Notch, Gorham, NH 03581. Phone (603) 466-2333.

Base Camp Adventure Center. In Waterville Valley. Biking, hiking, in-line skating rentals and guided tours. Waterville Valley Resort, 1 Ski Area Road, Waterville Valley, NH 03215. Phone (800) 468-2553.

The Mountain Wanderer. New England Maps and Outdoor/Travel Books. Located in Lincoln, on the Kancamagus Highway. A wide selection of how-to and nature books, guide books, compasses, and maps, including USGS topographical maps. Box 485, Lincoln, NH 03251, Phone (603) 745-2594. E-mail: sds@linwoodnet.com.

Loon Mountain Resort. Located off Kancamagus Highway. Lodging, skiing, hiking, and tubing on the East Pemigewasset River. Rentals for skis, mountain bikes, and in-line skates. Guided tours. Lincoln, NH 03251. Phone (800) 227-4191.

Waterville Valley Resort. Surrounded by mountains in Waterville Valley. Rentals and lessons for boating, biking, golfing, and skiing. 1 Ski Area Road, Waterville Valley, NH 03215. Phone (800) 468-2553.

Saco Bound/ Downeast Whitewater. Guided canoe and raft trips on the Saco, Swift, Rapid, and Kennebec rivers. Rentals, shuttle service, camping, and retail shop. Box 119WM, Center Conway, NH 03813. Phone (603) 447-3801.

Cannon Mountain Peabody Base Lodge. Rentals of bikes, skis, canoes, and paddleboats. Access to recreational trail through Franconia Notch. Located off Franconia Parkway Exit 3. Cannon Mountain, Franconia, NH 03580. Phone (603) 823-5563.

LAKES REGION

Gunstock Mountain Biking Center. Gunstock Mountain Vicinity. Mountain bike rentals and trails. NH 11 A, Gilford, NH 03246. Phone (603) 293-4341.

Dive Winnipesaukee. Downtown Wolfeboro on Lake Winnipesaukee. Marine and fishing supplies, windsurf boards and canoe and sailboat rentals. Dive gear and scuba lessons and charters. Box 2198, Wolfeboro, NH 03894. Phone (603) 569-8080.

Gadabout Golder Guide. Sport fishing guides and boat rentals. Middletown Road, Wolfboro, NH 03894. Phone (603) 569-6426.

Winnipesaukee Kayak Company. Kayak lessons, rentals, and tours. Box 2163, Wolfeboro, NH 03894. Phone (603) 569-9926.

WESTERN HIGHLANDS

Eastern Mountain Sports. In Peterborough, NH. Extensive retail and catalog store for all season sports, camping, and backpacking equipment. 1 Vose Farm Road, Peterborough, NH 03458. Phone (603) 924-7231.

Summer's Backcountry. In Keene, NH. Suppliers of cross-country ski, backpacking, hiking, and camping equipment. Books, topographical maps, canoes, kayaks, and bikes. Ski and snowshoe rentals, and kayak clinics. 16 Ashuelot Street, Keene, NH 03431. Phone (603) 353-0151.

MANCHESTER AND CONCORD

All Outdoors. In central Manchester, selling cross-country ski and snowshoe equipment, backpacking, camping, and rock climbing equipment and supplies, Books and topographical maps. 321 Elm Street, Manchester, NH 03101. Phone (603) 624-1468.

Gibson's Bookstore. In central Concord, selling sporting guidebooks and topographical maps. 27 South Main Street, Concord, NH 03301. Phone (603) 224-0562.

E. Glossary

Acidic—Characterized by an excess of hydrogen ions; typically detrimental to soil fertility or lake inhabitants.

Bog—Peat-dominated wetland, generally acidic, poor in nutrients.

Boreal—Descriptive of a northern coniferous forest and its inhabitants.

Coniferous—Cone-bearing trees; evergreens or softwoods.

Deciduous—Trees that lose their leaves in winter; hardwoods.

Delta—Fan-shaped deposit of river-borne sediments that forms at the mouth of a river as it enters a lake or ocean.

Eutrophic—Nutrient-rich; in lakes, usually characterized by heavy algae growth.

Fen—Peatland that is relatively rich in nutrients brought by a water source, either a river or a spring.

Gneiss—Banded metamorphic rock.

Iapetus—Ocean separating ancient North America from other continents.

Kame terrace—Sediments deposited by running water that fill the space between a glacier and an adjacent hillside.

Kettle pond—Pond formed where blocks of glacial ice are left behind by retreating glacier and buried in sediments before the block melts. When the ice block melts, it leaves a depression that fills with water and forms a pond.

Krummholz—German for twisted wood; used to describe stunted trees that grow in alpine areas.

Marsh—Wetland dominated by grasslike herbaceous vegetation such as sedges and cattails.

Metamorphic—Rocks formed from other rocks under intense pressure and temperature, typically due to mountain building.

Monadnock—A hill or mountain of resistant rock that stands above the surrounding low-lying area.

Oligotrophic—Nutrient poor.

Outcrop—Exposed bedrock.

Orogeny—Mountain-building event.

Pangaea—Super-continent formed from Laurasia and Gondwanaland about 350 million years ago.

Pluton—A body of molten rock that solidifies deep in the Earth.

Quartzite—Metamorphic rock formed from sedimentary rocks, typically sandstones in which the main element is quartz.

Roche moutonée—Literally "sheep rock," a form left when a glacier advances over a rock and shapes it asymmetrically, with a smooth slope on the upstream side of the glacier and a steep face on the downstream face. The smooth slope is abraded by the glacier, and the steep face results when ice shatters and plucks rock away from the cliff.

Striae—Parallel scratches or grooves in a rock outcrop, cut by the sandpaper-like passage of a grit-filled glacier.

Schist—Layered metamorphic rock formed from shales and characterized by parallel layers of platy minerals, such as mica.

Scree—Accumulation of stones, typically fist-sized and smaller, at the foot or base of a cliff, resulting from stones that weather from the cliff face and tumble down.

Sedimentary—Rocks formed when sediments— sand, mud, plant material, sea shells—are deposited in a place and accumulate over millions of years.

Shale—Rock formed by weak metamorphosis of muds and clays. Typically very fine-grained, dark gray. Breaks into thin layers.

Succession—A change in vegetation over time, with new tree and plant species replacing older ones, the pattern of which is determined by seed source, soil type, moisture availability, and amount of light.

Swamp—Wetlands colonized by perennial trees or shrubs.

Talus— Accumulation of stones, typically larger than a fist, at the foot or base of a cliff, resulting from stones that weather from the cliff face and tumble down.

Till—Silt, sand, gravel, and boulders frozen into or on top of a glacier that are left as an unsorted mixture on the earth after the ice melts.

Understory—Shrubs and nonwoody plants that live underneath trees in a forest.

Index